D1882676

HINDUS
of
INDIA

HINDUS *of* INDIA

BRIGADIER JAGDEV SINGH A.V.S.M.

GYAN

GYAN PUBLISHING HOUSE

New Delhi 110 002

HINDUS OF INDIA

[*Archaeology, Culture, History, Philosophy, Religion*]

ISBN: 81-212-0599-9

© BRIGADIER JAGDEV SINGH A.V.S.M.

All rights are reserved. No part of this book may be reproduced in any manner without written permission.

Published in 1998 in India by
Gyan Publishing House
5, Ansari Road
New Delhi 110 002

Laser Typeset at Alphabet, Delhi
Printed at Mehra Offset Press, New Delhi.

Contents

Preface

Hindus of India are a remarkable phenomenon, if not the most remarkable social growth in the history of the human race. Their religion and culture have defied time. No other civilization has had such a tenacity to its credit. They are a multicultural, multiethnic, and multilingual people, and even though its constituents have had some differences in their religious and cultural concepts, these have not generated any significant tensions.

Generally the Hindus are not inclined to use religion for mutual political or financial benefit. It has no in-built political element and has seldom served as a rallying point for any cause other than the cause of religion. Its concern is wholly and solely with guiding its followers along the path which, it believes, secures for them happiness in this world and in the hereafter, and while doing this its emphasis is on personal experience, on mature and sagacious reasoning, and not on blind faith, for the belief is that the mind has a cosmic dimension and an infinite capacity to comprehend. This is not a faith that coerces its followers to follow any set of tenets, for it has no tenets as such, only guiding lines which, according to it, if followed with sincerity and persistence, lead to the 'experience' and, eventually, to emancipation. It does not believe in proselytization, and for this reason, while missionaries of other religions go about constantly seeking conversions to their faiths so as to secure a clout in the running of the affairs of the state, the approach of the Hindu missionary is totally concerned with the affairs of the religion. He believes that the religion is an individual's personal affair and must remain so if it has to serve its purpose.

An important thought of the Hindus, in which, possibly, the majority of them believe, lays stress on truth and non-violence.

Both Jainism and Buddhism are the results of this thought; even Gandhi's non-violent movement to secure freedom from the British, was born from this source. The Aryan belief, which constitutes the second major strand of the Hindu culture, however, favours aggression in support of a just cause, so long as such an aggression is not committed for personal gains. At the personal behaviour level the guiding line is that one should do nothing unto others which if done by others unto him, is not likely to receive his approval.

Up to the end of the first millennium A.D. Hindu influence and rule extended up to Central Asia and the Far East. They had trade and commerce with all the major countries of Asia and Europe. Even during the period of pre-history their sea faring people sailed to the far off lands, particularly the islands of the Pacific Ocean, and left their stock there, going as far as South America. Right up to the middle of the nineteenth century they were amongst the leaders in industrial production and prosperity. The invading Muslims ruled some parts of India from about the first millennium A.D., but made barely any distinguishable difference upon the religion and culture of the people. Today it is this culture which is visible in the lives of all the people inhabiting the Indian subcontinent. In spite of the tribulations and vicissitudes that it has gone through, this, the oldest civilization of the world, stands intact, in content and form, even today when the contemporary civilizations of the Sumerians, Egyptians, Greeks, Hittites are all gone for good, for ever obliterated from the surface of this globe, leaving behind but scattered traces in evidence of their having once existed.

The Indus Valley Civilization flourished in the north-west of this subcontinent around, 5500-6000 years ago. But there is enough evidence to suggest that equally well-organized societies existed, at least in the north-western areas, even earlier, may be even 7000-9000 years back. All these people have contributed to form what goes as Hinduism today. It is a growth of concepts and ideas, and over these thousands of years these concepts and ideas have been examined and tested and selectively accepted, by wise and discerning people. For this reason there has been little scope for extra-religious concepts to make inroads into what existed already.

The Hindus have been a brave, hardworking and Godfearing people, who prized their professions and strove to achieve excellence; even their religion emphasized the pursuit of excellence. They also valued honest and healthy living, and followed dharma, as advised by their religious preceptors; any activity which brought unhappiness upon others was rejected. They produced great kings like Ashoka, the Guptas, Harsha Vardhana and great men of arts, crafts and sciences and other branches of learning. They established great kingdoms beyond the borders of the subcontinent, in almost all the countries of the Far East, and exerted decisive influence in shaping the cultures of the Central Asian and the Middle Eastern countries. They lived amidst plenty; the climate was salubrious and the soil fertile.

Then, after having ridden the waves for thousands of years, the open, outward looking, assimilative outlook of the Hindus began to turn rigid, conventional, ritual-bound and inwards. There was a decline in every field of activity, be it science and technology, engineering skills, military capability, trade and commerce, lack of abundant scientific, cultural and social activity, development of financial institutions, law and administration. They received their first major jolt with the Muslim invasions in the beginning of the second millennium A.D. The invaders went after them 'hammer and tongs', and even though they were second to none in their determination to oust their enemies, they lacked the latter's battle-field skills and the sophistication of their weaponary. The second major jolt was given by the British when, during the course of one century, from 1757-1858, they captured the whole of the sub-continent and literally enslaved the whole of its population. This country, which right up to the middle of the nineteenth century, had a noteworthy output in industry, and trade and commerce, became one of the poorest in the world by the time it got rid of its British masters in 1947.

Five decades ago the country gained independence from the colonial rule after a long struggle and is striving to find its feet in the present day complex world order. The years of slavery and alien rule have taken their toll. It has been ruthlessly plundered, and its masses have been rendered abysmally ignorant and poor. Neither the Muslim rulers nor the British captors did anything about the education and medical facilities for the people at the grass roots level. The population has increased outstripping the means of sustenance. In their ignorance people have multiplied recklessly, not possessing the capability to appreciate the inherent dangers in this growth, adding gleefully to their own poverty and the poverty of the country as a whole. Poverty has hindered development. Infrastructure for industrial growth is poor, industrial productivity is low and of substandard quality because an inadequately trained labour force. Problems posed by the complex caste system are virtually intractable; it will be some effort and time before the Hindu society manages to get them under control.

Thanks to the total deprivation inflicted upon by the British rule, the country today is placed in the third world. There has to be a lot of hard work and many miles of travel, before it can break out of the barrier and hold a noteworthy status amongst other nations, as it indeed did during its not too distant past.

New Delhi **JAGDEV SINGH**

One

The Subcontinent and the People

The continents of the earth have drifted apart since their coming into being. Gondwana land, named after the Gond tribals of Central India comprised one land mass having present day South America, Africa, Madagascar, India, Antarctica and Australia, while the single largest northern continent of Laurasia had North America, Greenland, Europe and Asia (less India). Over 300 million years back, as a result of the forces emanating from the core of the earth, the southern continent of Gondwana land started breaking up; about a 100 million years ago the land mass of the Indian subcontinent started drifting northwards at a speed of seven cm per year; and about 50 million years back it locked itself with the southern edge of Eurasia, closing up the ancient Tethys sea and folding up the earth's crust along the line of collision into what are now called the Himalayas. This break began during the age of the dinosaurs.

The old world, South America and Australia broke away in the course of time and carried their own flora and fauna which later developed into their present day mammals. For some inexplicable reasons the dinosaurs (except, possibly, the group now called birds) went extinct all over the world, but, otherwise, the evolution pattern remained the same in the three areas even though these areas evolved their own variety of mammals, the marsupials (born before being ready for birth and kept in the pouch) dominated Australia while placentae were the norm in the rest of the world.

The earth saw its four ice ages during the Pleistocene geological period, beginning around 1.9 million years back. Genus "Homo" arrived about one million years ago, during the currency of the ice age. During the early stages of this period the main features of the geography of the Indian subcontinent had been formed, except for the land immediately south of the rising Himalayas which was a large trough of marshes and salt water lagoons. With time the area got filled by the alluvium brought down by the fresh water from the high mountains; the process also eliminated the salt water lagoons. Finally the 80,000 square kilometre area of the Indo-Gangetic plain became firm and dry enough to be liveable; this happened some 7,000 to 10,000 years back. Comprising basically river water alluvium, the area is bereft of any mineral resources, although agriculturally it is the most fertile part of India and, consequently, the most thickly populated. Thus, as compared to the southern peninsular India, the Indo-Gangetic plain has evolved in recent times, the former being of great antiquity, going back to the early Gondwana period. Along the foot of the Himalayas the river system originally drained from west to east, till the earth movements of the post-Shivalik times in north-west Punjab caused the break and brought about the river system as they exist today; there is evidence to suggest that Yamuna, during the early times, discharged into the Indus system through the now near-extinct bed of the Sarasvati river of the Hindu tradition, and that its current flow pattern is a development of recent times.

The fertile Indo-Gangetic plains have attracted, over the millennia, migrants and invaders from other lands. These plains are protected in the north by the mighty Himalayan circumvallations, while any ingress from the east was made difficult by the jungles and hills of Burma (now Myanmar). From the west, however, the approaches over the low Sulaiman Range, and passes across the Hindu Kush, along almost all the main rivers, have provided many entry points for the people from Central and West Asia. An important approach from the west runs along the valley of the Kabul river and finally descends to Peshawar through the Khyber Pass, a winding and narrow defile of about 30 km length. This route leads directly into the plains of the Punjab, to the gap between the hills in the north and the Thar desert in the south.

This gap becomes the narrowest in the Panipat-Delhi region, and that explains why India's first line of defence had to be astride the Khyber and the second in the Panipat-Delhi area. The extensive network of rivers has provided ample amount of subterranean and surface water for large-scale cultivation and, thus, growth of civilizations.

South of the plains and the Thar desert are the low mountain ranges of the Vindhyas and the Satpuras, running east-west, and further south is the great plateau which covers most of the peninsular India. A number of major and minor rivers flowing through the mountains and the peninsula discharge into the Arabian Sea in the west, and the Bay of Bengal in the east. However, unlike the rivers of the northern plains, which are mostly snow-fed, these rivers are rain-fed. The deltas of the rivers flowing eastwards are extensive and fertile and play an important part in the economy. The eastern coastline stretches southwards from the Gangetic delta, going down to the Coromandel coast and is much broader than the western coastline coming southwards from the Gulf of Cambay all the way to the Malabar coast. Both the coastal strips are plain and fertile and are flanked by the sea on one side and the high ground of the Deccan plateau and the coastal Ghats (hills) on the other.

The Indian subcontinent is as large as Europe, excluding Russia, and has a variety in terrain which ranges from the highest mountains of the world to the most fertile plains, the desert of Rajasthan and the largest plateaus made up entirely of volcanic eruptions. It is criss-crossed by numerous rivers and streams, and hills and low mountains, and is dotted (at least was till the other day) with dense jungles, which made inter regional movements difficult. It is a land, tailor-made to nurture life, till this too has been made difficult by the unbridled growth of human population in recent times. It is believed, when Moses undertook to lead his people to the promised land, the land of milk and honey, he had the Indo-Gangetic plains in mind. Ever since the emergence of man, this land has provided shelter to the hungry, needy, and the oppressed and afforded them rich life and the means to generate wealth, which, naturally, has attracted invaders. Self-sufficiency in the different regions, the slow moving modes of transportation and the inter-regional obstacles, tended to isolate the regions from one-another, and this led to the differences in the development of regional languages and dialects, customs, cultures, and religious persuasions, conceptions and thoughts. The people of different regions seldom aspired to dominate vast tracts of this subcontinent or establish empires subjugating whole or most of South Asia. This, however, is understandable considering the size of the sub-continent, its topography and the very poor communications systems which existed till the very advent of the British rule. No wonder then that the Mauryan empire did not complete even 140 years of its existence, and the Mughal empire got pushed back to the gates of Delhi within 70 years of the death of Aurangzeb. There have been other reasons too for the regions to have stayed insulated from each other. Ethnicity has been one factor and the fairly rigid caste system another. Many tribes arrived in this country from outside, bringing with them their own cultural patterns, their own dialects, religious beliefs and social customs. All this influenced the overall culture of this country.

But, inspite of the problems imposed by the terrain and communications systems, the interregional exchange of ideas, customs, habits, did take place, even though slowly, over a long period of time. There were people who travelled between regions, and preachers who went about talking about their social and religious ideas, and the regions had states which interacted with one another, fought with one another, sometimes, fought wars, and that got the people to interact, exchange views, and this continued over the millennia, and resulted in a kind of a mix which today can be recognized as the culture of India, minor regional variations notwithstanding. In the accounts of history and myths of the earliest tradition dating back to the third millennium BC, accounts of sages and kings traversing the four corners of this country have been narrated. Indeed in the early second millennium BC the country has been called Bharata-varsha—the land of the Bharatas. Originally the name covered only the area ruled by the Bharata clan of the Indo-Aryans but, with time, it got to embrace the whole country, "the country lying to the north of the ocean and the south of the Himalayas". Today it bears this name in the Indian constitution.

Life sustaining elements abounded within the country, and migrants, or invaders, from the north-western arid lands of Central Asia and Middle East poured in. Even as early as the fifth century BC, Herodotus observed that India had the largest population amongst the countries of that time. Whenever the subcontinent had a strong central rule, or there were strong states along its borders, the invaders were held in check, though they were at its doors all the time, and at the slightest show of weakness launched themselves to secure ingress. Most major invasions, as stated earlier, came from the north-west; only the Europeans, including the British, invaded from the direction of the sea. Still, it did not mean that the submission of a border state placed the whole of the subcontinent at the mercy of the attackers. In fact, the states lying along the route of the invader offered their own resistance and this amounted to almost fighting in depth, and made the task of the invader that much more difficult. Alexander, the Macedonian king (356-323 BC), defeated Darius, the Emperor of Persia in two battles, in 333 and 331 BC, and took the whole of the Persian empire, in almost one go, but when he attacked India he faced an entirely different situation. The country was divided into small states, generally comprising territories lying within adjoining river systems, and each of them offered stiff resistance. Ambhi, the Taxilan king, cleared his path without offering a fight, and the older Paurava king, ruler of the territory between rivers Jhelum and Chenab, in spite of a formidable force of elephants, chariots and infantry got defeated by the superior manoeuvers of Alexander's cavalry. But beyond Paurava territory the going became tough, and by the time Alexander got to river Beas, his army simply refused to fight and forced him to abandon his plans to advance to the Gangetic plains. Even his withdrawal was stiffly resisted and he lost heavily while trying to extricate from this area of bristling hostility. The fighting was grim. Thousands of people, including women and children, perished in the struggle. During one of the encounters Alexander himself got a grievous hurt, the injury from which he never fully recovered.

Babar (1483-1530) acquired the whole of the territory of the Sultanate of Delhi after just one encounter at Panipat. The small states, which were generally protected by difficult rivers or dense forests or marshes or deserts, thus, had their own role to play, at least in those times, and because of them no foreign invader, except the British, ever managed to subjugate the whole of this country. Muslim invaders made a fair dent into the Indian defences and for the best part of six hundred odd years; ruled over substantial parts of the subcontinent. This happened at a time when the Indian culture and religion and its progressive scientific thought, had reached its nadir and lost its vitality and vigour after having been in existence for over 5000 years. In the recorded history the zenith of this civilization was reached during the Gupta period, and the decline commenced after Harsha Vardhana, hitting the rock bottom by the beginning of the thirteenth century AD. The Hindu civilization at this stage had lost its freshness that marked its rise from the Rig Vedic days to the days of the Guptas, (a time span of about two millennia), essentially because it fell under the stranglehold of the priestly class, the Brahmins, who, while anxious to perpetuate their own interests, came out as poor leaders. Their overcautious attitude to fresh and dynamic ideas arrested the growth of tradition, philosophy and religion, and threw up an impotent, ignorant, caste ridden social order. It was a confused civilization, steeped in sorcery and superstition, e.g., its people set out to defend the Somnath temple by chanting Vedic hymns and taking shelter behind a herd of cows, who, they believed could, with their supernatural powers, put their enemies to flight. The decay ate into the confidence of the people, their bravery and sanguineness, their pride, character, their ability to stand on their own feet. It turned them into a frightened, cowering, grovelling, beggarly lot of people caught in the web of an acute struggle for existence.

In their heyday the Hindus were a vigorous, dynamic people who believed in free exchange of ideas and strived constantly to improve their living conditions and environments, their arts and culture, their scientific and engineering knowledge and skills, and believed that knowledge had to be spread down to each member of the society. They had faith in themselves and in their God. But, as the society became static the emphasis shifted from learning to rituals, and it had to pay a heavy price for this. Militarily it became a weaker country and thus vulnerable to invasions from outside, particularly the north-west during the early part, and the sea along its western and eastern coasts during the latter part of this millennium. The Muslims arrived in large numbers from about the end of the 12th century AD and that brought in a significant change in the style of the Hindu society. It became even more insular. Large areas of the country went under the Muslim rule, thanks to the pacifism of the Hindus, and superior skills and manoeuvrability of their enemies in the field of battle. Yet, for most of the time, a large portion of the country continued to remain under Hindu sway, and, in spite of the adverse times, only about 10 per cent of the total Indian population adopted the Muslim faith, and that too, basically in areas which stayed under Muslim rule for longer durations.

In fact, their weaknesses notwithstanding, Hindu society at this stage of its history was fairly well organized. The religion, and the philosophy had made a deep impression upon the minds and hearts of the people, and, barring a few aspects, Islam had very little to offer which could better satisfy the emotional and religious aspirations and needs of the people. The priestly class, the Brahmins, were highly educated and well versed in the details of their religion. In fact, they were better equipped to resist religious conversions compared to those who were dead set upon securing them — their message to the people went across in dialects and languages that the latter well understood. In the history of nations, the governance of a country has always been difficult for people who profess a religion different from that followed by their subjects, and its goes to the credit of the Muslim rulers that they managed to follow their faith in the midst of almost hostile population. Here and there some Muslim rulers secured the willing cooperation of their Hindu subject by being soft and beneficient towards them, but such rulers generally got pushed down the cliff by the hard liners who advocated a fundamentalistic approach. But the fundamentalists did not survive either, because of the hostility of the subjects. So, the history of India during most of the current millennium, till the establishment of the British rule, has been dotted with emerging and vanishing rulers. The British succeeded in annexing the whole of South Asia because the population of different regions had been thoroughly disillusioned by the corrupt fundamentalist Muslim rulers on the one hand and the corrupt, incompetent, and the easy going Hindu rulers on the other. Naturally, the British thoroughly exploited the weaknesses, and with the resources they secured with the conquest of the subcontinent, they established an empire which was the greatest in the annals of the human history.

The People

Just who is a Hindu? The dictionary says he is a believer in Hinduism, which is the religion and a social institution of the great majority of the people of India. The word possibly is derived from Sindhu, the old name of river Indus, and was used by the Iranians and the people of the countries to the north and west, to designate the people inhabiting the Indus basin. From Sindhu it became Hindu, and Hind, their country, Hindi the people of Hind, Hindia, country of the Hindi, India. In the Veda and Vendidad terms Sapta Sindhavah and Hapta Hindu have been used to designate the country of the Aryans. The name India was used for this country by the Greeks. In the Hindu religious literature, the subcontinent is said to be part of Jambu-Dweepa, which was considered to be the inner-most island continent of this earth which was supposed to consist of seven concentric island continents. Most accounts of this Dweepa are pure myth and fancy, but early Buddhist chronicles use this term to designate the countries in South and South-East Asia. Thus, the original use of the word Hindu was basically in a geographical sense, like Arabi for a person from Arabia, or Englishman for a man from England. But, with time, the term got tied up with Dharma, Arya Dharma, Hindu Dharma, since Aryans lived in Hapta Hindu. Today Hinduism means Hindu religion and its social institutions. The argument that Hinduism has no fixed scriptural canons like those of Islam or Christianity, and, therefore, is not a religion in that sense, has some weight but not of any consequence in the present day context. This religion has a homogeneous character, its own philosophy and beliefs, methods of worship, and customs and rituals, most of which are at variance with those of other religions. It has its own distinguishing features and is, thus, a distinct entity.

As the Homo Erectus spread to the various parts of the world during the ice ages, he found his place on the Indian subcontinent as well, and the early *Homo sapiens* in north-west India were probably contemporaneous with the last two ice-ages; on the basis of the evidence from the finds of pebble and flake tools, it can be surmised that the Homo Erectus inhabited Punjab from the end of the first inter-glacial, right through the three succeeding glacials and two inter-glacials. One thought is that he had possibly originated in the favourable environments of the east coast in the south and moved northwards. During the Mesolithic Age man had fully evolved to his present form, and, typically, made small tools, an inch or so in length, and from the finds it can be concluded that he had populated the length and breadth of this subcontinent. But since all finds have been only from surface it is not possible to say exactly when he was here or whether he inhabited all places at the same time or during different periods.

Neolithic Age in India is indicated, by the finds of the polished stone tools and pottery, but so little has been found by the archaeologists that, again, it is not possible to give the dates of the beginning and end of this period. All that can be said with any degree of certainty is that the early man went through the same stages of development on this subcontinent as he did elsewhere. There is evidence that he made the stone age tools, hunted, did rock/cave paintings, possibly with the same intention as his cousins in Europe, but it has not been possible to say when all this happened. In some parts of the country, for example, like Gujarat the finds have been considered to be of considerable antiquity, while at other places these appear to have just preceded the Iron Age.

Even in the case of metals it is difficult to say when these began to be used in this country; not much work has been done in this regard, nor finds indicating definite periods have been discovered. Copper for tools and weapons could be had from copper ore deposits in Singhbhum in Bihar, and from the mines in Rajasthan, Chotanagpur and Orissa. Finds from different places include tools, weapons including axes, swords, daggers and harpoons, and ornaments like rings. Generally the workmanship is of primitive type, except in a few cases where European or Central Asian manufacture has been suggested, and on the basis of this evidence it can be said that Copper Age in India's Gangetic basin was extant at least before 1200 B.C. In the south, Iron Age appears to have followed directly from the Stone Age, without going through the intermediate Copper Age, and, unlike Europe and Central Asia, India seems to have skipped the Bronze Age altogether.

The Racial Groups of the Subcontinent

For reasons which are difficult to explain, the skeletal remains of the early man have been rare in this country, and therefore it has not been possible to reconstruct, with any degree of accuracy, the movements of different groups that inhabited it. The general view is that most people of the subcontinent have emigrated from outside, but have developed their characteristic traits during their stay here, and that, in course of time, some of them have detached from the parent bodies, and have moved on to settle in other lands. These groups can generally be put in the following classes:

(a) *Negritos*

Brachycephalic, probably from Africa, have all but vanished from the mainland except for small groups surviving in the Andamans, Cochin and Travancore Hills, Assam (Angami Nagas) and eastern Bihar. Being of black complexion and height on an average reaching around five feet, physically they are unattractive. They have been a restless kind of people who moved extensively. Their contribution to the development of the Indian civilization has been marginal. They seem to have been overpowered and generally absorbed by the people who followed them like the Proto-Astroloids, the Mongoloid groups and, possibly, the Dravidians of the Palaeo-Mediterranean class, although, on the evidence of frescoes, it does seem that they survived on the mainland even up to the Gupta period. They were essentially food gatherers rather than food producers, and developed some skills, one amongst them being their ability to cross the sea, which eventually got them to the Andaman islands. They travelled to other lands as well by land or sea and still survive in Malaya, Indonesia, Philippines and New Guinea. Their original speech seems to have survived in the Andamans, but, barring a few words connected with the flora and fauna, it does not appear to have made any contribution to the present day Indian dialects. They worshipped trees for fertility, and believed in the human being possessing a soul; they also narrated accounts of travel of the soul after death to paradise guarded by an avenging demon who inflicted punishment on the basis of the "sins" committed, before permitting entry. Such ideas were widespread in Europe, Africa and India of those days.

(b) *Proto-Australoids*

Dolichocephalic, probably an offshoot of an earlier Mediterranean race, possibly from Palestine. They have almost black complexion and an average height of five feet and six inches. There is, however, a greater possibility that these people evolved from a subhuman species, over the Indian subcontinent itself, and then moved outwards in all directions. The aboriginals of India are almost entirely of this stock, diluted by intermingling with other groups. Part of this group moved over to Australia in very early times, and formed the base for the Melanesians and Polynesians, spreading to the Pacific islands and, possibly, to South and Central America, inter breeding with other racial groups during its long march eastwards. They are a very important group in India, and it does appear that, at some stage, they moved in large numbers into this country from the west, which could also have happened subsequent to their having moved out of here initially. These groups from the west appear to have arrived over a number of lines of migrations and intermingled with other groups, like the Negritos and the Mongoloids. Of those who emigrated eastwards, some came back in later times as Melanesians and Polynesians, and contributed to the culture and economy of certain areas of this country — these elements have since been totally absorbed. The outrigger canoe, head-hunting, disposal of the dead by exposure, communal housing, and coconut, appear to have been their contributions.

The spread of the Proto-Australoids over this subcontinent has been wide, although in their near original form, their number is pretty limited and can be identified only amongst a few aboriginal tribes, like the Mundas and Kols of Chhotanagpur. But they have mixed extensively with other groups and imparted their traits and characteristics to a large variety of people. A majority of rural India of today carries, to a large or small extent, the Proto-Australoid strain. The languages they speak are grouped under the head "Austric" and these have made a substantial contribution to the development of Hindustani language. Since there is evidence that at some stage they have moved from the west, in large numbers, into this country, there have been other views also, as to their source of origination: William Hevesy places them in Hungary-Western Siberia area and believes that there was a major offensive/immigration into India by Finno-Ugrian or Ugrian tribes during the prehistoric times and that Kol and Mundas are the result of the inter-breeding between these tribes and the original local inhabitants, like the Negritos. The generally held view, as put forth by Jean Przyluski and others, however, is that Proto-Australoids are a very old offshoot of the Mediterranean race, that during their trek to India, moving gradually, over a period of time, they left their kind on the way, all along the route of immigration, including Mesopotamia and Iran; they believe the Sumerians of Mesopotamia and the Austric Australoids of India are closely connected, although the latter became fully characterized only on the soil of India. Pater W. Schmidt has given the view that Austric family of languages have two main streams: one, which is spoken by Melanesia and Polynesia and the peoples of the islands of the Pacific, and the other as spoken in South Asia and South-East Asia. This view is generally accepted.

The transition in the subcontinent from the Palaeolithic culture to the Neolithic was the achievement of the Proto-Australoids, as also the development of pottery and the use of the boomerang. Cultivation by the hoe and the digging-stick was also developed by them; this later brought in terrace cultivation of rice in many parts of South and South-East Asia. They, apparently, had a good knowledge of the human anatomy and the characteristics of the organs in the body, and as food gatherers, which is what they were initially, they were well acquainted with their flora. They possibly had a system of treating ailments with medicines made from extracts of herbs; this later developed into what is called the Siddha System. They devised the count upto twenty (*kodi*) which was in vogue for transacting business in most parts of India till the other day. The main occupation of these people, and others in their blood line, during the Neolithic period has been agriculture, from the sowing and harvesting of which they, perhaps, got the idea of the immortality of the soul and of its transmigration. They cultivated rice, sugar cane, vegetables, areca nut and betel vines, and extracted sugar from the cane, and weaved cotton cloth and lived in thatched dwelling units. They recognized red colour as the colour of life, of rosy health. Being the colour of life-sustaining blood, they regarded it as sacred and smeared their sacred stones and whatever else they worshipped, with vermillion and turmeric; In keeping with this view, colour of marriage ceremony and married life was red, and so was the custom of married women having vermillion in the partings of the hair on their heads.

Hindu religion and culture have interwoven strands of ideas and beliefs of different people who settled on this subcontinent, and of all these, three ideas stand out prominently being the contributions of the Aryans, the Dravidians and the Proto-Australoids. Proto-Austroloid ideas of cosmic and creational myths have found their way into the Hindu religion through the Puranic writings after varying modifications by their writers — the mythical story of *Amrita Manthan* wherein the good and the bad strive against each other to secure the ambrosia for eternal life, appears to be Austric based. Enumeration of the days by the phases of the moon, *tithis*, the system which is still used by the Hindus, is of Austric origin, as also some other ideas on astronomy; corresponding ideas can also be traced amongst the Melanesians and Polynesians. Myths and ideas about the creation of the world from an egg, *avtaras* or the incarnations of Vishnu, Nagas as serpent spirits of waters and the under world, Zoomorphic deities born out of tribal totems — Nagas, the snake deities, the tortoise, *makara* or the crocodile, the monkey god Hanuman, Ganesha with the elephant head — all these are Austric. Also Austric are some of the magico-religious rituals of some of the Hindus of today, like removal of evil eye by performing *neochhawar*, or observance of some taboos. Linga-worship, taking the idea from the "digging stick used for ploughing the fields", was possibly a contribution of these people. A lot of material relating to magic spells incorporated in black Yajur Veda is based on Austric tradition.

As has been stated earlier, Austric Proto-Australoids were spread throughout the length and breadth of India, and there were pockets of them all along the routes they took initially, may be, to get out of this subcontinent, and subsequently to return to it. Those of them living in Afghanistan and the northern plains of India became Aryan speaking during the second and the first millennium B.C., and, one can say, got extensively involved in the activities and culture of their regions. The fine mix that their language(s), religion and culture made with what later came to be called the Aryan civilization, to which the contributions of these people are not easily recognizable, has misled many a modern investigator into believing that, perhaps, the Aryans themselves originated in this subcontinent.

Today it would be difficult to identify the specific traits and characteristics of the Austric Australoid people as such, but generally it can be said that they were a gregarious lot, happy-go-lucky, superstitious, and timid, though it has been said that they were not coward. They were simple folks, generally quite content with their lot, a trait they evolved as food gatherers where they had little control over what grew naturally on food yielding trees and plants, and, may be, for having this trait of contentment ingrained into their character, they, by and large, have been easily dominated by whatever people came to this land, and have generally served as the underdog. Aryans ridiculed their comparative ugliness, their snub noses and dark colour, and called them Nishads, the dark skinned Austric dwellers of the forests. Their contribution to progressive activities, or the development of civilization, in the regions under their influence, has been noteworthy. It has not been in their temperament to aggressively take on the challenges of time and surmount the problems; they have believed in solving them by adopting passive means. They did not have to fight the rigours of the Ice Ages, and when challenged by those who had to, they were not able to hold their own, for, at least physically, they were not up to them. Though pacifists in character they have stuck to their values doggedly, and in areas where they predominated, they have managed to convert the aggressors to their way of thinking and convince them that aggression solved nothing. They have the capability for excellence in performance, but have generally been condemned to poverty, even destitution, because of deprivation inflicted upon them by physically superior and temperamentally more aggressive classes. They have been an important strand in India's social, cultural and religious fabric.

(c) *Dravidian Speaking People*

Dolichocephalic, colour of skin varying between wheatish to dark, these people came from the Mediterranean region over a long period, basically infiltrating through whatever openings for ingress into this country they could find along its north-western borders, or in the Indus delta, or even along the coast to the south of it. There have been African infiltrations too along the western coast, but those people have since merged with the Dravidian stock and are no longer recognizable. Although infiltration into this country has been an almost continuous process, and to a lesser extent continues even to this day, three major categories of Dravidian speaking people have been identified by the anthropologists, being the Palaeo-Mediterraneans, (very dark, bordering almost on black), the Mediterraneans, and the Orientals; this last category includes people of light complexion from areas east of the Mediterranean. The Mediterraneans and the Orientals were highly civilized people, coming from areas which were economically, culturally and in statecraft, the leaders in about the most developed area of the civilized world of that time. The proper Mediterraneans, taller and fairer than the Palaeo-Mediterraneans, inhabit the Punjab and the upper Gangetic plane. They were a part of the Indus Valley Civilization, but were later Aryanised, at least in so far as the language was concerned, and played a significant role in the evolution of Hinduism in Northern India. As for the Orientals, they can be recognized by the pronounced longish nose and fair skin, and inhabit Punjab, Sind, Rajasthan and Western Uttar Pradesh; infact, a fair scattering of this variety is found almost all over India.

Of the Dravidian speaking people, Palaeo-Mediterraneans, were about the first to arrive here and spread far and wide in the four corners of this subcontinent intermingling freely with the inhabitants, the Negritos and the Austric-Australoids. Down south, along with some Mediterraneans and the Orientals, they formed a solid block in what in the modern times are known as the states of Tamil Nadu, Kerala, Karnataka and Andhra Pradesh; together these states are considered as one block by the people of northern India, mostly because of the similarity of their languages — otherwise, as stated above, Dravidian mix is extensively present throughout the whole country; those in the north, however, no longer speak the Dravidian languages, their current speech mode being thoroughly Sanskrit-based. In Baluchistan there is an area where people speak "Brahui", which is Dravidian, and there is enough evidence to support the view that at some time in the past the Dravidians inhabited a large tract of land which in the north-west extended as far as Afghanistan and Iran. The mix of their language with the Austric-Australoid languages and Sanskrit, is mainly responsible for the evolution of the regional languages of the northern parts of this subcontinent.

The words *Dasa* and *Dasyu* that the Aryans used for the Dravidians, apparently were used by them during their inhabitation in Iran as well, and possibly meant "country", and were not derogatory references as they came to suggest in later times; the meaning possibly changed after the two racial groups had turned mutually hostile. It is quite possible that the fusion between the two groups had started in Eastern Iran itself, before the Indo-Aryans entered India.

In his book *Hinduism*, A.C. Bouquet says that ancient and longstanding elements in institutional Hinduism are such as also existed in the Mediterranean and Asia Minor of that time, and the megalithic culture of early India is closely allied to what prevailed in Bronze Age Europe, including Britain. Likewise the snake cult is similar to that of Crete, and the Indian bull-worshipping and bull-fighting practices resemble those of early Mediterraneans. It is almost certain that the Fire-walking ceremonies of South India were associated with the cult of Artmis in Cappadocia. Attention has also been drawn to the slender waists of males in Cretan paintings which are very suggestive of the males in some parts of South India. In religion, Dravidian thoughts and practices have made a notable contribution to Hinduism as it is practiced today. When Aryans came to India they worshipped a vague set of deities, like the Dyaush Pita (Zeus in Greece) — the sky father — and the *Prithvi Mata* — the mother earth. Austrics, similarly had Sun god (Sin Bonga) and Moon goddess (Ninda Chando). Only the Dravidians had the concept related to the cosmic energy creating the universe and within that the rise of the force of life. In common parlance God was represented as father, the Creator, and Mother Goddess, the life creating force. These concepts they seem to have brought from their homeland in the islands of the Aegean Sea and the countryside bordering it, comprising Greece and Asia Minor.

As opposed to the practice of *homa*, the fire worship of the Aryans which was generally accompanied by animal sacrifice, the Dravidians worshipped with offerings of grain and flowers — *puja* — a practice followed today almost all over India in most variations of Hinduism. Siva is a Dravidian god and Durga their goddess, while Vishnu and Krishna are only partly Aryan; a part of the concept has arisen from the Dravidian thought. The phallic symbol of Siva is basically of Austric or Proto-Australoid contribution, but the concept, possibly, has been modified under Dravidian influence. Aryans did not have idols for worship and worshipped only the fire. But the Dravidians had. As stated earlier, zoomorphic deities were mostly of Austric contribution, but the monkey god, Hanuman, in his final concept appears to be of Dravidian origin. All in all, it can be said that in the present day Hinduism the major part of culture, religious thought and practice, is based on the contribution of the people of non-Aryan origin.

Of the early Tamils it is said that they had small city states ruled by kings, who lived in palaces and had courtiers and other fanfare to bolster their image. They had a language and script, and they wrote on palmyra leaves and compiled books, and believed in God, and made temples in His honour. They had framed laws (but had no lawyers) and followed prescribed customs, and had the institution of marriage. They possessed a good knowledge of common metals, and astronomy, and knew agriculture, and lived in well organized dwelling units in properly planned towns, and knew weaving, spinning, dyeing and pottery, being well versed in martial arts and the use of bows, arrows, spears and swords.

(d) *The Mongoloid Group*

Of this group, the tribes living in Assam and along the Indo-Myanmar border, with dolichocephalic heads, constitute one part, while those with round heads found amongst the less primitive tribes in Myanmar and Chittagong Hills, form the other. Then we have the Tibeto-Mongoloid group who amongst the Mongoloid groups are more modern, and live in Sikkim and Bhutan; they seem to have immigrated from Tibet in comparatively recent times. However, not much importance is attached to these groups as they touched only the northern and eastern fringes of the subcontinent and made little contribution to the development of Hindu religion and culture; they have evolved from the intermingling of the Proto-Australoid and Mongoloid stocks. Till recently, isolated in the jungles and mountains of the north and the east, they lived like people of the Neolithic times. Christian missionaries took advantage of their isolation, particularly along the eastern borders, and converted a number of them to the Christian faith, establishing churches in their villages and generally educating them. They also secured financial support from their governments for the proselytization process. But in spite of the efforts of these missionaries and host of other agencies, north-eastern India continues to be inhabited by tribes which are primitive and live under social and economic conditions which their more civilized cousins in most parts of the country experienced thousands of years back. Even the Tibeto-Mongoloids, though more advanced compared to the tribes of north-east India, have subsisted under conditions which may be classified as primitive, with modern science playing a mere nominal role in their day to day existence. These people inhabit generally the Himalayan foothills, though in recent times they have started moving further south and are getting assimilated in the Indian cultural, economic and social main stream.

(e) *Western Brachycephals*

Another group which spread almost all over India, is classified as *Western Brachycephals*, and comprises the Alpinoids, the Dinarics and the Armenoids. Of these, the Alpinoids are a subdivision of the Caucasian race who lived mostly around the Alps. In India, the majority of them are in Gujarat; their broad-headed variation live along the west coast. They arrived in this country before the Aryans but, possibly, spoke the Aryan dialect. The Dinarics are originally from the Yugoslavian mountain region and have settled in this country in Bengal, Orissa, Kathiawar and Kannada and Tamil lands. In their near original form they can be located in Coorg. As for the Armenoids, originating from Armenia, they possibly arrived with the civilized Mediterraneans, that is the Dravidians, and spoke their language. The Parsis of Mumbai are a typical example of them; they are different from the long-headed Iranian Zoroastrians still living in Iran.

(f) *Nordic Aryans*

The last of the major groups are the Nordic Aryans who, apparently, originated in the Eurasian steppes and arrived in India during the middle of the second millennium B.C. A majority of them inhabit the north-western plains and highlands, including parts of Rajasthan, Punjab, on both sides of the Indo-Pak boundary — and the hills and plains of west Uttar Pradesh. But further east they have intermingled with other racial groups. They were of fair skin, possibly with blond hair and blue eyes, and tall, but with time, under pressures of natural selection and intermingling with other groups over a long period, they are now light brown in complexion and the colour of their eyes and hair is black, although long headed Nordics of light eyes and hair are also to be seen in many parts of the country. They were a dynamic people and major contribution was in the synthesizing of different cultures into one whole. They organized the religion, the society, the sciences, arts and crafts, and almost every vocation that men of those times followed. To an appreciable extent the Hindu society of today is still governed by the rules, laws and traditions that they set out during the second and the first millennium B.C.

In addition to the people described above there have been others, like the Scythians, Huns, Greeks, Mongols, Tartars, and the like , who arrived in this country and stayed on. Their number has been small and, consequently, their contribution to the evolution and development of the structure of the Hindu civilization, has been limited. Nonetheless, while they interacted or merged with this structure, their ideas and cultures imparted to it their own hues and flavours. Hinduism is not at all averse to assimilate ideas from other sources, for this religion is not based on the tenets or dictates of any single individual or a body of men. It claims to be *Sanatana* or eternal, having its origin in the bottomlessness of the past: it has no point of start. It just evolved as the human awareness of itself and the world and the universe around improved; and this process continues unabated.

Broadly it can be said that north-western India has a larger number of the Nordic types, mixed with the Mediterraneans and the Orientals, while the peninsular people are predominantly of the Palaeo-Mediterranean stock. To the east and west of these groups we have the Alpo-Dinarics and Armenoids, some in fairly original form while others visible as intermixtures of other groups. The dark Australoids are visible everywhere, in most cases with blood from other strains, predominantly from Palaeo-Mediterraneans; they constitute the poorer sections of the population. People with Mongoloid features inhabit the east and most of the mountainous north, although in some cases their strains can be recognized in far-off lands as well, like in Bengal and Orissa. The racial groups as discussed are today grouped in one or the other speech families, like the Austric (Kol or Munda), Sino-Tibetan, the Dravidian or the Indo-European (Aryan). But in spite of the differences, the common type of economic life based on agriculture has substantially brought the different groups together and ultimately evolved a common Indian culture and religion, and a common Indian archetype.

With the exception of the Aryans, most racial groups of this subcontinent did not have to face the rigours of the ice age. Any racial group with a superior capability to weather the effects of environments has a better chance to dominate. But there are other factors too that contribute to the collective strength of a racial group. Diet is one. Paranthropus, a human-like vegetarian primate, was possibly eliminated by the hunter, meat eating, Australopithecus, another type of primate, who made tools and was, therefore, cleverer and more intelligent compared to the mere food gatherer. Likewise the Australopithecus went out of the scene with the arrival of the advanced variety of the same species equipped with better tools and brains; tool developing capability improved the intelligence of a community, and vice versa, that is better intelligence produced superior tools, and higher dominating skills.

In the midst of harsh and existence-threatening environments, the communities of the north had to expend a considerable effort in the survival struggle, while those living in softer climes in the south could afford to pay more attention to the development of their civilizations; they, thus, developed earlier than the northerners. Gradually, however, the environment became more congenial and as the northerners emerged from the shackles of the survival process, they were more ingenious, hardier and better disciplined than the southerners, for as hunter-gatherers their survival was conditioned by their capacity to work in close cooperation with their kin and other people of their community, alongwith high quality of physical and mental robustness. In the harsh conditions of the north it was difficult for them to survive on their own; collective community effort was needed for this. But the southerner, living under salubrious environment, were not faced with such compulsions, and could survive even without having to bother very much about the community diktat. Additionally, the surplus wealth that the south had created with favourable geographical and environmental conditions, greatly tempted the north, and equipped as they were with superior discipline, physical fitness and martial skills, they took it. Right from their inception, the human being have fought for possessions every where: northerners have fought northerners and so have southerners fought southerners. But this difference in the aggressive capabilities between the people of the south and the north was one major factor prompting the southward movement, in search of easier pastures and richer possessions.

As stated above, the first to arrive on this subcontinent, from the west, were the Negritos. At the time of their arrival some habitations of food gatherers might already have been there, but little is known about them; they possibly got assimilated by the newcomers, or might even have gone extinct over a period of time. The country had enough vegetation in terms of food, and the climate was gentle. The arriving Negritos sprinkled themselves in small groups, in tiny settlements, and found life to be sufficiently comfortable, and they stagnated. Before, after or alongside them appeared the Proto-Australoids, who were probably already present on the subcontinent partly, and partly arriving from the west. They were much better organized, and were constantly on the move, and spoke a branch of Austric languages, ushering possibly the neolithic era where ever they went. They possibly ushered the era of land cultivation and organized themselves into village based societies. They easily overpowered the Negritos, taking possession of their lands, possibly enslaving them, and having easy access to their women, and setting in motion a process which ultimately resulted in their assimilating the Negritos into their own stock. Likewise Proto-Australoids were assimilated into the stock of the Dravidians, and so the process continued, and the victors and the vanquished continued to merge till a fairly homogeneous mix of the interracial groups had materialized. All migrants must have felt contempt towards the people they had overpowered and must have resisted intermingling with them, for they must have considered them mentally and physically inferior. That was how the caste system was born. But this system notwithstanding, with the passage of time, as the moderate climate and abundant food softened their dynamic traits. The sanguine edge they possessed at the time of the first arrival, blunted and they succumbed to the lure of easy life and multiplied with impunity in the company of local women, raising a stock which ultimately, over a long period, almost completely overwhelmed them.

The caste system was in practice in this country long before the advent of the Indo-Aryans; the latter, because they had a viable language at their command, made a go at formalizing and systematizing it. But the whole system as it existed , was so complex that even they could do hardly any better than give it a broad brush treatment; they left the system as it was being followed in the villages of their time, though they put the entire artisans' class in the category of Sudras, which may not have been the kind of status this class enjoyed earlier. The complexities and the compulsions of the system precluded any attempt to tamper with it, and the Aryans were no exception. Instead they devised the

Varna system which was a distinction based on the colour of the skin and the profession one followed.

Like no two animals are equal in strength and wits, no two human beings are identical in any one aspect: looks, colour, physical strength, or intelligence. While continuous movement and interbreeding has ensured homogeneity, the impact of the environmental factors impinging upon the genetics, has produced a variety within the species. When compared to the people who arrived in this country later, the stock of the Proto-Australoids has demonstrated a subtle mental and physical inferiority, and they have passed this on, to a greater or lesser degree, to whatever other groups or communities they came in contact with. This inferiority has adversely affected the people of South and South East Asia over the millennia. A large number of people of these regions are of smaller built, have narrower frames, smaller skull size and have demonstrated lesser ingenuity or determination for progress as compared to the people of northern regions of the Euro-Asian land mass. Hindus of India have not remained unaffected by this deficiency.

The Dravidian element of the Hindus comprising the Palaeo-Mediterraneans, the Mediterraneans proper and the 'Orientals', were basically people of the seas. The Palaeo-Mediterraneans who were the first to arrive in this country, mostly in search of means of survival, and who interacted and interbreed freely with the local people, got relegated to the bottom rung of the social order. The later Dravidians — the Mediterraneans proper and the Orientals — were a highly developed lot, with fairly clear ideas about religion, social institutions, customs, traditions, trade, arts and crafts and systems of governance. They basically arrived as traders and eventually established colonies which they ruled efficiently and with the required degree of strictness; the process was almost repeated by the British 5000 years later, except that the Dravidians lived on in this country while the British never really considered it as their home; but considering the means of transport and communications available then, the Dravidians hardly had any option.

[illegible] the extent of the [illegible] was a distinction based on the colour of the skin and the [illegible]

Like no [illegible] the equation [illegible] human beings' evidence [illegible] expectation, [illegible] and strength, [illegible] intelligence. While [illegible] and interior [illegible], they ensured [illegible] the [illegible] conflict [illegible] ancient Indian groups, not the people [illegible] variety within the species. When compared to the people who arrived in this [illegible] place, the [illegible] and they [illegible] greater or lesser [illegible]

[illegible] and the people [illegible] However the [illegible] large number [illegible] people of these regions [illegible] small [illegible] have [illegible] small [illegible] had [illegible] opportunity of determination for [illegible] the people in northern regions of the [illegible] Hindus of India [illegible] this determination.

The [illegible] the [illegible] the Muslims [illegible] and the [illegible] were basically people in [illegible] Indo-Muslim [illegible] that [illegible] mainly [illegible] with the [illegible] the [illegible] The [illegible] the Muslims [illegible] highly developed [illegible] about role of social institutions, customs, [illegible] trade, arts and crafts and systems of governance. They [illegible] arrived as traders and eventually established colonies which were ruled efficiently and with the required degree of [illegible] the [illegible] British 500 years [illegible] the [illegible] lived on in this country [illegible] the British [illegible] their home, [illegible] and [illegible] the [illegible] hardly had any option.

Two

The Indus Valley Civilization

Many centuries before 3500 B.C., people from the Mediterranean region and areas east of it, were emigrating to the western parts of India. The area over which this west to east movement was taking place extended as far as the lower Mesopotamia (Sumer) in the west, and included the areas of Elam, Southern Iran and Baluchistan. Basically the whole area is arid, with scanty rainfall, and the settlements depend upon rivers for their water supply. This movement is an event of the Bronze Age, as in the absence of iron tools, clearing of wooded areas, or levelling the slopes of rough hills, habitation was not an easy proposition. River valleys were level and not wooded, and were fertile, and could produce enough grains and other agricultural produce to support large populations; in fact, the valleys generated surplus for export and trade and commerce. Once the settlements had stabilized, the situation automatically lent itself to the exploitation of mineral and metal resources in the closeby areas. Industry, trade and commerce, thus, became the main sustaining force of these settlements, and gradually they took larger areas under their influence; the strategy helped them to gain wealth for themselves, and the leasure they enjoyed as a result, enabled them, over a period of time, to develop their own language, religious concepts, social order, system of government, and so on. They were the earliest known civilizations in the Middle East, Central Asia and in and around the Indian subcontinent; some of them even made important contributions towards the progress of the human race.

Before the emergence of Mohenjodaro and Harappa, settlements possessing remarkable organizational skills had sprung up in South East Afghanistan, Baluchistan and Sindh. These were almost at their prime around 3500 B.C.; they must have started a few centuries earlier. Some of the better known amongst them are Mundigak in South East Afghanistan (Quetta), and Rana Ghundai in North Baluchistan, and Nal, Nundara and Kulli in South Baluchistan. There were a number of them located in the present day Sindh province of Pakistan, starting from Bahawalpur in north Sindh, and then along the Indus river, going down south as far as Somnath in Kathiawar, and Mehgam, Telod and Bhagatrav in the Deltas of the Narbada and Tapti. Up in the north, in the Punjab, these extended as far as Harappa and Ropar.

All pre-Harappan settlements were located in the close vicinity of established water sources, and there is evidence to suggest that the whole of the region received more rainfall then, than what it does at present, that the hill slopes had more trees and that rivers Ghaggar, Sarasvati of earlier literature, and Drisadvati, carried substantial perennial water. At the time of Alexander's invasion, however, as deduced from the accounts of the Greeks, climatically this area was as it is today ; Alexander came to India almost 2500 years after the peak of the Indus civilization, or even later when compared to the earlier settlements. The majority of the people migrating eastwards were the Mediterraneans and they had amongst them labourers, agriculturists, artisans and men of trade and commerce. They laid out their settlements with meticulous care, in a well planned manner, testifying to the high quality of their earlier knowledge, discipline and organizational skills, and their faith in orderliness and their resolve to make use of their experience to the best advantage of every member of their community. Their houses were organized in blocks of buildings constructed out of mud bricks or stones, and provided with wooden doors. In some cases the houses had stone foundations, or flat roofs with stairs leading to them. Roadways between houses could be six to eight feet in width while in more densely populated areas the narrow alleys could barely be two feet six inches to three feet wide.

Interesting information has come from the cemetries of these pre-Harappan civilizations. Burials were mostly 'fractional' that is, burial after the bodies had been exposed and disintegrated and only part of the skeletons were left. Some graves had remains of more than one body interned together. Other than the remains, the grave consisted of pottery ware, bones of animals sacrificed, killed possibly to support the soul during after-life — number and type of animals slaughtered possibly depended upon the status of the person(s) buried. Some graves had implements like the axes. Most had red pigment, while women graves had bangles of pottery and shell; this was mostly in graves in Sindh. Pottery made by these pre-Harappan settlements was of high quality. Nal and Amri ware are of fine soft buff or pinkish paste, while in other settlements some are of grey or, sometimes, of brown or even black colour. The excellence is vouched for by the very thin walls of the vessels. Pottery is wheel turned. Figures on the wares include several types of geometrical designs or animals including lions, fishes and birds, occasionally ox, sometimes leaves of the pipal and the sacred fig. Tools and implements are of copper which contains a small percentage of lead, nickel and arsenic. Stamp seals, even though these were prevalent during the Bronze Age cultures of Iran and Mesopotamia, are conspicuous by their absence, except for a lone steatite seal recovered from Nal cemetery; this seal is of irregular shape, and has etched upon it the like of a kite, with a snake held in its claws, — could this be the Garuda, the vehicle of a later deity Vishnu!

The Kulli settlement was located on the western banks of the Hingol river, in southern Baluchistan. This settlement precedes Harappa by a couple of centuries, and at the time of its prime its culture seems to have evolved pretty much like the Harappan culture or one might even say, the culture of north-west India till almost the early years of this century. It had baked clay figurines of women or cattle, a possible pointer towards Mother Goddess worship, and also, may be, towards regarding the bull as a sacred animal; there are numerous figurines of the humped bull, some of these figurines, no doubt, served as toys, but there are clear pointers that some also served a religious purpose. Most female figurines found at Kulli culture sites terminate at the waste in pedestals of flat bottom. Little attention has been paid to facial details, but the necks have been shown as adorned with strings of beads and necklaces; some figurines show ornaments as are worn by Indian ladies of wealth even to this day, particularly in Gujarat, Kathiawar and Sind and western parts of the north-west area of the subcontinent. Likewise, in the hairstyles, the high curls piled up in front and supported by a fillet above the forehead, and the hair at the back resting on the nape in a heavy tress, or the hair arranged in two braids resting on the shoulders, or the forearms carrying a number of bangles, sometimes going above the elbow, are recognizable amongst the women of the western parts of India of today. Soft stoneware of the Kullis, and copper and bronze objects made by them and other village cultures along the river — of particular significance being the five inches diameter bronze mirror from Mehi — bring out the existence of important links between these village cultures and Mesopotamia and Syria in the west. In fact, there appears to be remarkable similarity between these settlements and the smaller communities of Mesopotamia, Elam and Iran. Even the trade in the original phases was amongst these people only and it was not till about four or five centuries later that it got expanded to cover the Harappans.

Apart from the figurines of women, possibly representing Mother Goddess as the guardian of the dead and the patron deity of fertility, no other evidence of fertility cult has been found in southern Baluchistan. However, in northern Baluchistan, a carved stone phallus was recovered from Moghul Ghundai area, and in a nearby site a female figurine with an exaggerated vulva and thighs was found; Ghundai precedes Kulli by six or seven centuries. It is only at Harappa that similar evidence of fertility symbols has been unearthed.

By early fourth millennium B.C., village life in most parts of habitable India, including Baluchistan and Afghanistan, had fairly developed. People cultivated and weaved and made pottery and polished stones into microliths for use in implements like arrows, knives and swords. During the latter half of the fourth millennium B.C. there was further immigration of tribes whose culture was similar to that of the people of Sumer. They cultivated barley and wheat (strains of grains cultivated by these tribes were about the same as were cultivated in the north-western India till recently); bred cattle; used bronze implements; engraved or painted their pottery (turned on wheel) and worshipped a nude fertility goddess. They were, in effect, the people of the pre-Harappan village cultures like Kulli or Rana Ghundai.

The Rise of the Cities

The cultures of settlements in Baluchistan and south Afghanistan, though broadly similar, varied a great deal from one another in finer detail, for example, they did not have a common system of weights and measures nor was there any uniformity in the designs of their buildings or housing blocks, or in the detail on their pottery, and, possibly, in their religious concepts as well, although no definite information is available on this last aspect. Actually these settlements were fairly displaced from one another in time and space, and hence the difference, for example, Rana Ghundai preceded Kulli by nearly seven centuries, and then Kulli, being closer to the sea and with fairly level land around it, was better equipped to have good means of communications and transportation as compared to the uplands of Rana Ghundai. But migrants moved on, eastwards, and once they were out of the difficult areas of the Makran coast, Baluchistan and south Afghanistan, the environments were easier. Evidence has it that the area received more rain compared to the present, that the rivers and streams carried abundant water, and the soil was fertile and level, and inter-settlement communications and movements were easier. Thus, the conditions were ripe for the rise of a central authority which could coordinate the trade and commerce amongst the settlements and secure profits, though this authority had to have the necessary business acumen and be well versed in the art of trading on a large-scale, including the documentation for it, and drawing specifications and imposing the necessary discipline for securing quality control.

By about the middle of the first half of the third millennium B.C. a city civilization was operating in the Indus Valley; it was then at its prime and must have taken some time coming up, although it has been generally suggested that transition from village settlements to organized city life was almost abrupt, and possibly this was caused by a take over by a class of people who had drawn their inspiration from Sumer, to which they had either originally belonged or with which they had strong affiliations. From over one hundred settlement sites, a centrally administered state was raised which extended from the Makran coast in the west to Kathiawar, and in the north included Punjab, covering Harappa, Ropar, and went right up to the Himalayan foothills, while in the east it covered the Ganga-Yamuna 'doab', all in all a vast area enclosed by a rough triangle measuring around 1.3 million square kilometres; compared to 3.3 million square kilometre area of the present day India! The central authority had standardized almost every aspect of the life of the people, their arts and crafts, designs of the pottery they made, the weights and measures they used, the houses they lived in, including the details regarding the blocks formed by clusters of houses, the width of streets, the design of sewage disposal system, the systems of defence and communications and movement, and so on. In the midst of these settlements, separated by about 550 kilometres, stood the two cities of Mohenjo-Daro and Harappa, the two capitals of this trading conglomerate, each in an area of at least a square mile and almost identical in design and detail, each developed with baked bricks of standard dimensions. In later times Sakas and Kushans also ruled their state in north-west India from the twin capitals of Taxila and Mathura, but then that happened almost three millennia later.

The near absolute uniformity of products of Harappa culture suggests the existence of a well organised central authority which meticulously oversaw the enforcement of rules and regulations pertaining to the different aspects of the commercial activities, including the techniques of production, e.g., for items like bricks, or designs for houses, or weights and measures. Artisans and workers' guilds must have fully cooperated, or else they would have had to face the prospect of losing their wage earning capability. Mohenjodaro was built nine times, and the lower most level has yet, perhaps, not been reached, for at this stage the excavators hit the subsoil water and further digging was not possible, while at Harappa six successive settlements can be traced, one on top of the other. As Indus carried far more water, its floods inflicted greater punishment on Mohenjodaro, located on its western bank, than did its tributary, Ravi, on Harappa, located on its eastern bank. As a result more information has come out of the diggings at Harappa, although information about the layout of the cities has almost wholly been obtained from Mohenjodaro (city of the dead). Located near Larkana in central Sindh, this city was laid out into roads and streets running almost parallel, in east-west and north-south directions, creating blocks of buildings which were again subdivided by smaller and not so regular streets meant to provide access to the individual houses. The size of a block was around 800 feet in the east-west and 1200 feet in the north-south direction and the width of the main streets, which were unpaved, could be as much as 30 feet. At the river end of either city there was a large citadel, and what exactly the function of these citadels was, is not clear. May be, in the style of Sumer, the high platforms within the citadels had temples standing upon them, although there is no evidence of it. Also there is no evidence to show that the cities were originally provided with any fortifications. At Mohenjodaro the architecture of the citadel seems to have been dictated by the Great Bath, the Collegiate Building, the Pillared Hall, and, may be, by the Temple which, some believe, lies underneath the stupa — the stupa, as is obvious, came up at the site at a much later date. The existence of the temple is deduced from the presence of the Great Bath, a kind of a structure which has normally accompanied a temple, right from the ancient times. Most Hindu temples of any reckoning, and the Pillared Hall which some experts believe, were centres for community prayer or meditation. At Harappa the Citadel seems to have had ceremonial terraces approached by a processional pathway leading from a ramp; terraces have been provided with guard rooms along the periphery. It appears the terraces had a ceremonial function which required a processional approach, but such a function could be religious or secular, or both.

Most buildings were erected with baked bricks; sun-dried bricks were used for inner walls and for filling of platforms or other places where large volume of construction were involved, for example, protective works, or ramparts. The striking feature of the Indus civilization has been the high standard of workmanship in any kind of construction job, including houses where brick laying and arranging skills could match the skills of modern times, and its almost modern system of sewerage running under the streets into which an elaborate system of house drains emptied. The main drains could be cleaned by lifting brick-made manhole covers. All sewage emptied into soakage pits and not in the river, a remarkable measure to arrest pollution. There is no evidence of lavatories having been provided, unless these were located at the roofs of the buildings. A house was built around a courtyard; it had rooms of varying sizes around it or on its three sides; bathrooms were located in the corner closest to the street drain, and so was the kitchen tucked in another corner — this kind of arrangement was also followed by the Babylonians. Houses had two or more storeys and were provided with vertical drainpipes, possibly for draining the kitchens and bathrooms at the higher floors. Some houses had doorless chambers at the bottom-most level, which could be for use by servants, unless those were cess pits for latrines, or storage vaults, or were meant to strengthen foundations against floods. Almost all houses had their own wells, and every two houses had a common well. Numerous sherds found around some public wells show that the custom followed by the Hindus till the other day (to some extent even now, by the orthodox) whereunder drinking twice from the same cup was not approved and after each drinking the clay cup was discarded, was very much in vogue even then. Rubbish-shoots emptied into rectangular bins outside from where, possibly, the refuse was removed under municipal arrangements. Wooden beams and rafters and columns were used for roofs, which were generally flat and had bamboo and rush matting covered with earth for protection from the elements. The sizes of the houses varied, apparently in keeping with the position and status of the owner. Small houses for workers, some for labourers, have been located. Granaries were near the rivers and had loading ramps, quays, labour quarters. The flour mills must also have made use of the labourers. There is every indication to show the existence of a well organized industry and a powerful bureaucracy deciding on what was to be produced, and how much, and about the distribution of the produce, including its export. In the opinion of Stuart Piggott (author of *Prehistoric India*), Harappa must have possessed the first really organized industry in Western Asia.

The Indus civilization comprised numerous small and large towns and villages, and at quite a few sites burnt bricks were not used, though wherever they were used they were of the standard size of 11 inches by 5.5 inches by 2.5 inches; here and there, however, some variations in the sizes of the bricks have been recorded. At some sites, stone has been used for the foundations, or stone walls have been constructed for five feet or so from the foundations, and thereafter the construction is in mud bricks. There has been no indication of fortifications in the layout of towns and villages except at Ali Murad where a three to five feet thick wall surrounds the housing complex, or at Sutkagen-Dor in the Makran where more massive fortifications, duly provided with batter to the outer face, protect the living area; this probably was a strongly defended outpost the like of which may have existed along the overland trade routes.

There is evidence to suggest extensive trade links between the Indus people and Mesopotamia; in the textual references of the latter the former has been referred to as the country with the name 'Meluhha', which has been given as source of many valuable commodities including those required to support inter-city wars in Mesopotamia or Elam. Trade was apparently over sea routes through the Gulf of Oman. Dilmun, probably Bahrain, was, it seems, an important staging post along the route. But trade with Elam could have been possible along the land route as well, although movement of goods over such a long distance, over hundreds of kilometres, would indeed have been an achievement of some significance. Indus civilization flourished during the Bronze Age, and for its trade and industry it collected raw materials from far and wide. It got bitumen, probably even steatite, from Baluchistan, silver from Afghanistan, and gold, silver, lead, tin, semiprecious stones including *lapis-lazuli* from Iran. It also had plenty of its own resources: semi-precious stones from Kathiawar, copper and lead from Rajasthan, wood from the Himalayan hills, and so on.

Indus trade and industry must have been backed by a strong merchant community. There is considerable evidence to suggest the export of Harappan items to the west, to Mesopotamia, Syria, Elam, but, very strangely, very little has been found in the Indus Valley diggings which might indicate that it came into this region

Steatite Seals Unicorn with a Standard

Shiva Pashupati

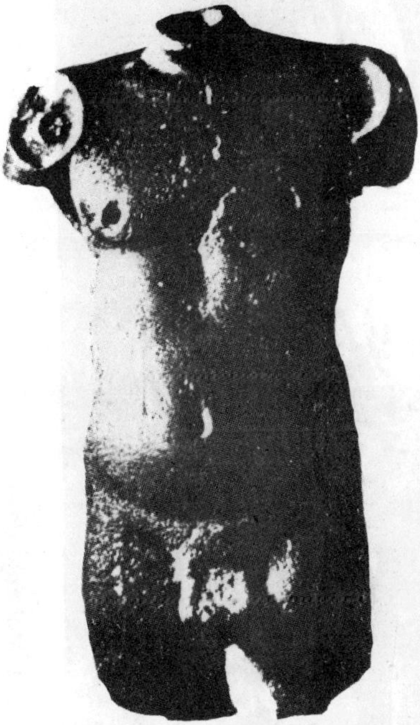

Red Stone Statue Harappa

Steatite Male Head, Mohenjo-daro

Clay Figurines, Possibly Representing Mother Godess

Great Bath, Mohenjo-daro

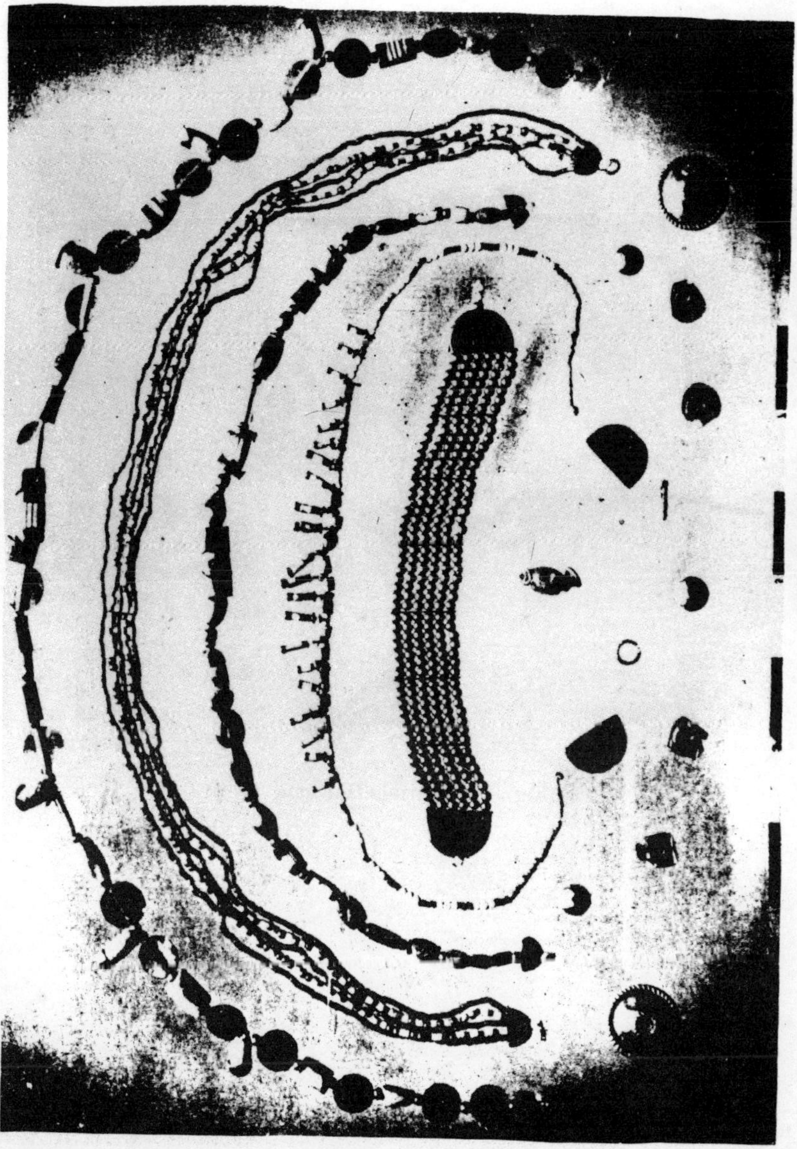

Jewellery-Necklaces, Mohenjo-daro

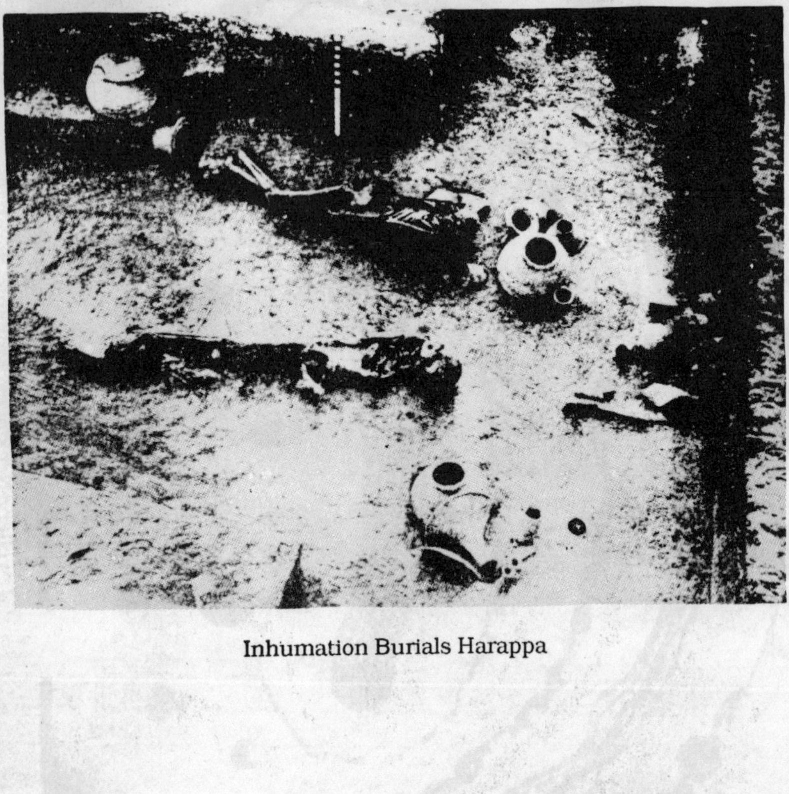

Inhumation Burials Harappa

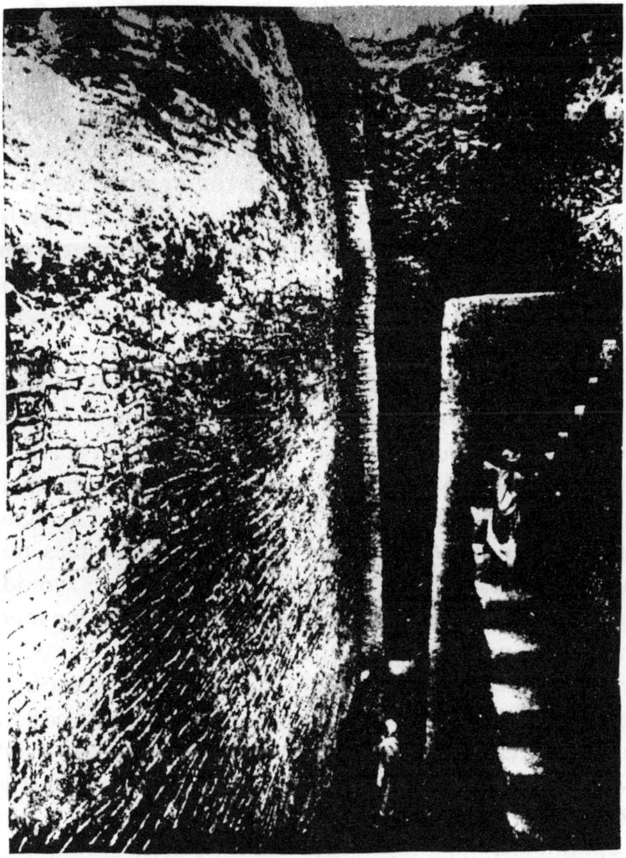

Section Through Mud-Brick Defences of Citadel.

from outside. One might, therefore, suspect that the trade was, in the first instance, organized at the initiative of the western traders, who, in the course of time, colonized the region, basically with a view to thoroughly exploiting its raw materials and abundant labour. The diggings have shown us the Indus Valley at its prime; it must have taken some time to develop it to that stage, considering the slow pace at which anything could happen those days, and during this time some of the merchant community must have got used to the environment and gradually settled down in this region. But their prime interest must have remained in the parent country, and even subsequently, after their links with the parent country had been severed and they had established themselves in commanding positions, as rulers of the region, trade must have continued to be their prime interest and their interest in local inhabitants, or the country in general, must have been restricted to an extent as would have ensured their continued prosperity in the conduct of trade. No big palaces were constructed, as happened in Sumer, Akkad, Syria or Elam, all of which existed contemporaneously with Indus Valley. There were no major temples, nor, any dominating priestly class, only, perhaps, as much as would have been necessary to satisfy the spiritual aspirations of the merchant community. Conservatism is the hallmark of this class, more so after it had set sails on a seemingly successful course, profits being the main goal. Any break with the past practice would be accepted with a lot of reservation and skepticism, for this could result in a loss of the established markets. Needless to say that priestly class can be equally conservative, if not more, particularly if progress tends to threaten their position or standing in the community. But in this situation there is no evidence of the existence of any dominant priestly order, nor of any major temples, nor of any other activity which might suggest established priesthood. It has been suggested that underneath the Buddhist stupa at Mohenjodaro there might be lying the structure of the ceremonial temple. This is unlikely, for if the striking feature of the Indus culture is uniformity in whatever it planned or did, and if it did have a powerful priestly class who thrived around big, ceremonial temples, then the evidence of that would have been forthcoming from the diggings at other sites as well. Nothing of the sort has happened.

It is also possible that there might have been no empire as such, no centrally run or administered territory. The workers of the areas concerned might have just attained a degree of excellence in whatever they manufactured, and that could have attracted the attention of foreign traders. These people were located in the midst of plenty in so far as food and other resources were concerned and this would have given them sufficient leisure which they would have devoted to produce items of high merit. Considering the quality of the goods and the high demand for them, the traders must have arrived from the west, from Mesopotamia Syria and/ or Elam, basically with the object of cultivating business activity, and in course of time, extended this activity to other areas of the vast Indus basin. To begin with they would have established themselves in key geographical positions which were strategically important for the viability of their trade, like Mohenjodaro and Harappa, both located on the riverine communications systems so essential for the movement of goods, particularly downstream. Considering the movement and communications patterns of those times, the traders probably selected the areas to be exploited on the basis of utility, from the point of view of availability of labour, or of some important raw material, like metals — silver, copper, zinc — or agriculture produce like cotton, wheat, barley, or precious and semiprecious stones, including jadeite, lapis-lazuli, onyx, and so on. Initially, possibly, only the traders quarters, and the segment of the town or village they lived in, was well organized. But with time, as nexus between the traders and their local agents and the producers/growers/ manufacturers grew and it became necessary for the latter category to operate in close proximity of the former, requirement must have arisen for a larger number of people to live in the developed sector. Developed villages turned into towns on account of the prosperity that visited them, and as the hum of activity multiplied further, the cities got evolved, carrying the multifaceted responsibilities for the smooth flow of trade within their organizations.

Was there a state at all? There is no evidence to suggest there was one. The countryside had villages and they, or a cluster of them together, existed on a self contained basis. Land was plenty, and its produce was enough for anyone who was prepared to work for it. People had fewer demands, located as they were in a temperate region; generally a thatched mud shelter, and some cloth to wrap around the torso and the loins and some kinds of food to fill the belly, was all that a person needed, and there should have been no serious problem in securing these basic needs. The governance process would have devolved upon the village chiefs, the headmen, or the Sarpanches of the later times, who might also have performed the functions of the shaman. It is difficult to guess how the leader got selected and whether he held an inheritable rank, but a study of the practices followed by the later day Indian societies, would suggest that the position was generally held at the pleasure of the members of the community, though inheritance factor did play its own part. So these self-contained village societies were there, and they produced competent workmen, and these people had leisure which they devoted to improving their skills and producing articles of high quality, which had a good demand in the countries of the west. To make the best of this situation the western trader moved into the area. He probably organized a series of cooperatives to get the optimum results.

Terrain configuration could be one reason why a viable state, let alone an empire, could not have been formed over this vast tract, criss-crossed as it was by a number of streams and rivers, some ranking among the major ones on this subcontinent. Elaborate policing arrangements would have been necessary to keep the assorted tribes together, on one course, and this, it would appear, was not possible. The mode of transport on the arterial rivers and streams was the peddle boat which could be really slow moving upstream, though near the delta it should have been possible to use sails. On the land it was the bullock cart, almost of the same dimensions and design as is in vogue in Sindh and Punjab even today, and this too was a time consuming mode of transport, certainly not suitable for the swift movement of law enforcing agencies, particularly when it came to movement over long distances. Although both the camel and the horse were known to the people of the Indus Valley, there is little evidence to suggest they were extensively used, although there is indication that horses were possibly used by Rana-Ghundai for carrying goods and people in that difficult country. But it is odd that even though extensive river trade is visualized, the finds do not provide much evidence to show this was indeed so. There has been enough proof of the use of the bullock cart — any number of clay toy carts and bulls have been found, and besides, there have been drawings of these on pottery and on the engravings on the seals — but regarding boats there has not been much, barring two representations: one on a pottery sherd, showing only a rough drawing of a boat with high prow and stern, and another, an engraving on a seal, again showing a vessel, apparently made of reed, with high prow and stern; both the representations resemble vessels from prehistoric Mesopotamia. It is possible that the boats were not a major mode of transportation, that basically movement was achieved through the use of the cart, and, of necessity, that movement could be over short distances only; over long distances the men and materials must have moved in stages. Bronze models of the present day *ekka* have been found at Harappa and Chanhudaro. This vehicle was generally used, as now, as a conveyance for a single person; the uniformity of the culture is stressed by the identical designs of the two models found at the two different places almost 650 kilometres apart.

The tribes generally settled around water sources, for existence without water was unthinkable, but the network of meandering rivers and streams would have been a serious impediment in the way of establishing inter-village/town communication and movement facility, so essential for any centralized governance. Considering the modes of transport available then, it would have taken an unrealistically long time to move troops and munitions of war to a threatened sector, whether the threat arose from an external aggression or an internal revolt. So, how could the centralized authority of a state having some of its towns and border-posts as far apart as 1500 kilometres, ensure that its writ ran throughout the length and breadth of the country? This was clearly not possible.

To take care of the security of as large a state as the Indus Valley and to enforce law and order amongst its citizens, there would have been an organized force, suitably armed with modern weaponary. In the diggings at different places no weapon troves have been unearthed. What has been found are chisels, flat axes (without shaft-hole), spears (without the strengthening midrib), knives, fish-hooks, and razors. In fact, this variety of tools was produced by the western states, like Mesopotamia and Elam as early as fourth or fifth millennium B.C. Obviously what was produced did not constitute weapons of war, but were mere tools for the day to day working; possibly the spears were for self protection or hunting. In fact, what is striking is the complete lack of improvement in the designs of these implements, even when improved designs were available in the countries with which Indus Valley had trade relations of long standing.

Another striking feature of the finds is the rarity of the silver-ware, like bowls and vases. There are plenty of bronze items, but even here the designs are not exactly attractive, or comparable with those of other contemporaneous cultures. In fact, they are as dull as the pottery designs of the time, the emphasis being on utility rather than aesthetics. There is, thus, a strong suggestion that there was, in fact, no ruling class as such, a class of aristocrats who live in high places and have an extravagant lifestyle, and infuse aesthetics in the structure of the life of the citizens. They are the cause of whatever is big and shining: the big building works, religious works including temples, and the like, irrigation works and roads. None of these have been revealed by the explorations. No doubt we have the two 'citadels', one each at Harappa and Mohenjodaro, but the precise function of these complexes is unclear — these may well have been the high pedestals wherefrom the merchants guilds worked out their trade strategies, laid down the specifications for the goods and services they would accept for purchase and resale within the country or abroad: kind of secretariat. It has to be appreciated that Indus Valley, if it was a state as wide as it is made out to be, would have been full of cities, towns and villages developed in their typical style and not have comprised just 100 odd towns and villages and the two cities. The merchant class, possibly, decided on the pattern of trade and, based on that, the pattern of development, and all this must have been considered and finalized at the secretariat at the citadels, where some other aspects of the daily life of the wealthy community must also have been considered. The ramp, the guard-posts, the level area at the top at Harappa, might have been the components of a venue for some kind of ceremonial observations or celebrations, annually or more often, by the mercantile community itself. The secretariat not only coordinated the trade and industrial activity but, possibly, also regulated and coordinated the activity of the different merchants' guilds operating in the different fields of trade, commerce and industry. Nothing in the Indus Valley could be called kingly or aristocratic. All that can be said is that a section of its inhabitants, with their knowledge and experience, original inspiration for which may have beamed from abroad, had developed some villages, towns and two cities to a high level of utilitarian standards, and the people who could be identified for having done this could be none other than the merchant class.

But let this not cast a shadow on the achievements of the people who organized the Indus culture. The emphasis on hygienic and comfortable living is unmistakable. The organizers seemed to be well aware of the fact that, of all the species on this earth, the human being caused the maximum pollution, and their designs of their habitats fully took care of this. They ensured that their rivers and water streams were not sullied, and disposed of their sewage in soakage/sullage pits. Indus Valley alluvium was eminently suitable for this. To secure uniformity in the designs of their products they laid down specifications and for that they worked out a system of weights and measures, a system which worked in many of the north-western parts of this country till pretty recently. Writing is an essential element in the development of trade and commerce — it is so essential for book keeping — and the Indus community had a script having about 400 characters, which, excluding the variants, could be reduced to about 250 different symbols. This certainly shows that at this stage the community was at an advanced stage of its development — compare this with 900 characters in the early dynastic Sumerian script, and almost 2000 during the Uruk period for as the writing and the language develop the number of characters reduce. But the disturbing feature is that throughout the time this civilization lasted there was no further development in their language or script.

The script appears to be pictographic. In this type, to begin with, stylized pictures of items may be used to indicate the item and the quantity, for example, stylized pictures of two bulls standing side by side may indicate two bulls, or, as the script develops the indication of two bulls may be given with one picture and two dots next to it. With further development the stylized picture could get associated with a sound value, and this could reduce the number of characters in the script. While Sumerians impressed wedge-shaped marks with a reed stylus on clay tablets — script is called cuneiform — and the Egyptians did their writing on papyrus also with a script which was essentially pictographic and developed into what is called the hieroglyphic script, the Indus Valley writing is available only on seals, pot sherds and, rarely, on small copper tablets, and at no place has anything been found exceeding twenty symbols. It seems the writing is done from left to right but the following line is written from right to left, and the one following that again from left to right, and so on. No monumental or public inscription has been found, nor anything which might be a business document or a letter or a historical account. The script is unique and without descendents. Though inspiration for it must have come from Mesopotamia, its initiation seems to have followed the Egyptian pattern (Egyptian script is of a later period compared to Harappan writing and also appears to have drawn its inspiration from the Mesopotamian scripts). But its development is entirely indigenous. A lot of work has gone in the attempts to decipher the script. Some of the assumptions are that it might be related to Sanskrit, or some West-Indogermanic language like Hittite or Latin, or that it might be an early form of Dravidian language like Brahui which is still spoken in Baluchistan, but there has been no success; from time to time scholars have claimed to have deciphered the script, but their claims have not stood the tests of detailed scrutiny and examination. Interestingly, in recent times, a team of two bureaucrats from Bihar have claimed success, although the experts have felt that more proof is necessary in support of their findings. According to the findings, the script is still being used by the Santhals of Bihar, particularly during their festivals and prayers, and has words from Sanskrit, Hebrew, Arabic and Persian. The sound value of symbols, according to this team, is the same as that of the alphabets of Devnagri script, and the writing varies from left to right, from right to left, from top to bottom and from bottom to top. Every letter has a legend and most of them are related to Indian deities. The team's findings are that even today several script words are used by Santhal tribes in their folk songs which also give an account of their migration from the Indus Valley to Bihar. However, the details of what the writings on seals and pot sherds mean, have yet to be worked out.

From the script too the conclusion is unmistakable: the Harappans had no kings. Their script, apparently, was for use by the business community, basically to establish ownership of items and commodities, and record trade transactions, and not for kings whose characteristic trait is to issue proclamations or leave behind monuments with their notable deeds recorded upon them for posterity to admire and emulate, nor for common citizens wanting to express their inner feelings to friends and foes, nor for the litterateur, poets or academicians. Even the business community did not use it to put down the results of their deliberations or studies, or even the details of their business deals or contract agreements. Apparently, ownership and numbers were the main concern, although short lines of the script may have details like the specifications in terms of weights and measures, sizes in terms of lengths, widths and heights, and such like matters. Most business transactions must have been oral, as is the custom followed even upto the recent times by the business communities of Gujarat and Kathiawar, and the Sindhis, and the Bania community of Punjab and Rajasthan. There is no evidence to indicate any dynamism in the development of language or script.

The weights they used were cut in chert and accurately graded in the ratio of l, 2, 4, 8, 16, 32, 64, 160, 200, 320, 640; the weights were related to each other in multiples or fractions of 16. The Indian reader knows the system whereunder 8 rattis made one masha, and 12 mashas made a tola, and 5 tolas made one chhatank, while 16 of the latter made a seer, and 16 seers made aumund (man-kacha) and 40 seers made the heavier maund (man-pacca). This system of weights was followed in the whole of South Asia till the Governments of the countries changed over to the metric system after 1947. Even in coins the system which was in vogue on the subcontinent till recently had 3 pies equal to one paisa, and four paisa equal to one anna, and four annas equal to a quarter

Lakulisha, god of fertility, the forerunner of Shiva.
Bhubaneswar, around 12th century A.D.

rupee, and eight annas equal to a half rupee and sixteen annas made one rupee. Undoubtedly, the system was based on what was followed by the Harappans. The weighing scales consisted of a bronze bar with two copper pans suspended at its two ends and having a central fulcrum device. For heavier weights bigger scales, possibly using wooden beams, must have been used, though nothing of the sort has been found at any of the dug sites. As for the measurement of length, the evidence is scanty, but from whatever has come out, it appears they used a measure where a foot was equal to 13.2 inches, a system which was widely used in western Asia and in prehistoric and Roman Europe. The other measure they used seems to have been based on the standard cubit (*hath* in India) of 20.62 inches; this was widely used in the ancient world. The accuracy of weights and measures, and indeed the whole layout of the cities and towns, suggests not only the existence of a highly organized mercantile system but also the fact that the system was backed by a sound knowledge of engineering, practical geometry and land surveying.

One find of Harappa civilization that has attracted a lot of attention is the steatite seals. Basically these are stamp seals used for marking property. The surface is precisely carved to make figures and letters, and then the seal is heated to give it a bright white face; it is pressed directly on the soft material used for sealing. The figures on the seals are of animals or are religious symbols, and they throw some meaningful light on the religion of the Indus people. The sizes vary between 3/4 and 1½ inch square. Clay being fragile, very few specimens using this material have been found. Some terracotta sealings have been found and it appears those were used for some specific purpose. It appears every citizen, rich or poor, had them, maybe even to establish identity. Cylinder seals which were fairly extensively used by the people of Sumer, do not seem to have been popular here; only three samples have been found.

Very few real sculptures and bronzes have been found; only thirteen statuettes or fragments thereof are on record. They are made out of steatite, limestone or alabaster, and the biggest is no more than 16½ inches. Of these eleven are of elderly bearded men clad in a loose cotton garment, shown as possessing protruding noses like jews, and narrow heads of the brachycephalic, dolichocephalic or the intermediate variety. The work generally is of high quality, and has a mature dimension, considering the time when these were made. Mention has to be made of the two torsos from Harappa, whose heads and arms, which had been fastened with pegs have since been lost. One of these is of red stone and looks like the miniature of a later day 'Greek athlete', while the other, of grey limestone, is in a dancing posture and could be Siva Nataraja. The noteworthy point is that the red stone figurine later became common as Kayotsarga pose of Tirthankaras of Jain religion who claim their Tirthankaras go back thousands of years into antiquity from the time Mahavir first preached the religion. Even today most Jains are traders, and the fact to underscore is that even non-Jain traders follow the Jain way of life and food habits. Of the bronzes the most notable is the 4½ inches statuette of an Austro-Asiatic dancing girl, the model for which was possibly from south Baluchistan. It is a piece with a sensitive modelling of the body and limbs, and shows in good detail the hairdressing and adornments. Kulli pottery showed similar figurines but in a rough style, and this could lead to the conclusion that there existed regular trade between the two areas. It also shows that the naturalistic human sculpture of Harappa was the forerunner of the later day Indian art and was entirely indigenous in content. But Harappa had no monumental or public compositions. The output is on a dimunitive scale and it does not appear as if this art form had any major interest for the people who ran the affairs.

Sculptures do not give much information regarding the clothes people wore except that men supported short beards, wore a loose robe, sometimes embroidered, over the torso and left shoulder, leaving the right shoulder uncovered, and wore ornaments like rings for the fingers and ears. Below the waste they wore a piece of cloth like the present day dhoti. Apparently women were similarly clad. The garments were of cotton or wool, and apart from the apparel that just wrapped around the body, people also had items which were stitched, as the needles found at the sites would suggest. They had their hair long, with short locks at the back of the head, and parted them in the middle and used a fillet to keep them in place, or they just coiled them in a ring on top of the head; sometimes part of the hair at the sides were plaited. Fillets could be woollen or of gold, silver or copper. Women had their hair *coiffured* as some of the figurines suggest, though details are not so obvious. But on balance it would appear that a majority of the women plaited their hair at the back with a bow at the end, as is the practice followed in most parts of India of today, or they had a number of small plaits hanging on either side of the head or woven together into one or two bigger plaits. The ornaments they wore were of numerous varieties and designs, made of gold, silver, copper or faience, depending upon the status and prosperity level of the individual, and included anklets, girdles, bangles and bracelets, finger and earrings, necklaces with or without pendants, made of precious and semiprecious stones or beads of pottery or faience, fillets or head-bands for the forehead, metal or shell cones for the side of the head. No evidence has been found for any nose ornament.

In cosmetics and toiletries, the vanity case from Harappa has an item which is a combination of a piercer, possibly for use as a toothpick, the ear-scoop, for removing wax from the ears, and a tweezer, all of which bear a striking resemblance to similar items found in Sumer and northern Mesopotamia. Then there are toilet jars of ivory, metal, pottery, stone and faience. Mohenjodaro women had shell containers for rouge, face-paint, kohl and lip paints, and other item like shampoos and eye-ointments. They had bronze mirrors and ivory combs of various shapes and designs. Men's razors were made of bronze.

Kitchenware included dishes, saucers, goblets, beakers, cooking-pots and a host of other items, and these were made of pottery, metal, faience, stone, even ivory, depending upon the financial position of the family. There were needles, awls, axes, sickles, knives, fish-hooks, and so on. House furniture included *charpais* or bedsteads, reed mats, wicker stools, lamps of metal or pottery, candlesticks — apparently wax or tallow candles were also used to light the houses. Marble balls and dice were used for playing and gambling, possibly some kind of a board game was played. Men hunted and watched bullfights, and kept birds for fighting (cock-fights), and fished extensively. Children had clay toys. It seems that there was a substantial market for toys which had ingenious designs and were also exported like, bulls made out of stiff fibre and having a nodding head, little clay carts, pottery rams, monkey with a movable arm, monkeys moving up and down a string where the speed of movement could be varied by tightening or loosening the string, models of men, women, birds, animals, rattles, and so on.

Very little information is available about the medicines used by the people or their medical system, but there are indications that *silajit* was used — the substance is used as a general tonic and for diseases of the liver — as also other substances like the horns of animals, cuttle fish bones, coral, leaves of the Neem tree; kind of items which are used in the Ayurvedic system of medicine even today. However, it does appear, though there is no evidence of it amidst the Harappan finds, that the *Siddha* medicines, popular even today in Tamil Nadu in the south, were already in use. The *Siddha* system had, as borne by the present day evidence, identified around 4500 diseases, and these, it is claimed, were cured by 64 medicines, administered singly or in combinations. The aim of *Siddha* system, it is claimed, is to strengthen the body, and through that, the mind. Siddhars, who are the doctors of the system, claim that their medicines and the regimen of do's and don'ts that they prescribe, which includes yoga, bestow longevity and disease free life. They say their system has evolved after observations and experiments spread over millennia and is potent and reliable. Besides physical health, the system, they claim, can generate spiritual power if it is followed with ardency and devotion, under the guidance of a master, Guru.

The people, particularly the traders, interacted with the people of distant lands and the range of activity went as far south as the Nilgiris, and as far to the north as Kashmir, while in the west the Indus traders were maintaining close relationship with Sumer, Elam, Crete and even Egypt and Iran; there is evidence of pockets of Indus people in Sumer. In fact, there is such a lot of similarity between Sumer and Indus regarding layout of cities and towns and the general architecture of the buildings, that it may even be said that the authors of Indus were Sumerians or people from nearby lands. Possibly people from Mesopotamia, pressed by the floods and droughts in their country, or by pressures of increasing population, set out looking for areas having more stable climate and water resources, and travelling by land and sea, establishing colonies enroute in the Arabian peninsula along the Persian Gulf, arrived in the Indus basin over a period of time. Or maybe they did not take that long, for they might have already heard of the 'promised land', and made straight for it after the living conditions in their own land had become difficult because of the population pressures, scarcity of ploughable land, uncertainty caused by the floods or droughts, and the internecine inter-city wars. But they, it seems, maintained their contacts with the parent country, and, maybe, even during the peak of the Indus civilization the bureaucrats and trade advisors and top clergymen came from the parent land. Whatever the case, the great wonder is that there has been an almost complete lack of interest in propagating history. Not a shred of evidence is available from the Harappan sources that they had people who believed they had achievements to their credit and were proud of them and wanted to leave a record of that for the generations to come, or who might have built monuments, great temples, stadia, universities and the like, of dimensions which could show they were a people who thought big, had a broad horizon and operated from commanding heights. No doubt their performance was magnificent, more so when we consider the time when they appeared on the world stage, but the output has basically been utilitarian, not splendorous or regal as is the wont of ambitious, energetic people. One reason could be that the people who ran the affairs, made the cities, organized the trade, harnessed the resources, and mobilized the local manpower, in fact, were complete strangers who had little interest in this foreign land apart from their interest in trade and commerce. May be the first few generations of the freshly settled foreigners — Mesopotamians, Assyrians, Elamites or Anatolians — cultivated and trained their cadres who ultimately produced what the findings have revealed, but the subsequent generations appear to have just followed the original pattern, showing little spontaneity, or innovative variation; they appear to have been too cautious to break away from the established stereotype. With time this kind of attitude must have depressed the level of verve and vitality of the community and deprived them of the force of self-assertion, and, maybe, turned them into kind of run-of-the-mill variety who had little interest beyond their trade and, possibly, religion; they possibly were interested only in such religious practices as they believed helped them in becoming prosperous.

Experts on Harappan culture tell us that in its developed state it, probably, existed from around 2800 B.C. to around 2200 B.C. Added to this is the period which it took to develop from infancy to its full maturity, and another span of time it took to finally break down. Indus civilization is said to have vanished from the Indian scene by about 1500 B.C. At the face of it this is a very long period indeed for any state to have lasted unchanged and unmolested. As we have surmised earlier, in essence the Indus civilization appears to have been the handiwork of traders, and its founding fathers must have been foreigners from Mesopotamia and other countries of that region. A parallel example in recent history is the arrival of the Europeans during the seventeenth century and subsequently, in the Indian subcontinent. They also came in search of markets and raw materials, and established themselves in small colonies, which they subsequently expanded and defended. As the level of their prosperity improved they became vulnerable to the depredations of the local contenders. It is another matter that in course of time, with the increase in the size of area over which they conducted their trade, and this is particularly true of the British, the size of the defence force that they had to maintain became large, for it had to have the capability to withstand pressures of the forces maintained by the rulers of the states with whom they were doing business. To maintain the large defence force they needed money, and for that they needed to expand the trade and that, since they had the wherewithal for it, it put them on the conquest course. Ultimately the process lead to the formation of the British empire. But the basic function of the empire continued to be the augmentation of trade with a view to enriching the mother country. Other European nations too decided to enrich themselves and made plans to acquire colonies, and it was after two bloody world wars, that human conscience awoke to the havoc caused by the profligate exploitation by human beings who had developed scientific resources, of sections of people who were not that fortunate. In the historical process this has been an oft-repeated development: countries show interest in trade and commerce, and then their traders arrive, who, with time, become rich and raise forces to forcibly snatch the basic resources.

Around 100 odd sites of Harappan civilization have been located. There may have been quite a few more whose existence has not been established because, maybe, enough digging in the areas of likely sites has not been done. Yet it can be stated with certainty that there were any number of villages and towns which did not attract the interest of the Harappan ruling class. Such habitats either belonged to people settled in villages and engaged in agriculture and raising domestic animals, or nomadic tribes forever wandering with the cattle and kin, hunting and gathering food and pillaging and plundering the agricultural settlements whenever an opportunity afforded. How the Indus traders safeguarded themselves against this ever present menace, is difficult to say, but they must have raised some kind of a police force or even an army of sorts, or even bribed the potential enemies to keep them at bay. All this must have worked very well during good times, but during difficult periods, brought on by heavy floods, or droughts, or otherwise dwindling trade because of closure of certain markets because of wars, disease or other calamities, an entirely different situation would have precipitated, which in some circumstances would have invited the hovering nomadic desperados to pounce upon and lay waste the villages, towns and cities. A study of the history and life pattern of the people of the area where Indus civilization existed, gives out clear and interesting pointers. There is very strong evidence to suggest that there was little change in the way of life of the people right from the Harappan days to almost the beginning of the twentieth century, except that the Bronze Age got superseded by the Iron Age, and the implements and weapons used were of iron. Otherwise time stood still over this land for the best part of 4000 odd years; the potter still turned out the same kind of ware, and people still wore the same kind of jewellery and clothes, and lived in the same kind of habitats, living in houses built on the same old pattern — made of mud bricks in villages and baked bricks in towns and cities — following almost a similar pattern in so far as the sewage disposal was concerned. The mode of transport still was the good old bullock cart with bronze parts replaced by iron. The fields were cultivated with ploughshare pulled by draft animals or, pretty often, with human labour using appropriate implements including a stick fitted with a sharpened steel edge at its one end. There were no armed forces worth the name except in the town or city where the ruler lived. In the countryside police force was virtually non-existent and whatever of it was there was at the disposal of the trader to afford him security and help him in carrying out the banking and usury trades. Often traders raised small protection forces of their own.

So it must have been during the Indus civilization. During stable times it must have been the trader ruling the roost, his interest in the well being of the common man was restricted to the extent as would further his own interests, like in later times, right upto the time of departure of the British in 1947, and to a gradually decreasing degree even after a national government was running the affairs of the state. At the lower levels, in villages, he must have basically been a usurer, besides being a petty shopkeeper, and in collusion with others of his kind in nearby places, he could play havoc with the economy of the area and well-being of the people, for example, he could refuse to buy the surplus grains from the farmers, or withdraw his patronage afforded to the weavers. He must have hoarded and sold at exorbitant rates when there were shortages. His major concerns must have been with his trade and profits, and he could not have been bothered about his popularity with the people amidst whom he lived and operated. He would have ensured the security of his operations by proffering bribes to bands of organized brigands, or raising his own little army or police, or getting the religious heads to issue proclamations in his favour. All this while the brigand nomad was watching him keeping a greedy eye on his wealth, waiting for the centres of power to weaken. Not that there was anything out of the ordinary in this; this has happened throughout the world, in all kinds of societies, during all historical periods. But the notable aspect of the situation in this area — where Indus civilization flourished — has been that the pattern has persisted almost right up to the present day. There was this pacifist trader, always preaching for peace, for that situation was conducive to his well-being and trade, and there was this nomad, all the time waiting for conditions which would enable him to loot and plunder with impunity. All excavations of Harappan towns have shown multiple layers of foundations, indicating the number of times the towns, villages and cities have been destroyed and reconstructed. The destruction has mainly been the work of the nomadic tribes or villagers around the prosperous areas created by the Indus trade, and this must have happened, almost invariably, when the central authority had weakened. The towns and cities were abandoned and people fled to safer areas, to the south or the east, and the abandoned places got occupied by the nomads who, bereft of the engineering skills and capabilities to keep the economy going, and accustomed to survive essentially on loot and plunder, eventually also gave them up. Possibly the sites remained unoccupied for long periods, for that alone can justify burial of whole buildings which were under sand and silt brought by the riverine floods, or by shifting and blowing sands where habitations were located away from the water courses — and the soil having become firm enough, with the passage of time, to completely support new structures. In course of time newer generations would have arrived on the scene, from south or the east, if they were the progeny of the earlier traders, or from the west if they were new adventurers in the field. But whoever came, managed to achieve only as much as the previous people had done; possibly they could reach only that far before the plunderers overtook them. This pattern has stayed throughout the prehistoric and the historical period, right down to our own time. The last time this happened was in 1947 when, once again, on the weakening of the central authority, a depradation of almost an unimaginable dimension was enacted, ostensibly for religious cleansing but primarily for looting the wealth accumulated by the trader community.

The Indus trader, and his progeny, right up to the present times, has been an effective businessman; trading is in his blood. But he is not an industrialist, or a scientist, or someone who might be called an inventor; he has little interest in such professions. He is a plain sales and purchase man, and in this field he is highly skilled. His Muslim counterpart left behind at the time of the partition, is no less manipulative. He is aware of the threat to his safety and security that the non-trader class holds against him, but has played his Islamic card with ingenuity and cunning, and partially managed to divert the attention of this class by raising the bogey of threat from non-Islamic India and partially by exhorting them to follow the fundamentals of Islam. But he is not likely to make it for long unless there are basic changes in his system of government, or his relations with other countries of the region.

So this pattern has stayed since the days of Indus, or, may be, even from earlier times. The business communities in the Punjab — Khatri Lalas, Aroras and Banias and their equivalents in other religious groups who accepted conversions essentially with a view to securing benefits — and most of the Sindhi urban communities, and the Gujaratis, and the Marwaris from Gujarat (Kathiawar) and Rajasthan, and corresponding business communities from the south and east established governments, monarchies, oligarchies, democracies or whatever other form of government, and provided finances to build their strength. So complete was their hold, and so dependent were all segments of the society upon them that, in the gradations of the Varna system, the engineers, inventors, scientists, workers, have all been placed below them, the business class. They were powerful and prospered but, with time throwing all restraint to the winds, became rapacious, and weakened the structures of their governments, providing the opportunity to the nomadic tribals to pillage and plunder them and lay waste the villages, towns and cities, upon which their trade and commerce depended. Then, after a gap of years, during which the drifting silts and sands, brought in by water and winds, had time to sufficiently firm up the soil, a new crop of entrepreneurs arrived on the scene to start afresh, and dig out the remanents of the old towns and initiate the process of rebuilding.

The nomad looted, but the Hindu trader came back, tenaciously, and restarted and reorganized the business, and once again brought prosperity to the area. Right up to the time of partition of the country in 1947, he was the chief organizer of business, even in the most remote areas, even when surrounded by near hostile or religiously inimical populations; they had to respect him, for, otherwise, the whole trade of the area could turn chaotic. But the nomad made little effort to change his way of life. He has plundered, and right up to this day that is all he has done. He is basically a cross between the Australoid and the Proto-Mediterranean, and possibly also carries the blood strains of numerous other groups and tribes that passed through this north-western area of the subcontinent. He is brash, audacious, cunning, but not brave. He has little capability to meet organized resistance, but definitely tries to frighten his adversary with loud noises and grunts. This helped his masters and mentors in their effort to form Pakistan, and again, subsequently, when India lost almost half the territory of its State of Jammu and Kashmir.

Indeed, right from 1947 through 1950, the record of these tribesmen has been noteworthy. They were one of the major factors that contributed to the split of the country. They profoundly nonplussed the Hinduized leadership that was spearheading the independence movement against the British, and with a remarkable show of unity and daring, caused the formation of Pakistan within a short spell of a few months. In the face of their show of force, the Indian leadership caved in, possibly fearing a civil war, particularly when the marauding hordes were enjoying the support of the rightist elements in the British hierarchy who were hell bent upon frustrating the Indian struggle for independence; they were out to create total anarchy on the subcontinent. Even the people of the newly formed Pakistan were astonished at the success of a half-baked, not so serious a demand for the bifurcation of the country, and some amongst them got so emboldened as to urge their government to try their hand in Kashmir, again with the help of these tribesmen. The Indian leadership was once again non-plussed, and sought the mediation of the newly formed United Nations to secure the withdrawal of the tribals, in the process making a laughing stock of themselves, making the nations of the world wonder how a country could be so overwhelmed by another which was barely 10 to 15 per cent of its strength in terms of manpower and resources. Obviously their admiration was for the plucky little newly born state, and the prolix cant poured by the Indians at the United Nations, at best, only amused everyone. Indians lost every time, and were saved only by the vetoes exercised by the Soviets in their favour. After braving many years of humiliations piled upon them by the world community, Indians eventually realized the folly of having come to them in the first place. It dawned upon them, howsoever faintly, that peace was never secured through begging, that it indeed, as Mao Ze-dong said, flowed from the barrel of the gun: there was no alternative to being strong!

But the barbarian has stayed where he was — a barbarian, nomad and a poor exploitable sucker; the trader community in Pakistan has ensured this. When exactly the day of reckoning for the two segments of the society shall arrive, shall depend upon how long Islamic fundmentalism shall hold there, and manage to keep the exploited lot in a state of frenzy — a ploy relentlessly pursued by the privileged segment — and thus, keep their attention off the essential values of life. It will also depend upon how firmly India manages to handle them in their incursions into Indian territory. A weak India is to the advantage of the privileged classes in Pakistan. A strong one will probably put some rational sense into the heads of the deprived class and induce them to demand their rightful place in the affairs of their society.

However, it is not to be surmised that the trader was the only operative prop in the social milieu of the Indus people; he, no doubt, played the cardinal role. But a society comprises persons of various callings, like landlords and tenants, contractors and artisans, scribes and bureaucrats, godmen and priests, jugglers and charmers, and so on, and surely the Indus people must have had their share of the mix; indeed the hand of the bureaucrat is amply visible in areas which had been selected and developed for trade. No evidence of collective military activity has been unearthed; no weapons or munitions of war on scales suggesting existence of armies, have been located. The Indus people seemed to believe in peace and orderliness, and this, their strongest point, could also have been their weakest, although opinions would differ on this. But it definitely afforded them an effective safeguard against a quick burn-out. Their culture lasted for a period of over 1300 years, and even then it did not get smothered or obliterated by the numerous ideas and ideologies that invaded it after it had ceased to be visible on the screen of history. Infact, it lived on, displaying a degree of tenacity which is not matched by any other culture in the history of the human race. People uprooted by calamities and disasters, and raids and pestilence, abandoned the land they had considered their home and made for other places, in the south or east of the subcontinent, and with them they carried their culture, traditions, thoughts, religious ideas and philosophy. Today all these are firmly embedded in what may be called the South Asian civilization, irrespective of the small differences that might have become apparent with the passage of time, with the induction of different religions and creeds, for example, a marriage in a Muslim house is almost identical to a marriage in a Hindu house except for the bare minimum variations incorporated to accommodate religious ordinances. The works produced by the Indus people, the designs of their buildings, the layout of their towns, the close attention paid to the development of the infrastructure, surpass similar efforts put in by other civilizations of their time. The emphasis appears to have been on simplicity rather than pompous and wasteful aggrandisements. Although evidence suggests that their diet included meats (beef, mutton, pork), poultry, fish and selected aquatic animals, it appears the stress was on vegetarian food.

In their approach to the problems of life, they seem to have believed in the wisdom of following the middle course in everything they did. Petty traders and officials might have harassed the simple folk at the village and town level, but their general lifestyle seems to have been based on simplicity, even though the idea of providing for themselves the optimum physical and mental comfort seems to have been followed. Improvements and innovations might have come slowly, and deviations from the beaten track must have been disapproved, for such an activity could only strain the existing achievements and cause hardship to workmen surviving on extant techniques and methods; alternatively such improvements could have been resisted by the workers guilds. In essence it was a civilization which favoured good performance but was afraid of excellence, for excellence could come their way only through hard competition, and that could generate stress, agitation and, finally, unhappiness. They seem to have been the people who appeared on the world stage at a time when human society was emerging from barbarism and entering the era of civilization and history. While the essential element in history is writing, civilization is far more complex to describe, for it is a healthy mix of sound political organization, a stable social and economic system, continuous pursuit of knowledge in all fields of science, technology and arts, development in the skills of artisans, engineers and other professionals, a good law and order umbrella to provide security to citizens, unhindered trade and commerce, and so on. The leaders of Indus had a good grasp of the essentials of civilized living. They also seem to have favoured the idea of the middle course, a direction which they felt essential to follow in all pursuits of life, for they felt that on either side of this lay misery and suffering. This realization possibly sustained their civilization in the land of their choosing for the best part of a millennium, while elsewhere contemporaneous civilizations did not last even a quarter of that duration, and almost invariably got snuffed out after a period of anarchy and violence.

However, the middle course created its own problems. Bereft of towering ambitions, these people seem to have withdrawn into themselves, seem to have been content with the way of life that they had evolved. Within their social order, time hung still for hundreds of years, and it did not bother them. The son went into the profession of his father and was content if he had reached latter's performance level, and for this reason the patriarch was held in high esteem. If we observe the way of life of the people who even in modern times can be recognized to be carrying the traces of the old civilization, it would appear that those people were essentially pacifists; this attitude might also have become necessary in order to safeguard the interests of trade and commerce which are best promoted during conditions of peace. Even otherwise their society seems to have emphasized nonviolence, politeness, cooperation, and obedience to those who were senior, or better placed in life, respect for family and society, eating simple and, as far as possible, vegetarian food, and wearing not too highly elegant or expensive clothes; in fact, the trend, it appears, was to wrap simple, unstitched garments around the body, though, during the colder winter months, warm clothing, duly stitched, appears to have been used. What the way of life was in areas which were out of the control of the Indus society, we do not know, for nothing has been unearthed; there could have been nothing to unearth in those mud constructions. But it can be presumed that life there must have been at a down-to-earth practical level, and not encumbered by the tedious rules and regulations that the organized sector had drawn for itself. This is, however, not to suggest that there were two types of civilizations operating side by side in two watertight compartments. What is suggested is that there was a developed sector which was highly urbanized, even at the village level, and followed a more sophisticated way of life, compared to others in the country. But there must have been extensive exchange of ideas, trade, communications between people, irrespective of their geographical locations or professions or stations in life, for, overall it was one culture which had its own variety in people, and its own ups and downs during the period that it lasted. Again, it is not to be presumed that all kind of fresh thinking was taboo, or that the people were so dull that they were incapable of it. There must have been a lot of inputs, otherwise a fine civilization of this stature and duration just would not have been possible. It was a unique civilization, with a near fanatical faith in its philosophy and way of life, and even after it had been trounced and beaten, its people held on to that faith in what might be summed up as the 'middle course', a course of non-violence, of truth, and of respect for all life, and they handed it down the line, over the millennia, so that even today there is as ardent a belief in it amongst the Indians who are the inheritors of this culture, as, perhaps, it was when this culture had grown to its full stature. This civilization had a character of its own, its own flavour, its own so called 'personality', and all that has lived on through all the vicissitudes of time.

We have already seen that the first to come into the sub-continent were the Negritos, a class of small, diminutive, black people who almost never managed to get beyond the hunting and food gathering stage. Even today whatever of their class has survived in their original, unmixed form, they are doing just that. In other words, this has been a class of human beings who have been satisfied with the mere process of existence and did not develop any ambition beyond this. Then came the Proto-

Australoids, dark, and taller and broader than their pygmy predecessors, innovative and more intelligent, for ever moving, hunting and food gathering. They would have had no problem in subjugating the Negritos and then extensively interbreeding with them. They continued their movement eastwards in search of food and animals, almost following the footsteps of the Australopithicus some two million years earlier. They did not stop when they came to the end of the land mass and continued the eastward movement in their reed boats, intermixing with the inhabitants of the small and large islands—in some of them settling down just by themselves — till, possibly, they had touched the shores of South America. They spoke a form of Austric language, and wherever they settled they organized village life, cultivated crops and tended animals. They lived through the Mesolithic and the Neolithic Ages of the north-western parts of this country. A number of words from their speech stand incorporated in the present day Indian dialects, and a number of Hindu social and religious customs and beliefs have originated from them. They seem to have been a striving lot, forever on the look out for fresh horizons. They appeared to have pondered over the ideas about divinity, and evolved a code of conduct and customs and practices, which can be easily recognized at the level of the grassroots Hinduism of today. Of the various racial groups that the subcontinent received, the Australoids were amongst the most numerous ; even in the Far East, in the Pacific islands, the number of people with Australoid strain is high.

Following the Australoids were the Palaeo-Mediterraneans, again dark complexioned, but hardier and stronger than their predecessors. They also came in large numbers, and were the masters of all tribes and races who had preceded them, and intermixed freely. The fourth major group to arrive was that of the Mediterraneans proper. Of dark colour, they were an agile, energetic and an intelligent lot, originating possibly in the islands and eastern coastal belts of the Aegean and the Mediterranean Seas, much like the later day Minoans and Mycenaeans. They, apparently, had a civilization of their own at the time of their migration and had some clearly developed concepts of religion and philosophy. They, together with the 'Orientals', the fifth segment of the class we call Dravidians, appear to have been the mainstay of the Indus culture. The Dravidian group as a whole is widely spread over the central, peninsular and southern India, while in other parts it is heavily intermingled with other ethnic groups, like the Aryans in the Gangetic basin, mostly in areas north of the river, and the Mongoloid people in the Gangetic delta, the Sythians in Sind, Gujarat and Kathiawar and all along the Western coast and the Ghats and the territory immediately to the east of it, right down to Mangalore and Calicut. Southern parts of Sri Lanka possibly have a mix of Aryo-Dravidians while the northern parts have only the Dravidians. Baluchistan and North West Frontier of the subcontinent have a majority of Turko-Iranians, but even here the presence of the Dravidian stock is not insignificant. The colour of the Dravidians varies from wheatish to dark, depending upon the pattern of interbreeding. Where the mix is between the Dravidians and other stocks like the Aryans or Scythians or Mongoloids, people are light complexioned. In the fairly unmixed Indo-Aryan belt also, from Kashmir in the north to south of Rajasthan, people have fairer complexion. But where the major concentration is of the Palaeo-Mediterraneans or the Mediterraneans proper, particularly south of the line from south of the Sind province of Pakistan in the west and the Yamuna river in the east, the colour of the skin is generally dark. In effect, because of the extensive spread of the dark complexioned racial groups over the subcontinent, majority of the people in most parts of India generally have darkish complexion.

The Indus civilization survived even when it does not appear to have made any serious attempt to keep itself abreast of the technology of its times. It continued with the manufacture of tools and weapons which had been outdated in other countries for scores, if not hundreds of years. It possibly collapsed only after the appearance of the horse as the primary means of movement; this had made a qualitative difference in the communications capability. In spite of an almost total lack of preparedness against any major external aggression, this civilization took its own time going down, possibly because the means at the disposal of the major nation states of the time, were not sufficiently overwhelming to smother it in one go. the problems of logistics were simply too formidable to attempt anything big, more so in the intricate riverine terrain and the wild mountains of the north-west. But it is quite possible that this culture was against the idea of war on the basis of a deliberate, well thought out philosophy. They were well aware of the destruction, pain, suffering, that wars cause; the internecine wars between city states of Mesopotamia, Sumer, Persia and also the fact that wars solved no problems, only created them. May be Jain Tirathankaras had already preached their philosophy of non-violence by this time; this could be quite in keeping with the claims to the antiquity of Jain religion. It is noteworthy that major following of Jain religion is amongst the trader community, and the major Jain monuments, even of later times, have been erected in the land which was earlier in the occupation of the Indus people, like the one at Mount Abu. Also, this country's, if not the world's, biggest concentration of traders is in the old Indus area. How widespread was their influence to make an impact on the social and cultural life of the people of their time, that is on the people of the non-trader communities, it is difficult to say, but the evidence does suggest that the lifestyle of the people of their kind, that is the traders, has not changed much even in the modern times; in fact all classes of people of these areas still adhere to the ways of the old culture. The conclusion is that the traders, the dominant community, were essentially pacifists. In everything that they did or planned, they emphasized moderation, and that has been at the core of the thoughts expressed over the millennia in some of the acknowledged political, social or religious literature of this country. The philosophy based on these thoughts has extolled contentment, complacence and, possibly even mediocrity, as virtues, and has broadly disapproved strife of any kind, including that which might bring about improvement.

But the main pressure for the evolutionary process is exerted by natural selection, that is if the danger to a species from another one is from the latter's better running speed then the former has to either develop itself to run even faster or devise some other strategy to neutralize the effect of latter's superiority. In other words, for survival, any of the two methods have to be adopted, viz., the species either has to constantly improve itself to cope with the unfriendly element in the environment, or adopt some other strategy to negate the effect of the threatening element. Trees grow big and to offset the destructive effect of the high speed winds, their roots go deeper in the ground and draw more food and, thus, improve their girth, and strength. That is how they survive. But grass and small plants survive by staying small and supple so that the high speed winds do not succeed in damaging them; at their level there are also the folds in the ground and other low-height objects which help to break the damaging effects of winds. Then there are plants which are extensively hunted upon by other species for food and forage and in order that they do not go extinct, they develop a prolific rate of growth. This, it appears, is the pattern of growth for species which are small and vulnerable and have little direct capability to resist the unfriendly elements in the environments. However, competition for survival is not only an inter-species phenomenon, it goes on even within the species itself; the example of trees in a dense wooded cluster outgrowing each other in a bid to catch sunlight, is well known.

In the northern countries the cold weather hung on a while longer as compared to the south, as the north had virtually been buried under the snow during the last ice age, which started a slow withdrawal around 20,000 years back, a process which is still continuing, and not until around 10,000 years ago did the old stone age come to an end in the northern countries. In the southern countries, this had happened a couple of thousand years earlier. Right through the duration of the ice age, the northern man had to struggle much harder as compared to the one of the south, for not only did he have to be physically tough to combat the elements but also had to be intelligent and innovative to secure food and shelter in the terrain which was totally snow covered. Though 2000 years or so behind the southern man in starting the Mesolithic Age, the northern man soon caught up and was looking for greener pastures to secure more power and comfort for himself. Backed by his superior innovative and survival capabilities he developed effective transportation and communications systems and superior weapons of war. And then he set out to dominate the world.

The western domination was a gradual process and in their march towards modernism, Europe led the way, although the Asian northerners were equally competitive. During the first millennium A.D. the kingdoms in northern and central China had beaten the rest of the world in the race for securing supremacy in armaments and other munitions so necessary to wage successful wars. Chinese invented the gunpowder, but, in course of time, Europe made the best guns. Genghis Khan of Mongolia (1162-1227) developed an absolutely masterly and novel technique to utilize the mobility of the horse to produce telling results during his wars in Asia and Europe. These examples are from recent history, but conquering and defending nations were invariably backed by strong contingents of scientists, industrialists, financial geniuses (for war is an expensive venture), and well-trained, disciplined and rehearsed armies. Even in the most distant past, success has visited only those who worked for it, and that meant development and acquisition of the best munitions of war, and manufacturing items of such capability and quality as would capture the trade markets for them. Only then could they hope to possess that degree of security which would permit them to be prosperous. Without adequate security the gains of business cannot be safeguarded, and without adequate business gains, resources to build the necessary security cannot be mobilized. How did the Indus people fit into this kind of an aggressive scenario? The fact is that the day the horseman appeared at their doorstep to snatch away the accumulated surplus, they really had no answer. The rulers of the cities, after their initial burst of innovative talent, business acumen and organizational and engineering skills, seem to have simply shut their minds off in so far as the developments for waging aggression were concerned, and just concentrated on preserving whatever they had. The process rendered them ineffective against the hostile forces pitched against them, and they lost, every time, right through the recorded history, right up to the modern times.

The important point is that the people of this civilization spread themselves throughout the length and breadth of this country and provided the base for the development of the subsequent cultures. And the important question is as to why were they defeated and beaten, by one and all who decided to go for them? During the pre-history of the Indian subcontinent and for most of the duration of its history, Europe was involved with themselves, their ethnic groups having common interests were aligning into bigger communities, leading to the formation of nations which, in course of time, started asserting, and there were wars, and so on. In Asia, Persians were about the first to take on the Europeans. Their great king Cyrus (559-529 B.C.), founder of the Achaemenid line, captured Babylonia and Lydia and made the Phoenician cities on the east coast of the Mediterranean, and all the Greek cities in Asia Minor, tributary, and had, thus, created an empire which was larger than any the world had seen till then. His son and successor, Cambyses (died 522 B.C.) defeated the Egyptians in a battle at Pelusium in 525 B.C. and conquered their country. He then planned the conquest of Ethiopia and Carthage but, unfortunately, did not live long enough. So when Darius I came to the throne of Persia he was indeed master of a formidable empire. The Achaemenids and the ruling minority in Persia were from the Aryan stock while their subjects were a mix of Greeks, Semites, Phoenicians — they constituted the elements who provided the essential support to the government in terms of the trained manpower and a host of other groups and tribes of local extraction.

What bugged Darius I the most were the Scythian horsemen from southern Russia, an area north of the Black Sea, and he decided he had to go for them with a view to destroying the very roots of the problem that continuously demanded his attention. He led a great army, and crossed over at Bosphorus, then marched up to the Danube and crossed it over a boat bridge, and further advanced northwards. But the essential element of his army was the infantry, and the hardy and very mobile cavalry of the Scythians kept them under observation all the time, and, in due course, cut off their routes of supply, and harassed and sniped at them whenever they got an opportunity, till the Russian winter became a serious threat, and the Persian army had to pull out, suffering heavy losses. This failure emboldened the Greek cities of Asia and they revolted, with the tacit support of the European Greeks. Darius was infuriated beyond count and he decided to attack the main land Greece to teach the Greeks a lesson. With the Phoenisian fleet supporting him, he launched his force from Asia Minor and eastern Mediterranean and landed at Marathon, north of Athens, where he was resisted by the Athenians. There was a bitter fight in which the Greeks eventually carried the day, but not before they had requested their arch rivals, the Spartans, to forget the mutual differences and come to their aid and save them from a defeat from the Persians. The youth who carried this message covered the distance of more than a hundred miles, over a rough terrain, in less than two days; marathon races in modern day sports are essentially to commemorate this event. Spartans responded positively, but by the time they arrived it was all over. Darius I was highly disappointed and shocked at his defeat, and died shortly thereafter.

His son and successor, Xerxes, decided to avenge the defeat of his father and in a period of four years assembled an army the like of which the world had not seen before. In 480 B.C. the army crossed the Dardenelles on a boat bridge, but further on, while the army was negotiating a defile it was challenged by a small force of mere 1400 Spartans, who inflicted severe losses upon it, although in the process they all perished, right down to the last man. Thebes surrendered. Athens was abandoned, then burnt by the Persians. But, just around then, the Persian fleet in the Bay of Salamis was caught off guard by the Greek fleet, who, though much smaller in numerical strength, nonetheless attacked it, and succeeded in destroying it. Persian supply line was thus cut, and they had no alternative but to withdraw ignominously. That was the end of any major Persian challenge to Greece, and also of South's challenge to their hardier northern neighbours, people from areas that had seen the hardships of the ice age. Arabs also, during their hey day, ransacked a part of southern Europe, but they were beaten back to their boundaries.

In 359 B.C., a very competent and ambitious king, Philip of Macedonia, ascended the throne, and the first thing he did was to reorganize his army. He divided his infantry into groups of compact and solid mass of men, each group having the capability to bear heavy pressure upon the opposing enemy infantry, or resisting their attack effectively by providing depth to the defence at any and every point. He organized his horsemen into disciplined formations which could charge as one solid block, capable of placing the point of attack under enormous pressure; he invented what in the modern parlance is called cavalry. His mind was set upon Persia, the country he wanted to attack to capture its vast treasures; it was about the richest empire in that part of the world. In 338 B.C., through a hard fought battle at Chaeronea, he became the master of all Greece, and by 336 B.C. his advanced guards had already crossed into Asia. Unfortunately he got murdered, apparently at the behest of his queen, Olympias, Alexander's mother, who was furious with him for his having taken a second wife. Alexander, who succeeded him, took a couple of years to consolidate the kingdom, and then in the year 334 B.C., set out on the conquest course his father had chartered earlier.

He crossed into Asia Minor, and met a fairly formidable contingent of the Persian army and defeated it. Then in 333 B.C., he met a large force under the command of Darius III himself, and smashed it too; Darius had arrived for battle with an almost unwieldy administrative train, including his harem, courtiers, sundry camp followers, and the like. City of Sidon surrendered to him, but Tyre resisted and was eventually destroyed. Then he took Gaza, and by the end of 332 B.C. he had thrown the Persians out of Egypt and taken hold of that country. In 331 B.C., he marched out of Egypt after having built the cities of Alexandria and Alexandretta, and went for Babylon, via Tyre. Enroute, at a place called Arbela, Darius challenged him again, and a great battle was fought. But Persian chariots did not make much of an impression on the heavily armed Greek phalanx, while Greek cavalry charges proved decisive. In fact one factor that precipitated the outcome was the oblique march manoeuvre carried out by the Greeks under orders of Alexander. Darius fled the field towards north Persia, to the country called Medes but he was pursued, and by the time Greek army caught up, he had already been murdered by his own people. Alexander now wanted to take over the whole of the Persian empire, and to do that he went up and down the vast territory, after first capturing Babylon and then Susa. He skirted the Caspian Sea, then went to western Turkestan, then came down and founded the city of Herat, then took Kabul, and via the Khyber pass, entered India. Here he conquered the whole of the north-western territory, right up to the line of the Beas river, but, at this stage, his battle weary troops put their hands up and just refused to proceed further, and he was left with no alternative except to turn back. Alexander had wanted to capture the heart of the Magadha empire at Patliputra. During the return journey, partly on account of the grievous wounds he had received during a battle in India when, during a difficult situation, he had to personally lead an assault, and partly on account of his drunken bouts, he became very ill and died at Babylon in 323 B.C.

The historical events narrated above are of recent times when compared to the period of the Indus civilization. The days of the big armies arrived with the induction of the horse, and the art of warfare assumed a totally different dimension with the advent of the Iron Age. During the Indus Valley the pace of activity was slower, but it cannot be said that there were no wars: histories of Akkad, Sumer, Elam of those days bear ample proof of wars. The Indus people had the resources to organize a strong military force and embark upon a conquest course and establish a formidable empire. But the oligarchy of the traders just did not move in that direction. Eastward movement was difficult on account of the dense forests and marshes of the Gangetic plains, and movement southwards, over the Rann of Kuch, or the Thar desert of Rajasthan, or the forest laden mountain ranges of the Vindhyas and the Satpuras, was not easy either. Thus this civilization had little impact outside the Indus basin or south of the Kathiawar peninsula, till it was broken by aggressions, or natural calamities, and the people were forced to flee to other areas.

Historians tell us that this civilization went extinct with the arrival of Aryans from the north-west during the first half of the second millennium B.C. Apparently the resistance offered to Aryan incursions was not stiff. But the evidence, whatever of it is available, does not suggest of any serious contest between the Aryans and the people of the Indus civilization. Apparently this civilization just collapsed upon itself; a minor jolt, perhaps, was all that was necessary to precipitate this. The idea of narrating a few historical events relating to Persia and Greece was to bring out the fact that when it came to the contest, it was the man from the north who, almost always, managed to overpower the man from this sub-continent. Obviously this had a lot to do with the quality of man-power present in the two regions.

Greeks flowered into a great civilization which made a solid contribution to the materialistic foundation of the western world of today. But the Indians offered to the human race the alternative system of survival, a system which, they believed, made the survival process a richer and more rewarding experience as compared to the western system based on the belief that matter and not the mind, was the primary reality. For the Indians, the mind and spirituality were of prime concern. In their view, faith in materialism led to negative situations, creating contention and strife, and exploitation, and war, and unhappiness. And for holding these kind of views, for negating strife and activity, they have been at the receiving end for a significant duration of their recorded history. But it does appear, however, that in his last days Alexander had accepted the Indian view and had come to the conclusion that no amount of strife for material gains could bring happiness to a human being, or a society, or a nation, that only by bringing happiness to others, and not by bringing suffering, can personal happiness be attained, and to convey this point, he had directed, from his death bed, so it is said, that on way to the final destination of his body, his bare hands be displayed out of the coffin, to stress his conclusion: on the material plane, you come empty handed into this world, and you depart from here empty handed!

It is not that civilizations do not stagnate, or all of those who appeared on the world stage made contributions to the movement and momentum of the present day world. Some did, while some perished without a whimper. Some made contributions, even if in a small measure, which enriched the experience of man along the course he has for the present adopted for himself. Others produced stuff which, though it appeared meaningful when it was there, fell by the wayside as time marched ahead, and got consigned to the dustbin of history, not so much because there was any fault in what had been put across, but, mostly, because of the ennui the humanity felt in general in hanging on to the same or similar set of values. Change is the essence and proof of creation. In stillness it is death, the end. The greatness of a contribution can be assessed only from its lasting value. No doubt the Greeks appeared on the world stage almost two thousand years after, as the evidence suggests, the peak of the Indus civilization, and during the time of the latter, western Asia and the Middle East were in quite a ferment. Egyptians had a culture of their own which in fact had been on the ground more or less unmolested for over a millennia, and so had Mesopotamia, Sumer, Elam, Persia — but the point is: what lasted? There can be no denying the fact that the Greeks, or for that matter any other civilization, did not appear on the globe in just one burst of activity. It was an evolution, physical, mental, in every way. Humanity has climbed up to whatever level they are at today, rung by rung, each rung having been placed in position by the preceding generations on the basis of their experience. In different parts of the world different groups of people have grown up cherishing different sets of values, so different at times that there appears to be no meeting point. What Indus valley left behind, apparently, was an emphasis on following the middle course, negation of violent activity, respect for life — all life — contentment with one's lot, kindness, gentleness, passivity, orderliness. Western emphasis, on the other hand, has been on values which were almost the opposite of these. Their stress is on achievement oriented activity, on competition, on striving for excellence, on merciless liquidation of all opposition. Experience of Indus, it would appear, was conditioned by the prevailing environment, the physical and intellectual capability of its people, their prowess, hardiness, capability to withstand adversity, the degree of their fearlessness in the face of danger to life. In fact, it was conditioned, apart from the environments, by the stuff its people were made up of, stuff in terms of their genetic built up. In the final analysis, the output of people is not so much dependent upon the exhortations and compulsions that they might be subjected to by those who might be their leaders. What counts is their mental and physical built up, their character, and their threat perceptions, and all that decides for them the way of their life, their philosophy, and, maybe, even their religion.

Ulysses (or Odysseus) of Ithaca best represented the western thought, way of life or philosophy. He is a cunning king, a man of action, and for him life is a series of challenges which have to be faced and surmounted, using all the means at one's disposal, including physical and mental robustness, guile, cunning and whatever. The aim is to secure success. He fights in the Trojan war, using every trick in his bag, to eventually secure the fall of Troy for the alliance of its enemies. The homeward journey took him ten years of wandering in the seas where he is confronted with several difficulties, and he fights his way through, using force when there was no other way to get over the obstacles, and guile, intelligence, alertness, when these served the purpose, taking on even the gods when that became necessary, braving all difficulties as an adventurer, without flustering, or losing heart, or being penitent of omissions and commissions, or ever feeling sad or bad or run down or demoralized, or afflicted by defeatist emotions, or ever wanting to give up. During the course of the journey his ships get wrecked, his crew drowns, and he is forced to tackle problems single handed. But he is there, fighting through it all. When he finally arrives at Ithaca he finds his wife, Penelope, besieged by suitors seeking her hand. Ultimately she says she would marry the man who would bend and string Ulysses' bow; only Ulysses could do it (any resemblance with the story of Rudra's bow that only Rama could bend and string to win Sita's hand?). Disguised as a beggar he was present at the assembly, and he strung the bow after others had failed to do so, and with the help of a companion killed all the suitors. The story ends with Athena, the Greek goddess of wisdom and prudent warfare, and patron of arts, and protectress of agriculture, reconciling the hero with the sorrowing kinsmen of the suitors who were thirsting for revenge. But the end of Ulysses was not a happy one either. He got killed during a fight with his own son, from Circe, who, out of filial devotion, had been looking for him (Ulysses), and had got down to plundering latter's territory when he had run out of resources (like Hanuman in Lanka) and not recognizing him, had entered into a fight during which he killed him. He is in great sorrow when he realized what he had done, and took Penelope with him and married her. The Greeks believed in the material aspect of the creation, and yet they were conscious of the tragedy inherent in materialism. The belief was that, that was how the world was a package of tragedy and comedy, and that had to be accepted and whatever stood in the way of material happiness had to be resisted with strength, vigour and cheer. They were outgoing and outward looking, and they laid the foundations of the modern day western culture, including its science and technology. They have supported mental and physical robustness at the individual, social and national, even global level.

On the other hand, the Indian role model is Gautama, the prince of Kapilvastu. Gautama (later Buddha) saw only suffering and sorrow in the journey of life, and pinpointed desire (including lust and zest for life) to be the cause of all sorrow, and came to the conclusion that if desire was eliminated, sorrow would end. He withdrew from the world of his possessions, from his kin, parents, wife and child, and set out on a meditation course, to think and find out things for himself, and, after spending more than ten years in intense austerities, wanderings, discussions and meditations, came to the conclusion that desire evoked karma, action, and that, in turn, caused rebirth. Essence of his teachings was negation of desire oriented action, including avoidance of violence of any kind, mental or physical. All contentions, he advised, should be sorted out through dialogue, through justice and fair play, by showing maximum compassion and understanding, without the interference of personal desires. For desires would precipitate karma and cause rebirth and delay the attainment of nirvana, the final emancipation.

During his lifetime, or in the immediately preceding period, there were two major ideologies which governed the political, social and religious life of the people. One was based on what the Aryans had brought into this country during the early part of the second millennium B.C. and was closer to the later day western ideology, and could be placed under the general heading of 'Brahmanism', while the other was of indigenous origin dating back to the Indus civilization, or even earlier, which repudiated any kind of aggression for solving any kind of problems. The latter thought was, perhaps, more popular amongst the common people, possibly because the non-Aryans far outnumbered the Aryans. Buddha also approved this way of life. Although a Kshatriya of Sakya extraction — Sakyas possibly were not Aryans — and even though he had grown up in the midst of traditions and customs and religious practices mostly laid down by the Aryan social and religious order, he was disenchanted because he found this order to be too ritualistic and mechanical, even hypocritical, and did not emphasize honesty and sincerity. There had been a sea change in the Aryan religious concepts too, from their earlier belief in the pantheon of deities representing the natural elements, like wind, water, rain, earth, and so on. In fact, there had been a fair amount of convergence of views on the basic thoughts of most religious groups. They all understood existence to be a continuum of cycles of birth and death, or temporal, a bondage in the phenomenal world, or *sansara*, a journey through time and space, mostly in pain and suffering, and agreed that to secure freedom there had to be cessation of birth, and since cause of birth was the karmas, its elimination had to be secured, and that could be done only through good and noble deeds. The basic differences between different philosophies were about the methods to be adopted for the elimination of karmas. There were differences on the speculative aspects of the religion too, as to how the universe was created, what was its final destination, how it would behave during the course of its existence, whether there was God, and if He was there how much influence could or would He exert in the day to day life of an individual, and such like matters. Since the majority of the people were of the pacifist Austric Australoid background, Buddha's ideas immediately appealed to them. This all but ousted Brahmanism. Even in other countries where Austric Australoid culture predominated (generally Far-Eastern) Buddhism was readily accepted.

Though the cohesiveness of the Indus civilization was no longer visible after the advent of the Aryans, its spirit lived on, even after the passage of another millennium, and even today it is very visible. At its one end lies compassion, magnanimity and break from worldly attachment, emphasis on justice and righteous and religious living, at the other is passivity, ultimately deteriorating into lack of committed, sincere and vibrant activity. This is the philosophy of the people who evolved from fruit gatherers. To them the life sustaining necessities were available directly from natural sources, that is food, shelter and clothing; in the non-rigorous, salubrious climate of South Asia, shelter and clothing did not have to be as protective against the weather as in the harsh weather conditions of the snow infested regions of the west and north. These people did not have to move extensively in search of food; nature presented it to them, in whatever quantity. But when there was a lack of it, no amount of agitation could secure it for them; droughts infested the whole land and without adequate means of movement there was not much they could do; they just had to endure the suffering in the precipitation of which they had no part. Fed essentially on non-proteinous, vegetarian diet, they developed milder physique and temperament as compared to the western hunter who was clearly ahead in guile, tenacity, and mental and physical robustness, and was under high pressure to discover and invent.

The philosophies and cultures of the two people were, thus, evolved from their environments. The western man believed in physical strength and all that went to develop it, and all that it secured. He lived at the absolute materialistic level. The eastern man of placid environments, on the other hand, living in the midst of nearly predetermined resources provided to him by the nature and not so much through his personal efforts, got used to being less concerned about his basic requirements, and more philosophic about the problems that confronted him; he felt that punishment, or reward, depended on forces over which he had little control, and learnt to accept the hardships with equanimity rather than fight and devise the means and methods to get the better of them; it is not that he took it all lying down, but was not as sanguine as was his cousin in the west, or north.

Being somewhat limited in physical performance and not under much pressure to innovate or invent to secure the better of the negative elements of his environments, he was prone to look inwards and concentrate upon developing an understanding of the meaning of life, ontology, eschatology, religion. His living conditions suggested to him that nothing was to be gained by unrestricted violence, or by any gesture or activity that might bring harm or injury to other people. His worries were not related to availability of food and other necessities of life, but to disease, old age and death, and he generally concentrated upon how the suffering caused by these could be mitigated or eliminated altogether. That was the essence of his culture. The essential aim of the two cultural streams was, however, the same, that is to secure happiness for the human being. The western stream could not do it, as the story of Ullysis would illustrate; according to Plato, the fourth century B.C. Greek philosopher, the island continent of Atlantis submerged into the Atlantic Ocean on account of the unadulterated materialism practised by its inhabitants. Also as the history of the last few centuries would show, western materialism brought untold misery and suffering upon the passive people of Africa and the Orient because of their being deficient in sciences and technology. But this knowledge also brought about the most destructive wars the mankind has ever seen, causing mutual destruction within the western powers themselves. Nor has the passivity and moral values of South Asia shown the way. Their way of life created a vacuum of performance into which the action oriented forces moved like a hurricane, smashing everything that was weak and fragile. The right course may be somewhere in between, but whether that balance or equilibrium can ever be reached, is any one's guess. Only in an action oriented, God fearing world can there be peace and happiness for the humanity.

Driven by materialism and armed with weapons which had higher destructive power compared to the weapons of stagnant societies, the western powers set out to colonize, and ushered an era of ruthless exploitation. Earlier, in most cases, the armies of conquest settled down in the conquered areas as a privileged class, lording it over the people they had vanquished, leading a life of luxury and dominance. They did plunder, but adopted the new land as their home and settled down, without unduly impoverishing the common people; the wealth of the state stayed within the state. They certainly challenged the ego and the pride of their subjects, but did not seriously disturb the local economic balance; it was in their interest to ensure this if they were to govern effectively. But with the advent of the machine all that changed. The armies were now based in the countries of their origin, and they plundered and carried the loot home, to the governments that had launched them. The military institutions, the instruments of aggression used to secure wealth and plunder, turned highly professional. The conquerors exploited the lands that they had taken so ruthlessly that they no longer remained fit for any kind of decent human living. About the British, Karl Marx observed in his paper of June 1853, that they had broken up the

Indian handloom and destroyed the spinning wheel, and drove the Indian cottons from the European markets, and in the end inundated the very mother country of cotton, with cottons. From 1818 to 1836 the export of cotton cloth from Great Britain to India rose in the proportion of 1 to 5200, being no more than one million yards in 1824, it was more than 64 million yards in 1837. Karl Marx also observed that India is "a country not only divided between Mohammedan and Hindus, but between tribe and tribe, between caste and caste; a society whose framework was based on a sort of equilibrium resulting from a general repulsion and constitutional exclusiveness between all its members. Such a country and such a society, were they not the predestined prey of conquest?" He further observes:

> If we knew nothing of the past history of Hindostan, would there not be one great and incontestable fact, that even at this moment India is held in English thralldom by an Indian army maintained at the cost of India? India could not escape the fate of being conquered, and the whole of her past history, if it be anything, is the history of successive conquests she has undergone. Indian society has no history at all, at least no known history. What we call its history, is but the history of the successive intruders who founded their empires on that unresisting and unchanging passive society.

Elsewhere he observes :

> England, it is true, in causing a social revolution in Hindostan, was actuated only by the vilest interests, and was stupid in her manner of enforcing them. But that is not the question. The question is: can mankind fulfil its destiny without a fundamental revolution in the social state of Asia? If not, whatever may have been the crimes of England, she was the unconscious tool of history in bringing about that revolution.

Karl Marx may be mistaken in some of his observations because of, may be, a deficient understanding of the people of this sub-continent, but it cannot be denied that the pathetic passivity of the Indian culture brought hordes of conquerors into this land, and brought untold sufferings upon its people. In effect the Indus culture may have been totally relevant during the time that it lasted, and it lasted a long time, may be, on account of its philosophy of passivity, but once the environments in the north-western parts of the subcontinent had become hospitable and emigrant-friendly and thus attractive to the people outside, this philosophy had become not only outmoded but distinctly negative and dangerous. From time to time, in the subsequent history of this land, this philosophy has emerged as a dominant thought, and whenever it did, the country as a whole went through a trauma which severely harmed the interests of its people.

But the universe does not operate in a fixed time-space frame; it is a process of constant, unremitting change. We have seen that in the beginning it was the strong and the muscular man, gifted with animal like qualities, who made it to the top. Wars, conquests and adverse environments, have been the major factors responsible for the progress of man from the old pithicus stage to that of the homosapiens. After the muscle-man came the stage when human intelligence started playing a role, and as time went by this role became more predominant, even though physical toughness and the toughness of the human will continued to be amongst the most important factors that made the difference between defeat and victory, survival and annihilation. These shall continue to be relevant even in the future, particularly the factor of the human will. But the factor of the muscle-gifted human being has been compromized to an extent, but only to an extent, with the coming in of the push-button, automated type of gadgetry which affords good chances of survival even to weaker groups of people, be it survival in the field of battle or in the economics field, or education or any other discipline. Vietnam is a typical case. Once the people had set their mind on securing a particular system of governance for themselves, and they had been adequately disciplined, there was nothing stopping them from securing their objective, even when their adversaries were better off in terms of physical strength, intelligence, scientific background and knowledge, and military capability. It would, thus, be wrong to assume that in the future, as in the past, only the physically stronger side, better equipped with weapons of war, will secure victory. As Jonathan Swift brought out in his satirical work *Gulliver's Travels* way back in 1726, even Lilliputians have a chance so long as they have the will and determination and a capability to act in concert.

Religion

About the religion of the Indus people nothing can be said with certainty. In fact, only surmises can be made about the various facets of the life of these people on the basis of archaeological finds, and the study of life patterns of the people who live in modern times, or were there till the other day, and who we believe were, at least partly, still following the Indus way of life. Figurines in terracotta, faience and other materials, of the semi-nude female, could be attributed to the cult of the Mother-Goddess. The *bania* and the *lala* communities of Punjab even today are the followers of this concept, and believe in the motherhood of God. Contiguously located people in the lower reaches of Himachal Pradesh and Jammu also subscribe to this belief. The only other place where this concept is prevalent is amongst the Mongolo-Dravidians of Bengal. Such figurines have been found in many places in West Asia, between the Aegean Sea and Persia, which shows how popular the belief was in the life sustaining attributes of the Goddess. She is Aditi, and she is Prithvi, the benefactress from whose womb emanate all that is essential for the survival of life on this planet. Then there is evidence that suggests the existence of tree worship, particularly of the *pipal*, the practice which is followed by a certain section of the people right up to the present times. A god, possibly a forerunner of the great Siva, also appears to have been worshipped. On some seals this god sits in a yogic posture, has horns, and has his 'member' erect, and wears bangles on his arms, and is surrounded by wild animals — possibly an early form of Pashupatinatha. The erect member, the fertility symbol, is the characteristic of another old form of the god: Lakulisha, of the Austric Proto-Australoids; the god is still held in veneration by some tribes in Orissa. Horns are a very common symbol of divinity in Egypt and ancient 'Near East'. Legends prevalent in some of the other countries of that time also find place on some seals.

However, there is a possibility that the Siva concept was finalized during the later period of this civilization itself. He is the god of fertility, and is also worshipped as *linga*; the phallic worship, as also the worship of the *yoni*, the female reproductive organ, possibly, originated with the Australoids. A number of animals have also appeared on the Harappan seals, leading some experts to conclude that some animals were regarded as sacred, like, for example, the bull, which even today, as Nandi, is considered to be the vehicle of Siva. There is no evidence to suggest that rivers, or water for that matter, were considered as sacred, but considering the prevalent customs of today, which consider water, as also the rivers, as sacred, and which enjoin people to take baths in rivers, particularly at the confluences, and tanks, during certain auspicious days, and the presence of the Great Bath at Mohenjodaro, it may be concluded that the water, of tanks and rivers, held an important place in the religious beliefs of the Indus people; in fact, in their layout of the cities they have taken care to ensure that their sullage did not pollute their rivers. It is not likely that the cow had a sacred status, for although seals have been found bearing figures of a number of animals, no seal has the figure of a cow.

Not much material is available as to how the Harappans disposed of their dead, but from the fact that only a few burial grounds have been found, it might be concluded that the main mode of disposal was cremation. The cemeteries, whatever have been found, indicate three kinds of burials, viz., complete, fractional and post cremation. Fractional burial means internment of the left-over bones after the body has been exposed to wild animals or birds. The urns containing post cremation ashes were almost invariably buried underneath a floor or a street. In all burials there is a suggestion of funerary offerings in terms of birds, animals, fish, or articles like beads, bangles and other household items, including cooking ware, and so on. The prevalent concept almost in all the countries of that time was, and this belief held on for a long time, that in the hereafter, for its comfort and happiness, the ethereal spirit needed offerings of those kind of items that provided it happiness and comfort during its human existence.

In some parts of the old world, like for example in Egypt, when a king or a person of status died, a number of animals sometimes even human beings including members of his retinue and other people he was comfortable with, and his favourite wives and mistresses, were killed in order to despatch them to the 'other world' along with him. He also carried treasures, and articles of food and other items of utility so that his and his retinue's needs were amply taken care of. How many human beings and animals were actually killed depended upon the power and position of the deceased person; whereas a king took hordes of material, herds of animals and a large number of human beings, a small-time chief had to be content, maybe, with just his wife and a few animals. The Indian custom of *Sati* was also, probably, a take-off from this belief. Considering the variety of funerary articles found and the fact that some graves had more than one skeleton, it is likely that at least some amongst those ancients believed in the 'other world' and, possibly, the need for material articles and a close companion to accompany the deceased for his general well being.

The Indus trader was a great organizer. He built his villages, towns and cities with an eye on his trade interests. He possibly arranged with people not directly concerned with him, to see to it that his agents and workers' guilds, which he had painstakingly organized, were not harassed and smooth flow of his business was not disturbed. He appeared to have a socialistic sort of an attitude towards his workmen. He housed them in clean, surroundings and must have generally looked after their well-being. In the collectives of artisans and specialized workers he left behind an institution that operates even today in the form of caste system, in fact, the system could even be older. Castes have been formed either on the basis of the professions, (like iron smith, carpenter, weaver) or tribal names, (like Lohana, Meena, Mahar), or religious movements, (like Arya, Bishnoi), or the localities people belonged to or had immigrated from. All these reasons were relevant during the Indus days, and there is every reason to believe that caste divisions existed then as well. There were, however, other classes, like the people who were the employers of the artisan class, such as the *vani*, the *bania*, the trader, or the priest (a priestly class must have existed then, although possibly, not as domineering as the later day Brahmins), or the class that held the weapons and looked after the law and order, or the bureaucrats, and all these, naturally, must have ranked higher than the people who made up the rank and file of the workforce. Amongst the *jatis*, the castes of the work-force, the relative gradation must have depended upon the status an individual's profession enjoyed.

INVASIONS AND MIGRATIONS OF INDO-EUROPEANS

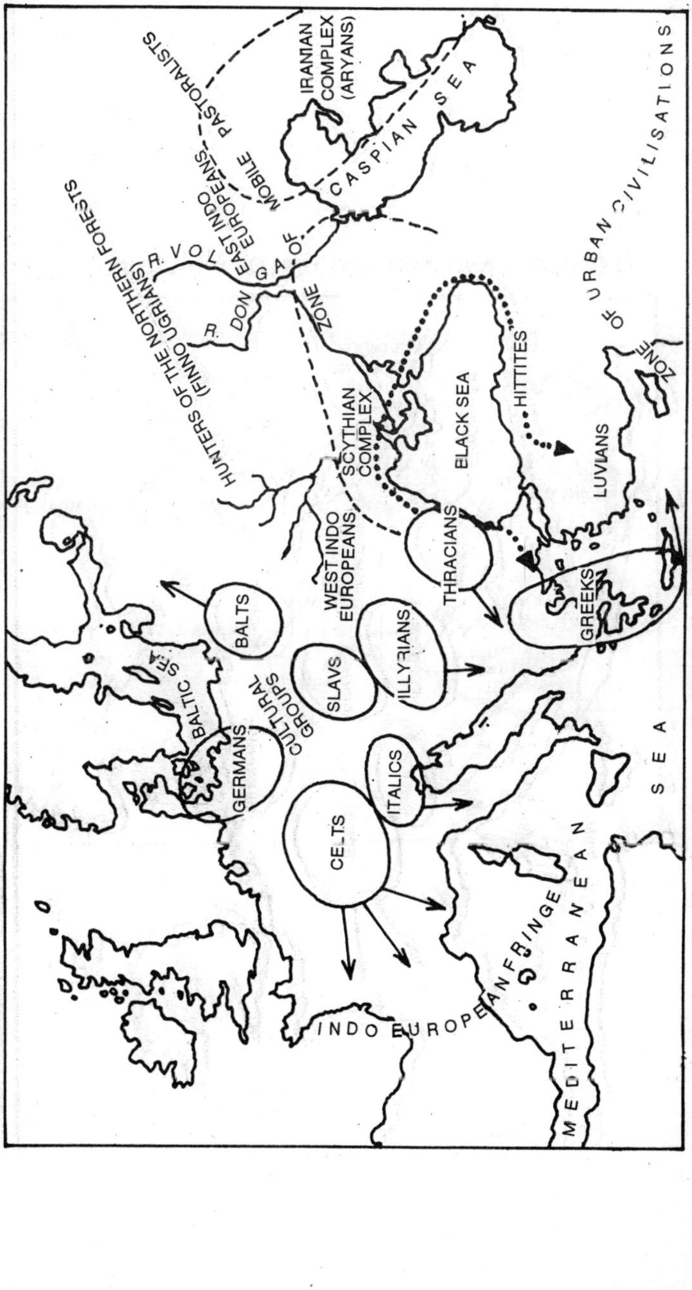

•3rd and 2nd Millennium BC ••••••••

•2nd and 1st Millennium BC ———

INVASIONS AND IMMIGRATIONS OF INDO-EUROPEANS

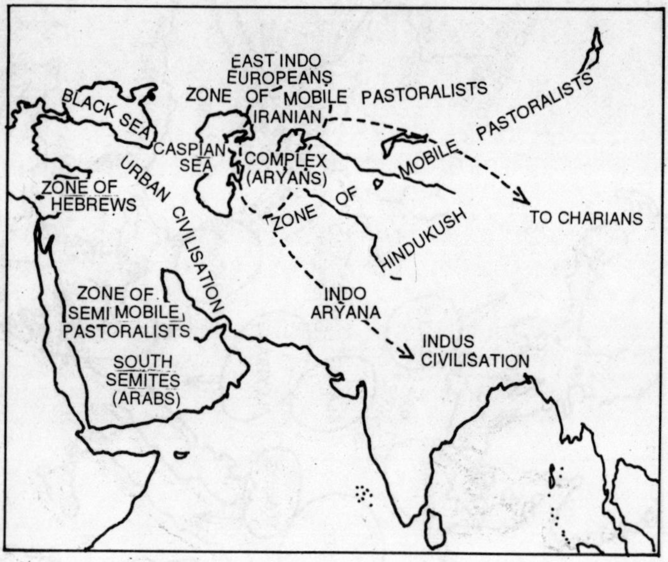

The End of the Civilization

It can be said that this civilization came to an end around the middle of the second millennium B.C., and as to how it happened, the views differ. Most scholars, however, believe that this was the time when the ancient civilizations in the west were breaking up under the pressures of bludgeoning populations of Central Asia. Tribes fought one another for grazing and cultivable lands and in the process of the fighting radically improved upon their battle field skills and weapon systems. Those who lost had to quit and migrate to other lands, and along with them some went just looking for fresh pastures and seeking better opportunities. They fell with ferocity upon the aging civilizations of West Asia and Middle East which just crumbled against the superior weapons, fighting skills and physical fitness of the invaders. The diggings at the sites of Harappan towns and cities render evidence of such kind of treatment at the hands of the invading tribesmen. At Rana Ghundai where there had been an almost continuous occupation from around late fourth millennium B.C., pockets of ashes in the later layers suggest that there was a large-scale burning of the place around 2000 B.C., and its reoccupation by a different set of people is indicated by the difference in the pottery style in the following layers; being coarser in style and painting, it suggests that the new occupants were barbarians. The evidence further shows that the settlement was burnt again, and yet again, every time being occupied by a different set of people with different pottery styles. Similar evidences have been unearthed at Nal and Dabar Kot, in north Baluchistan.

Some of the essential features of the Harappan civilization had long since been adopted by the north Baluchi cultures, and, at the face of it, there was little to distinguish one from the other; the point being made is that the two cultures were facing almost parallel ups and downs, suggesting that, possibly, approach to Harappa lay through north Baluchistan. In south Baluchistan, however, not much evidence of such destruction has been found. But in Shahi-tump cemetry a heavy copper axe with a shaft-hole, has been found amongst the grave-goods, and the pottery, in some cases, had the swastika or a similar motif painted upon it: clearly a new set of people had arrived. One burial spot carries a number of weapons along side a skeleton indicating that the person buried was a warrior. There is also evidence to suggest that in the later phases of the occupation of the two cities and some towns, defence works in the form of strengthening of breast walls, and the like were executed, indicating disturbed conditions. All this has led to the belief that the end of the entire Indus Civilization was violent, that it vanished from the surface of the earth under one surge of the pillaging and plundering Central Asian tribesmen.

Even though the possibility of this kind of a demise for a culture which had virtually stagnated for the last few hundred years, cannot be ruled out, it does not seem likely. For a civilization to blow out in this fashion, there had to be a well organized attacking force, under one command, which should have precipitated this event under a carefully thought out plan. There is no evidence supporting the emergence of such a force. All that can be concluded from the available evidence is that there was anarchy, that various tribes and hordes, separated in time and space, pillaged and plundered the relatively docile, but fairly affluent trading centres, time after time, till they had been virtually pulverized, and the leaders of Indus had abandoned them and moved elsewhere, to the east or south.

As stated earlier, it is most unlikely that Indus Valley was knit into a single unit in the shape of an empire, or even a kingdom. It possibly comprized an area of numerous tribal conglomerates, which had, over a long period of time, adopted similar customs, habits, and way of life, and, thus collectively given the impression of one culture. It is highly unlikely that the whole countryside had even one common language, though people of different geographical areas must have had dialects which were generally mutually understood, at least in the immediate neighbourhood. Into this social scenario stepped in a dynamic and a very competent traders class, and they provided the vital inputs to give a character to this civilization. Without their efforts not even a trace of the existence of the people of those times would have been found. Therefore, it was not like one state, which might have been brought down in one or a couple of battles. Tribal conglomerates would have provided depth to the total defence system, and should have taken time to get totally eliminated. It is, however, most likely that the various areas developed by the trading community were ravaged from time to time, and after each such incident a period of development and reconstruction followed. With better cutting tools, particularly after the onset of the Iron Age — which, however, at this stage was quite a number of centuries away — the areas to the east of the Indus basin and leading on to the river system of the Ganges, started getting cleared, leading to settlements which should have attained their own levels of prosperity, and attracted the attention of the Indus traders, who, in difficult times, would have emigrated there. Such times would have come during droughts or floods or when conditions of anarchy prevailed. However, the belief has persisted that even if not in one blow, the civilization burnt out over a fairly restricted period of time. It is possible that, considering the fertility of the Gangetic plains, and the disturbed conditions of the Indus basin, the whole, or most of the well-to-do people of the latter area just moved out, not in one wave maybe, but over a fairly restricted period of time.

An interesting hypothesis has been put forward by Professor M. Dmitriyev of the erstwhile Soviet Union. According to him Mohenjodaro was destroyed in a black lightning explosion which literally caused it to disappear from the face of the earth in one go. He says there is an account of the tragedy in *Mahabharata* where it is stated that there was a powerful explosion which was followed by a dazzling glow, and by fires without smoke, and that, almost instantly, the temperature of the water reached the boiling point and the fish looked as if they had been scorched. Such explosions, says the Professor, have occurred from time to time in various parts of the world, and are caused by physicochemical formations. Under the effect of the cosmic rays and electric fields, chemically active particles are formed which occupy large expanses in the atmosphere. These expanses get compressed by the electromagnet fields. Apparently, the atmospheric conditions in which the physicochemical formations appear, activate the formation of toxic agents, and these pollute the air. Possibly the people of Mohenjodaro were affected by poisonous gases to begin with, and then a powerful explosion caused the complete destruction. This phenomenon is possible only when a large number of black lightning discharges occur simultaneously; after one explosion has taken place others follow in a chain reaction.

Whatever the cause of destruction, it appears quite possible that the end at Mohenjodaro was pretty abrupt; evidence suggests that there was no time to collect even the bare essentials before death struck. Once Mohenjodaro was gone, what was there to hold Indus Valley together? Over the time, wandering tribes settled there temporarily, erected dwellings, then, after a stay, abandoned the area. For, essentially the place was significant only from the point of view of trade; being located at a nodal point on the land and riverine routes. With time, due to the neglect of the river training works, the rivers receded substantially from the ramparts of the cities so that cargo carrying boats could no longer off-load directly on to the market place, and the land routes fell into disuse for being under threat due to lack of adequate security. The horse had made the plundering tribals far more mobile and powerful, and enabled them to strike at will. For people to live in a place, there have to be avenues in that place for generating income, and without trade, the cities had no avenues. Superstition and fright at the manner of the destruction of Mohenjodaro might have been a further disincentive. With time, the drifting sands from the rivers and land covered up these places in a manner that any further rebuilding was considered counter productive.

Thus the places went, but not before the people who had nurtured them, had been flung out in all directions, like the droplets of a cascading wave scattered by the force of wind, or the seeds in a dried pod getting tossed out on ripening. During their dying years, cities showed a distinct lack of the previous verve and organizing capability. Streets had become narrower and people, it seems, liked to live closer together in order to be able to come to each other's help at short notice. Slums had sprung up in the middle of the earlier well organized areas; even the manufacturing kilns, which earlier were located away from the inhabited areas, were not following that rule any longer. With laxity all around, the places ceased to fulfil the purpose for which they had originally come into being. When they closed finally, the inhabitants had moved eastwards, to the Gangetic basin, or to the south, or the valley of the river Ghaggar in the Thar desert, and to Saurashtra and Gujarat. They developed new towns, including the very important port of Lothal in the Gulf of Cambay, supplementing the old ports of Surat and Kinnarkheda in the area. Their spread southwards and eastwards continued over a long period of time, till they, or their variants, were present almost throughout the length and breadth of India. But the hard core of this community today lives in Rajasthan and Gujarat (Saurashtra).

The Ancient Cultures of South India

About the ancient cultures of South India, not much is known. The north-western territory of this subcontinent has been under pressure since the invention of the chariot as the war machine in the first place, and horse cavalry subsequently, and under this pressure movement of the populations southwards and eastwards has almost never ceased. It is still there even in the present times. Southern parts of India, possibly, received a much larger share of the Negrito, Proto-Australoid, and the Palaeo-Mediterranean stock, for, being the first to arrive, they were the first to be pushed out by the tribes and communities that followed them. But south have had other people too, from Persia, Iraq, Arabia, Syria, Egypt, who made it directly after crossing the Arabian Sea, or the Persian Gulf, or following the land route along the Makran Coast and thence to Sindh, Gujarat, and then southwards along the western coast, all the way down to the Tamil land. People from African countries along the Arabian Sea have also made it from time to time mostly to peninsular India, by directly crossing the sea. The cult of Siva and Parvati in the south, is almost parallel to the cult of the 'moon god' and the 'Lady of the Mountain' which was followed at Ur, the ancient city of Sumer in southern Mesopotamia, including the ceremonial nuptials of the god and the goddess, their palace-temple, the temple slaves, and the *devadasis*. South Indian painted pottery. often resembles that of Tepe Hissar in Persia. Egyptian alabasters were discovered in Malabar. There is a lot of similarity in the forms of burials, and funeral offerings and accessories, with those of areas along the coast of the Arabian Sea, or of areas in Egypt, Syria, Cyprus, even as far away as Britanny in north-west France. There is also evidence of direct trade between the South and countries like Mesopotamia and Egypt and other countries of their times. In so far as the population is concerned, peninsular and south India, like the north, also have had a mixed bag. While a majority of the people are of the mixed Negrito, Proto-Australoid and the Palaeo-Mediterranean stock, they also have Sytho-Dravidians, and a mix from areas like Egypt, Syria, Mesopotamia and even Persia.

The pattern of population movement towards the east followed almost the same lines as the southward movement, except that in the case of the former there was virtually no ingress from the direction of the sea, and during the movement along the land routes some interbreeding with Mongoloid populations at the northern and eastern fringes took place. Later, people arriving from the west intermingled with the people of eastern Punjab and western Uttar Pradesh and produced a synthesis which flowered into another ancient civilization, that of the Aryans, which evolved a common language, and a script, so essential for the development of social, economic, political, and scientific institutions. Northern India had at last entered history.

To come back to the Indus civilization! At the face of it, on the basis of evidence available, it seems reasonably certain that, being a trade oriented civilization, it was not theocratic in its outlook. There were any number of ideas about divinity amidst all kinds of clans and tribes and social orders, and, it appears, that the state, or whatever organ was there running the affairs, let the things be. There were worshippers of Mother Goddess, or some old version of Siva Nataraja, or ancestors, or trees, or stones, or just spots on the ground, but this does not appear to have caused any mutual acrimony or friction. Religion is an activity one pursues to seek mental peace, or material progress, or better living in the next life, if there is belief in next life or in the well-being, happiness and health of ones family, or, rarely, that of the clan, tribe or nation, or even humanity at large, and on all counts this was regarded as a purely personal activity. To achieve whatever one had set out to achieve, they followed one of the methods entitled to follow whatever they considered to be the most efficacious. It seems fairly certain that religion was a personal affair of a person and no one was overly concerned about how he went about it, except, maybe, when he wished to tell the community or his friends how, while following a certain practice, he gained or lost in terms of worldly prosperity, or spiritual enlightenment.

In fact, that had been the broad attitude in India till the arrival of Islam and Christianity, where the prophet, or the messiah, had fixed all the details regarding the speculative aspects of the religions they were preaching, and given out rigid codes to their followers, covering almost all aspects of the daily life, including their dealings with believers and non-believers; the code covering the latter aspect, that is dealings with non-believers, created a psychosis of acrimony, hatred, distrust, and almost all other conditions that contribute to the fragmentation of the human family. The approach to religion on the Indian subcontinent was almost just the reverse of this. Hinduism became a religion essentially to identify those who were not the followers of Islam or Christianity. Otherwise it is not a religion in the same sense. It has a very broad spectrum of philosophy, as well as ideology. At one end of the spectrum are complete non-believers, while at the other those who believe in absolute monoism, which implies that the entire creation, and much more than we as mere human beings can comprehend collectively, is what could be called God, if a name has to be given to the power that creates or manifests itself as the creation. Then there are people who believe in gods and goddesses, believe in the Motherhood of God, believe in personal God in personified form, believe in their family gods, *graam devatas* or village deities, *isht devatas* or personal gods, and so on. In between there is also the faith in dualism, in a God who runs the universe like an emperor would run an empire, the essential characteristic of this faith being the feeling of complete devotion to God, a total submission to the divine will, unqualified love for the divine grace. The list could be large. And no one minds this, for, as stated earlier, the aim of religion is to provide psychic and psychological comfort to an individual, help him in building confidence in himself, get him to rough out the hardships of life with grace and fortitude and how he achieves this is for him to decide! There are scriptures, *Geeta*, epics, and other literature to guide, and there are masters and gurus, to advise, but ultimately it is the person himself who has to decide what course he wants to follow. For, as the belief goes, life is a chain of a series of problems, and has a lot of hardship; for some it is a long, arduous journey right from day one, to its very end. It is here that a person needs God's help, and Hinduism does not bind him to visualize his God only in one particular shape or form, he could do it in that form which would elicit maximum response from his heart and mind. The point being made is that the foundation for this kind of a broad and open approach, which could touch the very limits of eternity, were, possibly, laid by the Indus people. They had neither the time, essential activity being trade and commerce, nor the wherewithal in terms of communications and transportation, to force a particular point of view or a way of life. It does appear, though, that they had amongst them people who had given a lot of thought to the aspects of human psyche and personality, and to the phenomenon of creation, and made some lasting contributions to the fundamentals of Hinduism. Yoga is there contribution, and so is the Siva Nataraja, the cosmic energy engrossed in the creative and the annihilative processes, and the concept of the Mother Goddess, and the purificatory baths in rivers and tanks at the auspicious spots and confluences during certain specified auspicious times. The ideas form the different aspects of Hinduism today, even though they are not entirely complementary to each other in their detail. But, generally, there is a common thread, the belief that absolute goodness is essential for human happiness and growth, that God's kindness and grace is there for anyone who seeks it, irrespective of the person's religion, class or sex, irrespective of whether he secures it through the worship of Mother Goddess, or a tree, or stone, or *gram devata*, or *Dyaush Pita* or whatever, and irrespective of the shape and form he attributes to his God that there is no heaven or hell, but only karuas, deeds, which cause rebirth, and consequently, suffering, that absolute purity is essential to attain freedom from the hold of karmas and the birth cycle - once freed, the divine spark and the soul, flies off to the cosmic centre to merge with it forever, forever to be freed of the painful process of birth and death, forever to be part of that infinite whole whose essence is ecstasy, that no matter how hard the wrong doers work, the ultimate triumph shall have to be of the forces which are on the side of goodness and justice. This basic thought appears to have existed during the days of the Indus people.

But then all this talk of peace, morality, goodness, this emphasis on life on earth being nothing but unadulterated pain, this longing for an escape forever into a realm where it is all joy, could just be a defeatist talk of a people who might have been at the receiving end for most of the time, who might have been periodically subjected to unbearable pain and humiliation by their tormentors. Essentially most religious attitudes flow from a weakness of its followers to cope with the problems arising out of failures, failures to achieve, to perform, to look after, to stand up to certain beliefs, failures to secure wins in the day to day life. There, perhaps, is a lot of truth in the saying that essentially religion is the opium of the people. It is a crutch of the weaker sections, an idea that can put them in a world of make belief, and mitigate their pain, drudgery, hopelessness, humiliation, and fear, that life has brought upon them. But on pragmatic considerations we can say that this is but one facet of religion. It has many others. Most of all it generates fellow feeling, kindness towards one another, a sense of justice and fair play, a resolve not to ever harm any one for selfish ends. It helps in bringing forth in relief what by the modern thinkers are termed as the positive attributes of the human character. No doubt, the origin of religion is sourced in fear. It was the fury of the elements, the pain of death, the tribulations of the living process and the total mystery of the creation that surrounded him, that forced man to think in terms of a power superior to him, which could harm or benefit him, and whose patronage, good wishes and cooperation, he had to secure to ensure his and his clan's survival. But with the passage of time, man came to know better, and though he still recognized a power running the entire show of the creation, of which he was but a minuscule speck, his fear got transformed into confidence, hope, love, into his understanding of the other human beings, and he learnt to regard them as his friends and comrades, and not enemies out to destroy him. In any case, at this stage, so far away from the Indus time, it is difficult to say whether the evolution of the Indian religious thought was based on fear or wisdom, but the ultimate result that it has produced is the core of Hinduism today. Of course, there is a lot of extraneous stuff, some of it floating around from pristine times almost unchanged, which has found place in the Hindu thought, but then, as stated earlier, Hinduism has no dispute with that; it gives full freedom to its adherents to follow whatever practice they cherish, although the process of guiding, advising, educating, continues.

Three

The Aryans

Origin and Traditional Evidence

Who exactly were the Indo-Aryans, where did they come from and when? Their cradleland has been placed variously between India in the east and Germany in the west, going as far north as the Scandinavian countries. While their origination on the Eurasian land mass has been dated by some as not earlier than 2500 BC, some have put the period as far back as 10,000 BC. Unfortunately not a shred of evidence has been found anywhere which might throw light on the land of their origination or the time when they moved out, or the route they followed, or when exactly they arrived in India, and why only a part of them. Had it not been for their religion, and the literature for it, there, perhaps, would have been no direct evidence about even the existence of these very dynamic people. Even pottery seems to fail, probably because of the semi-migratory life they seem to have lived for a long time. In India some scholars have identified them with Painted-Grey-Ware culture which existed between 1100-500 BC. in the western parts of the present Uttar Pradesh, along the western reaches of the Ganges. These people lived in thatched houses and used copper, and, in course of time knew the use of iron as well; this corresponds to the descriptions contained in the Vedic literature. At Hastinapur, on the banks of the Ganges, digging has revealed that a part of the town was washed away in floods around 800 BC. This occurrence has been narrated in the *Puranas* and is given as having taken place in the reign of the seventh successor after Prikshat; the latter was the first king after the *Mahabharata* war; this would suggest around 1000 BC as the date for the war. The evidence of the 'painted-grey-ware' culture at Hastinapur ends at this level.

The Traditional Story

The traditional story in the Aryan mythological lore begins with Manu Svayambhu and is recorded in the *Puranas* and the *Brahmanas*, and covers the flood which is supposed to have occurred thousands of years ago; according to a seventh century AD inscription of Pulakesin II at Aihole, the *Mahabharata* war took place in the year 3102 BC. Apparently the estimate is based on the accounts in the traditional history. During the late eighteenth and early nineteenth century, evidence based on philology came to be developed and the results thereof diminished the importance of the traditional evidence.

The Language Similarities

In India, European scholars of Sanskrit realized, with some surprise, that the language bore a fairly close relationship in structure and, possibly, in sound, to Greek and Latin. On further study it came out that most European languages, including Sanskrit, were interrelated. At present these languages are divided into two broad groups, namely, the Satem and the Centum. In the former group the velar k became s and labiovelar kw became k, while in the latter, velar k and labiovelar kw have been retained. Most languages of central and western Europe are Centum. The Satem group has two divisions, viz., Balto-Slavanic and Indo-Iranian. Balto-Slavanic languages are of eastern Europe and the states around the Baltic sea, and the Indo-Iranian include Iranian, Baluch, Kurd, Afghan and all the languages of northern India, like Punjabi, Bengali and so on. The unmistakable conclusion is that originally the Indo-Europeans had a common language, and as sections of their population wandered away in different directions there developed modified versions of the original language after these sections had come in contact with other people and intermixed with them.

Archaeological Findings

In 1921-22 the archaeological finds at Harappa and Mohenjodaro revealed the existence of a pre-Aryan civilization in the north-western parts of India — the Indus Valley Civilization. The culture period of this civilization could have been between c. 2800 BC to 2200 BC although it could have existed in a fairly characterized state between c. 3500 to 1500 BC. This discovery puts serious doubts about the veracity of the early parts of the traditional history as recorded in the *Puranas* and the *Brahmanas*. It now appeared that the Indo-Aryans could not have arrived in the country much earlier than 2000 BC, that in the early stages they, probably, arrived as nomads in search of pastures for their animals and settled down in different areas in groups and tribes, and their emergence as conquerors of the local people could not have taken place much earlier than c. 1800 to 1500 BC.

The European, Asian and Russian Origins

On the basis of philology, one school of researchers, led by Brandenstein, has concluded that Indo-Iranians were the first to separate from the main body of the Indo-Europeans. This school believes that the original home of the Indo-Europeans was in the Kirghiz steppes to the south of the Ural mountain ranges, and from there the Indo-Iranians moved to the east, while the rest of the people, at a somewhat later date, moved to the west. The westward moving lot, however, split on the way, with one part moving north to be identified later as Nordics, and the other making for Ukraine and thence to south and west.

Another view, put across by Eduard Meyer, designates the area of the Pamir plateau as the original home of the Aryans. This is based on the established presence of the Hittites in Asia Minor around 1950 BC—Hittite is the oldest known Indo-European dialect. This leads to the suggestion that Indo-Iranians not only moved to India but also westwards, from their common home in the area of the Pamir plateau, or in Russian Turkistan (as suggested by Herzfeld). But if they moved in different directions and arrived in India and western and central Asia Minor almost at the same time, it stands to reason that the area from where they moved must have been equidistant from both places. This would place the original home in Russian Turkistan.

It has also been argued that all Centum speaking areas are to the west and east of the Vistula and Satem respectively. Thus, the conclusion is that before their final dispersal Indo-Europeans were settled on either side of this river, although discovery of manuscripts in Tocharian — a Centum language — in Chinese Turkestan in this century, has put a question mark on this view. Another point of focus has been Lithuania, for Lithuanian has been regarded as the most archaic of the Indo-European languages. Possibly the language was brought to this land by the Indo-Europeans who came to settle here after the Centum-Satem split, and if this hypothesis is accepted then the cradle-land could not have been very far away from Lithuania, unless Lithuania itself was the cradle-land.

Another view put across by some important European scholars is that Germanic countries — particularly Scandinavia — are not known to have ever been overrun by an alien race, and they all speak Indo-European languages. The obvious conclusion is that the original home of the Indo-Aryans was in this Germanic region. Penka, the chief exponent of this view, was an ethnologist and believed that term 'Aryan' represented a race comprising people from Scandinavia. However, it cannot be conclusively proved that the people of the interior of the Germanic countries remained totally static over the millennia, in their homeland and did not intermingle with any other group. That would go against the very grain of the evolutionary process which, as we know, has come into play with the ceaseless movement and intermingling of the different groups of a species. Professor Max Mullar has expressed the view, which is totally different from that of Penka, that term 'Aryan' is language related and signifies only people speaking one of the Indo-European languages and is utterly inapplicable to a race. This may be the other end of the spectrum of views on the issue, for we know that a language belongs to a group of people who in the initial stages occupy a common geographical location, and who, at least a majority of them, must possess common racial characteristics. Thus the term may have meant people speaking any one of the Indo-European languages or following the Aryan way of life or their religion (based on sacrifice and worship of their gods), but in the initial stages the term had to signify a racial group. But it is hard to believe that the Scandinavians were just static for such a long duration, that no other racial group ever arrived in their country and there never was any interbreeding; the outsiders may well have dominated the original inhabitants and their present language may well have developed as a result of the intermingling.

On the basis of pottery finds which were dated in the third millennium BC, Nehring formulated the view that the original land was in south Russia since the place of the finds (Tripolje) is located there. Other scholars, on the basis of the age of languages spoken in various parts in South Russia, also came to similar conclusion. Besides, there are similarities between the Indo-European and Finno-Ugrian languages, and it is certain that both groups of languages had influenced one another in very early times, and since the Finno-Ugrians originated in central Russia, the probability of the area of the Urals being the homeland of the Indo-Aryans is high indeed. It has also been established, by Moller, that there is evidence of similarity between early Indo-European and early Semitic languages, which goes to show that Semites had, possibly, immigrated to Arabia from the north, via Iran or Asia Minor, and that there must have been some sort of early contact between the two groups, and this, when viewed in the light of the fact that there was contact in early times between Finno-Ugrians and Indo-Europeans as well, would place the location of the cradle-land in south Russia.

Towards the end of the nineteenth century, B.G. Tilak, the famous Maharashtrian leader of the Indian freedom movement, published a paper (in October 1893) to establish the age of the *Rig Veda* on the basis of astrological calculations, and put across the hypothesis that the original home of the Indo-Aryans was in the arctic region. He based his arguments on a few statements and accounts contained in the Vedic literature. A hundred years have elapsed since he published his findings, and since then a lot of ground has been covered in so far as this subject is concerned, but what he said has not been convincingly refuted. Russian art scholar Svetlana Zharnikova has lately expressed the view that Tilak's findings had substance. Vedic hymns have told tales of great and forbidding mountains in the far north, stretching from west to east, and the plains covered with snow for most part of the year, and of the golden tops of the mountains around which the sun rotates throughout the year, and of the Great Bear shining above them during dark nights, and of the Pole Star as the centre of the universe. The hymns sing of the great rivers foaming down from these mountains, some northwards and others southwards, to the white ocean in the north or the warm seas in the south. The name of these mountains which separate the milky sea and the blessed northern land from the rest of the earth is Meru. Mount Mandara is the tallest of them all. The flow of time beyond the Meru is different from the way it happens in our world: there a day lasts as long as our half year. And so on.' A similar corroboratory account is found in the Avestan tradition, the mountain there is called Hara Berezaiti. The question that arises is: how could the plains men of Iran and north-western India know of the cold and snowy countries, and how could they see the Pole Star above their heads, unless the land of their origin was in the arctic region? Greek accounts also mention the northern mountains, they called them Rhipeans and assumed their location to be in northern Europe.

In Tilak's view the Aryans had emigrated from the arctic region of northern Russia. The view of prominent Russian scholars is that Indo-Iranian language and culture developed in the third and early second millennia BC and their cradle land lay in the south Russian steppes, while Gornung amongst them places the cradle land in the middle reaches of the Volga. Svetlana Zharnikova has given the view that Russian steppes in the south of the Urals was the home of the Indo-Iranians, that they had emigrated to this area along with other Indo-Europeans, from the north, from around Vologda (east of St. Petersburg) and lands to the south of a series of low hills (marked on the map as a number of yellow dots) stretching eastwards in the shape of a crescent for a distance of around 3700 km from Vologda all the way to the northern Urals. The small hills are the Meru Mountains. Obviously, the Indo-Aryans when singing about their original homeland many centuries later, attributed loftier dimensions to these hills, maybe on account of fading memory or under nostalgic impulses. But other details as narrated in the hymns tally well with the ground situation: the hills run east-west, the streams are big and foamy and drain north and south, the days are as long as six months in the arctic regions and Pole Star is right on top of the observer. The names of the places too are similar to the ones mentioned in the Vedic accounts even after the passage of thousands of years. The conclusion, thus, is that the original home of the Indo-Europeans was in the Russian plains, to the south of the low mountains stretching between Vologda in the west and the northern Ural range in the east, that many thousand years ago these people wandered off from these areas to the south Russian steppes, and after a stay there of many centuries, branched off in many directions, the Indo-Iranians having eventually made it to Iran. There is no doubt that during their wanderings these groups interacted with many other races and communities and as such ceased to be ethnically homogeneous, and developed cultures and languages which widely differed from group to group, though retaining some aspects of the original basics. This concept does not contradict the prevalent view. It only adds to the existing dimension by suggesting that south Russian steppes was not the original home of the Indo-Europeans but was the interim location which these people occupied after their emigration from north-western Russia, and before they branched off into different lands to the east, west, south and north.

B.G. Tilak in his book *The Orion* has stated that the relevant hymns in the *Rig Veda* show that the sacrificial ceremonies were well developed during the time of the early Aryans. Therefore, during those times there must have existed a reliable calendar to regulate the sacrifices, for no sacrificial system could be developed without the knowledge of months, seasons and the year. The exact nature of this calendar is not known today, but a study of the sacrificial literature shows that the phases of the moon, the changes in the seasons and the southern and northern courses of the sun were the principle considerations in the measurement of time. Aryans originally commenced their year, which was luni-solar and sidereal, with the vernal equinox. Sometime latter the beginning of the year was changed to the winter solstice but the sacrificial year continued to be reckoned from the vernal equinox. Thus, at this stage they had two calendars: one for sacrificial purposes and the other for civil use. This system has been followed right up to the recent times. On the basis of the calculations of astronomy, Tilak has brought out that the oldest period of Aryan civilization was when both the civil and the sacrificial calendars started from the vernal equinox. This period lasted roughly between 6000 BC and 4000 BC. During this time the hymns were not in a finished state and apparently the sacrificial formulae were partly in prose and partly in poetry, and mentioned the principal names and epithets and feats of the deities invoked. Though Greek and Iranian traditions corroborate the Indian tradition for the subsequent period of the Aryan history, in so far as the calendars for sacrificial and secular purposes are concerned, they have nothing for this period, for, apparently, they carried with them only the calendar which was in force when they left the common home, which, it would appear, happened much after the Indo-Aryans had left the flock.

Next, says Tilak, is the Orion period, extending from 4000 BC to 2500 BC. This is from the time when the vernal equinox was in the asterism of Ardra to the time when it receded to the asterism of the Krittikas. This is an important period in the history of the Aryans and their civilization when many *suktas* were composed and many legends were either formed afresh or developed from old ones. Greeks and Iranians left the common home during the later part of this period and have retained most of these legends. This is essentially the period of the hymns.

The third, according to Tilak, is the Krittikas period which starts with the vernal equinox in the asterism of Krittikas and extends to the period recorded in the *Vedanga Jyotisha*, that is from 2500 BC to 1400 BC. This was the period of the *Taittiriya Sanhita* and many of the *Brahmanas*. Hymns of the Rig had already become antique and unintelligible by this time and Brahmavadins indulged in speculations about the real meaning of these hymns and legends. During this period *Sanhitas* were probably compiled into systematic books, and Indians came in contact with Chinese who borrowed from them the Hindu *Nakshatra* system.

The last period of the old Sanskrit literature extends from 1400 BC to 500 BC or till the birth and rise of Buddhism. This was the period of the *Sutras* and philosophical systems.

The beginning of the Aryan civilization has to be placed in a time long before the people were able to conceive and formulate the calendar, but it is difficult to decide how far back did this happen. It is true that initially the Vedic hymns were passed down through word of mouth and it is possible that during the process some modifications might have got incorporated, but to suggest that hymns were composed thousands of years after the stories narrated in them were first conceived, would be wrong, for by the time of the *Taittiriya Sanhita* and the *Brahmanas*, even the *Rig Vedic* hymns had become unintelligible. The hymns must have been composed over a long period of time; the calculations in astronomy suggest that this must have happened during 4000 BC to 2500 BC. This would mean that some Vedic verses must have existed when the migrants to India, Iran and Greece lived together. According to Tilak this conclusion is supported by the comparative philology and mythology. He further suggests that we have a continuous record of the year beginnings, right from the oldest times down to the recent years, in the literature of India, and this is the main and reliable factor in determining the antiquity of the Vedas. According to him Zoroaster lived around 1800 BC (modern historians place him around the beginning of 600 BC), and the Indo-Aryans separated from the Iranians during the later part of the Orion period, that is between 3000 BC to 2500 BC. This conclusion supports the results arrived at via the astronomical calculations. However, if Zoroaster had lived at a considerably later period then, according to Tilak, some Greek writers of fifth century BC would certainly have spoken about it. In fact Xanthos of Lydia in 470 BC considered Zoroaster to have lived about 600 years before the Trojan war, that is 1800 BC. The issue is relevant to our consideration because, apparently, the split between the Iranians and Indo-Aryans took place on account of the former having accepted a different religious creed. In Aristotle's time, around 320 BC, Zoroaster was supposed to have lived at a very remote period of antiquity, and if that was so, the period of the Vedas must be older still. Even according to the general belief of the Hindus, Vedas have come to them from a past the antiquity of which cannot be fathomed; they are supposed to have existed from the beginning of all known things. As stated above, according to Tilak, the Vedic period should be placed at about 4000 BC.

Some Indian scholars have put forth the view that the homeland of the Aryans was none other than the north-western area of the Indian subcontinent itself, particularly the Punjab and Kashmir. The main argument is that the Indian Aryan literature does not at any stage mention about the fact of Aryan immigration, that, in so far as the language is concerned. Vedic Sanskrit has the largest number of vocables found in the languages of the Sanskrit family in different parts of India, whereas outside India, in parts of Europe and Asia, where Aryans are supposed to have settled down prior to their moving here, the number of vocables left are only a few. The explanation given is that the Aryans belonged to India, and the Indian languages that developed here had the maximum number of vocables, and that other foreign Aryan languages came about when Aryans migrating from India came in contact with non-Aryan population in other countries. The argument is not convincing, for during those times it would not have been possible by mere immigrants to influence the languages of people spread over such vast area of land. It has to be borne in mind that the Aryan movement took place over a very long period of time, gradually, and was not taking place in a vacuum but to areas which had people, language(s), and their was extensive intermingling. Different environments, flora and fauna, and working conditions, gave rise to languages, cultures, religious perceptions which differed substantially from one another, and after a lapse of a millennia all that was left out of the common whole was barely recognizable. In his essay on the Aryan problem, B.K. Ghosh, a philology expert, has rightly pointed out that the largest number of Indo-European languages are found in Europe, almost in all the countries, while outside Europe there are only scatterings which end up in Punjab in the Rig Vedic age. Besides, it is Lithuanian and not Sanskrit which has kept closest to the basic idiom reconstructed by comparative philology. Had India been the original home, the whole of this subcontinent would have been Aryanized. But that did not happen. In fact the position has been that instead of Aryanizing the subcontinent, the Aryans got converted, to a fairly large extent, to the Indus culture. There possibly could have been a case if it could be established that Indus civilization was in fact Aryan, for, strictly speaking, there is no definite proof of the existence of an Aryan race or language outside India prior to the advent of the Indus culture. But it can be said with fair amount of certainity that Harappa people were not Aryans, since the culture patterns of the two are totally different, as also their scripts. But Indian Aryans could be even older than the Harappans, and that would be the case if one was to accept the findings of Tilak. But, as can be ascertained from the language of *Rig Veda* and *Avestan Gathas*, the two had a relationship in time, and that tends to indicate 1000 BC as the approximate date of the *Rig Veda*, although the culture represented by it could be considerably older, going, maybe, as far back as 1500 BC. However, there could be other possibilities too, as very little direct and indisputable evidence is available in support of the different perceptions. For example, when the Indus Valley people were flourishing in Harappa, Mohenjodaro and other places along river Indus and its tributaries, up in the north, in the Punjab, it could have been the Aryans, operating in village democracies, and the two might have known of one another, but might not have been sufficiently close in terms of trade and commerce. It is not necessary that Aryans should have arrived in India as attacking, plundering, marauding hordes. There could have been quiet migrations, and it could have taken a long time for the groups, at the level of family, clan, community, to have reasonably urbanized themselves, or organized themselves to conquer territory and push eastwards. On balance, on the basis of the opinions of the scholars, it can be said that the earliest period when Aryan ingress into the sub-continent started could be around 2500 BC, and latest 1500 BC, and the age of the *Rig Veda* could be 1000 BC to 1500 BC or even upto 2000 BC. The finds relating to the Indus civilization were unearthed in the year 1921-22, and when Tilak gave his conclusions he was not aware of this. But it may be said that on most issues raised by him his views are abundantly rational and logical; only on a few of them there is room for disagreement.

The Iranian and the Indo-Aryan Split

Why did the Iranian and Indo-Aryans split? The question is directed at the happenings in remote antiquity and, in the absence of authentic data, is almost impossible to answer; only conjectures might be made. It is true that the religious perceptions of the Iranian-Aryans developed on different lines compared to those of the people who eventually migrated to India, and generally the scholars are of the view that this caused a bitter hostility between the two groups and resulted in the parting of ways. In other words, the cultural and religious differences were the cause of the parting, and not the result of it. Indo-Iranians were probably the first to leave the Indo-European group after the Proto-Tocharians, and moved eastwards to find a home in Eranvej, an area coinciding roughly with modern Turkmenistan, having borders with the Caspian Sea, Afghanistan and Iran. They stayed in this area for a long time, at least from the late fourth millennium BC to about the middle of the third, during which time they expanded their activities towards Mesopotamia and Syria as well. Iran, particularly the eastern part of it, and north-western India, at this stage had people of the Austric Proto-Australoid variety and also comparatively light skinned people from areas south of the present day Turkmenistan, and the Mediterranean people, the Orientals and a host of others like the Alpinoids, Dinarics, the Armenoids; these light skinned people were apparently the leaders and perhaps contended for supremacy along with the Aryan tribes, the comparatively passive element of the population, possibly, being the most numerous Proto-Australoids.

What aspects of religious diversity caused the divide, it is difficult to say. Indo-Europeans worshipped deities based on the elements of nature, like sun, moon, sky, wind. But, with time, the Iranians who, possibly, had been affected by the culture, thoughts and religion of the pre-Aryans in the midst of whom they were living, had started evolving new gods and, apparently, on this issue the followers of the different pantheons clashed, and so determinedly, they decided to forever part company. To begin with, it seems, the *Daiva*-gods of the Indo-Aryans and the *Asura*-gods of the Iranians coexisted, but by the time of the Avestan (dialect of old Iranian) *Gathas*, which, amongst others, laid down strict instructions against the system of animal sacrifice, bitter antagonism seems to have developed.

On balance, however, it might be stated that religious intolerence could, at best, only be one of the factors contributing to the divide. The Indo-Europeans had been on the move for a long time, like all other groups of people the world over, for as we know, movement is the essence of evolution. Species move in search of food and shelter, in search of easier life, and they intermingle to maintain uniformity and homogeneity in their characteristics. Indo-Europeans moved from their homeland in south Russia, or even further beyond, not because they comprised groups with varying religious perceptions. They moved in search of better life. It hardly matters whether the *Daiva* and *Asura* gods coexisted in Iran before the departure of the Indo-Aryans, as is borne by the finds of a treaty record at Boghaz-koi; the treaty mentions the *Daiva* gods, Indra and Nasatya, alongside the *Asura* gods, Varuna and Mitra. Besides, the claim to antiquity of Zoroaster and his Gathas is not sustainable. It can be stated with certainty that the Gathas were not contemporaneous with the *Rig Veda*. Date accepted for Zoroaster by the modern historians is c. 628-551 BC which would put him just a few decades ahead of the Buddha, c. 563-483 BC but no way near the Rig, the latest date for which could be c 1000 BC while the earliest could go back considerably. The Iranian Zoroasterianism, therefore, would not have precipitated a split. The most important reason for the eastward movement of the Aryans from Iran, thus, would be search for better life, and this could have been possible only after the desired advances in the methodology and technology had been made, like in metallurgy and other related fields, which could facilitate travel over long distances, crossing difficult mountains like the Hindu Kush and the Sulaiman ranges, and camping for prolonged durations in the open, inhospitable climate and terrain, and in a country bristling with hostility. They did not arrive in the Punjab as an army out on conquests, but as simple migrants, and possibly settled down on whatever land was then available. There is evidence of westward movement too of the Indo-Iranians, to Anatolia and northern Syria, obviously for similar reasons; the westward moving people came to be known as the Hittites.

In course of time, in the north-western part of the Indian sub-continent, they organized themselves into small states, probably the size of a village or town, and then expanded outwards, subjugating the local tribes. Around 2000 BC they were in contact and, maybe, even in conflict with the Indus Valley settlements. Possibly due to poor communications and movement facilities, the Iranian and the Indian factions did not develop uniformly. In north-western India it was the Vedic civilization. In Iran, till the spread of Zoroasterianism in the sixth and fifth centuries BC, the civilization was, presumably, pretty much the same as was there at the time of the major exodus of the Indo-Aryans. It is possible that in Eranvej there was a preponderance of the worshippers of *Asura* gods and they might have made it hot for those who revered the *Daivas*. However, there were large population of non-Aryans in both the lands, more numerous than the emigrants', and these people exercized a decisive influence in shaping the two cultures. The Indus culture could be taken to be the archetype of the cultures prevalent in north-western India and the adjoining territories before the arrival of the Aryans. Broadly speaking the people then were pacifists; the land and other resources were adequate to meet their needs and, it seems, they did not possess much of an urge to accumulate surpluses to highlight the importance of wealth and, thus, create a capital oriented society. They appear to have been living in self sufficient village communes. The moral values, apparently, tended to deprecate aggression in any form, aggression being the hallmark of a capital oriented system.

There is no indication from the *Rig Veda* that the Aryans believed they were entering a new country when they came to India. The non-Aryan population in both the countries comprised the Proto-Australoids and their cross whom the Aryans named as Nishads, and the lighter skinned people from the Mediterranean, and the 'Orientals' and the like, whom they called Dasyus. The fact that the Vedic literature gives no indication of the migration from Iran tends to suggest that, firstly, the process of formulating the Vedic lore started strictly in India (Punjab) and, secondly, it possibly also had literature incorporated in it which had been, wholly or partially, the work of non-Aryan elite. Two great things that the Indo-Aryans brought with them were the language, Sanskrit, and the horse. Both these provided mobility to the pace of the cultural change. Otherwise, on arrival they were, at best, only semi-nomadic, and their culture rated below that of the Indus people.

The cultures in the north-western subcontinent were ahead of the Aryans in certain aspects: they were urbanized, had a better socio-economic structure, a fairly developed system of medicines, balanced and defined moral code and perceptions of religion. In course of time, before the middle of the second millennium BC, as the pressure of Aryan migrations mounted, a conflict with the local people became inevitable. The Aryans dominated the northern parts of the subcontinent as far east as the western parts of the present Uttar Pradesh, including the hills to the north, and Rajasthan. With more time, taking advantage of the language Sanskrit, and duly aided by the horse for swift movement, they managed to colonize or dominate some parts of central India as well, as is indicated in the *Ramayana* epic, and extend their influence, perhaps, as far south as Sri Lanka. In the process of this catalysis, which possibly had been caused in this intensity in this part of the subcontinent for the first time, they came across the customs and habits of the people they had befriended, or dominated or vanquished, and exchanged ideas with their intelligentsia, even intermingled with them, so that what ultimately emerged as the Vedic culture was, in fact, a hybrid of the original Aryan ideas and the ideas of the non-Aryans. There must have been a sizeable infiltration too in the rank and file, of the people from other races and classes, particularly of people following similar vocations, for example, not all the *Rishis* whose contributions are incorporated in the Vedas could have been pure blooded Aryans. What got incorporated in the *Rig Veda* were inspired writings of learned men; the race or sectarian considerations do not seem to have influenced the selection process. If fair skin was the essential requirement to get admitted or sneak into the Aryan fold (during their ascendency any non-Aryan would have preferred being identified as an Aryan), there was no dearth of people who would have easily qualified. Thus, when the four *Varnas* got formed the people constituting them could not have been the pure Aryans. Perhaps all the fair skinned people got together to put themselves in the upper three classes of the Brahmins, Kshatriyas, Vaisyas, while all the rest got put in the Sudras and other classes. No doubt the vocation of an individual had its own impact on deciding the *Varna* and the caste; almost the entire of the traders community of the pre-Aryan time got enlisted as Vaisyas irrespective of their colour; the Aryan community had, perhaps, to accept this, for the Indus trader was ahead of them in matters connected with trade and commerce, and without his willing support no community could have raised enough resources to run the affairs of the state. This must have happened with other *Varnas* too, to some extent atleast. The learned Brahmans, keen to maintain the ethnic purity, had little hesitation in nearly bracketing together the Vaisyas and the Sudras. The Kshatriyas faced almost a similar fate. During wars there was a large requirement for soldiers and other personnel for running the affairs of the government, but when it was peace there had to be large-scale demobilizations. So what were the Kshatriyas to do during this phase? They naturally took to other professions in order to sustain themselves and their families, and when it was war once again, not all of them could readily give up their vocations which they had cultivated with so much trouble and care, and the ruler had to recruit people from anywhere to meet the emergency, even from the communities which had been categorized as Sudras, or even below them. Later these people, powerful as they had become, claimed Kshatriya status for themselves, and a situation ultimately arose when there were Kshatriyas of all hues and colours, ranging from fair skinned to dark. Puritanical minded Brahmins again refused to accept the situation and declared that Kshatriyas as such had ceased to exist. According to a story in the Puranas, the axe wielding Brahmin sage Parshurama, an incarnation of Vishnu according to Vaishnava faith, was incensed at the hauteur and the overbearing conceit of the kshatriyas, and the unjust use of the power accrued to them. As the *Puranic* story goes, they had snatched his Kamadhenu cow which yielded unlimited milk, and had killed his aged father when he (Parshurama) was not there to protect him. He was furious, and vowed never to rest till he had wiped out the entire of this class from the face of the earth. This, the *Purana* says, he did. The only Aryans left then were the Brahmins, though they too had dark skinned people in their midst. But having raised themselves to positions of commanding heights in the Aryan society, they thought it prudent not to fan contention within their own ranks and did not agitate the issue. Besides, there were any number of coloured Brahmins who were better versed in the Vedas as compared to many others with fairer skins. And so the traditions, thoughts, and ideas, churned on in the crucible of time till, finally, the word 'Arya' had almost entirely lost its ethnic overtones, and come to mean a person of virtue and noble and divine thoughts. In earlier tradition it had, probably, been used to address a person of noble extraction.

Four

The Aryan Way of Life

No evidence of any kind is available which can conclusively project the way of life of the people who lived in the north-western parts of the subcontinent when the Aryans arrived here. Even pottery evidence is scanty, probably because of the near migratory nature of the people. The only source of information in so far as the Aryans are concerned, is their religious literature and, as Farquhar in his book *The Crown of Hinduism* has stated, had it not been for this literature, we would have been without any direct evidence about the existence of these most dynamic and gifted people. The Indo-Aryans first arrived as wandering graziers in search of pastures, and settled down in the Punjab and, in course of time, took to agriculture, like the Indus people. The hymns of the Rig Veda, the first work of the Vedic literature, were possibly composed and memorized during this period which, spans over a few centuries.

The traditional accounts of these people are set out in the *Puranas*, but these books were compiled between 500 BC and almost 500 AD, over 2000 years after the incidents they narrate. There are, therefore, discrepancies in the accounts, and a lot of mythical material has got incorporated alongside historical detail, the two so intermixed that it is not easy to make out the fact from fiction. *Ramayana* and *Mahabharata* also give some dynastic details and traditional accounts. Notwithstanding the problems in culling the facts from the traditional accounts, it does appear that at least the royal genealogies as set out in the *Puranas* bear some relationship to the history of Aryan antiquity. The earliest record is of Manu Svayambhuva who is the son of none other than Brahma Himself, and from the female form of His body gives birth to two sons and three daughters; the latter have elaborate legends woven around them connecting them to gods, sages, religious leaders and so on. Svayambhuva is the lord of the first Manvantara, a period which covers the rule of one Manu on planet earth, and is credited with the institution of the system of Varanas. The division of the society on the basis of the colour of the skin, giving duties to each division or segment, like, for example, Brahmins to teach and advise, Kshatriyas to be soldiers, Vaisyas to be the traders, Sudras to do all kinds of manual work, and so on. The system of marriage, and a host of other customs and traditions covering different aspects of human living and social and communal behaviour are also credited to him. It is also stated that earlier these systems had been ordained by Brahma Himself but had fallen into disuse with the passage of time. In other, this Manu was brought forth by Brahma basically to re-establish in the world order, the Dharma. Following this there were other Manus, all there to see to the implementation of the laws of Dharma, till we come to Prithu, after whom the earth is named Prithvi; he levelled the earth and brought in agriculture.

Then there is Manu Vaivasvata of the great flood. It is said that he was informed of the flood by a fish who advised him to construct a ship, and when the mighty flood actually struck, the fish pulled his ship to a big mountain where Manu stayed and came out of the ship only after the flood had receded. The flood had swept away everything and only Manu had survived. Therefore, Vaivasvata is given out as the originator of the human race, the first traditional king, father of ten sons, the eldest of whom had the dual personality of a male, Il, as well as a female, Ila. The other nine sons were the originators of nine important dynasties, the most important of which, Akshvaka, of the solar line, was founded by Ikshvaku, the eldest of the nine princes; he had his capital at Ayodhya. From Ila, the female personality of the eldest son, was born Pururavas, the originator of the Lunar Dynasty. The traditional history accounts tend to suggest that the date of the great flood was around 3100 BC which tallies well with the dates given for the flood in the Hebrew and Babylonian accounts. In the Hebrew accounts it is the story of Noah's Ark and that is pretty similar to the account of Manu's Boat and it is likely that both narrations have emerged from a common source. But it is also possible that, as a phenomenon of the receding fourth Ice Age, there might have been near simultaneous floods in most major rivers of Asia in that distant past. Whatever the reason, the flood story brings in Manu Vaivasvata, but date, 3102 BC, is also the start of the age of Kali, though according to traditional history it starts after the Mahabharata war. However, taking into account other details in the traditional history the probable time for the Mahabharata war could be placed only between the years 1400 BC and 1000 BC.

Other important details from the traditional history would suggest the dates of Vishvamitra, Parashurama, Harishchandra between 2550 and 2500 BC, king Sagara of Ayodhya and Bharata of Hastinapur between 2350 BC and 2300 BC, of Rama, the king of Ayodhya, around 1950 BC and Dasarajana war around 1900 BC. These dates, so say the scholars, have been worked out taking the Mahabharata war in 1400 BC. But if the date of the war is brought down, say to 1000 BC, then all the other dates will also have to be lowered by the corresponding number of years. The details as set out in the traditional history suggest that the Aryans were in control of most of northern India during the time of the sons of Manu Vaivasvata itself, that is, during the early fourth millennium BC. It is possible that of the kings and dynasties mentioned in the Puranas, all were not pure blooded Aryans, and accounts of non-Aryan kings and lines have got incorporated for reasons already covered earlier, but the fact remains that the details as set out in traditional history suggest that in that distant past large parts of northern and central India were following a well defined pattern of civilization and had layed the foundations of a culture which had its own typical distinctive features.

From the important landmarks mentioned in the Rig Veda it can be concluded that at the time of the compiling of its hymns the Aryans were dominant in the land extending from Afghanistan in the west to the western parts of the present Uttar Pradesh in the east, while to the south the limit went as far as the present day Rajasthan and parts of Sindh and in the north as far as Kashmir. Saptasindhavah mentioned in the Veda could be the name of the country of the seven rivers: Indus, Sarasvati and the five rivers of the Punjab (Jhelum, Chenab, Ravi, Beas and Satluj), although it is possible that the western most river could be the Oxus and all the rivers of the Punjab may not have been flowing through the land under Aryan domination. Amongst the tribes of the Rig Vedic period, the most important are the Bharatas, initially established in the land between rivers Ravi and the Ghaggar of the present times; in course of time this land came to be known as Brahmavarta. Their king Sudas fought and defeated a confederacy brought together by Vishvamitra, who had been dropped by Sudas from the top position as priest in preference for Vasishtha, whom he considered to be better versed in priestly knowledge. This was to teach his erstwhile master a lesson of his life. In the Rig Veda the battle is referred to as Dasrajna, the battle of the ten kings, and was fought on the banks of the river Ravi of the present times. The Bharatas eliminated their enemy with ruthless ferocity. Sudas later had to take on another united army, this time of non-Aryan tribes, under King Bheda. He inflicted a decisive defeat upon them as well. Apart from the Bharatas, after whom this country is named today, there were other powerful tribes who have been mentioned in the Veda. Kurus got formed through the union of Bharatas, Purus and Tritsus, and later there was an alliance between the Kurus and the Panchalas, basically with a view to defending their interests against incursions from the north-west where there were powerful tribes like the Pakthas, Sivas and so on, forever straining on the leash to venture eastwards.

Apart from the inter tribal conflicts, Aryans had to contend with the people who had already arrived in this land before them. There were the Australoids and their admixture with other races, particularly the Palaeo-Mediterraneans, whom Aryans referred to as Nishads in contempt. They were black, short statured, flat-nosed people who served as the under-dogs of the society and generally gave in to the Aryan superiority with timidity. The other variety of people whom the Aryans called *Dasyus*, possibly belonged to the central Asian regions and possibly included a host of strains, some dark complexioned while others not so dark. Like the Aryans, these people too had been on the move, and both in

Iran and north western India they had been ahead of the former and, possibly, had clashed with them, resisting their ingress. But it appears that the Aryans fairly managed to overpower them, although as stated earlier, a number of powerful kingdoms whose accounts figure in the *Puranas*, could well have belonged to them, and they may well have been Aryanised after most of north India had adopted Sanskrit as their working language. But with time the word Dasyu or Dasa came to mean a 'servant' because of the hatred the Aryans felt towards their enemies; this was not unmixed with the frustration at being challenged at every step. Dasyus too may have had some kind of an expression of disgust for their enemies, but we have no record of it. Only the Aryans had a language which was well developed and capable of being put in writing, and today we have everything regarding how the Aryans felt about their environment, situations and the people they came in contact with, for their language still lives on. Dasyus had no such facility. Language conferred a special advantage upon the Aryans in the field of administration, state craft, law, trade and commerce, and military science. As Farquhar has said, ancient Sanskrit is one of the great groups of Aryan languages all of which show many common features, but this language is the only member of the family which has preserved its words in such form as to make their origin quite plain to the philologist. The linguistic consciousness of the people who developed Sanskrit must have been delicate and analytic far above the average.

No authentic details as such are available of the way of life of the people who preceded the Aryans, and whom the latter put in the general class of Dasyus. Aryans in their accounts have variously called them demons, *Rakshasas*, or celestial beings with evil designs, or uncouth barbarians, or just people fit to be consigned to the profession of servants. Panis are another group of people who are listed in the category of enemies of the Aryans and have been mentioned in disparaging terms in their literature. Of the various views given out regarding the identity of Panis, some put them down as Babylonian traders, others as non-Aryan caravan merchants, while still others consider them as the sea faring Aryans. Another possibility, a strong one, is that they were the Indus traders who had drifted northwards and eastwards during the existence, subsequent to the collapse of the Indus Civilization. Pani, also called Vani in some accounts, is, possibly, the Banya of today; these people got incorporated in the Vaisya category of the Aryan Varna system. There was another important class of traders who arrived from modern Syria and Lebanon (Phoenicians) in the period 1500-1200 BC. All these communities have played a major role in the development and progress of trade and commerce in the northern areas of this subcontinent.

The Aryans used the epithet *asura* for evil gods. The term was used for worshipworthy gods when Indo and Iranian Aryans lived together but came to signify evil gods in the Indo-Aryan literature after the separation. Some scholars have considered *asura* to be people, and not gods, immigrated from Assyria, who were the founders of the Indus Civilization. Maghadas, of south Bihar, too have been given a low rating right from the days of the Rig Veda. These people possibly created problems for the Rig Vedic Aryans operating in the Kurukshetra-Delhi region. Some scholars have suggested that these people were in fact Aryans but outside the Brahmanical fold. On balance, however, it would appear that they were non-Aryans who were hostile to the Aryan ingress in areas under their influence. Vangas, non-Aryans living in modern East Bengal, are not mentioned in the Rig but in the later Vedic literature their activities have been described. In fact, the area under the Aryan influence or occupation by the time of the Upanishads (c 800 BC) was the territory of the whole of north India, north of the Narmada river, with a few stretches to the south of it.

Political and Social Organization of the Aryans

The progress of the development of the political organization of the Aryans can be made out from their legends. When the good gods were fighting the evil *asuras* they realized to their surprise that they were about to be routed. In order to stem the tide they elected a king for themselves, and won the war. This and similar legends suggest the development of the ideas about kingship. Aryan tribes were organized in patriarchal groups, and as the requirement for the safety and security of the tribe grew, the most competent warrior amongst the tribal males was elected to be the chief. With time, with rising stakes in the security, the importance of the chief grew, and so did his responsibilities and privileges, and not before long he was enjoying the status of a king. The king in the tribe or a confederation of tribes, was assisted by a *sabha* and a *samiti*, the former, it seems, could have been like a council of ministers selected from appropriate tribal elders, while the latter could be a kind of a general assembly of the tribe(s). These assemblies, apart from performing other functions, also ensured that the king did not over step his authority. Where tribes did not have elected leaders, the functions of the government were carried out by the assemblies, though such instances were rare, for monarchy was the system followed in most places, as was to be expected in any highly patriarchal society. The Vedic king was essentially a military and a defence expert. He could impose no taxes; his assets were built on voluntary gifts that the well-off members of the community conferred upon him from time to time. He was, however, entitled to a share in the booty of war, and for that reason he was on the look out for any opportunity to pillage and plunder any other tribe whom, he felt, he could vanquish. He had practically no say in the matters of religion; the priests ruled supreme in this field.

The Rig Vedic king was generally addressed as Rajan, which term was also used for a chieftain enjoying a status not much above other elders of the tribe. But there were powerful kings too, living in imposing palaces and conferring imposing presents upon their priests and courtiers. With time, the conquests multiplied, and larger kingdoms came into being. There is mention of *samrats*, emperors, and *Visvasya bhuvanasya rajas*, the kings of the universe, and also of pomp and pageantry of some courts, and high life-style of their queens and ministers. The *Shastras*, the religious ordinances, pronounce that a Kshatriya who had received according to the rule, the sacrament as prescribed by the Veda, must duly protect this whole world. It is further stated in the *Shastras* that when creatures dispersed in all directions on account of fear, then the Lord created a king to protect his creation. Thus the idea of the divinity of the king got incorporated in the concept of kingship. Special sacrifices were worked out to bestow divinity on him, and for this the services of the priest became indispensable.

This brought the mutual interdependence between the king and the priest. In gradual stages, as the power of the king grew with the size of his kingdom, and he had at his disposal a more elaborate administrative network and a formidable war machine, the kingship became hereditary. The *sabha* and the *samiti* still exercised checks on the king but the latter's authority was supreme.

A small kingdom, *rashtra*, had tribes, *Jana*, and tribal units, *vish*, and villages, *grama*, where families, *kulas*, lived under the tutelage of their heads, *kulapas*. Tribal elders and the headmen of the villages assisted the king whose two most important officials were the chief priest, *purohita* who combined the functions of a priest, astrologer and adviser, and the military commander, *senani*, who was the chief of battles, though in peace time he, normally, took on the functions of a general administrator. Then there were the spies, messengers, the treasurer, the charioteers and even a superintendent of dicing; the office of this superintendent came into being mostly in later times when dicing and gambling had become widespread in the Aryan society. As stated earlier, the Rig Vedic accounts give out the king as essentially a warrior and he and the nobles and the officials of the army, the *rajanya*, fought from chariots while the common soldier did so on foot. The army possibly was organized in units and, not infrequently, marched to the battle to the beating of martial music, and accompanied by fluttering flags which showed its organizational structure. They used metal or poisoned horn tipped arrows, and lances, axes, spears, swords, sling-stones, and wore coat-of-mail and helmets to protect their bodies. Horse cavalary may have been used but there is no mention of it in the Rig Veda. Defences were based on forts, pur, which had ramparts of stones, or even of metal. Hedges of thorny bushes or stakes were used to defend individual defended areas. The assailants laid siege and pelted fire inside the defence and possibly also made use of special engines to demolish strongholds.

Brahmins brought in the Varna system, and with that they got the charge of imparting religious education to the upper three varanas, i.e., the Brahmins, Kshatriyas and the Vaisyas; Sudras and the women were not entitled to receive this education. However, specialised education pertaining to a varna, like education in the Vedic religion to the Brahmins, martial arts to the

Kshatriyas, trade and commerce to the Vaisyas, remained with the concerned Varnas, though there also were schools, run by Brahmins, where all types of education was given to all the Varanas. Priestly functions were entirely with the Brahmins as also the practice of astrology. Being better educated than the people of the other Varnas they were specialists in the art of state craft and generally served as the top ministerial advisors to the ruling hierarchies. They also interpreted religion, and Vedic and other non-secular literature. During the Rig Vedic stage the Varanas had not fallen into water-tight compartments and essentially signified the profession of a person, and there was no serious problem in changing the varna by taking on another profession; a Kshatriya, for example, well versed in the knowledge and practice of the Vedas, could qualify to be a Brahmin. In Muir's view, during this period the hymns could be composed, or the sacrifices could be presided over, or other religious functions, which during the post-Rig Vedic stage became functions exclusively of the Brahmin community, could be performed by any member of the three higher Varnas. In fact, initially the sacrificial system was simple and no elaborate training was necessary for offering obeisance to one's god. With the passage of time, however, it became complex and guidance by well trained Brahmins became necessary. A lot of emphasis came to be placed on small detail, like how the fire was to be ignited, with what type of wood, with what number of logs, how were the logs to be placed in relation to one another, and how the words were to be sung, and pronounced and so on. Any priest enjoying a reputation with a dignitary of consequence, added his own small variations.

In so far as their survival or, depending upon the capability of the individual, comfortable living, was concerned, the Kings and Kshatriyas of noble extraction, the *Rajanya*, had their wealth accumulated through pillage and plunder and taxation, while the Vaisyas, the traders, had the commercial activity taking care of them. Sudras were the working class, most of them artisans, so essential to the well-being of the society, and in their case also, depending upon the ability and the profession of a person, most of them made enough to take care of their needs. But the Brahmin community had problems. How were they to survive if the householder himself performed his religious functions and also took care of astrology in so far as it affected him or his family, and educated and trained his children in the professions they were to adopt on growing up? Being at the top rung of the system, Brahmins considered work of any denomination, other than what was of religious concern, as infra dig. The creation myth in the Veda says that when gods sacrificed *Purusha*, the universal spirit, his mouth became Brahmin, the arms the Kshatriya, the thighs the Vaisya and his feet became the Sudra. Having been created out of the mouth of the *purusha*, they claimed the top position in the Varna system, and the only function they considered fit for their vocation was the job of guiding and educating the community in religious and, to some extent, secular subjects. Having reasonably complicated the system of worship, they claimed they alone could perform sacrifices with the accuracy envisaged in the Vedas, or that they alone could bestow divinity on a king which was so essential to kingship. However, barring the issues relating to the functions of priesthood, the people of the Kshatriya varana, who lived in comparative leisure and had the time to think out the problems concerning the different aspects of living, did not always accept the Brahmin verdict and, from time to time, made their own contributions to the Vedic thought and literature, often disagreeing with the highly ritualistic cults. Their contribution to the Upanishadic literature has been significant. In much later times, Gautama Buddha and Mahavira Jaina, both princes from royal families, revolted completely against the Brahminic religion of sacrifices and caste distinctions.

Vedic religion was particularly harsh towards the Sudra class. They forbade them the study of the Vedas, whose denial in effect implied denial of any education to this class and resulted in forever keeping them in the category of the downtrodden. Normally this group could have made a solid contribution to the well-being of the society, had they received the right level of education in the fields of science and technology, and arts and crafts, and could have generated wealth and added to the strength of the nation against dangers and threats to security. But in actual fact they were bereft of education, and were deprived of fair wages for their work and thus of decent livelihood, being denied adequate self respect, they became a drag, a burden which the society often found difficult to carry, and this often crippled the society when it came under pressure facing external or internal threats.

However, it must be said in support of the Aryan priestly community that they were not any different from similar communities elsewhere in the world. On the negative side these priestly classes have exploited man's fear of the unknown, of his desire to steer clear of misfortunes by trying to keep favourably disposed, the gods that he felt or was told, commanded his destiny. Greater the intensity of the fear, more ardently did he clutch at the assurances advanced to him by the *shaman* or the priest; in the process he often entered into a rigmarole of rituals and ceremonies which ultimately turned him into a superstitious bundle of nerves and an ineffectually functioning human being. Priestly classes have maintained a tight control over their societies by placing the entire gamut of human activity under one religious ordinance or the other. This has been totally to their advantage.

On the positive side, however, they have kept the human hearts kindled with the light of hope, and urged the oppressed classes to face adversity with fortitude. Often they were amongst the front runners in revolts against excesses committed by despotic rulers. Aryan Brahmins were a highly educated community, and not all of them were outright exploiters. They expanded the Aryan sphere of influence by assimilating in their fold the non-Aryan people who had preceded them, or who came after them, by giving them status, even places of honour, depending upon their standing in the general hierarchy of tribes. Their contribution in the fields of sculpture, music, literature, astronomy, astrology, mathematics has been noteworthy, though not as much as would have been possible had the whole society, and not only a segment of it, been working jointly. There have been accounts narrated in the epics and the *Puranas* where Sudras have been punished, even mutilated, for excelling in performance in vocations which were the preserve of the higher Varnas. The caste divisions had tended to inject a negative element which, more often than not, acted to sabotage the potential and capabilities of the people, hanging like the millstone in their march to progress and prosperity, although on the positive side it can be said that the system lent a measure of stability and provided work and means of livelihood for everyone.

North-western parts of the country were wetter during the Rig Vedic stage; there was more rainfall, and rivers had more water and even the deserts of the present day had extensive and impressive forest cover. In the early stages this impeded the Aryan expansion, for copper and brass tools and implements were not as efficient for clearing the undergrowth and felling the trees as the iron tools, which came into use around 800 BC. This is the Upanishadic period of the Vedic age, a period marked for religious and secular effervescence, which became possible because of better inter-people contact brought about by improved communications.

Family was an important unit of the society, and the *kulapa* or *kulapati*, the eldest male, was its head. Normally people lived in joint families which extended over three or four generations. In a village, *grama*, in most cases, the people were generally inter-related, having originated from a common family a few generations earlier. Land was in plenty; it had to be only cleared and cultivated. In non-joint families, the sons developed the land for their own dwellings; other members of the family group helped. On the father's death, or his turning very old, the sons divided the inheritance amongst themselves; looking after the aged parents was their responsibility. During the Rig Vedic times the dwelling units were mostly wooden structures, but later, after the climate had become somewhat drier, mud bricks also came into use. Roof was of bamboo, superimposed by thatch. The accommodation for animals was either incorporated in the main dwelling itself or it was, where families were reasonably prosperous, located along side, though this latter practice exposed the animals to theft, which, considering their value, was not an infrequent occurrence. Cattle raids and lost cattle often led to inter-tribal fights. Cow was prized and considered a measure of value; some tribes regarded it as a totem animal, and it was generally venerated by all. Beef eating was forbidden except on some occasions when it was considered even auspicious. Horse was an animal an Aryan prized; it gave him status and in war a superior fighting capability. Amongst other animals lion was known before the tiger, while elephant was a curiosity, and snake was associated with evil; it was believed to have malevolent power, a possible outcome of conflict with powerful Naga tribes. As for diet, mention has been made of milk, *ghee* or clarified butter, vegetables and fruits of different varieties, and barley. On special occasions, religious or secular, such as the arrival of a guest of importance, special preparations of meat (beef, mutton or fowl), were served, washed with intoxicants like *sura* or *madhu*. Clothes people wore were simple, men wearing only a lower garment, or a cloak; clothing is essentially an item related to weather and environment. By the time of the Rig Veda, Aryans seem to have picked up a lot from the clothing habits of the earlier people. Both men and women wore jewellery, like the Indus people. Leisure hours were spent playing music, singing, dancing; an idea of the interest in music can be had from the number of instruments mentioned — the drum, lute, flute, cymbals, harp — and also from the highly developed knowledge of sound, tone and pitch used in chanting the Sama Veda; they were familiar with a heptatonic scale. Dicing too was a favourite pastime, as was chariot-racing, the latter, being a prestige sport, was always organized for special ceremonial occasions.

The family rejoiced at the birth of a son, for a son not only provided security to the parents in their old age, he also protected the interests of the society by cultivating food and rearing animals, and, most of all, by joining the fighting forces to defend and fight for the interests of the tribe. In the highly patriarchal Aryan society he completely eclipsed the girl and was endowed with the status almost of a demigod. His presence in important family ceremonies was essential; some of these were designed to provide happiness and comfort to the forebears in the hereafter. Girl's position, though secondary, was not inferior. In her childhood and during her nubility, she was trained by the females of the family to make a good housewife. She was given education in any discipline of her choice and upto the level she desired or the family could afford, e.g. music, dancing, or other arts and crafts. Not many girls seem to have opted for serious education as their primary interest; here and there we do have works of value compiled by female litterateurs but they are few and far between. Generally the society believed that during her life time a female was appended to a man: during her girlhood to her father, and then to her husband, and finally, if the husband expired, to her son(s). In a set-up of overly dominating males, this was necessary to protect the interests of the weaker sex; a sex related assault on a girl or a woman was regarded as an assault on the very honour of the community or the tribe to which she belonged. By restricting the exploiting capability of the overbearing males, the system also protected the society from moral corruption. But it was not as if the woman's own needs and desires were ignored, or she led a life of subservience, far from it, no religious function was complete unless the house wife participated in it, and her status during the participation was equal to that of the householder. The laws of religion, the *Shastras*, based on the Vedas, unambiguously lay down that women must be respected and honoured by their fathers, brothers, husbands and brothers-in-law, for where it so happens, there the gods are pleased, but where it does not, no sacred rite yields any reward. *Manu Smriti* says: A house in which female relations are not being duly honoured, is cursed and perishes completely, as if destroyed by magic!

The early marriage was not the practice and the girl had a good deal of choice in the selection of her spouse, even though arranged marriages, apparently, were the norm. The marriage systems, however, were not uniform; different tribes followed their own customs and traditions. Some permitted marriages between consanguine pairs except between brother and sister and the like, others ruled out alliances between pairs who might have had blood connection as far back as seven generations, or even earlier. Most, however, preferred the latter system; for it ruled out any possibility of interbreeding and thus ensured a healthy breed of offsprings. Besides, it forbade the males to view the girls or the women of their tribe as sex objects, so essential to keep the tribe free from sexual promiscuity. In fact, the honour of the womenfolk was considered to be the honour of the tribe and any attempt at sullying it was stoutly resisted. Some tribes paid dowry (mostly when the girl was plain looking), others charged bride-price (generally people lower down in the caste hierarchy), some made the widow go through symbolic self-immolation, Sati, at the death of her husband, others expected her to actually immolate herself on his pyre, while still others permitted remarriage, generally with an unmarried brother of the deceased husband or with any other male of the tribe whom the widow might appropriately select.

Not much is found in the Vedic literature regarding the practice of Sati. One important case quoted is in *Mahabharata*, that of Madri, the younger wife of Pandu. The Vedic Aryans knew of the practice, but it seems to have been restricted to the *Rajanya* class only, and there too it appears to have been practised sparingly, under very special circumstances, only when the widow asked for it and the society was convinced it would not in any way harm the interests of the family. The practice of widow remarriage varied with different tribes. Some permitted remarriage within the tribe, others only within the family — in some cases the younger brother of the deceased automatically became the husband of the widow even when he already had a wife. Some permitted *niyoga*, levirate, to widows who did not have a son, but only till she, after cohabiting with a brother-in-law or, in some cases, with a person of her choice, got one. *Niyoga* was permitted in other specific cases as well, like, for example, when a woman, because of a fault with the husband, was not likely to get impregnated in the normal manner, or when the husband was away from his wife for a prolonged duration. The permission was valid till the woman got a son, after that it ceased. However, most tribes forbade *niyoga* or remarriage, though they could consider remarriage in the case of very young widows. Some did not even do that. Polygamy was permitted during the Rig Vedic age, but seems to have been restricted mostly to the *rajanya* class. Otherwise monogamy was the prevalent custom. Polyandry is also mentioned but was very rare.

In the actual celebration of a marriage, it was the bridegroom's party that came to the bride's house. The two important events of a marriage were the feast and going around the ceremonial, sacred fire. Beef seems to have been the preferred item at the meal. In the final act the bridegroom took the hand of his bride and together they went around the fire to complete the marriage. Post marriage prayers and blessings were for the harmonious and happy life of the married couple; they describe the bride as mistress of the new house, and urge her to take charge of her husband's parents, his brothers and unmarried sisters, obviously by bestowing loving care upon them. The Vedic hymn emphasizes that the community rejoiced at the union of the two young people and prayed for their happiness, that the bride now belonged to a different house where she was to enjoy the status of a mistress and not that of a subservient being.

The sacrificial fire, *agni*, played an important part in the life of the Aryan householder. It is a god, *deva*, the master of the house, *grihapati*, and guest, *atithi*, a friend, a messenger for the gods. It was the essential item of sacrifice, for its highrising flames and smoke took the offerings heavenwards, and brought blessings and initiated the newly born. It is also performed important family functions, including marriages or for individual or collective tasks, or the fertility of cattle and bountiful crops, and it bore the spirits of the dead to the abode of their forebears, and also carried the offerings made to them. The householder performed these sacrifices all by himself (or he could engage the services of a priest, depending upon the importance of the sacrifice), by offering into the fire of the domestic hearth (which served as the altar) items like milk, grain, clarified butter, flesh and the like, while uttering simple prayers. Such sacrifices were offered by all, the elaboration of the arrangements and the offerings depending upon the means of the person and the importance of the sacrifice. This was the beginning of the Vedic religion. With time, however, elaborate sacrificial rituals came into being. Sacrifices by kings, or well to do people, were organized around three sets of sacred fires, conducted by a host of priests, with four of them superintending the entire proceedings. The essential purpose of the sacrifice was to secure favours from gods who were believed to be participating.

The custom of making offerings to the sacrificial fire is of Indo-European origin and, apart from the Indo-Aryans, was also followed by the Greeks, Romans and the Iranians, the basic underlying idea being that the gods could be made to yield to grant the wishes of the sacrificer as long as the latter knew the right method in terms of the items to be sacrificed, the accompanying incantations, the manner of organising the fire, and so on. The idea of making a sacrifice of the horse was that by so doing the sun-god, represented in the horse by its speed of movement, would be so pleased as to grant great strength and status to the sacrificer. This sacrifice was essentially performed by powerful kings during the period of their ascendancy.

As stated earlier, the role of the priest, or the *purohita*, was all important; the term Brahmin means one who possesses mysterious and magical power, Brahma, or, as some scholars have viewed, *mana*, a term carrying a similar meaning during a more primitive period. The belief was that during the course of the sacrifice the god, the priest and the offering became one. The feeding of the priest, (during a major sacrifice feeding of a number of them), was an important requirement. Equally important was the requirement that he, or they, in whom the gods invoked had dwelled, even if only during the conduct of the sacrifice, left with generous gifts, and generally beneficiently disposed towards the sacrificer. Gifts, besides foodgrains and other items of value, often included cows, even women when the sacrifice was performed by a king, after a battle where he might have enslaved a large number of people.

Sacrifice was a serious and a solemn affair, but it also was a social event when people of the clan met each other in an atmosphere of general conviviality, which marked the end of the ceremony when guests were invited to the feast and given a liberal intake of the Soma wine. As the system became more complex, the knowledge of astronomy and mathematics had to improve, for the time of the sacrifice and the position of the stars had an important bearing upon the layout of the sacrificial area and the items of the sacrifice. Alongside also grew an interest in astrology. Frequent sacrifices of animals led to the knowledge of animal anatomy, which was a dominant science for a long time, way ahead of physiology or pathology.

The *Rig Sanhita*, as we know, was composed over a long period. Its earlier portion has hymns which have nothing to do with sacrifices, although a number of them were later used for that purpose, while the later portion contains hymns which right from their inception were meant to be used as incantations. The former were generally used by the householder for simple household sacrifices during which he himself, or, at the most, accompanied by the family *purohita*, presided over the ceremony, while the latter were used for major occasions at the level of the village or tribe, or when sacrifices were performed by persons in high positions, or even by kings.

There were no organized legal institutions at the time of the Rig Veda, although later, after the formation of states and the establishment of the institution of kingship, the situation changed substantially. Law, Dharma, was evolved on the basis of customs, and the king and the chief priest were the arbiters, assisted possibly by the elders of the community. In the case of larger states, where it was not easy for a complainant to reach the king, most cases got decided at the village level, by the elders who, with time, formed a body for this purpose like the later day Panchayat. The main problems seem to have been related to thefts, particularly of cattle, burglary, highway robbery, cheating at gambling, and so on. Marriage of brother and sister was forbidden and considered as incest. As punishment, the criminals were usually tied to a stake. The punishment for killing another person was based on wergeld, or blood money, and could be a hundred cows or coins or something which would reasonably satisfy the aggrieved party. But even revenge was permitted, though it may not have been widely practised. Trial by ordeal was also in vogue whereunder a person had to prove his innocence by putting his arm in boiling water or placing his tongue on a heated axe-head; there were many variations of this mode of punishment, which are generally placed under the heads of water or fire ordeals.

In inheritance, from time to time the practice of primogeniture appears to have been followed, whereunder the eldest son inherited all the property. But it does not appear to have been a universal custom; it may have been practised only amongst the well to do *rajanya* families.

During the early Rig Vedic days the law was basically designed to provide satisfaction to the wronged person, but later the emphasis shifted to making the punishment more stringent and deterrant. The law started being formalized and encoded in the *Dharma-sutras*, manuals initially written by the teachers in Vedic schools for the guidance of their pupils, but later accepted as sources of the sacred law applicable to the Aryas. The first of the *Dharma-sutras* were, perhaps, compiled as the Aryan kingdoms expanded and it was no longer possible for the king to sort out the complaints and disputes of all hues and colours in a just and equitable manner. Some scholars, including Professor Max Muller, have dated the oldest of the *Dharma-sutras* not much earlier than 600 BC. But that does not appear to be correct. These could be older; there are practical problems in dating the ancient Sanskrit works.

Even though the people of the Indus Civilization had used a script, there is no evidence available today which might suggest the Aryans used one till as late as about 700 BC. To the Aryans the Vedic literature comprised the inspired sayings of very learned men and seers who had thoroughly understood the mystries of creation and had passed their knowledge to the ordinary people so that they could lead organized and happy lives within the society. The Vedas contained the ultimate truth, that which was revealed by the creating power itself, and there was nothing to be known beyond what the Vedas had revealed. The Vedas were sacred, and to put them down in writing, like any other secular literature, would be sacrilegious. Therefore, all religious literature was committed to memory, under a very carefully worked out system which was designed to avoid any chance of error when the knowledge was passed down the generations. The ancient literature of the Aryans was divided into *Sruti*, the revealed literature or knowledge, and *Smriti*, the traditional literature. The latter was not the revealed knowledge by itself but was based on it; it was not to be treated as secular literature, e.g., the *Dharma-sutras* have been formulated only on the basis of what has been stated in the Vedas, and are not the compilation of any one or more persons based on his or their experience or assessment on what the law of the land should be.

But it definitely is likely that the Aryans were using Sanskrit script for secular purposes almost soon after their arrival in this country, if not at the time of their arrival itself. All ancient secular literature of the period earlier than 700 BC. must have perished with time, written as it must have been on peels of tree barks or appropriately suitable leaves. Marauding, dissenting hordes must have done their bit to contribute to the general destruction; it was executed ruthlessly and wantonly during the invasion and the rule of the Muslims in this country. As for the religious literature, it survived because it was committed to memory. But the possibilities of interpolations or editing at the time when it was committed to writing, cannot be ruled out. Thus, a document might have originated during the prehistoric past. The learned pundit while committing it to writing many centuries later, may have inserted in the text certain terms and references which were relevant to his time. A modern scholar will presume the origination of the document on the basis of such interpolations or editing, and date it to the time of its being reduced to writing. Dating of ancient documents, thus, is beset with many problems, some of formidable dimensions. But it can be said with certainty that the Indo-Aryans had a language, Sanskrit, when they entered this country during the first half of the second millennium BC.. They possibly had a script too at that stage, or soon thereafter..

Veda is a *Sruti* and not a *Sastra*, the latter being the systematized knowledge in one particular discipline and would contain special terminology and definitions in relation to that discipline. In order to better understand the *Sruti*, the Vedic schools systematized and cultivated the six sciences which on account of their being closely connected to the Vedas, are called *angas*, limbs - *vedangas* -, and are (a) *shiksha* (orthography); (b) *vyakarana* (grammar); (c) *nighantu* (lexicon); (d) *jyotish* (astronomy); (e) *chhanda* (prosody) and (f) *kalpa*, (the system of rituals and ceremonies). The schools also evolved the four *upa* (minor)-Vedas, being (a) Ayur-veda (the system of medicines and cures); (b) Gandharva-veda (system of aesthetics); (c) Dhanur-veda (of defence science) and (d) Artha-veda (of wealth — the economics of its generation and distribution).

With time, as the subsidiary literature developed and the amount of material to be learnt and committed to memory increased, the Vedic schools which were the centres of the intellectual life of the Aryas, got divided into two categories: one, who committed the literature to memory, and just that, and the other who interpreted it. Following these came the schools of specialities, who concentrated only on the subsidiary literature, like the Ved-Angas or Upa-Vedas or law, and so on. The Vedic schools, thus, performed the function of committing the Vedas to memory, and correctly and accurately interpreting them, while the schools of specialities handled Ved Angas and Upa-Vedas and other specialized subjects, and concentrated on the Veda only to the extent it affected their subjects. In the Vedic school the student acquired full and accurate knowledge of the sacred texts and for that he had to learn the Mantras as given in the *Sanhita* texts and the *Brahmanas* and also *Pathas*, or the mode of recitation, and considering the knowledge he had to acquire, it took him almost all the four and a half to five and a half years that he spent at these schools, to do just that. This led to the need for bifurcation, and the specialized institutions. Thus, some Vedic schools, or *karanas*, became schools of special disciplines and ceased to be the centres of intellectual learning, enquiry and interpretation in so far as the general Vedic literature and thought were concerned.

The institution of the Vaidics of the recent times performed almost the same function as was performed by the *karanas*. The former, run essentially on charity, devoted themselves to memorize the sacred texts of the *angas* and other similar works, and recite them more or less perfectly, but they could hardly ever explain or correctly interpret them. For that purpose there were other specialists, e.g., *srauta* sacrifices could be performed only by the Sarotriya pundits. Gradually the fields of specialization narrowed down even further and we find that the pundit, while concentrating on a particular *anga*, committed to memory only that part of the Veda as was relevant to his discipline, so that while he was a specialist in the particular *anga*, his connection with the Vedic school as such was only nominal. But in his own field he was the authority.

This system of specializations applied to the law schools as well, and, over a period, a number of *Dharma-sutras* or strings of aphorisms, all, by and large, based on the *Dharma-sutra* of the *Manava Sutrakarana* came up; almost the final major work in this field was *Manu Smriti*; Manu's name derives from 'Man', which means to know (the meaning of the Veda). Sutrakaranas were the schools which first collected the different doctrines scattered in the older Vedic works and arranged them in Sutras for convenience of oral instruction. But, with time, as the schools acquired a higher degree of expertise in their respective subjects, new institutions came up, developing their subjects as independent disciplines, and claiming superiority over the Sutrakarana schools; all this happened during a period of considerable antiquity. For example, the science of astronomy is connected to the Vedic Sutrakarana schools on the basis of a few recensions, but the discipline of jyotisha or astrology, closely connected with it, was developed mostly independently on the basis of the work carried out by the new institutions.

The first to be compiled were the *Dharma-sutras*, or aphorisms about religious and social law and observances handed down by tradition, and the rights and duties of individuals, essentially to guide the students to lead a life free from sin, in conformity with the sayings of the Vedas. In course of time, these became laws for all Aryans. According to scholars, metrical Smritis, like *Manu Smriti*, are works of later period and are based on ancient *Dharma-sutra* texts. According to G. Buhler, it can be reasonably averred that *Manu Smriti*, the law book held in high esteem and containing the rules governing the life of the Aryas, was already there at the beginning of the Christian era; nothing more than that can be established. As stated earlier, there are practical problems in dating old and ancient Sanskrit works because in a number of cases interpolations and modifications have taken place, and these tend to misguide the scholars. *Manu Smriti* has a number of contradictions, no doubt as a result of modifications and interpolations; in some places it has supported *niyoga*, at others it has opposed it; some parts of it give an exalted position to the women, while some enunciate an unduly harsh code for them. According to the general belief amongst the Hindus, Manu was the first law giver and this implies that the work is of considerable antiquity. Some Indian scholars have placed it in a period even earlier than the Mahabharata war. However, whatever its antiquity, it was not the first of the law books, and even though to seek divine authority for itself it claims authorship by Manu, the descendant of the self-existent Brahma, in effect, as stated earlier, it is a recast, in metrical form, of earlier *Dharma Shastras* and Sutras.

While earlier laws contained in the Sutras and Shastras may have been compiled by Vedic law experts for a limited purpose — for a tribe, a kingdom, a republic — , the *Manu Smriti* broadened the scope. It attempted to give a law which was above modifications. A number of contradictions within it suggest that it has been tampered with. In the Sutras arrangement of subjects is pretty haphazard, and, barring the rules relating to inheritance and partitioning of property, their handling of civil and criminal laws is deficient of detail. However, one has to keep in view the fact that the laws pertain to a period of remote antiquity, when the legal cases were settled on the basis of customs. The Sutras gave only brief guidelines in terms of what was laid down in the Vedas, while the details were left to the *Dharmadhikarins*, the legal advisers to the kings, the judges and the lawyers. But the Smriti, on the other hand, sets down the law in greater detail and in a better logical sequence, unfettered by religious references and customs, laying more emphasis on the moral side of the duties of the administrators of law rather than legal technicalities. For this reason it was widely accepted, almost throughout this sub-continent. An important work on Aryan law which preceded Manu Smriti is the *Manav Dharma-Sutra*, apparently the oldest, properly laid out work on Dharma on which most subsequent works including *Manu Smriti*, are considered to have been based. Other notable Smritis which preceded or followed *Manu Smriti* are those authored by Bhrigu (mythically one of the ten mind-born sons of Manu), Narada, and Yagnavalkya. Dharmashastra of Vasishitha is also an important manual covering the laws of the Aryans.

The Vedic Literature

Rig Veda

The core of the Vedic literature is the Rig Veda, a collection of over a thousand hymns (*Sanhita*) of varying lengths, set out in more than ten thousand stanzas. Many recensions of this Veda are known, but the one which has come down in almost complete form, is the Sakala recension. This happened because only the hymns of this recension were used in rituals by the priests of the Sakala school. A number of them had become irrelevant after the rituals had changed, but were retained because, with time, their position in the Sanhita had become sacrosanct.

Rig Veda has hymns dating back to the Indo-Iranian time, and some of these throw light on the geography of the area of Aryan dominance, their way of life, the kind of opposition they encountered during their eastward move, the people they fought against and vanquished, the pattern of their movement, and so on. The hymns were composed by a number of priestly families, in the language the Aryans had been using for a long time for their sacrifices. The composers have been called *rishis* or seers, people with illumined visions who had fully understood the working of the universe, and who, consequently, were in a position to compose hymns, mantras or incantations, which, when recited, in a particular metre or chhanda or verse form, and accompanied by an appropriately designed sacrifice, could, so it was believed, force the natural phenomenon, or the gods concerned, to grant the wishes. The person concerned could do the recitation himself, or a priest could do it for him. Recitations were not always for self gains; often these were in praise of the gods, or God.

The whole of the Rig Sanhita has been organized in ten *mandalas*, and the hymns within each of these have been arranged systematically. The middle six *mandalas*, second to the seventh, are said have been composed by six different families of priests, *rishis*, or seers, their names being Gritsamada, Vishvamitra, Vamdeva, Atri, Bharadvaja, and Vasishtha. The eighth *mandala* is ascribed to Kanvas and Angirases, while the tenth appears to have been a later addition. In all family *mandalas*, the opening hymns are addressed to god Agni, immediately followed by one to Indra, then follow the hymns dedicated to other gods in keeping with a prescribed system. In the eighth Mandala the hymns have been arranged author-wise, while in the ninth the arrangement is metre-wise.

Some Rig Vedic hymns, like those addressed to Ushas, Goddess of dawn, are fine examples of lyrical poetry. The whole of the *Rik* (the term is used for one stanza of a Rig Vedic hymn or one mantra of it) Sanhita, including the late-added tenth Mandala, was in existence in the form we find it in today, before Sanhitas of other Vedas came into being.

Max Muller divides the period of the Vedic literature into four, being the periods of the *chhandas* (prosody), mantras (incantations), Brahmanas (where elaborate details for the sacrifices were worked out) and the Sutras (aphorisms). As Tilak has said, by the time of the Brahmanas, the hymns of the Rig Veda had already become antique and unintelligible, the institution of the *Brahmavadins* had already come into being with the sole purpose of finding out the real meanings of these hymns. The language of the hymns was the old Sanskrit which was scarcely understood then, and understanding which became even more difficult later.

Distinguished Brahmavadins wrote commentaries from time to time to give their views about what they thought were the direct or implied meanings of the hymns. These scholars were assisted by schools of etymologists and grammarians. Panini wrote *Astadhyayi* while great Patanjali wrote his own commentary, the *Mahabhasya*, and both authors based their works on a detailed exposition of common and Vedic Sanskrit in support of their interpretations, quoting extensively from the works of renowned etymologists. Vedic scholars of recent times, following the line of Dayananda, believe that the mantra (i.e., Sanhita) portion of the Vedas alone is self-authoritative. Brahmanas, being only commentries on the Vedas, are authoritative only where they agree with the Vedic revelations. In the last quarter of the fourteenth century Sayana, the famous Brahmin scholar and Vedic commentator from the kingdom of Vijayanagar, has described the Vedas as collections of hymns, essentially formulas, designed to perform rituals. This was widely accepted during his time, and even subsequently. Sayana believed ritual to be part of divine knowledge, and endowed with mysterious efficacy. He believed hymns invoked gods for the good of man, community, society, nation, and if the code of conduct that the ancient scriptures had prescribed, is followed, contributed to happiness, prosperity and general well-being. His views influenced Hinduism in so far as the place in it of the Vedic thought was concerned. Only in the nineteenth century, the curiosity of the western scholars about Vedic literature brought in a reappraisal which questioned Sayana's views and brought in other interpretations.

Dayanand (1824-83) was one of the prominent Vedic scholars to disagree with the ritualistic interpretation, and took on the task of writing his own commentries on Rig and Yajur Vedas, but his detractors poisoned him when he had completed the Yajur Veda commentary and covered only six Mandalas of the Rig Veda. A serious enquiry was already underway amongst the European and Indian scholars to understand the Vedic literature and its impact on the Indian culture and civilization. Vedic influence in the shaping of philosophy, as contained in the Upanishads, language and grammar, as illustrated in the works of Panini and Patanjali, astronomy, mathematics, surgery and medicine was recognized. The neo-Vedantists in India, led by Dayananda, claimed that the Vedic religion was essentially monotheistic, that Agni, Soma, and various gods sung about in the hymns were in fact the facets of the same God, that all the variations of *homa*, as prescribed in the Vedas, were, in essence, addressed to the worship of this same omnipotent and omniscient being. The concept of monotheism has also been advocated both by Ramanuja and Madhava during the twelveth and thirteenth centuries AD, but one suspects that Dayananda's views are the result of an influence of the Christian and Islamic concepts of monotheism.

A section of Hindu theologians of modern times find similarity in all religions, including Hinduism, in their emphasis on the social, moral and ethical values. This, no doubt, is a noble thought, more so in a country where people of different religious perceptions have to live together. But, it is not an entirely correct view point. No doubt all religions aim at mentally equipping the man to better serve the society and withstand the vicissitudes of life with fortitude, but their emphasis is on different sets of values, and it is this difference where reconciliation becomes a problem. Nor is the Vedic religion, as we understand it in this country, monotheistic. The Rig Veda alone, in spite of its antiquity which has come in the way of its correct interpretation, has ten *mandalas* of over one thousand hymns and over ten thousand verses. It is a vast storehouse of knowledge in theology and sciences. Its earliest hymns are in praise of gods named after the elements, like fire, earth, clouds, and other deities like Soma. Indra is the lord of the gods in the later hymns, and in still later ones the suggestion of one omniscient and omnipotent God has crystalized. In the ultimate vision (Vedanta) the concept has shifted to one creating energy, the power, of which all that we see, or do not see, are constituents. God as a separate entity has ceased: He is all, and all is He. It is monoism.

Within this vast spectrum of concepts, many views and concepts, in so far as the speculative aspect of the religion is concerned, are embraced by the Veda, and the lesson is that the Veda has no quarrel with different religious thoughts so long as they lead to the satisfaction of an individual's religious needs and guide him to a clean, just, honest and good life, a way that should bring him happiness and generally benefit the society. But this is not to suggest that the Vedic religion accepts all religious perceptions to be correct. What it accepts to be correct is what has been revealed, and is contained within the Veda, and the belief is that the revelations came to man right at the time of creation, that the Vedic religion is *sanatana*, without beginning, and is totally beyond the scope of any modification. It is a religion of *homa*, sacrifice to fire, of chanting of hymns (to suit different occasions), of faith in the divine origination of Veda (which is about the most important pillar upon which it stands), of gods who may or may not be considered to be the facets of one almighty God, of sacrifice which initially included slaughter of animals, depending upon the occasion, but in later times, particularly in India, got restricted to offerings of grain flowers, leaves and the like, and where the priest(s) played the cardinal role in its conduct. Its followers believe that their way is the surest one to get them happiness in this world, and emancipation in the hereafter.

But the Vedic religion did modify with time. It was a religion unencumbered by complicated labyrinths of philosophy, and stressed the practical process of living, emphasizing the pursuit of happiness and achievement of excellence as principal objectives for human existence. But, surrounded as these Aryans were by the majority comprising the earlier inhabitants, they could not remain indifferent to their way of thinking. From the simple concept of heaven and hell they moved to that of rebirth and Karma, that is, there is no separate world for the good and the bad souls in the hereafter; all that is there is the rebirth on the basis of the Karmas of the previous births. From the simple galaxy of gods who could be prevailed upon through the medium of the mantras and *jantras* to shower their benedictions they accepted the concept of the universe being a cosmic whole, run by Dharma, the sacred law, which, among other things, places the human destiny in the iron grip of the law of Karma whereunder the soul goes through an interminable process of births and deaths till release is secured through the medium of right thoughts and righteous actions.

By the time of the Atharva Veda, a complicated regimen of charms and spells had come into practice, which partly was due to the influence of the earlier inhabitants of the country, and partly a logical extension of the original sacrificial cult which was, after all, designed to bend the gods to the bidding of the worshippers. But the essential elements of the Vedic worship remained intact, and are still so in modern Hinduism, though there have been modifications. Alongside the Vedic religion, non-Aryan gods are also worshipped by a large majority of the people in appropriate temples, and that also is a facet of Hinduism. The Vedic religion was a religion of sacrifice. It had no temples and no concept of idol worship. The pre-Aryan concept, however, was that an idol helped a devotee in making a mental picture of the deity and, thus, concentrating upon it while offering prayers. It was based on the theory of *Dhyana*, mental concentration. In the sacrificial worship it is the mantra and the sacrifice that do the job, and performer's mental concentration upon the god he is invoking is not the primary consideration. But, as of today, most Hindus do both the things: they use the medium of the sacrificial worship for occasions like marriage, birth, death, or for fulfilment of cherished wishes, and also go to the temples and worship before the idols, praying for whatever they want out of life. Yet those who do not believe in the Aryan system of mantra and sacrifice and pray only at the temples, are also Hindus, as also those who do not believe in idol worship and visit no temples and believe only in sacrifice. Also those who believe in neither but carry a Hindu sounding name, that is, a name derived out of Hindu books by pundits, astrologers or just the elders of the family, are Hindus, or even those who practise no religion and just say they are Hindus! There is no mutual acrimony amongst them for following different concepts.

The Aryans were conquerors. They initially arrived as emigres but, with time, had organized themselves to subjugate the local population. They had a highly developed language, and the horse driven chariot. Their religion was well developed and they were so ardently devoted to it that they, possibly, parted company with their Iranian clans-men when the latter tried to impose modifications to the original concepts. They were fair-complexioned and handsome, better organized in statecraft and conducting warfare, and they had every reason to believe they were superior to the original inhabitants. Their lore has contempt for the people they overpowered, and even for those they had not been able to vanquish and who posed a constant threat to their security and well-being. It is not that they came in contact with the mixture of the Proto-Australoid/Dravidian stocks for the first time when they arrived in India, they had a good knowledge of these people even during their stay in Iran, and even there they had held them in low esteem. It is difficult to see how a people under such circumstances could have avoided racial segregation. They divided the people, including those they had subjugated, into four classes, being Brahmins (those who looked after the religion and education); Kshatriyas (soldiers and those who ran the affairs of the state); Vaishas (the traders), and the Sudras (artisans and tillers). Males of the first three classes wore a sacred thread, which came to them in an initiation ceremony conducted a few years after birth, and were classified as *Dvija*, the twice-born, the second birth being at the time of the ceremony of the sacred thread. The thread is in the form of a loop with three strands, and is worn across the body over the right shoulder. The Sudras and the women were denied this status; only the men wearing the sacred thread were entitled to the study of religion, including Vedas. Whereas inter Varna marriages between the twice-borns were tolerated (marriages within the Varna itself were considered to be the best), that between the twice-born and the Sudra class drew penalty. This class composition resulted in segregation, between the twice-born and the Sudras, and, to some extent, particularly in later times, between the Varanas themselves.

With time two distinct cultural and religious streams evolved, being the Aryan religion and culture based on the Vedas, and non-Aryan one of the Indus people and other earlier inhabitants, i.e., generally the religion and culture of the Dravidian and the Australoid groups. The two streams flowed side by side, and borrowed from each other now and then, but generally maintained their identity almost throughout the course of history. From time to time one stream or the other acquired predominance, and a study of the history of this country tells us that better times visited when the optimistically inclined and simplistic Aryan stream was dominant. The non-Aryan way of life and religion has stressed pacifism, peace and non-violence, and has indeed produced some great ideas. Both Buddhism and Jainism are direct results of this way of thinking. Though the basic ingredients of this thought are noble and friendly not only towards the human family but even towards the general environment, they tend to breed timidity amongst its adherants. Governments run on these principles break down under stress, leading to anarchy and disorder. This subcontinent has suffered enormously on account of this stream of thought.

The Rig Vedic society was strongly patriarchal and they worshipped no female deities, other than, may be, Ushas, the beautiful goddess which heralds dawn, and, Sarasvati, the goddess of learning. In the days of the early Aryans a river named Sarasvati flowed through the present Rajasthan, and, while living along its banks, these people composed a lot of their religious literature; the river discharge diminished substantially in later times because of tactonic changes in the upper reaches in the Himalayan foothills, and whatever of it remained, has since been lost in the sands of the desert. In the earlier Vedic society the woman enjoyed quite a status although she was always placed below man. In later days, however, her position dropped, basically for two reasons: firstly, because the Varnas and the caste systems became more rigid and to maintain the purity of the stock and discourage sexual promiscuity, a stricter control on her was considered necessary, and, secondly, with the acceptance of the rebirth theory in the Vedic religion came the belief that she was born a female and not a male, because of inferior performance in her previous birth(s). The result of this was that the Vedic education was denied to her, as it was to the Sudra class, who also were believed to have been thus born because of poor performance in earlier lives. In some communities even basic education was not considered right for her, for it was felt that it could broaden her mental horizon and loosen her moral discretions. Lack of education brought in ignorance and that not only made her more dependent upon man but also accentuated her apparent inferiority. However, in spite of such an attitude widow remarriage was not uncommon during the Brahmana period.

The view that the deeds of the past births had a direct bearing on the situation one faced during the present life, considerably influenced the Hindu attitude towards fellow human beings. It tended to turn them callous, for the belief was that a person's station in life was of his or her own making and there was little requirement for the society to take any action to improve the lot of the downtrodden or those lower down in the birth rating. In fact the higher castes considered it their privilege and right to exploit them to the full, like it was their right to exploit their animals, which advantage, after all, also accrued to them because of the lower birth status of the animal. One Brahmana text declares that if so required a Sudra could be killed at will. The woman was branded as the epitome of falsehood. The Brahmin secured the top place for himself in the order; he was closest to God and ripe for liberation. Next came the Kshatriya, and then the Vaisya. Undue emphasis on religion threw up wily, crafty but second rate religious leaders, and bred blind faith, a lack of open, secular education, ignorance, superstition, sorcery, witchcraft. Brahmanas and the black Atharva Veda, it was claimed, had formulas which could destroy any enemy. The decline was gradual but definite. The later day Vedic thought and literature in the form of Brahmanas, lacked the spontaneity, the richness, grandeur and loftiness of earlier times, and for most part, turned into cult language. The worship process became cumbersome, and the supporting literature unduly extolled the virtues of the Brahmin community, and deprecated any group, or language, which could pose a challenge to their supremacy. Any attempt to alter or improve the living conditions of the community, was opposed on the plea that it was caused by the deeds of the previous births of the individuals, and any attempt to change the situation would not only be useless but actually be a sacrilege. Under the same argument conversions to Hinduism were not accepted, nor any alteration in the birth status of a person. The emphasis was on the individual to bear his circumstances with equanimity, and perform his duties appropriate to the station of his birth, with diligence, and give his best to his profession and thus improve his merit, and hope for higher station in life in the next birth, and go on thus improving till the attainment of final deliverance. People of other religious beliefs and nationalities were held in contempt, because they did not have access to the Veda, the only revealed literature in the world, and the Aryan priestly class was not prepared to provide this access to them because of the same argument: that it was because of their past deeds that they had been placed in such an unfortunate situation! A fatalistic kind of view had gripped the society at large.

But the Brahmana texts had their positive points as well. There was a lot of emphasis on pious and truthful living, and this was impressed upon the laity through a series of meaningful and well compiled stories. As B.K. Ghosh says in his essay on Brahmanas, the five daily offerings (to gods, beings, fathers, the study of Veda and charity), the cornerstone of orthodox Hindu sociology, were stressed upon for the first time in the Brahmana texts. These works have also put forth thoughts of high intellectual content concerning religious order, philosophy and the speculative aspects of the religion.

Even though there have been contemptuous references to the Sudras, it was not as if they were treated like dirt by the society at large. Artisans, and those who had any part in the economy, were already organized in communes and guilds, probably from the days prior to the arrival of the Aryans, and they ensured that their interests, including social, were well protected; in fact, often the performing hands were better off economically, compared to the Mantra reciting Brahmins.

Even in the case of the women, any number of cases have been cited in the Vedic literature where they have excelled in learning and even in the knowledge of the Vedas. Some of them have even contributed to the sacred writings. But she has been placed below man. In *Ramayana*, Sita, the wife of Lord Rama, has, as the story goes, said that (translation, J.N. Farquhar):

> 'The woman who on earth below, Her parents on a man bestow, And lawfully their hands unite, with water and each holy rite, She in this world shall be his wife, His also in the after-life!'.

Thus, signifying that a Hindu woman marries not merely 'for better or for worse', but for this world and the next; the marriage cannot ever be broken. In actual life, however, though she has been enjoined to treat her husband as her lord, yet she enjoys power which adequately matches that of her husband. Sita may have been unjustly banished by her husband, but the very fact that she commands the status of a goddess because she took her banishment with equanimity, shows the respect the Hindu community gave her, and to womanhood. No one could deter Sita from accompanying her husband when he was banished, once she had made up her mind. In fact, the very banishment of Rama was caused by his stepmother, a woman, against whom the king, his father, was helpless. It would be wrong to assume women were treated with contempt during the later Vedic age either. They, generally, enjoyed a respectable status amongst the well-to-do upper classes, though amongst the poorer sections their position possibly was not that comfortable. This position held on right through the historical period, right up to the present times.

The Vedic religion believed that in the hereafter the soul travelled to the world of Yama where it was rewarded or punished in keeping with its deeds performed during its stay on earth. Yama, a human being and not a god, the ruler of the nether world and the twin brother of Yami — together they make the primeval twins —, had discovered the nether world after his death, and had established his rule there, rising to the status of a god because of the excellence he had achieved during his living days on earth. In that world, in the company of Yama, lived the fathers, in immortality, and in the midst of joy and plenty, having attained the objective they had cherished during their lives on earth that is, attainment of god-like status in the hereafter, by performing appropriate fire worship and sacrifices. In this process, the offerings from the relatives and their good deeds also helped the departed spirits. For this purpose the *shradhas* are performed. These are rites performed on specified days when, under the guidance of the *purohita*, the family priest, and with the chanting of appropriate Vedic incantations, offerings are made to the departed relatives; these comprise food, grains, clothes, sometimes even cows, depending upon the status of the family: offerings, in fact, have to be made to the *purohita*, for, the belief is that the god invoked; merges with him during the process of the sacrifice. The Vedic seers were essentially concerned with life, its vitality, energy, its capacity to provide pleasure and joy. They were not overly involved with the hereafter. The Veda says that the spirits of the dead travel either along the path of the Fathers, or the gods and the mortals, and in the paradise of Yama they have the best of the foods and drinks, and all the joys that the gods have. But all this is achieved by performing good deeds during the lifetime; amongst the deeds, performance of sacrifice has a pre-eminent position. The evildoers are punished and thrown into hell, and although no description of this place as such is given in the Veda, it is believed to be dark and suffocating, existence inside it would be miserable. After expiation, the soul moves to the higher world.

There are hymns in the Rig Veda which tend to suggest sexual symbolism, like the Yama-Yami hymn where Yami expresses sexual desire for her twin brother, or the hymn of the Virile Ape and Indrani where the latter seeks the sexual favours of the former because of deficient potency of Indra, or the horse sacrifice hymns. Horse sacrifice was a simple ceremony, not involving actual slaying of a horse during the Rig Vedic days, but, later, it required actual killing and acquired sexual overtones. A number of scholars have tried to work out the meanings of these hymns, and most have concluded that these and some other similar ones, were connected with fertility rites, though hymns like those for the horse sacrifice, were for the good and glory of the ruler who performed the sacrifice. Some, however, have tried to connect these with social customs of the Aryans, for example, suggesting that incestuous relations were not entirely frowned upon amongst these people. Nothing could be more preposterous. Although the fertility meaning, or that the sacrifice was performed for the glory and well-being of the king (all sacrifices, in any case, were performed for the well-being of the sacrificer) could be relevant, but in this distant time it is almost impossible to be sure about it. Sometimes the ancient wise men had the tradition of giving esoteric expressions to their inner thoughts, which they felt had much depth and could not be expressed and comprehended in plain language. Such a language, in any case, was meant for those high up in the religious order and not the laity. A lot of the *tantric* tradition has been expressed in this manner. There is no reason to believe this might not have been the case with these hymns of the Rig Veda. Anyhow, as stated above, because of the Old Sanskrit of the Rig, and the thousands of years that have elapsed since their first writing, it is not possible to comprehend the meaning and purpose of such compositions.

Sama Veda

Word Rik stands for knowledge, *Sam* for devotion and also for melody, while Yajuh stands for Karma, action. The Vedas have not been arranged subject-wise, though most of the hymns are related to the topic indicated by the name of the Veda. Sama Veda is essentially a collection of melodies which are designed to be used while chanting the ritual verses of the *Rik Sanhita*. Theoretically any melody could be chanted for any verse, but in practice it is not done this way. The verse on which a melody is chanted is called a *Yoni*, source, which suggests that the verse itself was regarded as the source of the melody. The core of this Veda, *Archika*, is a collection of 585 Yonis. Additionally it has other literature forming the text part, basic function of which is to assign melodies to the verses. The Vedic chants played a significant role in the Soma ritual.

Yajur Veda

Like Sama Veda, this too is a ritualistic Veda, essentially forming the guide book for the *adhvaryu* priests who perform all the functions in the sacrifice except reciting the Mantras and chanting the melodies; reciting is done by the *hotri* priests and chanting by the *udgatris*. Thus, while the Sama Veda apportioned the melody variations to the hymns of the *Rik Sanhita*, Yajur Veda laid down the actions to be performed during the recitations, like pouring clarified butter or other ingredients of sacrifice, into the sacrificial fire, or drawing signs or symbols at or around the place of sacrifice, or going around it, and so on. Six complete recensions of this Veda are extant today, being two of the white Yajur Veda and four of the Black Yajur Veda. The Black Yajur Veda is the older of the two and is preserved in the *Taittiriya*, *Maitrayani* and *Kathak* recensions, while the former is preserved in the *Vajasneyi* recension. The *Vajasneyi* recension has around forty chapters, and of these the last twenty-two appear to have been added later, the basic text comprised the first eighteen chapters only. The formulas given in these chapters occur in the *Taittiriya Sanhita* as well, while those in the last twenty-two chapters are found in Taittiriya Brahmana. Chapters nineteen to twenty-one are for expiation of sin of excessive indulgence in Soma, and twenty two to twenty five are for horse-sacrifice. Actually, in the Veda itself there is no direction as regards *Viniyoga,* that is, indication as to which of the verses are to be recited on what occasions. This has been left to the judgement of the priests, though, over a period of time, a fair amount of uniformity in this regard has evolved. In the Black Yajur Veda the Mantra and the Brahmana are mixed up throughout and, therefore, the Sanhita is more like a Brahmana than a Sruti. The sacrificial prayer has not only the hymns taken from the Rig Veda but also original prose formulas for the Adhvaryu-priest.

Atharva Veda

Originally only the three Sanhitas, *Trayi* (threefold knowledge), were recognized as the canonical scriptures. In course of time, however, at a period much later than that of the three Sanhitas, a fourth one, Atharva Veda, the book of magical formulas, attained the canonical status. Though the recognition came late, much of the matter in the collection is old. Quite a few hymns are of popular rather than priestly origin and could be as old as the earliest hymns of the Rig Veda, or even older, maybe of a time earlier than the arrival of the Aryans in this country. It is a book of songs, spells and incantations against disease, dangers and enemies of many kinds, and to bring evil upon those who are hated. The book has a large number of what are called the khila hymns, that is, hymns which do not enjoy a high sacred status. These, obviously, were put in under the popular pressure, suggesting adulteration of the Brahminical religion with the non-Aryan literature. They must have found it hard to resist this as the majority of the people in the land were non-Aryans. But Sanhita does have hymns, the non-*khila* ones, of rare beauty, some extolling the power and omniscience of God, others beneficence of Mother Earth. Generally, it is the *Saunakiya* recension which is in use, although the other recension, *Paippalada* also has a lot of relevant material. Both recensions have a number of chapters which have been added later.

The Brahmanas

By the time of the Brahmanas, the hymns of the Rig Veda had become quite unintelligible, and the authors of the former texts had their own views as to the meaning of the hymns. The texts were compiled, apparently, a few centuries after the last of the Rig Vedic hymns had been composed — according to Tilak the time gap could have been as much as a millennium, though this view has not been accepted. They contain detailed directions as to how the sacrifices are to be performed, and since these are based on the understanding of their authors of the meaning of the Vedic hymns, these works could be regarded as commentaries of sorts on the Rig and the Atharva Vedas. Each of the Vedas has its Brahmana, like the *Aitareya* of the Rig; *Jaiminiya* of the Sam; *Satapatha* of the Yajur and *Gopatha* of the Atharva Veda. Although most Brahmanas have been assumed to be works handed down in the form in which they were first composed, in effect it does not appear to be so. It seems they contain works of many authors and have been edited and re-edited from time to time. Apart from the details of the Brahmanical sacrifices, the works also have the duties of the priests, the mantras to be recited, and other relevant detail considered essential for the sacrifice. In effect they have tended to mystify the whole sacrificial ritual, including the role of the priests. They also have illustrative stories to emphasize the importance of the ritual and the benefits the sacrificer would draw from it, sometimes dealing with speculative aspects like how the world came into being and the part sacrifice played in this. The modification of the texts continued long after the Brahmanas were first composed.

The literature of the Brahmanas had its own beneficial impact on the language, leading to the evolution of a more polished and forceful writing and speech, with more attention being paid to the rules of grammar (mostly Paninean). Besides, the complex ritual designed by the clergy got other literate and concerned elements of the society to think; a lead in this was given by the Kshatriyas, who not only were responsible for running the affairs of the state, but were also well educated (by their Brahman teachers) and had the necessary leasure to think upon what direction the religion was taking and whether that was the correct course. Then, the earlier inhabitants of the land had a very strong voice and their views could not be ignored altogether. The result of all this was the Aranyakas and the Upanishads.

Shrauta-Sutras

The prolix and complex jumble of detail of the Braḥmanas often tended to be lacking in coherence. In the Shrauta-Sutras the sacrificial detail has been arranged concisely and in a systematic manner. *Shrauta* means, according to *Shruti*, the revealed knowledge. The Vedic tradition was untouched by later additions. A Shrauta sacrifice is performed strictly in accordance with the Vedic injunctions. *Sutras* are aphoristic texts, generally expressed so pithily that to understand them, separate commentries have become necessary. Brahmanas defied proper understanding because of a lack of coherence, but the Shrauta-Sutras are equally difficult because they are just too brief and assume too much of the sacrificial detail to be already well known and understood to need any mention. They have, however, separated the common and the special features of the sacrifices and expressed them in digits, in a kind of a coded manner, computer-style — a remarkable arithmetical achievement!

Each Veda also has its Shrauta-Sutras and they bear relationship to the corresponding Brahmanas, i.e., Brahmanas appended to the particular Veda. Normally the Atharva Veda, which has nothing to do with the Shrauta rituals, should not have had its own Shrauta-Sutra, but it has, and possibly this has been done on the insistence of its followers who must have felt the necessity for it in view of their claim to its being of canonical status. But, in fact, it is Shrauta-Sutra only in respect of its twentieth chapter, which has a Sanhita status anyway. A considerable interval must have elapsed between the compiling of the Brahmanas and the Shrauta-Sutras.

The Aranyakas

These are sacred 'Forest Texts' which contain religious secrets which could be taught only in the seclusion of the forests. Though considered to be extensions of the Brahmanas, they, in effect, were not stressing the sacrifice or explaining its details. They were more concerned with its mystery and the meaning of the symbols which came to be used during its conduct, leading to the unfolding of a philosophy which in effect said that sacrifice was not the only way to attain the realm of the Brahma, that meditation without any sacrifice accompanying it, was an equally, if not more, effective method. They advocated meditation for securing *Moksha*, in preference to ritual and thus initiated a new, almost revolutionary, thought which, in essence, went against the grain of the established religion; meditation was an important ingredient of the pre-Aryan worship. No doubt they skilfully established the basis of the new thought in the sayings of the Veda. Otherwise it was virtually impossible to secure its acceptance, since the belief in sacrifice was deeply ingrained and widespread. For the same reason the need was felt to impart the new knowledge in the seclusion of the forest, where the hymns of the Veda which supported the Aranyaka thought could be emphasised, and where, even if the student was not convinced of the arguments, he was not in a position to organize a collective revolt, and where he could be trained in meditation so that he could himself assess its efficacy. The sacrificial ritual as expounded in the Brahmana texts had become so complex, complicated, time consuming and expensive, that it had almost fallen out of the reach of the common people. This must have been demoralizing.

A sacrifice as elaborated in the Brahmana texts, required a minimum of four priests, namely, the Hotri, who invoked the gods by selecting the relevant verses of the Rig; the Udgatri, who sang the hymns as laid down in the Sal, the Adhvaryu, who performed the sacrificial acts with appropriate mutterings from the Yajur Veda and, finally, the Brahmin, the supervisor, who ensured that the ceremony was conducted in accordance with the procedures as laid down in the Brahmana texts. *Shiksha*, instruction or education in phonetics, the correct pronunciation, intonation and so on, while reciting the Mantras also played an important part. The head priest had to ensure strict compliance of the *shiksha* instructions. Though the Vedangas, the limbs of the Veda (and *shiksha* is one of them), are not a divine revelation — these have been written for the proper understanding, recitation and sacrificial use of the Veda —, a good knowledge of these works is essential for the correct conduct of the sacrificial ceremonies. The head priest who supervised the sacrifice, therefore, had to be a man well versed in the Veda and the Vedangas. A *Shrauta* sacrifice was even more complex, requiring three fires going at the same time and employing sixteen or more priests. The number went up manifolds when more than one gods were invoked at the same time or when invocation of even one god was required to be emphasised. Whereas such sacrificial proceedings could be possible when they were being conducted on a joint basis, like for the invocation of the rain god by the people of a region, or by rich patrons like prominent *Rajanyas* or flourishing traders, or by kings, at the level of the common man the requirement was for simpler and workable procedures. The authors of the Aranyakas were essentially concerned with this basic deficiency in the argument that considered sacrifice to be the only way of realizing happiness in this world and the hereafter. Aranyakas have stressed that self-realization through the development of one's spiritual self, is the goal of man, and have allotted this method of reaching the Brahma Lok (the abode of Brahma), a place higher than that of the ritual method (of sacrifice). The Upanishads have taken this refrain a step further and have stated that this would progressively lead to the liberation from the birth cycle and ultimately to the unity with Brahma. As stated above, the Aranyakas are extensions of the Brahmanas and are their appendices and, therefore, like the Brahmanas, they also are attached to particularized Vedic schools, e.g., Aitareya Brahmana of the Rig Veda has an Aranyaka of the same name as its appendix.

Kalpa Sutras

These oldest Sutra works, systematized the sacrificial procedures by dividing sacrifices into three broad classes, namely, (a) elaborate sacrifices based on the Brahmana and Shrauta texts, as explained above; (b) simple domestic rites, like for marriages, conception, births, deaths, and so on; and (c) rites to regulate the conduct of a person with a view to purifying him morally and making him fit to reap the benefits of the sacrifice. Works falling undercategories (b) and (c) are in the *Grihya Sutras* which also have the details of the five sacrifices prescribed for the householder, already described earlier. In fact details of all sacrifices performed at the level of the householder, for any and every occasion, including house building, or digging of wells, or effecting cure from illness or warding off evil omens, are contained in these Sutras. The Shrauta Sutras are so called because they are based on

Shruti, the revealed knowledge, while Grihya Sutras are Smarta, that is, based on Smriti, tradition.

The instructions regarding the responsibilities, duties, conduct and behaviour of an individual, as a member of the family, society or a citizen of the state, are contained in the Dharma Sutras which are a part of the Grihya Sutras. In its broad sense Dharma is what holds together, that is, it is the basis of all order. In the common parlance it has the overtones of morality which leads to good results. The usual meaning is religious merit for securing good in the future, here as well as in the hereafter. Rituals of the Dharma Sutras are for securing wealth, children and all else that contributes towards attaining happiness in life, and heaven after death. Their instructions can be put in two categories, namely, (a) general, meant to develop and improve the character of a person, like self-discipline, kindness, consideration towards others — not only towards fellow human beings but also towards animals and plants —, speaking truth, altruism, and such like qualities; and (b) those for the people in the four Varnas and the four Ashramas, their duties and obligations. We know that the society had been divided into four classes, viz., Brahmins, Kshatriyas, Vaisyas, and Sudras. It is not entirely clear how rigid this Varana system was during the Vedic age; it certainly was not as rigid as it became during the second millennium AD.

The Ashrama System

By the time of the Brahmanas the Ashrama system for the male population had also taken firm roots. The system divided the life span of a hundred years, into four parts, each of twenty-five years, as follows :

Brahmacharya Ashram

During the first twenty-five years, known as the *Brahmacharya Ashrama*, i.e. the stage of celibacy, the individual was to grow to healthy manhood, allowing himself no sexual liberties, and solely devoting to full education, and training in religion, crafts and sciences.

Grihastha Ashram

During the second stage, called the *Grihastha Ashrama*, i.e., the stage of the householder, he was to raise a family, and strive to make his contributions to the society. During this stage the four prescribed injunctions were to receive his full attention; these in the order of importance are, (i) *Dharma* (this has been defined above), (ii) *Artha* (economics: generation of wealth through work of any kind and trade, commerce, industry; but the activity must not at any stage violate the injunctions of Dharma), (iii) *Kama* (participating in and enjoying arts, music, poetry, the beauty in general, including sex — but all within the ambit of the first discipline: Dharma), and finally, (iv) *Moksha* (acquisition of knowledge and performing worship and meditation and such other noble deeds as would help him to attain freedom from the cycle of births). All these instructions are for the male only. The female takes the cue from the male, and was expected to lead a chaste and truthful life, tending to the household chores with loving care, standing steadfast next to her husband, if she was married, both in this world and the next.

Vanprastha Ashram

In the third stage, called the *Vanprastha Ashrama*, i.e., the stage of the forest dweller, the individual abdicates from the performing world and devotes himself to the study of religion or any other discipline of his choice, conducts research where he can, hold discussions with other people following the same or similar vocations and, where possible, imparts the knowledge so gained to the other members of the society. To ensure that he is not disturbed in his pursuit of knowledge, he may, sometimes, decide to retire to a life in the forest, with or without his wife; that was how the Aranyakas came into being. Like in the first stage, he is a student again, studying, but with a broader horizon, and with a view to making his own contribution.

Sanyas Ashram

The last stage is the *Sanyas Ashrama* or the life of the ascetic, of renunciation. The person has now completely abdicated from all social obligations and retired from the affairs of the world, to some place of his choice where he might indulge in contemplations of his liking, or take on the life of a wandering monk. But being in a stage of infirmity it might not always be possible to accomplish this. Some Dharma Sutras have denounced asceticism and enjoined upon the members of the family, those in the *Grihasth Ashrama*, to take care of their old and infirm relations, and allow them to perform the duties of this stage in the security of their homes.

To the person in the third stage of his life, in the *Vanprastha Ashrama*, who was devoting his time to the study of religion or other sciences and crafts, or the hermit, in the fourth stage, the *Sanyas Ashram*, who had completely renounced all worldly activity, and who, therefore, did not have all the facilities at his disposal to fully follow the sacrificial rituals, the only course open was that of study and contemplation, and by experience, gathered over a period of time. These people, possibly, found this mode of worship to be more effective and rewarding. They were also influenced into accepting some of the ideas of the people of the pre-Aryan cultures, with whom they must have had extensive contact during the period of the hermitage. As we have seen (on the basis of the Indus Valley seals), pre-Aryan cultures emphasized meditation and, it can be deduced, self-realization, in their modes of worship. In fact, even the induction of the Ashrama system amongst the Aryans, seems to have been effected under the influence of the older cultures. Thus, it appears that during the Brahmana period, while the Aryan priesthood was emphasising sacrifice, definite inroads were being made by the earlier cultures into the Aryan way of life, and the complexities of the sacrificial system was making that ingress easier.

The Brahmana and the allied literature has laid greater stress on the duties of an individual towards the society as a whole, of which he was but a small part, rather than the aspects which promoted his personal well-being. No doubt, during the *Grihastha* stage he is permitted to delve into *artha*, economic activity, which brought wealth to him, but here too he was required to create in sciences, technology, trade, commerce, primarily for the society, partaking only a part of the produce to enable him to raise his family. Same is the case with *kama*. He patronizes arts, cultural activities, music, song, drama to bring joy and happiness to himself and to the people amongst whom he lived. He indulged in sexual activities to bring forth children who would, when they grew up, be the asset of his people. Besides, all activities connected with *artha* or *kama*, were to be within the overall limitations of the first and primary and all encompassing activity of *dharma*. No activity might violate the injunctions of *dharma*. Such was the burden of the instructions contained in the Dharma Sutras.

The Upanishads

These are the last of the works of the Vedic literature, and, for that reason, their teachings along with those of the Aranyakas, are termed as the *Vedanta* — 'Ved Anta', the last or the final teachings of the Veda. The burden of the teachings of these works is that Brahminic ritualism has little merit, that the ultimate goal of human existence is unity with Brahma, the self-existent, omnipotent, omnipresent, omniscient God, and that the entire creation is in effect a manifestation of Brahma and each part of it, howsoever small, is but a constituent of the Whole, i.e., Brahma, and also that the human being is stuck in the *Sansara*, the phenomenal world, because of his ignorance about this truth, and that this truth can be realized by following the *Gyan Marga*, or the path of knowledge, by doing meditation and contemplating upon the Self. The learned people from the earlier cultures appear to have played a cardinal role in bending the Brahminic beliefs to this way of thinking. Amongst the Aryan community the sections which promoted Vedanta were either the Kshatriyas, upon whom the Brahmin priestly class was dependent for survival, and who, because they ran the affairs of the state and fought for its integrity, came in extensive contact with people of different backgrounds, including those from earlier cultures, or they were those who were extremely unhappy with the pattern and philosophy of the rituals, the *Karma Marga*, like women, or almost the whole of the trader community, or the whole lot of the people classified as Sudras by the Brahmins.

The Ashrama system, possibly an idea emanating from the earlier cultures, logically precipitated the demise of the pre-eminence of rituals. The large number of people joining the *Vanprastha* and the *Sanyas Ashramas*, were carrying out an intellectual investigation into the thoughts and philosophies in vogue, and they had all the time in the world to ponder over the issues and wander around and exchange their thoughts with other people, including the non-Aryans, and then preach their ideas to listening ears. They preached the supremacy of Brahma, not of the rituals or the gods. They preached supremacy of the word and not of mere incantations. However, once the being of gods had been accepted, acceptance of the idea of one God running the universe could not have been far away, for their had to be a being to control and coordinate the activities of the gods, otherwise, instead of order, which is the essence of the process of creation, it would all be chaos. The idea must have suggested itself with all the force after the Aryans had acquired skills in the art of governance: the functions that the king performed *vis-a-vis* his council of ministers and other functionaries responsible for running the affairs of the state, had to be performed, in the realm of the gods, by some power which had to be superior to them. Likewise, the idea of one force manifesting itself in different forms, shapes, phenomena, ranging from a particle of dust to a most minor germ or virus, to different forms of life, to the formation of stars and galaxies was a natural take-off from the concept of the Brahmanas which claimed that sacrificial ritual, when performed properly, could force the gods to the biddings of the sacrificer. The concept allotted to the man a place even higher than that of the gods, provided he followed the path of ritual shown to him by the Veda. From here the move to the idea that in fact he was a part of the power that causes creation, a varied manifestation of it, *tat tvam asi*, that thou art, was only but a logical step.

Five

The Vedic Thought

The Word

The Veda is the revealed text, the primordial word, *Vak*, of which no human being is be the author. In fact the word itself is an aspect of the Supreme Being. It is closely connected with the life-force, the senses, the mind and is like the ocean—deep, endless and unfathomable. The Veda is not to be regarded as having been authored by God, or as a kind of a message from God communicated to humanity through some sage or holy man. It is the Word itself. In essence the Word is a part of the phenomenon of creation. It kind of pervades the creation as a dimension, like the dimension of time, *kaal*, and gets revealed through intuitive minds when such minds are attuned to the process of creation. Even the Supreme Self becomes visible only through the medium of the word. According to Atharva Veda, it is limited to four stages, and the people with insight know them; three of them are dormant and hidden, while the fourth appears in the form of speech. Sayana, while commenting on this explains that the Original Word is the Inner Immortal Light, and when this is realized all frivolous activities of the body and mind cease. In the middle stage it becomes an object of the intellect, and takes the form of thinking and brooding, and in the final stage, of course, it is just speech. Rig Veda gives the four stages as: *para* (the original and the highest); *pashyanti* (the visible); *madhyama* (the middle) and *vaikhari* (the articulate). Words have vibrations, which generate beneficial or deleterious effects. The words of the Mantra came down to man to create the desired effect; those words have power. The Vedic seer, the Rishi, discovered the word after practising rigorous austerities, after he had discovered the working principles of the cosmos and became conversant with the Universal Order, and had become a part of the divine speech. It was at this stage that the words came to him, the right ones which when arranged in proper Mantra forms, and uttered in a specified metre, and accompanied by an appropriate sacrifice, endowed the Vedic seer, and subsequently, any person who followed his directions, with the requisite power. The word, thus, is a facet of God, and when turned the right way round, it is God. It is *Naam*, name of God, and when dwelt upon, generates a sound current, a vibration, which, in effect, is the same as the essence of creation, an experience which is transporting, and which, if practised over a period of time, depending upon the concentration put into the word, could eventually lead to union with God. Humanity communicates through the word, transacts its business with its aid, makes use of it in prayers and so on. Life would be devoid of meaning if it was not supported by word.

Om

The word most sacred for the sound vibrations is Om, composed of three sounds, A-U-M, where, by one account, A is considered to be standing for Brahma and His activity which essentially is to trigger the process of creation, U for Vishnu who is the great sustainer of the universe, while M stands for the Great Siva, the supporter of all knowledge. Taken together it has been given as standing for the Hindu Trinity of Brahma, Vishnu, and Siva, creation, desire and knowledge, (*kriya-ichha-gyana*), which represent but the three facets of the Supreme Being. In another view M represents Siva not so much as the bestower of knowledge, as the great destroyer unto whom everything ultimately folds up. Thus, as the sound emerges, it is creation, and this goes through the process of sustenance during the second stage with the sound flexing to U, till with M it is all over, and it is the end. Then there is the long silence, *shunya*, when the primordial atom has completely withdrawn unto itself, till, once again, the process of creation starts with the utterance of sound A. The word (*om*), thus, represents the creation and the annihilation processes. This kind of explanation, however, appears to have been designed basically to motivate the laity. Otherwise, it is just a word which is most efficacious when communion is sought with the kernel of the creation; it has no meaning and in essence represents no thought or idea. It is regarded as the most helpful sound in mobilizing concentration during meditation. Its oral vibrations are considered to be beneficial in every situation that a human being might face. The Buddhist lamas believe that this word is beneficial even on a fluttering flag. It is the original sound that comes to a person when he meditates, and concentrates on the Self. The Self is the origin of this word; it, therefore, is the Self. It has a mystical impact and is used at the beginning and the end of all sacred recitations.

Rta

While trying to comprehend the meaning of this term the reader must remember that the Veda is not a Shastra where the subject matter has been arranged in a logical sequence, properly laid out for ease of reference and understanding. It is a record of the transcendental experience of the Vedic seers (*rishis*), and the germs of different ideas, like those regarding the being of the Creator, or how the creation came about, or which way it is heading, or what constitutes Dharma, and so on, lie scattered all over the literature. Besides, the literature is so old that to understand what has been stated, it has to be approached with the right spirit and understanding. Earlier Vedic scholars have understood *Rta* to mean the Truth, but that does not appear to fully cover this expression. When some European scholars likened it to the Universal Order, this was opposed by others, particularly Luders, who said that the Vedic people had no idea of the universal order. He maintained that the word stood for Truth, i.e., non-lie. This appears to have been a biased assumption. In the earliest reference in the Rig Veda, *Rta* has been understood as the cosmic power which had the capability of expression in a variety of ways, both at the cosmic and the terrestrial levels. *Rta* has been described as energy that enlivens faculties like will power, perception, action, and so on. If *Rta* is harnessed, the essence of creation has been taken under control. Mantra achieved this and then bent the energy for the well-being of the people, including fulfilment of their cherished wishes. Most essential things come out of the abode of *Rta*, including Brahma, the creator of the universe. Agni, fire, resides in its womb.

What controls *Rta*? The answer is that by *Rta* is *Rta* controlled, although Mantra should influence it in whatever way the Rishi to whom the Mantra came, wanted it influenced. In certain hymns there is the suggestion that the visible aspects of *Rta* have invisible counterparts, e.g., invisible part of light, or fire, has been given as water. The assertion is that there is double *Rta*, implying that there is no visible entity which does not have its invisible counterpart. The hymn mentions about the balance being achieved in *Rta* by the interaction of the visible and the invisible entities: sun and its movements, right speech, even the right conduct, are the visible aspects, which are, in fact, being held in the perceptible form by the corresponding invisible constituents.

Rta has also been described as cosmic moisture, which brings rain and water on the earth, and the seer who, with his Mantric power, has got into the guts of the cosmic process, so to speak, is presumed to possess the capability to extract favourable response from this power, like, for example, the precipitation of rain. Possibly for this reason, viewed over a narrow spectrum, the tradition understands the term to mean just water. Sayana, who sees nothing in the Veda beyond the ritual and sacrifice, has also given it the same meaning. This view, no doubt, is myopic. Amongst the European schoiars the views have differed. While some have understood it to mean 'the holy power', others have understood it as a 'ritualistic formula' used to excite the cosmic power in favour of the person performing the sacrifice. Some of them have interpreted it as 'the absolute power in the whole nature' that, among others, also constitutes nature. After all, Brahma has origin in *Rta*.

Brahma, according to the views of some scholars, is 'a mysterious fluid, or potence, that fills the whole world (universe). It can be induced to make itself manifest in a given substance through charms, incantations and scientific and magical movement.' It also is given out as 'the midway process of giving form in expression to the thoughts that arise in the mind, i.e. speech (*Vak*)'. It pervades the cosmos and is its inner core (that sustains it). The concept has a broad connotation and cannot really be summed up: among others it covers the 'Mantra and the prayer' or the 'inner power', or the superhuman results that the Mantra can produce, or the manifestation of the super wonder and its myriad and complex activities, that is, the total universe. But, as stated in the Rig Veda, Brahma's origin is in the abode of the Rta.

The Vedic Content

Veda has sometimes been viewed as the literature of rituals. But in effect it is much more than that. It is also intensely speculative, and literature of contemplation. The Vedic seer, while in the contemplative mode went through certain intuitive experiences which gave him an insight into the process of creation, how the creation sustained, wither it was heading, and such like matters. But, he had the problem of language, for he felt there just did not exist the vocabulary for giving a simple, coherent expression to his experience, and he designed some kind of esoteric expressions for this purpose; Tantric literature freely used such expressions. Tantras are treatises wherein, in some cases, highly learned and accomplished men of religion and philosophy have described intricate and difficult aspects of rituals, and their own meditative and contemplative experiences, in a manner as to make them comprehensible to their selected disciples. For this purpose they used even sexual symbolism. With time, however, some sects took to the practice of performing rituals in accordance with what was actually written, without bothering about the intent behind the use of the sexual expressions. This set in motion a process of degeneration that took the practice of ritual to the limit of absurdity, making almost a mockery of the ancient religion, the process continued till almost the present times.

The knowledge about the Creator, it is claimed, is attained through the Veda and the Tantra; the latter, in fact, in general terms, is regarded as an elucidation of the Vedic experience. The process of creation has been explained in the Tantra by a diagram called the *chakra*, the Circle (shown in Fig. 5.1) — it could also mean the Universe or the Cosmos. The centre of the diagram is the dot, *bindu*, and around it are two triangles, one with apex upwards and the other with apex downwards, and this total arrangement is within a circle which has eight lotus petals marked around its circumference, each lotus petal having two filaments. The dot in the centre stands for absolute consciousness, *chitta*, 'the all pervading Universal Force, the Supreme Being'; its nature is absolute joy, the supreme bliss, and it expresses itself 'in the form of knowledge, desire and action.' These are represented in Fig. 5.1 by three points around the central dot, and when these points are joined, they form a triangle, of which the dot becomes the centre, and this triangle is referred to as the *yoni*, the place of origin, the source, of all consciousness in the creation. Immediately around it are the static force, *sthiti*, represented by the triangle with apex upwards, and the dynamic force, *gati*, represented by the other triangle. The two, in effect form one unit, and are inseparable.

Fig. 5.1 : The process of creation represented by the chakra

Somewhere in this matrix is the primordial atom in repose, that which is the potential universe(s), and beyond this is the abode of the Absolute Being, represented by the dot. The creation process is activated by the intense heat in the womb of *Rta*, which is a characteristic of the Absolute Being, and it reaches a stage, may be after an explosion (the Big Bang!) or otherwise, when it propels into action the static and the dynamic forces (the two inseparable opposites), and expands; the expansion is represented by the circle. This is *mula prakriti*, the primal matter. This is also the *hiranya garbha*, the golden germ, the primordial egg, or seed. Hiranaya means heat, light, brightness, splendour, energy, effulgence, the fire-ball of the Universe immediately following the activation of the static and the dynamic forces, and it is the *garbha*, the Womb, for the creation in the form of primordial matter and consciousness comes out of this. For, simultaneously with the explosion of the primordial atom, the source, *yoni*, comprising knowledge, desire and action, also gets activated and pours forth consciousness in an unending stream. Rta, the ultimate dynamic and harmonic structure of the Reality, which operates alongside the creating energy, is what controls this process. Though Agni, Fire, the visible aspect of *Rta*, resides in *Rta*'s womb, its non-visible aspect is water, out which is born Brahma, the mysterious fluid which pervades the Universe, and is the cause of its creation. The things pick up shape and form because of the dynamic and static aspects of *Rta*, in that the static aspect moves in a direction opposite to that of the dynamic aspect, or matter and anti-matter particles interact with each other, till, ultimately a state of stability is reached and shapes and forms are discernible in the unidirectional flow of energy. That is how 'by *Rta* is *Rta* controlled', or the veracity of the statement is established that for every thing seen there is that which is not seen. Thus is *Rta*, the abode of Brahma, the creator, canalising the creating process along harmonic and dynamic lines, and thus is Dharma, the law, born. This is the law that governs the functioning of each single entity of the creation, including the functioning of human beings and their institutions. It is the *Rta* aspect of the Creating Energy that ensures that the activation of the static and the dynamic forces takes place at the right level of heat so that once the matter has been projected into time and space — which, incidentally, are also the aspects of *Rta*—, it goes on along its projected course till the time comes for the Universe to fold up and ultimately recollapse into the Primordial Atom. *Rta* ensures uniformity in the expansion of the Universe, and no matter what stars and galaxies get formed, the process initiated once is sure to complete its course without ever degenerating into chaos. *Rta* thus is the force of creation, while Dharma is that which sustains it. The dividing line, however, is hard to see, for in all non volitional activity, Dharma appears to be the same as *Rta*: it has its modes of creation, sustenance, and annihilation. It assumes significance essentially in the volitional human activity. Violation of Dharma is the sure-fire road to annihilation.

That the Universe is governed by predetermined laws in all its activity, and that the shackles of these laws just cannot be broken, is the burden of the later Vedic thought. This is also the basic idea that runs through the heart of Hinduism. Karma philosophy, and the idea of the transmigration of soul is the outcome of this thought. What it implies, in effect, is that there is no God as such, or there are no gods, keeping watch on the activities of the living beings. It is the Law that takes care of everything. The Law, or Dharma, is active and effective not only in the physical realm but also in the sphere of speech and thought; these are constituents of the Word, a dimension of the Creator, one amongst many known and unknown dimensions. Bad or evil speech or thought will precipitate bad results while the reverse is true of the good thoughts or speech. Prayer has effect, as also meditation, contemplation or singing of hymns or devotional songs, for Word influences *Rta*. The system of Vedic rituals is essentially based on the same idea. Rituals and invons, in the shape of, we might say, formulas, are designed to influence the gods, representing different aspects of the energy, *Rta*, even though they are, strictly speaking, not prayers as understood in the normal mode of worship.

To come back to the *chakra*, in the beginning it is pure consciousness and pure primal matter, *mula prakriti* and, the two have not mixed, and, therefore, there is no presence of form. But as the process expands, a stage arrives when conditions are right for the *mula prakriti* to split; in this split state it is called the *bhinna prakriti*, i.e., split up *primal matter*. The splitting is in eight elements, five being earth, fire, water, air and *akaasha*, and the three, *manas*, mind, the seat of all emotions, *buddhi*, intellect, including thought and understanding, and *ahankaar*, ego. The term *akaasha* means space, ether, vacuity (emptiness); it is all-penetrating and infinite, like the Creator. This split is represented on the circle by the eight petals of lotus. Two filaments in each lotus petal represent sentinence and insentinence. This is the stage when name and form appear on the scene of the universe. With time and continued expansion, the conditions become right for the further split of the

Primal Matter, and the eight lotus petals get increased to twenty four, representing the new elements that get evolved in nature, like sensory and motor organs and subtle and gross elements, all of which combine to evolve life.

The Creation hymn in the *Nasadiya Sukta* of the Rig Veda (X.129) goes somewhat on the following lines:

> Then even nothingness (Asat) was not, nor existence Sat. There was no air then nor the heavens beyond it. Who covered it? Where was it? In whose keeping Was there then cosmic water, in depths unfathomed? Death was not then, nor any sign of day or night. That One-Thing, breathless, breathed by its own nature, *svadhaya*; apart from that there was nothing whatsoever.
>
> Darkness, *Tamas*, there was; at first concealed in this darkness, this all, *Sarvam dam*, was indiscriminated chaos (plasma, *aparketam salilam*). All that existed then was void and formlessness: By the great power of warmth, *Tapisah Mahina* was born that unit, *tat ekam*.
>
> Thereafter rose desire, *kama*, in the beginning; Desire, the primal seed and germ of spirit, *Prathamam retah*. ...
>
> But, then, after all, who knows and who can say, whence it all came, and how creation happened? For gods themselves are later than creation.

The technical terms in the creation hymn could be differently interpreted, and this can bring the description of the creation process surprisingly close to what modern sciences are discovering today.

The expansion process of the universe goes on and a stage is reached when, what till then appeared as chaos, gradually starts showing orderliness and movement towards stability. The idea underlying the Chakra diagram is that through knowledge and right experience is the understanding of the Reality achieved and it is possible to get past the net cast by the *Bhinna Prakriti* (the net which is the cause of all ignorance), and understand the truth in its most magnificent form, and ultimately reach the Reality, the Dot, *bindu*, and merge with it and be freed of the Birth-Death cycle. The *chakra* has influenced the design of the sacred structures of the Hindus, including the temples and the sacrificial altars, or the pillars supporting the structure of a place of religion. Even the Sivalingam is representing the same idea; the Buddhist stupa is just a magnified form of Sivalingam, or the pillar.

All the while when Brahma, the mysterious fluid, which is pure energy and consciousness, is causing the expansion of the universe, or the Creation, what remains unmoved is the Dot, the ultimate source of everything, including Brahma; it reposes in its pristine purity as absolute consciousness, embodiment of *Ananda*, pure bliss. Time is born when, impelled by the infinite heat in the womb of *Rta*, the primordial atom begins its expansion, along with the pouring forth of knowledge, desire and action; like *Rta* these too are the constituents of the Absolute Consciousness. Time, *kaal*, is a constituent, or an attribute, of the *mahakaal*, who is also referred to as *akaal*, That which is not bound by time, which creates time but is not affected by it.

Mula Prakriti of Brahma expands till it breaks down into *Bhinna Prakriti*, the primordial matter split into different constituents, and conditions become ripe for the evolution of life.

The expansion process of the Universe goes on and a stage is reached when, what till then appeared as chaos, gradually starts showing orderliness and movement towards stability. The idea of the diagram is that by acquiring knowledge by studying the Vedas it is possible to understand the reality and get past the net cast by the *Bhinna Prakriti* (the net which causes ignorance), and understand the truth in its magnificent form, and ultimately reach the Reality, the Dot, *bindu*, and merge with it, and be freed from the life-death cycle. The diagram has influenced the design of most sacred structures of the Hindus, including temples, or sacrificial altars, or the pillars erected to support any sanctified place, i.e., the design incorporates the relative positioning of the *bindu*, the square, the circle and the lotus petals. Even the Sivalingam is representing the same idea; some scholars believe that the Buddhist stupa is just a magnified form of Sivalingam or the pillar.

All the while, when the Creator, Brahma, the mysterious fluid which is pure energy and consciousness, is busy in the creational process, the Dot, the ultimate source of everything, including Brahma, is unmoved, and stays in its pristine purity, as absolute consciousness, embodiment of *ananda*, pure bliss. According to the Vedic religion, the time is born when, impelled by the infinite heat in the womb of *Rta*, the Primordial Atom begins its expansion along with the three forces of knowledge, desire and action pouring forth from the divine source; like *Rta* these too are constituents of the absolute consciousness. Time is *kaal*, and from whom the time is born is *Maha kaal*. He is also referred to as *akaal*, that which is not bound by time, which creates time but is in no way affected by it. The universe of the Brahma expands, and as has been stated earlier, at some stage the *Mula Prakriti*, the primordial matter, breaks down into *Bhinna Prakriti*, the broken down constituents of the primordial matter, and conditions become ripe for the evolution of life. According to *Vishnu Purana* this activity of Brahma, from the time of the first explosion, or stirring, starting the process of creation, to its reaching the zenith, and its final collapse, when everything gets wrapped up and all that remains is the absolute consciousness and the primordial atom (which is an attribute of the former), lasts for the duration of one *kalpa*, which is one day of the Brahma. Thereafter it is the night, *pralaya*, of the Brahma, when it is non-existent, more or less. With the rise of the next day, the creation begins again, like it did the previous day. In this fashion The Brahma is on the job for one hundred years, at the end of which another Brahma is born, and the process is continued unabated. However, at the end of one *kalpa* only the finer, delicate, fragile, constituents of creation get eliminated. The gods, sages and the substance of the universe stay intact. It is only at the end of the life of a Brahma that there is complete annihilation when the elements merge with the primary substance, 'besides which only one spiritual being exists'. A *Kalpa*, comprises *manvantras* and *mahayugas*. A *mahayuga* has four *Yugas*, time cycles, and out of these the *Sat Yuga*, the time cycle when absolute virtue prevails over the universe, is the first, and is of 17,28,000 years. *Treta Yuga*, when the virtue element has been reduced to about 75 per cent, is the second cycle, of 12,96,000 years. Then is the *Dwapara Yuga*, of 8,64,000 years, with the virtue element reduced to about 50 per cent, and finally it is the *Kali Yuga*, the time we live in presently, of

4,32,000 years, where the virtue element is down to around 25 per cent. What it boils down to is that the human being has evolved in the final yuga and the enquiring intelligence is at full play, and has a role in the evolutionary process. The inert morality has limited relevance in the existence of the human beings and even everything else of this earth which is influenced by the human existence. The total of these four yugas, 43,20,000 years, is one *Maha Yuga*. Seventy one *maha yugas* make one *manvantra*, during which the different worlds of the Universe are under the care of one Manu. Planet earth is said to have come into being during the period of Manu Svayambhu. Fourteen *manvantras* plus six *mahayugas* together make one *kalpa*; this works out to 1000 *maha Yugas*, i.e., a day of Brahma is equal to 4.32 billion years. His night pralaya, is of the same duration. Thus creation and annihilation of the finer and fragile constituents of the universe, *bhinna prakriti*, takes place during a cycle of 4.32 billion years, and this is followed by a period of an equal interval of time when the process reposes. It again springs into action with the start of the new *kalpa*, and so this process of making and annihilation goes on till the stage is reached for complete annihilation at the end of the life of Brahma, which is $4.32 \times 2 \times 360 \times 100$ billion years; one year of Brahma has 360 days (*Kalpas*) and an equal number of nights.

What is one to make of the *yugas* and the *maha yugas*? There have been various thoughts, some as naive as suggesting they represent the four seasons of the year, ending in the deluge — monsoons — after which the cycle begins again. Traditional history based on the accounts recorded in the *Puranas*, states that the four ages, namely *Krita*, *Treta*, *Dvapara*, and *Kali*, flourished during the times of kings Sagara, Rama and Krishna, respectively, not taking into account the *Kali* age, being the current one, and that the first age covers roughly 40 generations; *Treta* 25 generations; while *Dvapara* covers 30 generations. Obviously this is being given out in a context different from that which is dealing with the age of the universe. Other accounts in the same history give out the beginning of the *Dvapara* age with the coronation of Rama after his return to Ayodhya, and its end, and the beginning of the Kali age, with the end of the Mahabharata war. This too could not have anything to do with the speculation of the age of the universe. However, some accounts place the end of the Mahabharata war and the start of the age of Kali in 3102 BC. There is an obvious confusion here, for, as stated earlier, the Mahabharata war cannot be placed much earlier than 1400 BC.; But it can be inferred that some event of great historical value took place at this time. This date, on the basis of the accounts of the traditional history, also works out to be the date of the great flood and the start of the period of Manu Vaivasvata (Manu of the seventh, the present, *manvantra*), who is believed to be the originator of the human race, although the legend about the flood would suggest that Manu Vaivasvata was not the originator of the human race but a member of it who, after the entire of his clan had perished in the flood, restarted the process of raising the clan along with Ida, the female. He has been remembered well and with respect by the following generations, and was, apparently, a man of great character, wisdom and foresight. He is thus of the present age, the originator of the age of competitive materialism when dialectical, achievement oriented activity has gradually overtaken activity based purely on virtue and religious ethos. Therefore the year 3102 BC., or there abouts, is the start of the *Kaliyuga* (this is supported by the astronomical tradition represented by Aryabhatta).

In the calculations about the age of the universe one *Mahayuga* has 4.32 million years, and 71 *Mahayugas* make one *manvantra*, i.e., the period presided over by one Manu for taking care of the universe. This period would be 306.72 million years. A *kalpa*, i.e., a day of Brahma, has 14 *Manvantras*, and there are six additional *Mahayugas* during which the collapse of the *Bhinna Prakriti* takes place; this is referred to as the evening of the *kalpa*. A *kalpa*, thus, has a total of 1000 *Mahayugas*, and is of 4.32 billion years. Thus, while total annihilation takes place after 100 years of Brahma, the annihilation of the finer and delicate constituents is once in every 4.32 billion years; subtle variations in the creation pattern get effected during each *manvantra*. The creation process is highly dynamic, and changes are taking place all the time; there never is a stage when any of its constituents is static. But one *manvantra* differs from the other, may be, in terms of the flora and fauna, and other aspects. *Yugas* and *Mahayugas* too signify stages of changes in the structure of the universe. Evolution is a gradual process. To begin with the matter (*Mula Prakriti*) and consciousness are floating side by side. With the evolving of the *bhinna prakriti* the interaction between *prakriti*, or matter, and consciousness begins. The direction of this interaction is towards the evolution of the three subtle attributes of matter, namely, intellect, mind and ego. In the beginning these attributes are almost dormant, but gradually they become defined and definite, and get mixed with consciousness, and then there emerges life which has all the three attributes pretty well developed. The ultimate development of this process appears to be the human being. We are in the period of the seventh Manu, in the seventh *manvantra*, which is almost the mid-point of the *kalpa*. The earth has already gone through the first three *yugas* of this *Mahayuga*, but of the *Kali Yuga* of 4,32,000 years, we have done only around 5000; there is thus a long way to go. The typical characteristic of this *yuga* is the continuous sharpening of the subtle attributes, namely, intellect, mind and ego. Therefore, there is a lot ahead. *Vishnu Purana* says that towards the end of the Kali age an incarnation of Vishnu in the form of Kalki shall descend upon the earth to rid it of rapacious, self serving tyrants, and the people shall be awakened from wrong concepts and shall be rendered as pellucid as crystal.

That life was first formed in water is borne by the concept of the *Dasha Avatars*, the ten reincarnations of Vishnu, whereunder He appears on earth, from time to time, in appropriate forms, to protect His beings from inimical developments. The first time He came down was in the form of fish, an indication of origin of life in water, then as a tortoise, when life moved from water on to dry land, then as a boar, when herbivores had evolved, and then as lion, when carnivores came into being. The remaining *avatars*, (incarnations), namely, Vaman, Parshurama, Rama, Krishna, and Buddha, appeared to rid the humanity from evil despots. The last one, Kalki has yet to appear; the manifestation shall take place at the appropriate time, towards the end of the Kali age, to rid the earth of highly rapacious, overly materialistic and self serving tyrants.

Creation is a manifestation of a mysterious power, energy, which, in a matter of speaking, spills out of the *Hiranya Garbha*, the golden germ — golden because it is absolute fire —, and which has two constituents, namely consciousness and matter. Pure energy has no name or form. It is just energy, invisible, like, let us say, electricity flowing through a conductor. But the two attributes of the energy that manifests as matter, namely, *stithi*, the static aspect, and *gati*, the dynamic aspect, finally combine together to produce name and form. The function of the former is to interact with the dynamic force, and create the illusion of static forms, of creation, and impart name, form, shape, to things that then appear created on the infinitely vast canvas, so to say, of the Creator.

In the Hindu thought, the Absolute Creator is the Reality comprising absolute bliss, the ocean of consciousness. One of its attributes is the creation of the universe, and that is represented by the Brahma characteristic, the Creator. The aspects of the sustaining and annihilation of the universe are represented by the Vishnu and Shiva characteristics respectively, and together the three form the Hindu trinity. But the core idea is the ocean of consciousness and bliss, and the attribute of creation. Thus the Creator as such is visualized in two modes, that of bliss in which state He is free of Karma, the need to perform, and that of the Creator, in which state He is energy manifested as the working universe. In the Hindu pantheon the blissful mode is represented as the male symbol and the creator mode as the female symbol or *shakti*, the absolute power or creating energy, which also takes care of what it creates. The blissful mode is the infinite sea of consciousness, and peace and tranquillity, the very core out of which everything comes, including the creator mode. This is the abode the soul attains after it has been freed of the birth-death cycle of the matter in which it is trapped. The Hindu iconography as evolved over the centuries, thus, depicts God as a male-female pair, the male aspect representing the absolute God, the abode of peace and bliss, above the tribulations caused by Karma, and the female aspect representing creation; the examples of this iconography are Radha-Krishna, Vishnu-Lakshmi, Sita-Rama or Shiva-Parvati. The Saivas visualize Him as *Ardhanarishvara* also, i.e., half male and half female, to emphasize the fact that what creates (the female aspect) has its roots in the abode of bliss and tranquillity (the male aspect) and that part of Him (the male aspect) though not directly in the process of creation, sustenance or annihilation, is ultimately the very source and the cause of it all, all this creation, that while an attribute of Him is the activity of Creation (the female aspect), the whole of Him is just actionless tranquillity and bliss (the male aspect). Visualizing the creating energy as female is particularly helpful in devotional form of worship. Here God is mother, and it is much easier to love the mother than father or any other relationship. In fact, the basic idea of Mother worship is the worship of the active principal of the Creator, the aspect which, it is believed, is actively concerned and involved with the well-being of the creation, including the human beings. This distinction between the two aspects is essential, for, if it is accepted that after being delivered of the *sansara*, the soul eventually merges with the eternal Creator, then there cannot be much to speak of in favour of merger with a force which is always in activity. In deliverence the requirement is for peace and bliss and not for entering a sea of perpetual activity. This same concept also holds good for the Buddhist *shoonya* or void.

The dynamic and the static forces combine together to produce the impression of things and this can happen only when things have attained some kind of a static status. But the things being in a static state is only an impression; otherwise there is nothing static as such. It is the interplay of the two forces which is what the manifested creation is all about. And where such interaction has not taken place, and it has not in the case of a fairly high percentage of the energy that emanated out of the *Hiranya Garbha* —, the phenomenon of the name and form is missing; no creation is visible. This possibly happens because the attributes of the creating energy that precipitate manifestation of creation, are not present any and everywhere.

The power that creates, the Brahma, the unknowable and incomprehensible, is understood to be *nirguna*, without attributes or qualities, transcendent Absolute. When we talk of Brahma without attributes, the meaning is that the attributes of this creating force are so many and so complex that it is neither possible to enumerate them, nor to understand them, so that a definable, comprehensible picture cannot be made in our minds about the form or shape of this energy. In Bhakti, or devotional worship, God has attributes, for it is not possible to develop devotion for anyone or anything that cannot be conceptualized. For this purpose the being of devotion has to be visualized in human, or near human, image and as worthy of respect, even awe, for its great powers, and for being omnipotent, omniscient, beneficient, kind and merciful. It has to possess appealing looks, and be visualized as the destroyer of the oppressors, one who is mighty and can fulfil the wishes of the devotees and generally look after them. This is Brahma with attributes of Ishvara, the personal God. But this is only a modification permitted essentially to help develop devotion and love in the heart and the mind of the worshipper. Otherwise the real Creator is only *nirguna*, the one without attributes, and the followers of the Bhakti mode have no doubt that as the intensity of devotion develops, the object of devotion gently and gradually changes from the *saguna* to the *nirguna*.

As has been stated earlier, Brahma, the force, power, energy, that creates, is, on the basis of the narrations in the Vedic literature, the cosmic fluid, and the myriad things that the human eyes see, or for that matter the eyes of all the sentient beings see, from the smallest germ to the stars and galaxies, and much more that is not perceived, is a phenomenon precipitated by the interaction of *stithi* and *gati*, the static and the dynamic forces. Where the interaction is successful, manifestation takes place, but where there is no interaction, or where it is not successful, nothing is perceived, and the cosmic fluid, the combine of matter and consciousness, flows on, unseen, though in full potency. The question we can ask is: whether the flow of energy is basically for the purpose of creating a manifested universe? May be, may be not. Manifestation could be purely incidental, although to us human beings it appears to be the only reason, for it is not possible for us to comprehend any other purpose. However, the entire flowing energy does not convert into manifested universe. Take the example of seeds contained in a pod on a tree. All the seeds that the tree produces do not fortify into trees; hardly an odd one does. Nature does appear to possess super abundance, but when it comes to creating something which has a presence and is visible, useable and viable, its capacity seems to get restricted, possibly because so much goes into making completed objects. The inter-dependence of the created entities is the major cause of the restrictions in the proliferations in their growth. But why does this great fluid spill out in the first place? For whose benefit? Vedas are silent on this. But the Puranas state that all this is a divine play, the *lila* of the Absolute Consciousness. He seems to have been conditioned to these cycles of creations and dissolutions, and, may be, He likes it this way. Otherwise there does not appear to be any reason, which might suggest to the infinitesimally small human mind as to what this, that he witnesses around himself and experiences, is all about.

Thus, according to Hindu thought, the consciousness that spills out of the divine source, an attribute of the absolute consciousness, and which has knowledge, desire and action as its constituents, mingles with the *bhinna prakriti*, the split up primordial matter, at an appropriate stage, and we have seeds of evolution, which ultimately bring forth the sentient beings. The process, in the form of birth-death cycles, with all the pains and rewards and the intense struggle that go with it, with the ego erroneously assuming a distinct identity for itself, proceeds at a feverish pitch, generating perpetual restlessness, from inception to dissolution in cycle after cycle of creations. There is only one place where there is complete serenity, peace, and, consequently, absolute bliss, and that is the seat of absolute consciousness, and that is where the freedom is from the febrile agitation which the *bhinna prakriti* inflicts upon the element of consciousness trapped within it. The role of religion is to guide the individual towards this seat of absolute consciousness.

Belief in the continuous life-death cycle is fundamental to Hinduism. Like matter, which is indestructible, consciousness too cannot be destroyed. It is not something which is part of matter or is evolved out of it. It is a separate mode of the creating energy, an entity by itself. What mantle the spirit takes on at each birth is dependent upon the karmas, the collection of deeds performed during different cycles of life. The resultant impact of the thoughts and deeds puts a kind of a wrapper around the spirit, the soul, and, imparts to it a distinct identity, which, no doubt, keeps changing with the accumulation of fresh karmas. Soon, as in the picture of Dorian Grey, the pristine lustrous form of the soul is no longer discernible. What is discernible is a distorted and ugly image of the karmic mantle within which the spirit has been trapped. The process of creation is so programmed that after the spirit departs from one material body, it picks up the next on the basis of the residue of its Karmas. The process continues even after the creation has ceased, for in the following cycle the process starts from where it was left off during the preceding one. Only after liberation from the debilitating and chokingly arresting influence of the karmas, does the spirit soar free in the zone of absolute bliss.

Buddha, who did not believe in the existence and identity of individual souls, has said that it is the collection of karmas alone which decides about the type of body which comes into being after the body that performed those karmas has perished. The ultimate aim, however, in both the cases, i.e. in the Hindu as well as the Buddhist traditions, remains the same, which is to secure freedom from the stranglehold of karmas so as to attain Nirvana, for the Buddhists, or *moksha*, for the Hindus; in the former case the deliverance is for the consciousness in general, while in the latter it is for the consciousness in the form of the individual soul.

Another issue which is fundamental to Hinduism, essentially to the Vaishnava sect, is their belief in *avataras*, i.e., the descent of God as incarnation of Vishnu (the ultimate Creator) with a view to putting right the wrongs that might be threatening to interfere with or dislocate the orderly movement of the creation in time and space. As has been stated earlier, *Rta* and Dharma take care of this. The concept of *avatara* implies that there is an inbuilt mechanism which activates an element of the Absolute Creator whenever the process tends to get out of hand. In the mythological and other religious literature this has been explained, for the understanding of the common folk, in the form of tales and stories of gods and goddesses, and their interaction with God, and His descent in an appropriate form to protect His species from the pressures of negatively inclined accumulations in the creation process. The first of the incarnations of God, Vishnu, is in the form of a fish, suggesting that under the divine scheme the first to appear on this planet was marine life, and so on, till we have incarnations in human form, essentially to protect the human species. While *Rta* and Dharma perform their own roles, corrective mechanism has to come into operation from time to time to fine-tune the protective process, particularly when it concerns a specific part of the creation and not the whole of it, e.g., a species, like the human race, or the humanity in a particular segment of the world. And these corrections, by implication, are not restricted only to this planet; they come into operation for the whole system of creation.

> Whenever, in any age, there is a fall in righteousness, and unrighteousness increases, then I incarnate myself, so as to protect the good and destroy all that is wicked, and re-establish righteousness'.
>
> *Geeta IV, 7,8.*

In effect God reincarnates Himself whenever or where ever the precepts of Dharma are ignored; the belief is that this would endanger the very survival of the human race. Dharma is what holds together. It is the basis of all order and covers in its ambit the religious or moral merit. In his translation and commentary on Bhagvadgita, Radhakrishnan says:

> It is the essential nature of a being that determines his or her behaviour. So long as our conduct is in conformity with our essential nature, we are acting in the right way. Adharma is non-conformity to our nature. If the harmony of the world is derived from the conformity of all beings to their respective natures, the disharmony of the world is due to their non-conformity. God does not stand aside, when we abuse our freedom and cause disequilibrium. He does not simply wind up the world, set it on the right track and then let it jog along by itself. His loving hand is steering it all the time.

However, the belief is prevalent essentially amongst the followers of Vishnu. Saivas do not have any such concept. For them Siva is the lord of creation, and the system of creation that has come into being is such that it automatically takes care of the negative influences. Such influences might exhibit temporary success, but are eventually overtaken by the system and get eliminated.

There are other accounts too of how the creation came into being. In one account in the Vedic literature — the essential items in Vedic worship are fire and sacrifice, i.e., sacrificial offerings into the fire, — the creation has come into being as a result of the sacrifice of Prajapati, the primordial God, who dismembers and immolates himself in order to create the universe and make it what it is. On the basis of this hymn there is none other than Prajapati to whom the sacrifice could be made, for there is no other existence. Prajapati himself is the sacrificer, the victim and the one to whom the sacrifice is offered; he is also the result of the sacrifice. The creation comes into being through the pressure of *kama* and *tapas*, desire and heat. 'Tapas is the primordial fervour, the original fire, the supreme concentration, the ultimate energy, the creative force, that initiates the whole cosmic movement.' Kama, desire in this situation, according to scholars, indicates the birth of consciousness, which is born alongside Tapas, the original fire, and incites it to the point from where creation is initiated, i.e., spills out of the *Hiranya Garbha*. This has been projected as the dismemberment of Prajapati.

The *Hiranya Garbha* hymn (Rv. X 121) describes God as the effulgent being, the Creator of everything, the mighty one, who has established the laws of movement, and the order in the universe, and the hymn enjoins that we should worship only that God. Hymn at Rv. X 190 states that from Tapas, or fervour, or heat kindled to its extreme, Rta, the eternal law, or the cosmic order, and *satya*, the truth, were born, and then was produced the night, *ratri, tamas*, and thence the ocean of cosmic intelligence from where came the time, and days and nights. The great Creator, *Dhata*, then, as in the previous creations, formed sun and the moon, the celestial heaven and earth, the regions of air and the *Svar*, the regions beyond.

As we have seen, the earlier portion of the Vedic literature comprises the Mantras, contained essentially in the form of hymns in the Sanhitas of the Rig and the Atharva Vedas. So much time has elapsed since their composition, at least of the earlier ones, that today it is hardly possible to interpret them satisfactorily. The Mantras are followed by the Brahmanas, which have laid emphasis upon the importance of ritual, laying down even small details for the performance of sacrifices. They also contained the roots of earlier Upanishads in the form of Aranyakas, the forest treatises compiled by people who had renounced the world and retreated to the forests where it was not possible to perform the elaborate rituals as laid down in the Brahmanas. The literature that they put forth was not related to the sacrifice, but bordered on interiorization. Both the Brahmanas and the Aranyakas are kind of appendices to different branches and schools of the *Sanhitas*. And finally came the Upanishadas, forming part of what is commonly termed as *Vedanta*, the end of the Veda, and contain the mystical and philosophical thoughts based on what their authors thought was the essence of the knowledge contained in the Vedas, including complex issues like the origination of the universe, whither it was heading, what was its fate, relationship between the Creator and the beings of the universe, and so on. Alongside the Upanishads came the Vedangas, the limbs of the Vedas, dealing with phonetics and correct pronunciation of the language of the Vedas, metrics, etymology, grammar, and astronomy (to determine the correct timings for the Vedic rituals). One of the Vedangas, Kalpa, deals with the details for the correct performance of the sacred rites. These details are recorded in the form of Sutras, aphorisms, and cover every phase of the life of an individual, like domestic rituals including *sanskaras*, sacraments dealing with birth, marriage, death and so on, public sacrifice, rules and duties of a citizen, obligations of a ruler and the state. The legal literature, the Dharma-shastras, are a part of this Vedanga.

In the early stages the Veda emphasized the Mantra, which along with the prescribed ritual and sacrifice, was all that was required to urge the gods to grant the wishes of the sacrificer. This is the stage when the reincarnation theory is not known and the belief is that after death the soul travels to the abode of the *pitris*, the fore-fathers, living and enjoying in the company of gods, and, possibly, equally powerful. Gods are natural elements, like rain, fire, earth, sky, and prayers are addressed to them essentially for worldly gains: wealth, sons, good crops, general well-being. In later hymns the idea of reward after death for good deeds and punishment for bad ones, seems to have taken root. According to this idea the good souls go to *svar loka* where they have a good time and the bad ones travel to *naraka loka* where they are subjected to suffering and hardship. Only in the tenth book of the Rig Veda, which contains late hymns, there are two passages which vaguely suggest the idea of rebirth. It seems the idea found place in the Aryan thought and literature from an earlier civilization.

In the later Vedic literature, i.e., the Aranyakas and the Upanishads, the importance of the sacrifice has diminished and the idea of devotion to the deity has caught on; a tendency towards this is apparent in the later Vedic hymns and the Brahmanas. The Aranyakas almost completely broke off from the way of sacrifice and emphasized the importance of Bhakti, i.e., prayer and devotion, while the Upanishads, laid stress on the importance of acquisition of knowledge, *gyan*, about the Absolute Reality. Without such a knowledge, Upanishads argued, it was not possible to fully practise even Bhakti.

In the later hymns of the Rig Veda and the Brahmanas, the attributes of all gods — they were earlier identified with the elements of nature — have become similar: they are *devas*, luminous, and maintain the world order, are omniscient, omnipotent, friends of the virtuous, and so on. The time is ripe for the emergence of one God. But this is not the God of monotheism, it is just that power that works behind all the gods, a Being who possesses the qualities of all of them, Prajapati, the 'Father god', who has created all beings as his children. A concept of *Rta*, the power that maintains the world order, has been worked out, and Prajapati is visualized as born out of it. Later, however, with the spread of Upanishadic thought, the Prajapati has been relegated to a somewhat secondary place; sometimes he has been referred to as Brahma of the Hindu Trinity.

There are many Upanishadic compilations, though only twelve or so are regarded as authentic Vedic literature. The point they stress is that the ultimate reality is spiritual in its nature, and everything else exists in it and through it. Everything created has this reality as its integral part; in fact, everything of the Creation is just a manifestation of this reality, an aspect of it, a facet, a version may be, there is nothing outside of it, be it the spirits of the sentient beings or the physical universe; all this is one whole that expands when creation is manifested, and goes back to the *bindu* stage, the dot, when it is the dissolution. And this process of expansion and contraction goes on interminably. This reality is *Sat, Chit, Anand,* i.e., being (existence, the reality), sentience, and bliss. This is the monoism of the Upanishads.

Six

The Systems of Philosophy

There are six orthodox systems of Indian philosophy, *Astika-Darshanas*, which believe in the authority of the Veda, and are called as the Vaidic schools. In addition there are three heterodox systems, *nastika-darshanas*, which do not accept the authority of the Veda, and are classified as Avaidic. The Vaidic schools are :

(a) Nyaya,
(b) Vaisheshika,
(c) Sankhya,
(d) Yoga,
(e) Purva-Mimansa; and
(f) Uttara-Mimansa or Vedanta.

The three Avaidic systems are Charvaka, Buddhism and Jainism. Out of the Vaidic systems Purva-Mimansa and Vedanta are strictly Vedic, while the other four accept the Vedic authority but are not dependent upon it, i.e., they expound their doctrines without reference to the Veda. In other words, the authors of these systems have given their own interpretations of the Veda which do not fully coincide with the commonly held beliefs. It is possible that some of these doctrines are of pre-Aryan times and were modified in the light of the Vedic writings. While discussing the systems, Nyaya and Vaisheshika are generally grouped together because of their similarity on most points. Likewise, Sankhya and Yoga are also grouped together.

As has been stated earlier, the generally accepted period for the Vedic age is 1200-1500 BC. Lately views have been expressed by eminent scholars, both western and Indian, which place the period as early as 2000-2500 BC. Earlier, western scholars had put the period just a few centuries before Christ, but that was mostly on account of limited information at their disposal, in fact the period could indeed be 2000-2500 BC. or even earlier. The systems came into being a couple of centuries after the Vedic age, i.e., after the dozen odd classical Upanishads had been compiled. During this time, regarded as the period of prolific intellectual activity, many philosophical treatises had come out and, in an attempt to systematize and preserve them, their *Sutras*, or aphorisms, had been compiled. Each system has its own *Sutra*, though in the case of *Sankhya*, the *Sutra* was compiled much later. Even the non-Vedic systems have their Sutras.

The systems have argued their cases on the basis of *parmanas*, or means of knowledge. The empirical *parmanas* are, perception (*pratyaksha*), inference, (*anumana*), and verbal testimony, or (*sabda*). Verbal testimony as *parmana* implies acquisition of knowledge from others, since it is not possible to get the whole of it through personal study or experience. The literature of study could either be revealed, *Sruti*, like the Veda, or man-made. The latter could have errors, depending upon the capability of its author to critically analyse the acquired knowledge, and cannot be fully relied upon. The knowledge obtained from *Sruti*, though more reliable since it has come from inspired minds, could also have faults, since the person to whom it was revealed, could have had defective understanding. Therefore, even such a knowledge could be accepted only if it had the approval of learned persons, granted on the basis of their knowledge of the *Sruti*, and their experience. Both Purva-Mimansa and the Vedanta accept this and for verbal testimony have taken the support of the portions of *Sruti* which the illumined minds have found to be totally acceptable.

Mimansa means enquiry, and Purva-Mimansa means enquiry into the earlier portions of the Veda, while Uttara-Mimansa (Vedanta) means enquiry into its later portions; Uttara means later or subsequent. The widely used expression is Vedanta, for Uttara-Mimansa, and just Mimansa for Purva-Mimansa. According to

Mimansa, action in the form of ritual, *Karma-Kanda*, is the means to *moksha*, while Shankra in his expositions on Vedanta has stated that the way to *moksha* is through knowledge, *gyana*. But what is Karma?

In a broad sense the doctrine of Karma visualizes;

(a) a soul,

(b) that it transmigrates and takes on another body after the one it is housed in has perished,

(c) that the type of body it adopts when reincarnated, depends upon the deeds performed during the previous births. In effect the soul is neither born nor does it die; it is eternal. But it is trapped in matter which assumes name and form depending upon the deeds of the previous births. The shapes and forms of sentience vary between vegetation at the lower end (grass is the lowest form of life according to this gradation) and man at the higher end (Brahmin male is the highest because he not only studies Veda but teaches it too).

The term *karma-kand* means ritual-action, i.e., recitation of Mantras along with performance of sacrifice as laid down in the Veda and the Brahmanas. The basic assumption in all systems is that it is the deeds which are the cause of the rebirth, and hence suffering. The systems have devoted substantial attention to the type of activity which does not contribute to rebirth, for it is accepted that all sentient beings have to be active, ceaseless activity being one of the most important attributes of the power behind all creation. *Geeta* in the 49th verse of the 18th Chapter, says that he whose understanding is unattached everywhere, who has subdued his self and from whom desire has fled — he attains, through renunciation, the supreme state, transcending all work. In other words renunciation and absence of desire are essential to spiritual perfection, and it is the spiritual perfection alone that destroys the effect of the deeds, or makes them ineffectual, in so far as rebirth is concerned. In the highest state of perfection there has to be complete absence of desire. This is described as the state of *naishkarmya*, that state which transcends all work. Some religious teachers have been of the view that, as given in verse 47, Chapter 2 of *Geeta*, mere renunciation of the fruits of action is adequate to attain the state of *nishkarma*. This verse says: "As a being of action, your right is only to act, but not to the fruits thereof. Therefore, let the fruits of action be not your motive; nor should there be in you any attachment to inaction."

Giving up the fruits of action implies giving up the ego, for ego makes a person believe he is the author of the deed, and this happens because the soul wrongfully identifies itself with the physical mind-body complex. It is this identification which is bondage. In other words, whatever a person does he has to do it as his duty towards the Creator, and consider that work as a sacrifice, without considering it as an achievement of his mind-body complex. Thus, the deed itself is performed as an act implementing the designs of God. Mere renunciation of the fruits of actions is not good enough.

The other aspect to which the systems have devoted attention is that of *moksha*, perfection, liberation, freedom from the bondage of *Sansara*, the interminable cycle of births and rebirths. For *Sansara* is sorrow; *sarvam dukham dukham*, all is misery, misery, as Buddha observed. This sorrow, however, is not the relative sorrow that human beings experience alongside the relative pleasure or happiness. We know from our experience that what appears as pleasure at one stage in fact is another facet of pain, for pleasure cannot be experienced unless there has been an experience of pain, a state of continuous pleasure ceases to be distinguished as pleasure, it possibly becomes a monotonous continuum. In effect all pleasures have their roots in pain. So the system believes that the entire life of the soul in the body and as conditioned by the mind, is of sorrow. This is because of the bondage. Freedom means a state where there would be no further embodiment of the soul, a state when the body will no longer condition it. In this state it is all bliss. This freedom is variously called *moksha, mukti, kaivalya, nirvana*, etc.

Nyaya-Vaisheshika

Vaisheshika system appears to be based on an earlier non-Vedic system, some essential aspects of which, relating in particular to Dharma, were accepted by the Vedic authority; it, thus, became *Vaidica*. Its views are very similar to Nyaya, hence the bracketing of the two systems under one head. Author of *Nyaya Sutra* is Gautama while that of *Vaisheshika Sutra* is Kanada. *Nyaya* is based on logic and dialectics. Nyaya-Vaisheshika believes that there is no identity between the material cause and its effect. This they call as the theory of new beginning, *arambhavada*. The effect is not pre-existent in the cause, like, for example, a weaver weaves cloth from the threads, but once the cloth has come into existence it ceases to be threads, or potter's wares cease to be clay from which the potter makes them. The universe comes into being through the interaction of matter, time and space; all the three are independent entities. Matter comprises *akaasha* (space), *prithvi* (earth), *vayu* (air), *apah* (water) and *agni* (fire). Except space, all the rest are made up of atoms, and different combinations of these atoms of different elements produce different objects, like hills, trees and so on. *Akaasha* is infinite and all pervading, a substratum of the quality of sound. Time is also infinite. The physical universe thus consists of an infinite number of atoms, or whatever is the smallest part of matter which cannot be further subdivided or reduced in size, of air, water, earth and fire, and two infinite, pervasive entities, viz., time and space. Though ordinarily *akaasha* should mean space but its philosophic connotation is somewhat mysterious; it is perhaps the equivalent of another mysterious term called ether. It is frequently identified with Brahma. So there is another infinite entity making up the physical universe, and that is *akaasha*. The atoms are indestructible and are different for different elements, but even in the same element there is difference between atoms though qualitatively they are alike. In all cases they are indeterminate and above the perception by the senses. The difference in the atoms of different elements is based on their qualitative nature: air has only the quality of touch; fire of touch and colour, water of touch, colour and taste; and earth has smell in addition to touch, colour and taste. One quality of each element is considered to be its principle quality, *vishesh guna*: air has touch, fire has colour, water has taste, and earth has smell. Sound belongs to *akaasha*. God is not considered to be the material cause of the creation of the universe, but only the efficient cause. The force that causes the manifestation of the physical universe by the interaction of atoms and the infinite entities is *adrshta*, the unseen potency, and the power that guides this unseen potency is God. In other words just like a potter makes pots out of clay, God makes universe out of the pre-existing atoms. The constituents of the world, the atoms and the infinite, pervasive entities, have not been made by any one, they have always been there, and, therefore, there is no question of who produced them, or whether they will cease to exist at the time of dissolution; they are eternal. God is like the potter: the clay has always been there!

The combinations of atoms produce binaries and triads — could be called molecules —, and at a certain stage there is interaction between molecules of different elements, and thus starts the process of creation of the universe. At the end of the cycle the process is reversed till finally the atoms are separated into individual entities, in which state they remain till the start of the next cycle. God does not create the atoms; they are eternal like Him. All He does is organize them into the visible universe. In support of the argument about the being of God, the systems say that there has to be a Being to bring this vast and diversified universe into existence, and from the evidence regarding the design and purpose and the method of the working of the universe, it is clear that God, the efficient cause of the creation, is not only a prescient and a just Being, but also one with infinite wisdom and power. The variety in creation is attributed to the past deeds of the beings that inhabit it, and the purpose is to afford the opportunity to reap the fruits of those past deeds, karmas, and make available to the human beings the occasion to secure release from the cycle of reincarnations.

The next important element in the creation is the self. It is the soul *atman*, plus *manas*, (heart, mind, intellect). Souls also, like the atoms and the three infinite entities, are eternal. They acquire knowledge, feeling and volition (psychic life) because of their association with *manas*; this is their characteristic, i.e., they have the tendency to get trapped by *manas*. Individually and collectively both the soul and *manas* are non-spiritual. The self (it has inbuilt psychical element, as we have seen) experiences only through the physical organs it possesses at the time of the experience. Selves are not identical, and this difference shows in the circumstances of the living beings. Even after release, the selves maintain their distinctions, like the atoms; each of them has its own distinctive *manas*, which stays with it till it has secured release. *Manas* is atomic but does not give rise to new products. Because of its association with *manas* (except during deep sleep) the self acquires knowledge and that gives rise in it to the feelings of love, hate, pleasure, pain and volition. These feelings are specific to the self like colour to fire or touch to water. To these are added *dharma* (moral merit) and *adharma* (that which is morally sinful). These are not felt directly like love, hate, etc. but are inferred from the effects, like the pleasure and pain they cause in keeping with the Karma doctrine: 'if the deeds performed have been good the feeling shall be of pleasure, and vice-versa'. The knowledge of love, hate, etc., is perceived through *manas* only. But this knowledge cannot reveal itself, and needs another kind of knowledge for this purpose. This is called after-knowledge. In any case knowledge is not the essence of the self; it (self) appears only when certain external factors — all non-spiritual — cooperate. Like God, self also has infinite bliss or happiness. The system is pretty close to the concept of materialism.

The things are of two types: (a) Derived, which are mere aggregates of atoms, a variety in objects; and (b) new creations, like the weavers cloth woven out of threads; this creates a totally new thing out of the parts which were the threads, and it exhibits totally different features. Causation is thus creative. The system enunciates two theories here, that of new beginning, *arambh-veda*, and that of effect not being pre-existent in the cause before it comes to be produced, called *asatkarya-vad*. But cloth cannot be woven through a combination of, let us say, yarn and bamboo sticks, even if the two are brought together as intimately as possible. The mutual relationship between the threads of yarn is intimate, *samavaya* or closeness, while in the case of bamboo sticks and yarn it is merely a case of conjunction, *samyoga*. It is the *vishesha*, or quality, of each atom that will decide whether any two or more will combine to form a new substance.

Movement can be effected only by atomic and finite objects — which is what action means in this system. All pervading primal entities cannot move, for they have already filled up whatever space there was, their spread is infinite. Movement of other things is initiated only by the sentient beings, by themselves they just cannot move. Such movement as the blowing of wind, is given out as having been caused by some supernatural agency. Atoms cannot move by themselves, so the creation of the universe requires a competent, conscious agency to initiate movement in them, this is the cosmological argument in support of the existence of God; the other is the universality of belief in Him, i.e., He is there because it is universally believed that He is there. Substance, quality, action and *samvaya* and *vishesha*, are five of the six positive categories of this system. *Samvaya* is one and eternal, *vishesha* are many but also eternal, characterizing eternal things like atoms of the same class, or selves, which cannot otherwise be distinguished.

The sixth positive category is the 'universals', *samanya*. The system believes that the eternal substances, like the four elements, selves, and manas, form the basis of the universe. Add to these many finite objects derived from the four elements, and we get fundamental and derived objects each of which possesses certain characterized features which provide shape and size to the object, like a ball, knife, or earth or water atoms or selves. These characterized features which provide shapes, etc., to the objects, like ball, etc., are the universals. They are considered to be real and eternal, and like atoms and the selves, are the fundamental aspects of the universe. They characterize not only substances, but also action and quantities. For example, a particular shape, or colour, seen in many objects is not just one thing but many, as many as the objects in which these characteristics are seen, though all of them share the distinguishing feature, colour or shape; this characteristic is eternal and unchangeable. *Samvaya* and *vishesha* have no universals. The means of cognizing universals is perception where corresponding particulars are perceptible, or it may be inference or other testimony. The system also accepts one negative category called 'non-existence', *ahava*. But it is not an absolute nothing. A thing not of one particular shape just means it is not of that shape — it may have some other shape. Absolute nothing is just not within human thought and is a false concept.

Non-existence can involve a reference to time, suggesting a thing has already happened, or is likely to happen in the future, with reference to a particular point in time, or space, or mutual exclusiveness, like we say a bowl is not a plate; this last aspect is eternal. The cognizance of the universal is through perception where its correlate is perceptible, and in other cases it is either inference or verbal testimony. For example absence of an item can be perceived when we do not find it where we expected it to be, but the absence of a thing like a germ can be known only from the information given by another person.

Self acquires knowledge through *manas* which is in contact with the object about which knowledge is being acquired, through the sensory organs. But in a case where existence of fire is being inferred from the presence of smoke, it is the past experience which comes into play. Perception is what enables the senses to know, and then pass the information to the *manas* where it gets transformed into knowledge for the self. There is an involved argument to illustrate how perception can err, like, for example, mistaking a rope for a snake. The error is attributed to some past experience where the individual has actually seen a snake. Thus, snake is a fact, though it is not a fact for this situation of the rope. The conclusion is that the basis of all error is objective, and error precipitates when some experience of the past, or the present, gets transferred to a situation under examination.

As for the validity of knowledge, the system believes that the truth or otherwise of all knowledge should be ascertained by appropriate tests, unlike some other schools which believe that all knowledge attained is correct, and only when there is doubt there is need for verification. It emphasizes the cognitive functions of the means of knowledge, *parmanas*. Error means ignorance of the true character of the object, and removal of ignorance is the primary purpose of knowledge; hence the need for validation by appropriate means. *Vaisheshika* accepts only two *parmanas*, namely perception and inference, while *Nyaya* accepts two more, being verbal testimony and comparison.

(a) **Perception** *(pratyaksha)*

This has already been covered broadly. The only other aspect that needs to be mentioned is 'transcendental' perception, which is beyond the reach of ordinary mortals and can be achieved only by mystics or *yogins*, and covers such diverse subjects as selves, atoms, moral merit (*dharma*) and so on. These people develop capability to perceive super sensuous entities through their mystical powers; this is developed the same way as the power to achieve salvation, i.e., with moral purity and meditation.

(b) **Inference** *(anuman)*

Fire can be inferred from smoke. This is a kind of an inference which will be of benefit to the observer and will satisfy his curiosity. But when the requirement is to satisfy another person regarding the incidence of fire deduced from the occurrence of smoke, language has to be used, and in such a logical manner that the other person can be convinced of the conclusion arrived at. But the language by itself is not the main element that convinces the other person; the language sets in motion a chain of thought in his mind, and it is this thought that eventually makes him accept or reject the inference. This method of deriving an inference is accepted by this system.

(c) **Verbal testimony** *(shabda)*

Only the *nyaya* system accepts this *parmana*. It traces it to the omniscience of God and views Him as its author. Veda too has come from God in the form of *shabda*, its authority, therefore, is unassailable. But the system extends this means of knowledge to secular matters as well, like the testimony of a trustworthy person who knows the truth and communicates it correctly. Though this kind of testimony cannot have the same authority as that of the Veda, for obvious reasons.

In essence *Nyaya-Vaisheshika* accepts God, who, with the help of the 'unseen potency' (*adrshta*), puts the eternal elements comprising the atoms, and the infinite, pervasive entities, and the non-spiritual selves, together to create the world after his design. To begin with atoms combine to form binaries and triads and then the universals give shape, size, numbers and movement. At the end of the cycle the process is reversed and dissolution takes place. Self experiences is through the *manas*, which is in contact with the sensory organs which communicate the knowledge to it.

All systems have worked out procedures to ascertain the truth closely and accurately regarding the coming of the world and its final destination, and the role of the sentient beings in this, and have suggested that the essential requirement for a human being is to secure freedom from the cycle of rebirths and, thus, from misery. The emphasis is on misery, and deliverance from it. According to some systems, this state of freedom has inbuilt in it the quality of bliss. Gautama, the author of *Nyaya Sutra*, does not agree with this. His argument is that bliss cannot be experienced unless it is preceded by pain. *Moksha*, according to him is a state achieved after the self has departed from the physical body, and in this state there is no pain, pleasure, thought, feeling or will. The point is as to how is bliss visualized. If it is a state of eternal happiness then that would not be possible, for the concept brings in the aspect of comparison, which in this situation has to be with unhappiness, for unless unhappiness has been experienced it is not possible to make out happiness. But if it is something which is inbuilt in the state of perfect repose, then it is a different matter, for that kind of bliss cannot be conceptualized by the human mind. *Nayaya* is visualizing a kind of a repose as it exists, let us say, in a rock, a kind of a state in which every part of the subject is bereft of any trace of animation; that, according to this system, would be the state of the self upon being delivered. However, some systems believe that the perfect state of repose for the self is nothing other than the state of absolute bliss. This is not like the happiness of the sentient beings on this earth, which comes only after pain and misery have been experienced. Heavenly repose is different. It is perfect peace, which in effect is perfect bliss. The system accepts perfect repose, but not the aspect of the bliss being inbuilt in it.

Mention has been made of terms like *parmana, vishesh-guna, samvaya, samyoga, samanya*, universals, and so on. It is not within the scope of this work to dwell upon these terms and demonstrate how these have been utilized to develop this branch of philosophy. The idea of mentioning them is to inform the reader that the theory has taken into account a number of factors and examined the issues from many directions, before arriving at its conclusions.

According to the systems, cause of all evil is the association of the self with the body-mind complex, and this association has been brought about because of the merits and demerits gathered by the self during the past lives. At death, the physical body gets destroyed, but *manas*, being eternal, remains connected with the self, and it leaves the self only after the latter has secured the freedom. Merit or demerit is acquired by deeds which fall in the realm of *dharma* or *adharma*. Initially the concept of *dharma* or *adharma* was purely moral, but later, after the systems had accepted the authority of the Veda, these started being taken as what is commended or condemned by the Veda. The cause of bondage (*sansara*) is attachment, (*moha*), which breeds desire and ego, and hatred and aversion; love has a strong element of self interest. Therefore, to secure freedom, detachment has to be cultivated, and there has to be intense moral training to overcome ego and selfishness. Simultaneously there has to be the study of the Vedic literature, and a lot of reflection so as to effectively pursue the philosophical ideal. In the final stage it is meditation, and yoga, to attain direct experience and banish all ignorance and realize the ultimate truth.

Sankhya-Yoga

These two philosophic systems are considered together, because their broad metaphysical views and concepts of ideal life are generally the same. They do, however, differ in their approach to realizing the goal of *moksha*. While Sankhya emphasizes the role of knowledge and reflection, the stress in the Yoga system is on meditation. The author of *Sankhya* is Kapila, and of Yoga, Patanjali, not the grammarian of the second century BC. In importance the doctrines are next only to Vedanta. Some experts believe these are based on Upanishidic thoughts, others consider them to be of totally independent origin. Not much literature is available about Sankhya; Ishvara Krishna's work on this is of 5th century AD., while Sankhya sutra was compiled around as late as 14th century AD.

The arguments and conclusions put forth by the systems are based on logic and reasoning and are not given out as revelations. Systems regard both matter and spirit as real and accept the plurality of the selves, whom they term as *purushas*. They believe the universe originates from a single, all pervasive substance, *Prakriti*, the primordial matter, and evolves through transformations within this substance, it is not a new creation as such. Causation is just a transformation of what was latent into what becomes manifest. In other words, unlike *Nyaya-Vaisheshika*, the view here is that effect is always there though in a potential form, and becomes visible when conditions like the efficient cause, like the weaver in the case of cloth, get into action. This is the doctrine of 'the pre-existent effect' (*sat-karya-vada*). Evolution in effect is change of form, and not change of place as expounded by *Nyaya-Vaisheshika*; the latter thought would imply involvement of time and space, the infinite pervasive entities, in the process of evolution.

It is not possible to perceive *prakriti*; it can only be inferred, as in the case of atoms in *Nyaya-Vaisheshika*. According to Veda, it is devoid of all attributes, but has an eternal existence with the potential material causality as its only characteristic. In its existence it is eternally real, but when it is non-manifested, and devoid of name and form, it could be considered as unreal. It has three *gunas* (qualities) as its constituents, being — *Sattava* (goodness, purity), *Rajas* (action, activity) and *Tamas* (inertia, that which offers resistance), these have no beginning and are eternal like the former. Although *gunas* may be referred to as qualities, but in fact these are constituents which possess certain characteristics. During the state of no creation the three *gunas* are in a state of equipoise and though somewhat antagonistic in their nature towards one another, can and do act in concert; though essentially distinct in their nature they are mutually interdependent. This prevents their mutual separation ever, and, thus, a break-up of *prakriti* by such a separation. Let it, however, not be visualized that *prakriti* is just these three qualities. It is much more, and while it is dependent upon them, they also are equally dependent upon it, dependence is mutual. The evolution emerges from these *gunas*, i.e., the *gunas* cause the change of form and create the diversity in things after *prakriti* gets into the creation mode. The equipoise of the *gunas* in this mode gets disturbed, and this results in the transformation of the latent into the manifest diversity. Unlike *Nyaya-Vaisheshika*, the *Sankhya* system believes, as stated above, that effect is not something different from the cause, it is the cause only that gets transformed into effect. This is called the theory of transformation (*pariniamvada*), which in effect is the same as (*sat-karya-vada*).

Prakriti, in this system, is not visualized as a static entity, but a dynamic force which does not need any other power to make it evolve into this universe. Thus, there is no need for God to be there; *prakriti* can evolve on its own and produce the diverse universe that we see around ourselves. Diversity is caused by the varying proportions in which *gunas* enter into the make up of the things created or manifested. *Prakriti* is changing continuously, and, as stated earlier, is all pervasive and complex, forever in motion, never static. In its creation process the need for the presence of an intelligent being or beings is met by the individual souls. *Prakriti* evolves in their presence. All things born out of *prakriti* have the three *gunas* ingrained into them, and these *gunas*, like *prakriti*, are complex and continually changing. The fact that the three qualities have the capability to operate in concert, shows that the universe is an orderly whole and there is no contradiction in it, though each of these qualities may possess ingredients which may be hostile to some ingredients in other qualities.

Every period of evolution (*shristi*) is followed by a period of dissolution (*pralaya*) when the entire diversity of the universe, caused by the *gunas* becomes latent and comes to rest in *prakriti*, so to speak; these cycles of creation and dissolution are endless. In dissolution too *prakriti* is not static (motion is conceived as being original to it). Only the *gunas*, instead of acting upon one another, because of loss of equipoise, now regain their equipoise, and reproduce only within themselves; during the state of imbalance they generate heterogeneous transformations resulting in visible universe. The belief of *Nyaya-Vaisheshika* is that matter has no activity beyond what has been communicated to it from outside.

Prakriti produces three kinds of substances — firstly to adjust to the needs of *purusas*, or selves, it evolves the organs of thinking (*mahat*), which in turn give rise to ego (*ahankara*), i.e., development of the feeling of individuality in the self. Then comes the mind (*manas*), which has the five sensory organs of hearing, sight, smell, touch and taste, and five motor organs of speech, handling, walking, evacuation and reproduction. Then there are the elements, in two phases, being subtle and gross. Subtle elements are sound, colour, touch, taste and smell, and these combine to produce the gross elements — from sound comes *akaasha*; from *akaasha* and touch comes air, from *akaasha*, touch and colour comes fire; and from these and taste we have water; and from these four and smell there is earth. Thus *akaasha* is characterized by sound; air by sound and touch; fire by the last two plus colour; water by the last three plus taste; and earth by last four plus smell. *Nyaya-Vaisheshika* does not recognize division of elements into subtle and gross. The Sankhya system visualizes continuous evolution in progress, starting from intellect and evolving into things that ultimately form the universe.

Gross elements are the ones that get transformed into things, like rocks, trees and such like natural objects. These objects, however, do not produce any new category of items, which might contribute to further evolution. They do interact with one another, and also with subtle elements and *Manas* or mind, and intellect, and make their contribution to the variety which is the hallmark of creation. But otherwise they are at the lowest wrung of evolution; beyond them nothing evolves, e.g., intellect will not turn into egoism, or sound into *akaasha*. The things, constituted out of the gross elements, do not endure throughout a cycle of creation: once their life expires they just break up into the constituent elements, and are not further reduced. Subtle elements and other evolutes, on the other hand, last throughout the cycle and disintegrate only at its termination. *Manas*, the sensory and motor organs have mostly the *sattava* aspect of the ego, while the subtle and gross elements, the *tamas* aspect. *Rajas* cooperates with both *sattava* and *tamas*.

By itself the spirit, or the self, is passive and unable to know anything; it acquires its knowledge through the medium of *manas* or mind, ego and intellect; collectively these could be called the internal or the psychical organ. The constituents of the organ receive impressions from outside and respond to them, in which act they are assisted by the sensory and motor organs. In other words, there is this internal organ and then there is the total nervous system, both physical entities, operating together to impart experience to the self. This constitutes the 'subtle body' which, less the sensory and the motor organs (which perish with the gross body at the time of death) stays with the self throughout the cycle of rebirths and is cast off only after the self has attained the freedom. The 'gross body', constituted as it is from the gross elements, perishes at death and disintegrates and has nothing further to do with the self or the subtle body. Thus, in this system, apart from the self, everything else that makes up the universe is materialistic, a manifestation of *prakriti*, which is primordial matter.

The doctrine allots independent and equal status to *prakriti* and *purusha*. While the existence of *purusha* (self) has been established on the basis of logic and reason, the existence of *prakriti* is postulated on the principle that effect presupposes a material cause. There are complex and tedious arguments in support of this contention; this is beyond the scope of this work. The selves are believed to be many while *prakriti* is just one; this is the doctrine of pluralism. The plurality of the selves is proved by the difference in the temperaments of the sentient beings, though this difference is restricted to only that state in which the selves and the primordial matter appear, duly integrated, in their *sansaric* or worldly manifestations. Otherwise in their liberated state there is no difference between the different selves. The *Nyaya-Vaisheshika* stipulates that each self has distinguishing peculiarity of its own.

Purusha is a simple, non-dynamic entity (*prakriti* is dynamic), and does not have the capability to know or will anything unless assisted by the internal organ (*manas*, ego and intellect). It is a mere onlooker, the one to taste whatever knowledge or experience is passed on to it; it is not the agent of precipitate action. But it is the essence of sentience, though its psychic life springs from its association with the evolutes of *prakriti* (which make up the internal organ). Since internal organ activates mental life it is dominated by *sattava* qualities; most things of the material world, as also a large part of the human body, have *tamas* predomination. *Prakriti* evolves for the selves, for the benefit of the sentient beings, and self and *prakriti* operate in unison most of the time; the fact of their coming together is verified by the day to day experience of every individual. But consciousness is not a product of matter — it is so considered by the materialistic schools like *Charvaka*; it is something through which the spirit manifests itself. When we talk of *purusha*, it is the spirit in its pure and unadulterated state. But self in the empirical sense is that which has been conditioned by the karmas since its beginningless existence. Therefore, it is not passive like the *purusha*, but is active, and reacts to the external object as it perceives it, depending upon the limitations imposed upon it by the past *karmas*, e.g., the universe is richer than what is perceived by the self, because the latter cannot sense the full richness on account of its limitations. When a person has followed the path of dharma and has totally rid himself of the human weaknesses and got rid of the cumulative effect of the past karmas, the self begins to shine like the *purusha*, and the person is freed from *prakriti*, even though he still has the balance of his life to live through. Thus, the character of a person, in every sense, and his perception capabilities, will depend upon the hold that *prakriti* has on the self on account of the performance of the past lives. For this reason no two persons can be identical in character, intellect, perception and so on. However, the visible universe is common to all and is real in its own way, and to that extent, at the visible or physical level, there is not much difference amongst individuals. But when it comes to non-physical, emotional or intellectual issues, prejudices creep up on account of differences in personalities, which, as stated above, are conditioned by the deeds of past lives; these differences in perception breed conflict, within the same person at different times, or different persons at the same time.

It is the knowledge of the truth (which knowledge is essentially intuitive and based on synthesis and is not so much a result of physical experience), that makes a person identify *prakriti* and see that it is distinct from *purusha*. It makes him identify the empirical self, and once that truth has been attained the *purusha* appears in its own lustrous self. This is release. In other words the knowledge has to first help in identifying *prakriti*, and then the empirical self, and once this has been achieved, the pure, radiant form of *purusha* comes into comprehension. The attainment of this truth is the goal of life, and the system believes that *prakriti* is ever helping the individual in attaining this goal, for, according to it, the reason why *prakriti* evolves is to fulfil the *purusha*'s purpose. It takes form and structure in accordance with the need of the self, e.g., eyes see because it is necessary for *purusha* to see, and not because sub-organs constituting it have combined in a certain manner. The experience along the course of knowledge is of two types, viz. temporal and eternal. The former is through common worldly or secular values (*bhoga*) falling under the head of *arth* (acquisition of wealth), and *kaama* (enjoyment of pleasures), while the latter comes through self realization or escape from *prakriti*, under the head of dharma (religious and moral merit) and *moksha* (the final release from the hold of *prakriti*) — *apavarga*. This implies that the way to the goal is through worldly life, the duration of which depends upon the moral and intellectual level of each person. In other words, man turns to the spiritual freedom only after he has learnt the futility of secular values.

Knowledge is the key to identify *prakriti* and realise its distinctive existence *vis-a-vis* the *purusha*. This knowledge can be direct, which, of course, is not likely to be of much use when the quest is for metaphysical entities like the *prakriti* or the *purusha*. The system accepts the knowledge acquired through psychic perceptions. It accepts three *parmanas*, viz., perception, inference and verbal testimony. There are two types of reasoning which the Indian philosophic systems recognize, being (a) syllogistic — inferring fire from smoke, and (b) analogical — deducing the existence of a potter from the presence of an earthen jar; a good jar with intricate and delicate work proves the existence of a competent potter. Likewise, the world, assuming it to be an effect, is brought into existence by a competent force *purushas* or, since they are identical in their pure, radiant forms, collectively they can be taken as one force, i.e., *purusha*. The other way to look at it is to visualize *purushas* collectively as one sea of consciousness from where individual *purushas*, as constituents of this force, depart to mingle with *prakriti* to effect creation. This is an inference based on likeness. Since the inference is about transcendental matters, the Vedantins are of the view that such reasoning can give only the probability and not certainty.

Like in *Nyaya-Vaisheshika*, in this system also the goal is to secure release from *prakriti*, attain *kaivalya*, solitude, detachment, the state of supreme freedom. And the way to achieve this is also the same as in the other system, i.e., cultivate detachment, acquire knowledge of the ultimate truth under proper guidance, and then reflect upon it, and practise meditation. In essence *Sankhya* covers the theoretical details of the system, while Yoga gives the practical side of it. The point, however, to note is that in the Upanishads Yoga is the means of uniting the self with the Creator, while in this system, which does not recognize any absolute self, it is the path which ultimately leads to the point where the individual self separates or extricates itself from the hold of *prakriti* and comes to be by itself. The system recommends an eight fold path of discipline, which includes (i) self restraint, (ii) observance of the rules of dharma, (iii) practice in learning the correct posture for meditation, (iv) regulation of breath, (v) withdrawal of senses and cultivation of detachment, (vi) steadying the mind, (vii) contemplation, and (viii) meditative trance (*samadhi*). The idea is to assist a person in his ascent from a narrow outlook to a broader vision, and this vision brings freedom with it.

Under self restraint and observance of the rules of Dharma, the systems recommend certain do's and don'ts to cultivate the discipline which is so necessary for the yogic training. They say that, to begin with, the human will must focus in the right direction to attain goodness and purity, physical and mental, as distinct from truth. The do's, which generally amount to the observance of the rules of dharma, are: purity of thought and deed, contentment, right aspiration, study of philosophic texts, and devotion to the power that is the cause of all creation. It is not God as such, as visualized in the Upanishads, but ,may be, a *purusha* of superior dimension, as visualized in the yoga system, or the total collective of the spirits or *purushas*, a kind of a sea of consciousness, or a combine of *prakriti* and *purusha*: it is the power that causes creation and sustains it. Don'ts are: non-injury, always speaking the truth and never speaking lies, no stealing, nor having any possessions, and celibacy. All these observances fall under the overall heading of 'restraints'. These rid the person of the ego which is the cause of so much evil, and develop impersonal attitude, which awakens the spiritual will. This is the stage of lower (*apara*) detachment; higher (*para*) detachment is almost the same as enlightenment.

Once the spiritual will has been awakened the person is ready to effectively practise the remaining stages of discipline. These, viz., posture, regulation of breath, and withdrawal of senses, control the physical frame in order to facilitate the control of the mind.

The next three stages, — steadying the mind, contemplation and meditative trance (*samadhi*), lead to revelation of truth-bearing knowledge. In the *samadhi* stage the individual attains the desired knowledge, initially he experiences the fact that the self and *prakriti* are two different entities, but eventually he transcends this and becomes oblivious of the world, even his own existence, and is face to face with the effulgence of untainted *purusha*. At this stage the operations of the internal organ are suspended and the spirit returns to its own pure form. The person, practising self discipline and living in total (para) detachment, has then secured the release and becomes *jivanmukta* or liberated, during the currency of his life itself.

It has already been stated that God is not integral to the doctrine of *Sankhya*. *Prakriti*, the primordial matter, is self creating, and the fact that the creation is orderly and follows a pattern, or design, is because it creates for and adjusts to the needs of *purusha*. Thus, the orderliness and design get evolved for the self; the doctrine denies any conscious designer. *Yoga*, however, accepts God, (*Ishvara*), but not of the Upanishads; the concept has a kind of a super *purusha* , eternal and omniscient, but not all comprehensive. He is not the God of the *NyayaVaisheshika* responsible for the creation of the universe. But he is unique and perfect, and the liberated *purushas* do not match his greatness. Disciplines like posture, regulation of breath right upto meditative trance, are meant to effect complete surrender to such a God. He may not be conceived of as the great Upanishadic God, but He is great enough to meet the needs of the sentient beings. According to *Patanjali* (of Yoga), mere devotion (bhakti) to God can secure freedom, for in His abundant mercy, He grants the wishes of those who repose their trust in Him and meditate upon Him. This path of release is simpler than that of knowledge. But *sankhya* attaches all importance to the knowledge of the ultimate truth, the belief in a supreme God is not organic to the doctrine.

Prakriti secures for the self either secular values, like wealth (*arth*) or pleasures of the senses (*kaama*), or it secures self realization through moral merit (Dharma) or final release (*moksha*). It adjusts its activity differently to meet the needs of different *purushas*. To achieve this it ought to have a mental or spiritual capability. This could be provided by *purusha*, but it is conceived as totally passive and external to *prakriti*. Thus we have, in this concept, insentient *prakriti* possessing a capability to exercise choice. Possibly the choice capability is not born out of some kind of an intelligent process, as in the case of the created sentient beings. May be it is conditioned by the law, Dharma, that which holds together, which is the basis of all order, and which is the essential ingredient of *prakriti*. Logically the problem could be overcome if the doctrine assumed a spiritual content in *prakriti* itself, and postulated that this element prompted and completely guided its evolutionary course from within. This could explain the rational order in the nature. The doctrine, like the Upanishads, would then maintain that main aim of life is to secure freedom from the cycle of rebirth, and that man pursues lower values initially because of his ignorance of the ultimate truth. According to scholars, this Upanishadic thought has been modified in this doctrine and the spirit and nature have been separated. Intellect (*mahat*) and egoism (*ahankara*) have been given as the evolutes of *prakriti*. As cosmic entities they represent the psychic organs of the universal self, but by itself the psychic organ is a product of *prakriti*. The thought that spiritual content ought to be immanent in *prakriti* as a whole, has been dropped from the doctrine, possibly after it had come out of the hold of the Upanishadic influence.

Dharma, as stated above, could, in fact, be that which gives *prakriti* the capability of choice to provide to the self the secular values, or the values that lead to self realization. Take the case of the insentient planet earth. Its substances, singly or collectively, react in certain predetermined patterns that ensure its continued functional efficacy, e.g., when floods are causing extensive erosions in the soil, the pattern that the process of silting follows is designed to maintain the erstwhile balance and keep the impact of the damage to the minimum. This is the behaviour pattern of the elements in all situations. The blowing winds, the flowing waters, the shifting earth: all these are continually engaged in the process of restoring the balance, the equilibrium, the moment a threat precipitates. The activity is triggered under the effect of Dharma, the law. In the same manner, possibly, does the *prakriti* act at its level. Its choice to bestow secular values or values for self realization, gets actuated on the basis of the signals that emanate from an individual's psychic self, signifying whether he is ripe to receive one or the other set of values; the signals, no doubt, would be conditioned by the deeds of the past lives, as also by the depth of the desire risen in the present life and the training the individual has received in this direction.

It is also possible that originally the doctrine was totally naturalistic, and the spiritual element was brought in later to match with other doctrines. Yoga has its origin in the Indus Civilization — it could be of even earlier times. The fact that the doctrine is closely tied up with Yoga, could suggest that, possibly, it had developed during pre-Aryan days, and the Aryan thinkers adopted it after it had been appropriately modified, and the spiritual element had been brought into it. Otherwise, there had been a firm belief amongst many thinkers of this subcontinent, from the remotest past, that earth itself is a living entity, a macro organism, that responds to the internal tensions and hostile extraneous interferences, in a manner that would conduce towards the survival of whatever it carries upon its surface. Often it is referred to as 'mother earth'. Its species evolve under environmental pressures, and it is not possible to establish any role of the spiritual factor in this process of evolution. In fact, it is difficult to even define life. It has been suggested that the origin of life on earth was based on self-replicating inorganic crystals, like crystals of silicates. All modern earth-based life has its roots in the organic component of the nature, but, it may not be true all over the universe, and may not have been always true even on earth. If so, organic replicators — eventually DNA (deoxyribonucleic acid)— must have taken over later. It is hard to imagine DNA and proteins which are the two pillars of evolution, developed out of a step by step process, unless there was something preceding it which is just not visible now.

Some kind of replication is in evidence in inorganic matter, and some scientists have concluded that, may be, it all started with clay replicators which, gradually, synthesized organic molecules and then used them for their own purpose. Whether the original replicators were mineral crystals or organic direct fore-runners of DNA, can only be guessed, but, apparently the power they exercised was direct and elementary, like, for example, stickiness.

Take the example of water flowing in a stream. The clay crystals lying on its bed are influenced by the flow of water, but these equally influence the flow. Successful clay crystals would not get washed by water but would, possibly, change the course of the stream. When stream has excess of water, it bursts its banks, but clay crystals gradually raise the bank height and contain the flow and, thus, save the surrounding countryside from undue damage. It does appear that a close association can exist between organic chemical synthesis and clay surfaces, and it is quite possible that clay replicators synthesised organic molecules and then used them for themselves. Eventually, however, organic molecules would have cast aside the clay replicators, and that, possibly, was how evolution of life as we see it, began; it would have happened from a relatively recent common ancestor, with a single uniform genetic system and largely uniform bio-chemistry. Thus, there is a paradox about the origin of life. If a sufficiently plausible theory in this context can be put up which might satisfy our subjective judgement, then it is too plausible to account for the paucity of life in the universe as we know it. We do not know how natural selection really began on earth.

Some protozoa, algae and fungi show very complex internal organisation but are not divided into cells. Viruses are midway between living and dead matter. Bacteria too do not possess all the properties of cells. There is, therefore, this problem of drawing a line between life and insentient matter. In 1979, Dr. James Lovelock, a British scientist, expounded the view, in his book titled *Gaia, a New Look at Life on Earth*, that life and the environment were two important constituents of the same whole, that the two together formed a single self-regulating system which allowed life to keep the environment to its liking. He likened the regulatory process to that which in animals maintains the stability of such vital aspects as the body temperature and the composition of blood. His conclusion was that the earth in itself was, in fact, a live planetary system which encompassed every living creature and other things normally considered inanimate. It is these regulatory mechanisms which maintain a relative constancy of climate, surprisingly moderate levels of salt in oceans, a constant level of oxygen over the past few hundred million years, and other things besides. Darwinians have generally not accepted the concept, for, according to them, life evolved under the pressure of natural selection, and as such earth cannot be called a live organism, for there is no evidence of natural selection playing any part in any of the phenomenon on the basis of which the idea of 'live planet' was being advanced.

However, it is not the intention here to decide whether or not the earth can be called a living organism. The idea is to emphasise the fact that there are self correcting mechanisms in the natural systems of the whole universe, and that is what Dharma, that what holds together, is all about. The authors of the *Sankhya-Yoga* systems came to the conclusion that *prakriti* it was that took care of the entire evolutionary process and also of all else that got the universe going and made it functional. It evolved an umbrella of protective environment to begin with, and then got going with the evolution of life under the cover of this umbrella. They have, however, conceded, in a later thought, perhaps under Vedic influence, that for sentient life, selves (*purushas*) come into the picture, conceding a spiritual content in the total creation process. But they have not veered entirely from their original thought and have continued to stress that the evolution of the universe is purely a *prakriti* show, even when conceding that the direction of this evolution is conducive to the growth of life based on *purusha*. Otherwise, according to them, this entity, *prakriti*, power, force, or whatever else you might like to call it, is entirely self evolving and self regulating.

Purva-Mimansa

Mimansa is enquiry, a systematic investigation, and Purva refers to the earlier portions of the Veda which deal with rituals (*karma-kand*). The system is, thus, based on the instructions contained in the earlier parts of the Veda, and originated during the *Brahmna* period; *Brahmna* means considered opinion of a priest of recognised authority. The works were systematised in *Kalpa Sutras* — aphorisms dealing with Vedic rituals. The primary source of the system is Jaimini's *Sutra* compiled during 300-200 BC. It is about the biggest philosophical work of its time, and, perhaps, even the oldest. The earliest known commentary on this is from Sabara Svamin (400 AD.), which has been explained in two different ways by Kumarila Bhatta and Prabhakra. Their works were compiled around 700 AD. and have given rise to two schools, which, though generally agreeing on fundamentals, do have minor differences in other detail. Like *Nyaya-Vaisheshika,* the system believes in the plurality of souls and multiplicity of the fundamental elements comprising the physical universe. In other words, it also believes that the ultimate reality is many and not one. During the early phase of the development of this system, heavenly happiness was considered to be the goal of human endeavour. The idea was to accumulate merit during one's life time to secure a place in the heavens after death. The belief was that if the rituals prescribed in the Veda were performed following the laid down instructions and procedures, then merit could be gathered which could entitle the soul of the person to a stay in heaven. Later, however, once the theory of re-birth on the basis of karma, was accepted, it became apparent that stay in heaven, on the basis of the rituals performed during one's life time, could not be the main goal, for such a stay would last only till as long as the merit gathered lasted. Once it was exhausted the self had to return to the world of the mortals and the sorrow-inflicting cycle of birth and death. Essentially this change in the concept took root during the later stages of the *Brahmana* period when the germ of the idea of rebirth had found its way into the religion; it got consolidated during the *Upanishadic* period. The authors of the system realised then that the final goal had to be freedom from the cycle of rebirth, *sansara,* and decided that even this could be achieved by performing the Vedic rituals in accordance with the laid down instructions.

This system of philosophy classifies the karmas (of the Karma Kand, the Vedic rituals) into different categories, one of which is *kamya,* which are optional rituals and are required to be performed only if the performer desires heaven. The Vedic prescriptions for this variety of karmas are called *kamya-vidhis;* they are also called the *jyotishtoma* sacrifices. Next are the *nitya-karmas,* the obligatory rites, the texts in respect of which are called the *nitya-vidhis.* These rites, like regular prayers in precise texts and at the prescribed times, are compulsory; the non-performance will attract demerit. Then we have the *naimittika-karmas*, occasional rites, which are performed during specified occasions, like birth, death, marriage, and so on. These are obligatory in the sense that they have to be performed, as laid down, during specified occasions; non-performance, in their case too, would gather demerit. In the last category are the *pratishidha-karmas*, the prohibited acts, the performance of which would, in any case, accumulate demerit.

The system believes that if good deeds are performed then one is born in good circumstances, in human form may be, while deeds of demerit cause birth amidst lower species, like animals or vegetation. But birth is the beginning of all suffering anyway, no matter whether one is born as a god or man or beast or vegetation. For absolute release there have to be no *karmas*, which means that the *karmas* have to be such as would leave no residue which might cause re-birth; it is accepted that activity is the essence of creation and, hence, cannot be avoided.

The system believes that the state of no-karma can be achieved by following the Vedic injunctions regarding the different categories of karmas. By following *kamya-vidhi* and performing the optional rites, one gains merit. But this will cause re-birth. The system suggests that such actions can be performed if one wanted heaven, or when in this life itself there was requirement for gain, like getting rain by performing *kariri* sacrifice, or a son through *putra-kameshti* sacrifice, or conquest of territory by performing *ashva-medha*. By performing the optional rites one gathered an appropriate reward, but, in the process, one also risked re-birth. Therefore, such rites are best avoided.

Prohibited deeds *pratishiddha-karmas*, assuredly cause re-birth and have to be avoided. As for the *nitya* and *naimittika* karmas, the system's stand is that such deeds do not afford merit, but their non-performance causes demerit. Therefore, to avoid gaining demerit, one has to perform the obligatory and the occasional rites. The doctrine, thus, postulates that by non-performance of optional rituals and prohibited deeds, and meticulously carrying out the obligatory and occasional rites, to the very end of one's life, one can achieve a state which will not lead to re-birth. According to the doctrine, the way to the final release is through the performance/non-performance of the Vedic rituals. The expression karma here has been used in two different contexts, firstly as acts of *karma-kand*, performance of Vedic rituals, and, secondly, to convey the meaning of activity other than *Karma Kand*, i.e., the general activity of an individual during the course of his life. Both expressions are relevant to this doctrine.

The system covers the whole gamut of the ingredients of creation as covered by the *Nyaya-Vaisheshika* and recognises all of them, like substance, quality, action, universals and non-existence. But it discards *samavaya* and *vishesha*; it considers the latter as arbitrary assumptions acquired by *Nyaya-Vaisheshika* to put forth its case. Then there are differences in the understanding of the ingredients as well. It does not accept that particles of fire, earth, air and water are super-sensible, i.e., beyond the perception of the senses. It believes they are finite and are not atomic. The conclusion by Kumarila is that relationship between these particles and the whole that manifests out of them is like a relation between substance and attribute — identity in difference: the whole and the parts are absolutely distinct, but distinct while being the same. He also differs regarding the precise magnitude of the ultimate material of the universe.

In respect of self also the view point is similar to that of *Nyaya-Vaisheshika*, though with some reservations. The qualities of the self are also similar, except that Dharma and *Adharma* are not there. The remaining six qualities, i.e., knowledge, desire, hate, pleasure, pain, and volition are accepted as internally perceivable, as in the other two systems. But knowledge disclosed to introspection is regarded as inferred and not direct. Unlike the other systems, the existence of an omniscient, super-excellent God is not accepted; otherwise how do we account for such abundance of misery in the world? This is explained by the past karmas, and, according to Kumarila, if karmas is the cause even after accepting the existence of God, then it is only karmas where full explanation can be sought. Thus the concept of a Creator and the cycles of creation and dissolution are not accepted. The physical universe is considered to be without beginning or end, self existent; it was never any thing different from what it is now; origin, growth, decay are attributes of the things of the universe, but not of the universe itself. The system believes in the selves and karmas and lays great stress on the ethical order of the universe.

Like *Nyaya-Vaisheshika* this system also postulates 24 qualities for matter and spirit, but with certain modifications. It omits sound — puts it under 'substance' —, and *dharma* and *adharma*. Of the new qualities introduced, one is *Shakti*, potency, causal power, like burning capacity of fire. This power is not visible, but its existence can be inferred from the effect it produces. Kumarila's views on universals too are slightly different. Like *Nyaya-Vaisheshika*, this doctrine too rejects intuitive perception. It accepts six *pramanas*, or means of knowledge, including perception, inference and verbal testimony. The other *parmanas* are: (a) comparison, (b) presumption; for example, Veda says that rewards for the performance of rituals come in a future life, and the karma doctrine says that the rewards are reaped only by the doer — conclusion: self survives the body, (c) non-apprehension (*an-upalabdhi*). *Nyaya-Vaisheshika* ascribes the knowledge of non-existence to perception and all else to inference, but Kumarila says perception can come only through contact with a sensory organ and it is impossible to think of perception when the thing is just not there. Hence the need for non-apprehension as *parmana*.

The doctrine has expressed opinion regarding the validity of the Veda, but before that there is an exposition on the nature of knowledge. *Nyaya-Vaisheshika* says that if the practical activity to which the knowledge leads is a success, then that knowledge is valid, not otherwise. In other words, knowledge can be validated only by more knowledge. But this can lead to a kind of an unending chain of bits of knowledge, each bit validating the one preceding it. These systems, however, say that there is no requirement for this, that normally one or two tests should suffice, and that for things of every day experience no test is called for. The view of *Purva-Mimansa* is that knowledge by its very nature is valid. Verification is called for only when knowledge has strayed from truth, like for example, when correct position may not be visible on account of poor light, or some other outside interference, or when an element of contradiction is detectable in one bit of knowledge on account of another bit of knowledge.

On the basis of the discussion on the validity of knowledge, the system expresses its views regarding the validity of the knowledge contained in the Veda. The view of *Nyaya-Vaisheshika* is that this knowledge is valid because it is a word of God, but they do not rule out its being questioned. Kumarila, who does not recognise God as such, has said that this knowledge is valid because all knowledge has the aspect of validity built into it. According to him, the error at source is not possible, for Veda, not being a work of any person, human or divine, has no source. Nor is any conflict with other knowledge likely as Veda refers to only the super sensuous matters which, in any case, are beyond the reach of human experience. But Veda does contain material of ordinary or mundane experience, and whenever there is conflict between what has been stated in the Veda and the knowledge gained through personal experience, credence has to be given to the latter. It will be seen, though, that if such contradictions are given liberal interpretations, their superficiality will become apparent. The need, therefore, is to interpret the Veda correctly. This aspect of correct interpretation is as important to this system as that of rituals or philosophy. The system says that the purpose of the revelation is to impart correct knowledge regarding dharma and moksha, which are the two supreme values of life; it, however, concerns itself mainly with dharma. In essence its view of the Veda is that (a) it is self existent or eternal, (b) it is concerned with supersensuous matters, and (c) it has portions that require liberal interpretation.

Kumarila and Prabhakara schools differ on certain matters of detail. The latter do not accept non-apprehension as a *parmana*, and explain every form of non-existence positively. They accept the remaining *parmanas* and add four more, making a total of eight. Differences are also there regarding concepts of knowledge, error and truth. There are a host of other details where the two schools have their own views, but all that is beyond the scope of this work and the inquisitive reader shall have to locate the details elsewhere.

Since the schools do not recognise God, their views regarding all world activity are based on dharma/adharama. In general terms dharama implies Vedic rites, and religious duties, including also the ethical conduct, and activity taken on for the good of others — in the five daily sacrifices (*maha-yajnas*), hospitality towards the guests is also prescribed. *Adharama* is the opposite. *Dharma/adharama* do not produce results directly, but serve only as vehicles. The actions produce an unseen effect, a kind of an invisible potency, which abides in the self till appropriate result in terms of pleasure or pain has precipitated. According to Kumarila, Veda promises heaven and other pleasant results for those who perform the Vedic rites and rituals. The guidance provided by the Veda is not available from any other source and should, therefore, be valued and strictly followed. Prabhakara, on the other hand, says that to view *dharma* as the means to secure heaven or other pleasant results, would be to deny what it actually is, or what it stands for. *Dharma*, therefore, should be followed for its own sake, and not with desires for rich results or for securing heaven; it should not be regarded as a ceremonial act, but an intrinsic value.

Originally the goal prescribed by this system was to secure heaven, which later got modified to securing *moksha*, absolute freedom from the rebirth cycle. Kumarilla's school believes *moksha* is not just freedom from misery; it is positive and un-ending bliss. But the emphasis is on *karma* and not on *gyana*, self knowledge, or even *bhakti*, devotion. To achieve the ideal one must purify the natural impulses and not yield to selfish inclinations, and should perform social and religious duties as taught or implied in the Veda.

Vedanta

The system is also called *Uttara-Mimansa*, i.e., enquiry into the later or subsequent portions of the Veda, which are the Upanishads; even amongst the Upanishads the enquiry is related to the final portions and the term implies 'the settled conclusions of the Veda taken as a whole': Vedanta. It also covers the *Bhagavad gita* and the *Vishnu Purana*, both of which are considered to be amplifying the Upanishadic doctrine. The *Sutra* which systematised the doctrine is by Badarayana; it is called the Vedanta Sutra. This *Sutra*, the Upanishads, and the *Bhagavad gita*, are the three pillars which support this doctrine. The *sutra*, aphorisms, is too cryptic and is not clear on many details, with the result that several different interpretations and view-points have emerged. However, the different schools agree on the fact of the eternity of the self, and the need for *gyana*, knowledge, for attaining *moksha*. The principal schools are: (a) Absolutist, which expounds *Advaita*, non-dualism; it represents Brahma as the impersonal principal; Shankra is the main exponent of this school; (b) Qualified non-dualism — *Vashishtadvaita*, the principal exponent is Ramanuja, and (c) Theistic, *Dvaita*, dualism; represents Brahma as personal principal; Madhava is the author of this doctrine.

Different views of the ultimate reality have emerged primarily because firstly, the *Vedanta Sutra* is too cryptic and lends itself to different interpretations and, secondly, even the Upanishads have not defined in clear terms the nature of Brahma, the self and the physical universe, and their mutual relationship. Bhartraprapancha, who was about the first person to have written a commentary on the *Vedanta Sutra*, said that Brahma is one, but that oneness includes variety which has been caused by infinite number of selves included within Brahma and numerous distinctions of the physical universe. This variety, which is implicit in Brahma, becomes explicit at the time of creation. Thus creation is not a new origination, like making something new or for the first time, but only an articulation of distinctions already subsisting in Brahma. The thought is almost the same as in the case of *Sankhya*, except that the evolving principal is not the insentient *prakriti* but the sentient, and all comprehensive Brahma. The liberated soul is not lost in Brahma but retains its individuality. To achieve liberation a person has to acquire moral and religious merit, essentially to eliminate selfish impulses and develop detachment, and, having achieved this, he has to acquire the right knowledge and dispel ignorance, *avidya*, about the oneness of the ultimate reality. The commentary extols the virtues of karma (of the *karma kand*) as the direct means of liberation, almost like *Purva-mimansa*; other Vedic schools also emphasise the role of karma, but not to this extent.

Shankra, however did not accept this view-point, and so downgraded it that it could never again be revived. His main objection was that Brahma, self and the physical universe cannot be identical and different at the same time; the presumption is mutually contradictory and hence incorrect. According to him the teaching of the Upanishads is only about the unity, and the stream of thought which talks of the reality of diversity is only at a superficial level, something experienced in the initial stages of contemplation. He is an exponent of non-dualism and not of monoism since he accepts the existence of variety; the question of unity would arise only if there is variety in the elements.

Shankra, a great thinker from South India, lived for barely 32 years, and in this time he wrote *bhashyas*, or commentaries, on *Bhagavad Gita*, and all the important Upanishads, and the *Vedanta Sutra* (also called *Brahma-sutra*). *Sutra* means an aphorism, or a work of aphorisms, short sayings which are required to be explained or interpreted; they are like paragraph headings. To write the commentary on the *Vedanta Sutra* he moved to Kashi, modern Varanasi in Uttar Pradesh. He travelled widely, extensively spreading the *advaita* doctrine, and established monastic institutions in the four corners of this subcontinent: at Sringeri in the south in Mysore; Badrinath in the snowy Himalayas in the north; Dwarka in Kathiawar in the west, on the Arabian Sea; and Puri in the east, on the Bay of Bengal; he was one of those men who visualized the people of this vast land as one nation. And all this he achieved in a short life of 32 or 33 years. Tradition places Shankra in a period before the birth of Christ, but modern scholars place him in the late eighth century AD. It has not been possible to pinpoint the time when he lived and worked but the generally accepted period is 788-820 AD, which, according to scholars, may be accepted as correct within limits of a hundred years. He was born in a Nambudiri Brahmin family in Kaladi village on the west coast of Kerala in South India. His father died when he was still a small boy, and he was brought up by his mother. He was a precocious child and learnt fast and sought to renounce the world when he was just eight. When at last he turned to philosophy he travelled north to the bank of river Narmada, and there sought the renowned guru Govinda, and received his initial grooming under him.

The basic thought of Shankra's *Advaita* is that self is not the body, nor *manas* (mind), or *ahankar* (ego). It is eternal, and non-dual; it is the absolute spirit: *Tat Tvam Asi*, that thou art, i.e., you are Brahma. Only *Maya* (the cosmic illusion) comes in the way of recognizing this fact. Otherwise this universe is a reflection of God-hood itself: he is the Creator and the Created, the sole essence. The matter exists not independent of perception; the substances appear real because of the ideas of the mind. Otherwise all that we see is *maya*. There are no two things in existence. It is only the spirit that exists, and not matter. The universe is not God, but there is nothing but God in the universe.

Regarding karmas, Shankra's views are in agreement with other thoughts, that karmas put the self in the cycle of rebirths, but he does not agree with *Purva-Mimansa* that karmas can be eliminated just by performing appropriate rites or not performing certain others. He believes that the karmas are caused by ignorance and nescience. These can be eliminated only by eliminating the effect that they produce, namely, the cycle of rebirths, *sansara*. Only knowledge of Brahma, the non-dual Self, — which is the same as the *atman*, (the individual self) — can dispel ignorance, and once that happens, the final truth is realized and freedom achieved. In the final truth, the ultimate state of perfection is not something which is created afresh, for if it were so then it would not be eternal, for whatever can be created is prone to destruction. Release cannot be non-eternal; if it is prone to destruction it would not be much different from *sansara*. But even *sansara* is not something which needs to be destroyed. It is just a false appearance, and its destruction implies only the destruction of ignorance. In the oft-quoted example of a rope mistaken for a snake, the person taking the rope for a snake is distressed and frightened and urgently moves to destroy the danger confronting him. But on careful examination he realizes his mistake and feels relieved and happy; after he has gained knowledge of the true position he knows that what he considered to be a danger was in fact not so. Likewise, if truth about *sansara* gets realized, through the medium of right knowledge, the same kind of happiness is achieved, and that is the state of *moksha*, complete freedom, also referred to as *jivan mukti*, that is, attainment of freedom during lifetime itself. A person does not have to die and then move into this state; he attains all that he has to attain during the lifetime itself, and continues to live on. According to *Advaita*, this state of freedom, or bliss, was in fact never lost, for the very essence of self is bliss, but the self, having got entangled with the body-mind complex, (called *jiva* in this state, that is, the soul in its individuality) became confused and ignorant and forgot about its real nature and, consequently, got plunged into pain and misery. But no sooner had it realized its true nature, and the veil of ignorance got lifted, it attained the state of *moksha*, freedom and bliss. The *jiva* is attaining this by shedding the limitations imposed upon it by the internal organ (mind, intellect, ego) which being of matter is unreal and illusory. But *jiva* as such is not illusory, only the internal organ enveloping it is. By itself *jiva* is Brahma.

According to Shankra, all diversity is illusory, *mithya*. Reality (*sat*) has to be eternal, and since only Brahma is eternal, He is the only reality. Non-reality (*asat*) is absolute nothing. The physical universe is neither real nor unreal. It is not real because it is not eternal, and because it is constantly changing. Born out of *tapas*, heat or the inner energy, or the spiritual fervour, and kama, the creative power of desire (personified as the god of love), it grows from the primordial atom to its full stature, and then undergoes the process of dissolution till it is back to the stage it started from. But it is not unreal (*asat*) either, for it has an appearance which cannot be regarded as a non-entity or be classified as absolute nothing. It is a non-permanent appearance which in the flow of time, when viewed at a particular instant, has an appearance, which is a reality during that instant, but the moment it has gone past, it becomes an illusion in relation to that instant; it was but is no longer! That appearance has been reduced to an illusion, like something that appeared and then vanished out of sight, for in the next instant what is visible is a totally different form of that momentary phenomenon impression. In the rope and snake example, for the person undergoing the experience the snake is neither there nor is it not there. To a certain impression in the mind which is born out of some experience of the past, it is there and affects the person accordingly, mentally, psychologically, but to a close examination it is not there, and he feels relieved and his mind is restored to its original state. In this situation a complete illusion turns into a reality for a while. But the things of the world, though not ultimately real, being non-permanent, follow certain patterns which suggest reality. For example, a tree does not grow with its roots in the air, or the pull of gravity always follows prescribed laws. These patterns and laws are for ever applicable, till as long as the universe lasts, and this gives the suggestion of reality. It is these laws which constitute *Rta* and Dharma, which hold the universe together. But the universe itself, being non-eternal, is not a reality, and, thus, we have a situation where a seemingly real thing exists within a non-reality, or, in other words, what appears to be a reality is, in effect a non-reality. This is the situation where reality turns into an illusion in the very next instant. Only Brahma is eternal, *sat*, changeless. *Prakriti* the primary matter, is unreal, for it is forever changing. Whatever reality may be ascribed to the manifested universe, it is derived from Brahma, it is not a part of Him though, since it is changing constantly: it is *maya*, the primary essence of which is ceaseless change, while that of Brahma is changelessness. He transcends all empirical attributes (He cannot be described as this, or that, and so on; he is *neti, neti*, not this, not this) and is classified as *nirguna*, without features or attributes, that is, His attributes are beyond comprehension. However, when placed within the ambit of human imagination he is *saguna*, with attributes or qualities, very much related to *maya* even though He still essentially is of the self.

The point being made here is that what is true of the part is also true of the whole. Self trammelled by the internal organ is *jiva;* internal organ is the cause of *avidya*, nescience or ignorance, the trap is *avidya*. In dreamless sleep the self is not involved with *avidya*, or the internal organ, but during dreams it is, while during the waking hours its association is chiefly with the physical body (matter), which is derived from *avidya;* in dreamless sleep self is in its original, pure form. As in the case of the self, Brahma also, when descending to the observable level of the created universe, is not the unadulterated absolute consciousness. He is *apara*, lower, and not the *para*, the higher power — which is eternal, unchanging, and the abode of absolute peace, tranquillity and bliss, and is untouched by *maya*. Thus Vishnu, the *para* Brahman, lies on the cosmic waters in absolute tranquillity and bliss, and the myth has it that it is out of His navel that *apara* Brahma is born; the latter is, in effect, an active principle and has *maya* as an inbuilt part. The manifested universe is the creation of this force, the *apara* Brahma.

Thus, just as Brahma has *maya*, the individual self has the internal organ. In fact the *maya* of the *apara* Brahma goes down to the individual self as the internal organ; the quality and nature of this would depend upon the karmas of the different selves. Thus, though *maya* is an essential part of *apara* Brahma it is lodged only in the pure consciousness, i.e., *para* Brahma, and, as one view holds it, both *apara* Brahma and the *jiva*, the individual soul, are reflections of pure consciousness in *avidya* and mind respectively. Another view is that reflection of pure consciousness in *maya* is *apara* Brahma, while its reflection in *avidya* is *jiva*. Some scholars however, are not happy with the concept of reflection, for, according to them, attribute of reflection could not be assigned to Brahma who is formless. *Advaitins* say that if the redness, which is without form, of a flower could be reflected from any reflecting medium, Brahma's formlessness could also be, and this could not be an argument against the reflection concept.

Maya is indeterminable. It is not real, if it were so it would not be removable. Yet it is not unreal either, for then it cannot serve as the tranformative material cause of the universe. Since it is real and unreal at the same time, it would violate the law of contradiction. Likewise, it cannot have parts, for that would suggest it had a beginning. But its not having parts means it cannot be the transformative material cause of the universe, only objects with parts can serve as the cause of the effects. Hence *maya* cannot be partless. But it cannot be partless and with parts at the same time, otherwise it will violate the law of contradiction. In fact *maya* is indeterminable.

The *saguna* Brahma is the *Ishvara*, or the God, of the *Advaitins*. The universe as we see it, is dependent upon Brahma; it is not a mental fiction, but is as real as the individual perceiving it. But it is not the ultimate reality. Self, *atman*, is the same as Brahma, the essence of self which is the deepest part of our being, is one with the essence of the universe. The universe cannot exist by itself, it is wholly dependent upon Brahma. The changes in the universe, however, do not affect Brahma. While the universe depends upon Brahma, Brahma depends upon no one. Ignorance, *avidya*, affects the self. It is removed once the truth has been realized. But nothing happens to the world as such when ignorance is removed; only the person's view of it changes. *Moksha* is not the dissolution of the universe but only a change of false outlook, *avidya*, by wisdom, *vidya*.

As for the means to valid knowledge (*parmanas*), the system accepts all the six of them, being perception, inference, verbal testimony, comparison, presumption and non-apprehension. Regarding the Veda, unlike *Mimansa* which believes it to be self existent and eternal, the system accepts it as having been authored by God, but, unlike *nyaya*, which also believes it to have been authored by God, it believes that at *pralaya*, the end of each cycle of creation, the Veda too disappears, to reappear again at the next cycle. The content of the Veda may thus be taken to be independent of God, but its reappearance is caused by Him. The belief secures self validity for the Veda.

As in other systems, here too the ultimate aim is to remove sorrow and secure *moksha*, freedom from the cycle of births, by acquiring the correct knowledge about the truth of the reality. Requirement is to realize that the individual self which is the inner core of a human being, is nothing other than the all pervading Brahma, that the self drifted away from Brahma on account of *avidya*, ignorance, which, in turn, has come about because the self got attached to the internal organ and forgot its true identity. Once this ignorance is removed the self sees its true and pure nature. That is freedom, for *avidya* no longer bothers it.

Let it, however, not be understood that just the knowledge that *avidya*, or the internal organ, is what prevents the *jiva*, the human soul, from realizing that it is Brahma itself, is all that is required to secure freedom. The knowledge has to be acquired from the correct source; there definitely shall have to be a guru and then this knowledge has to be experienced , and to be able to do that practical discipline is necessary, which includes non-killing, cleanliness, correct posture for meditation, control of breath, restraining the senses from their objects, learning to fix the mind for meditation, meditation, and finally *samadhi*, or attaining the state of super-consciousness. There has to be a lot of reflection on whatever is learnt, for unless there is complete conviction, progress towards realizing the goal is not possible. But once there is conviction, accompanied by an ardent desire to know, the truth is experienced, and the person is *jivanmukta*, free during this life itself. He now is above the internal organ, beyond the reach of ego, full of spontaneous love, and after he has left the world he is finally free. This achievement is possible in one life, or over a number of lives.

As in other systems, here too there have been elaborate expositions as to the elements that constitute the material world, including the sentient beings, and how the gross and the subtle bodies have been formed; universals, means of knowledge (*parmanas*), valid and invalid knowledge; and the result of all the arguments and considerations is the system of the Advaita philosophy.

Vashishtadvaita

Upanishads have not been categorical in explaining the relationship among Brahma, self and matter. It has been asserted that the self and the physical universe are identical with Brahma, and yet it has also been emphasized that Brahma is distinct and supreme in so far as the self and the matter are concerned. *Advaita* has sought to solve the problem by stating that self is in fact a part of a whole which is Brahma, and that the matter is only an appearance, *avidya*, the snare that traps the self, till the self has secured the true knowledge and understood its own reality, and, thus, attained complete freedom. Around 1100 AD, Ramanuja, a renowned Brahmin from a village near Chennai in South India, a follower of the cult of Vishnu, wrote his own commentary on the *Vedanta Sutra*, titled *Sri-Bhasya*. He postulated that the relationship between Brahma and the self on the one hand and between Brahma and the matter on the other, is of very intimate nature, in that it is not possible for the self or the matter to exist without Brahma or vice versa. According to his interpretation of the teachings of the Upanishads, Brahma, the individual self and the physical universe are inseparable from each other, but at the same time they are all real, and eternal, and are totally different from one another, unlike the Advaita of Shankra where the physical universe is not real, is only a reflection, *maya*, while the individual self is but a part of the whole that is Brahma. The three entities have been given by Ramanuja as different, but they stand together in a close relationship. The doctrine is referred to as *Vashishtadvaita*, signifying that the physical universe and the individual selves have existence only in the body of Brahma, that though these are essentially different from Brahma, they have no existence or purpose to serve apart from him. The doctrine is also called qualified non-dualism: one Brahma has two forms, i.e., selves and matter. The concept of matter is almost the same as of *prakriti* of Sankhya, except that it is not independent of God, and *satav, rajas, tamas* are its attributes and not constituents; it is described as the garment of God. According to Sankhya, *prakriti* is a dynamic force and does not need another dynamic agency to set the process of evolution in motion, it can evolve on its own. There is, thus, no need to postulate God as the prime mover in the evolutionary process of *prakriti*. There is a requirement for an intelligent Being or Beings for the evolution of sentience, but that need is amply met by the individual selves in whose presence *prakriti* evolves. God is out. Ramanuja, however, is of the view that *prakriti* cannot evolve on its own into such a complex universe which has so much of diversity and is so rich in content. There has to be an Intelligent Being, and not beings, for the becoming of the universe. God, thus, is not only the efficient cause of the universe, as affirmed in the *Nyaya-Vaisheshika* also, he is the material cause as well: universe is a transformation of God. The essential difference between the views of Ramanuja and the Sankhya doctrine is that while the former believes universe is a transformation of God, the latter holds it as a transformation of *prakriti*. Shankra's Advaita also considers God to be the efficient and the material cause of the universe, but does not regard it as the transformation of God, for transformation implies change, and only non-eternal entities change, not God who is eternal. According to his doctrine, universe has to be only an appearance, even though this appearance is only in God.

In *Vashishtadvaita*, salvation is defined as release from limiting barriers imposed by the internal organ. Self cannot be dissolved into God, but the released self has a permanent intuition of Him; self continues to retain its individual existence after release.

The doctrine accepts only three *parmanas*, viz., perception, inference and verbal testimony, and gives equal importance to both the sections of the Veda, i.e., the earlier portion relating to ritual and sacrifice, and the latter one which is concerned with Brahma. It says that the former deals with the worship of God and the latter with His nature. Shankra also gives equal importance but his view is that the former portion is for those who are trying to fit themselves for acquiring Brahma knowledge and the second for those who want Brahma realization. Vashishtadvaita relies heavily on Puranas for support; Advaita also does so but to a lesser degree. *Tat tvam asi*, meaning 'that thou art', has 'that' (*tat*) for God with the entire universe as His body and 'thou' (*tvam*) for God with the individual self as His body. Individual self is a part of the highest self just as the light issuing from a luminous body, such as fire or the sun, is a part of that body. Although the distinguishing attributes, and the thing distinguished thereby, stand to each other in the relation of part and whole, yet we find them to be different in essential character.

The doctrine is the work of Ramanuja, a Brahmin of Vaishnav faith, and, as can be expected, he has laid stress on devotion as the primary means of securing the goal of release from the birth cycle and attaining the world of Narayana (a term used by Vaishnavites for the Supreme Being), and enjoying complete freedom and bliss there. For this achievement a person has to completely surrender to, and have complete faith in the mercy and power of Narayana. The process has to be set in motion preferably under the guidance of a qualified teacher (guru), whose job it would be to impart the necessary knowledge, for, as stated in the Upanishads, knowledge is the essential, if not the only, method of securing release. Once that has been done, or along side this, other disciplines have to be practised which, include adopting correct posture, control of breath, restraining of the senses, reflection on the day to day occurrences and convincing oneself of the correctness of the course adopted. This should culminate in meditation so as to transform into direct experience the knowledge of the ultimate reality acquired through the study, learning and reflection. This course is open to every person.

Then there is the course of devotion or *bhakti* which is only for the higher castes. This progresses through the stages of *karma yoga*, *gyan yoga* and the *bhakti yoga*.

Karma yoga means performing one's duties in one's station in life in accordance with the teachings of *Bhagvad gita* with no thought of reaping the fruit; the duty is performed solely to please God. Karma here means much more than just performing good deeds and thus gathering moral or religious merit, or mere performance of Vedic rituals and sacrifices, it also means following Dharma, and all along performing the duties of one's station in life, even while seeking liberation, for this also constitutes Dharma. This implies that even a householder can achieve liberation. Renunciation, *sanyasa*, as advocated in the Upanishads, may secure early release, but that does not mean it is essential for release, or is the only method of securing it, or that the duties as enjoined in the Veda may be given a go-by.

Gyan yoga, is the realization of the true nature of one's self in relation to God and the physical world, and involves meditation upon one's self as a spiritual being, and as entirely subordinate to God. This yoga is the way to God-realization; in Advaita this itself is the realization.

Bhakti yoga is constant meditation on God, not blind faith, but in loving devotion based on highest knowledge. During its course, ego and the rest of the internal organ is demolished and the soul has the direct vision of God as its own ultimate essence. It cannot be termed as direct perception, for the operation of sensory organs becomes unnecessary at this stage, but it is a unique form of direct experience. Result obtained through the other two courses, detailed above, would also be about the same.

The doctrine does not recognize *jivan mukti*, i.e., liberation during the current life itself.

Dvaita

Dvaita is dualism. Madhva (1199-1278 AD), who lived in a village near the coastal town of Udipi in the present day Karnataka state of south India, was its renowned exponent; he has also written commentaries on important Upanishads, the *Bhagavad gita* and the *Vedanta Sutra*, and has left behind several other works. Like *Vashishtadvaita*, the doctrine is theistic and Vaishnav in content. God, Narayana of the *Vashishtadvaita*, is referred to as Vishnu here. It is pluralistic in that it believes that God, selves and the universe exist permanently, and are separate entities, though the latter two are subordinate to God; He directs the universe, is transcendent to it and is imminent in it; He is the ruler of all selves. Self by nature is blissful, but gets subjected to pain and suffering on account of its association with the material body; this happens due to karma. No two selves or two material objects, are alike. The doctrine claims the support of the Veda which, being revealed, cannot be inconsistent and should teach the same truth as the Upanishads. The exponents of the doctrine claim that it is as old as the Upanishads and maintain that Madhva was only its exponent.

The doctrine says that God is beyond the reach of the unaided faculties of man. He is the efficient cause of the world while *prakriti* is the material cause, as in the Sankhya doctrine. Everything exists, knows and functions finally at God's will. In support it quotes the Upanishadic statement: *sarvam khalvidam Brahma* (all this indeed is Brahma!). Everything is dependent upon God's will, but they are not derived from Him; God exists in his own right. Essential characteristics of an eternal entity are eternal while those of a temporal entity are temporal. God possesses all excellences, but it is not possible to know Him even with the aid of revelations, though He is not beyond the reach of the mind as in *Advaita*. He is above *satav, rajas, tamas* which are products of *prakriti* (and not its attributes as in *Vashishtadvaita*). He is infinitely powerful and has infinite mercy. He is the essence of knowledge and joy; is the creator and the terminator of the universe; and entirely controls its every aspect. Individual selves, matter, time, all exist by his grace and would immediately come to nothing if that grace were withdrawn. The complex, multifarious activity of the universe only reveals His perfection. He can assume any form, like *avatara* (incarnate form), and is the significance of all words.

Souls are infinite in number and are different from each other. Each has its own imperfections which put it in ignorance and suffering. It is essentially atomic but has some features which are common with God, like sentience and a degree of bliss. Upanishadic statement tat tvam asi (that thou art) does not mean identity of self with God but only resemblance. There are three types of souls, namely, those bound but may become free, those migrating from life to life within the mundane sphere, and those which are permanently doomed to the miseries of hell. It appears Madhva's thoughts had been formulated more on the basis of the Brahmana literature than the Upanishads. There is a distinct admixture of pessimism in his thinking. Even though he places much reliance on divine grace, he does not seem to believe in universal redemption. He seems to believe that evil will persist for ever, and scope for human freedom and divine grace is limited.

Prakriti, the ultimate source of the physical universe, is eternal but insentient. *Satava, rajas, tamas* are its first products (*gunas*), and from these come intellect (*mahat*), ego (*ahankara*) and *manas* (mind), and the sensory organs and the five elements, as in the Sankhya doctrine. The effect of the cause of the universe is both existent and non-existent; in material causation a thing may exist as a cause, but it may not exist as effect. To properly understand the ontology of the doctrine a good understanding of the *visheshas* i.e., special characteristics that distinguish things, is necessary. The doctrine explains knowledge as a transformation or a mode of the internal organ and, therefore, as characterizing it and not the self. But the self initiates the process of knowing and is not unconnected with the knowledge gained. All knowledge points to complex or qualified objects and there is, thus, no reason to admit any attributeless entity. Knowledge in respect of something is with reference to something other than the thing about which knowledge is to be gained. Anything that comes into relation with time and space, is necessarily real, no matter for how long and to what extent. There is no distinction between the real and the empirical or the empirical and the unreal. The distinction ontologically is between the real and the unreal. Advaita explains the absolutistic stand of the Upanishads by accepting only one reality; it accepts the universe only as an appearance of this reality. Dvaita postulates God as the supreme reality and everything else as totally dependent upon it.

Truth corresponds to reality, this is the realism of the doctrine. Object is apprehended as it is. Dreams and recollections are also taken to be true, but that part of the dream is an illusion in which the dreamer is not involved directly; dreams are real because they are not contradicted later. Recollection is also real, and right knowledge. The doctrine accepts three means to valid knowledge or (*parmanas*) viz., perception, inference and verbal testimony. Valid knowledge itself is a *parmana* as it points directly to a fact, though that fact by itself is not the means to valid knowledge. There are primary and secondary means to valid knowledge, the former indicating a fact directly and the latter mediately; inference as *parmana* indicates fire mediately while valid knowledge does so directly. Thus valid knowledge is the direct means of knowing, while perception, inference, and verbal testimony are seyoaders. When compared to Shankra, Madhva too, like Ramanuja, leans heavily on Puranas and connected literature to support his doctrine. According to him, seven senses are instrumental in acquiring knowledge, including *manas* (internal organ) and *sakshin* (the pure self as viewer of things). God and the selves are sentient, and this sentience is taken to be *sakshin* (viewer), i.e., it can know through one of the senses and also know directly; direct knowledge is invariably correct. Own-self, pain, pleasure, time and space, are known directly; all else is known through one or the other of the remaining senses. That self knows itself by itself, was dismissed by Shankra as a contradiction. In his view, if we say that pain, pleasure, time, space, are known by the self directly, then we reduce the internal organ to a mere aid in the process of knowing. It ceases to have its own specific role of making the self know, as given in other doctrines, like *Nyaya-Vaisheshika*; it becomes just an aid in the recollection process.

Sansara, or transmigration, is beginningless ignorance, *avidya*, which is specific to each individual; *avidya* is considered a substance. It obscures from man the true nature of God and of himself. Release comes by overcoming *avidya*. Correct self knowledge is obtained by study of scriptures, but this knowledge is only mediate, and becomes direct when final release is attained, through God's grace. True knowledge of God is more essential than that of the self, and this also is attained through the study of scriptures, and then conversion of the knowledge thus gained, into a personal experience by meditation. The best effort can bring bliss only in keeping with the intrinsic worth of each self; distinction between selves persists even in *moksha*. Bliss of the released souls is finite while that of God is infinite; bliss realised in *moksha* cannot be experienced in mundane life.

Final release comes through *bhakti*, unadulterated love for God, and this brings God's grace, and it is this grace which brings about the release. To achieve this there has to be detachment, performance of duties as enjoined in *Bhagavad Gita* (*karma yoga*), study of scriptures under the guidance of a teacher or guru and then reflection on what has been taught and, finally, meditation upon what has been learnt. Duties of one's station in life have to be performed till the very end, including rites as prescribed in the scriptures; these are considered to be obligatory. *Jivanmukti*, or liberation while still alive, a concept of Advaita, is rejected.

The non-Vedic System

In the preceding pages we have brief glimpse of the systems of philosophy which accept the authority of the Veda, the *astika darshanas* as they are called, or the Vedic schools, also called the orthodox or traditional systems. We will now briefly go through the heterodox systems, ones which do not accept the traditionally recognized authority of the Veda, also referred to as the *avaidika* schools or *nastika darshanas*. There are three such systems, viz., Charvaka, Jainism and Buddhism.

Charvaka

The main work on this system, which was compiled in the *Brahaspati Sutra* around 600 BC, has been lost. Therefore, not much is known about this system, particularly about its earlier stages. The system is also called *lokayata*, i.e., belief in the existence only of this world; that there is nothing beyond. It accepts only perception as one means to valid knowledge (*parmana*). It rejects inference and verbal testimony, for there is a lack of finality in reasoned conclusions, for the reasoning in such cases depends upon some inductive truth which is not demonstrable. But observation like 'North Star will appear at night in the north in the northern hemisphere', are valid and there is nothing wrong with this. As perception is the only form of valid knowledge, matter, which alone is cognized by the senses, is the only reality. The elements recognized are: earth, fire, water and air; space, the fifth element of the Upanishadas, is not recognized.

Ajita (nick name *Kesa Kambli* - hair blanket) was about the first historically recognized person who preached a materialist doctrine. He said good deeds and charity achieved nothing in the end, that the body dissolved into primary elements at death and thereafter Karma had no meaning. *Lokyata* school from which brutally practical theories of the Magadhan statecraft developed, borrowed from Ajita. Charvaka view is that consciousness is a material and transitory modification of the four elements, and will disappear after a duration when these elements have ceased to be together. The intelligence which is found to be embodied in the forms produced from the combination of the elements, is produced the same way as the green colour of the leaves or the red colour of a flower. Soul is only the body qualified by intelligence; it has no existence apart from the body. Postulates of religion, God, freedom, morality, are mere illusions. Nature is indifferent to good or evil, and history does not bear witness to Divine Providence. Pain and pleasure are central facts of life, while vice and virtue are not absolute values but mere social norms laid down by the society for its convenience. Therefore, the conclusion is that while life is yours, live it fully and joyously. Chastity and such like ordinances, and the rituals of religious practices, as also the ideas of religion, are mooted by misguided or cunning or weak and dishonest people; the latter, under the cover of such ideas, are doing nothing but furthering their own gains and interests. It is not logical to regard something as perceived unless it appears to be perceived; otherwise it would be an undue assumption. It is not possible to understand the relation of cause and effect. Knowledge is not different from the object of knowledge, as both are forms of existence and have no other form; in fact, they are one and the same. Only fools imagine that spirit is different from body, and that they would reap the rewards of actions in some future state. They assume existence of something that does not exist. Only sustenance and love are the objects of human existence. Death is blessedness. If victims slain in sacrifice ascend to heaven, why are parents not slain for this purpose? Some materialists are, however, inclined to recognize the internal organ as soul, so long as it is accepted that it has no existence after the body has perished. Besides, there is a tacit acceptance of the law, dharma, and the principal of 'as you sow, so shall you reap', for the duration of life on earth.

Jainism

Quite like Vaishnavism, this system too was a revolt against Brahminism and their system of animal sacrifice. It does not recognize any Supreme God. It came into being during the later Vedic period, during the time of the Brahmanas. The author of the doctrine is Vardhmana (599-527 BC), who is also called Mahavira (the great hero). The followers of the doctrine say that he was not the author but only the 24th prophet guide (*Tirthankara*: *tiratha* is religious order, and *ankara* the organizer who lays down its doctrine, disciplines, order, and other aspects of organization); they claim the doctrine is much older and already had 23 *Tirthankaras* before Vardhmana Mahavira. Mahavira followed four rules ascribed to his predecessor Parshava: possess no property of your own, take no property from others, take no life, and be truthful. The one he added was celibacy. However, notwithstanding the existence of earlier *Tirthankaras*, the exposition of the essential doctrine and laying down the structure of the organization of the religious order, was done by Mahavira only. He was from a princely family of Kundagram, in the Vaishali republic in North Bihar, and led the life of a householder till he was thirty. Then he left his home in search of the truth, and after nearly 13 years of study and meditation, he achieved the illumination and became a Jina — the spiritual conqueror; his followers founded Jainism based on his teachings. The religion has two sects: *Svetambaras* (dressed in white) and *Digambaras* (who go about naked); it is the belief of *Digambaras* that any kind of ownership of property, even a loin cloth, is in the way of achievement of enlightenment.

The essential belief is that the universe consists of two types of basic substances: the soul and the non-soul. A soul or *atma* bound by body is called *jiva* or an embodied soul. A free or a not embodied soul is *paramatma* or the perfect soul. That which transforms a soul into a perfect soul is *dharma* or religion. Spirit and matter (*jiva* and *ajiva*) have eternal, independent existence; neither the inanimate is born out of the animate, nor the vice versa. There are infinite number of souls, and each of these has independent existence. But the souls and the matter possess a number of common characteristics; that is how they interact. The animate, because of the exertion of its inherent force, consumes the inanimate, including karmas, and gets associated with it. This is bondage, and this matures into attachment and aversion, which causes the performance of good or evil deeds, and that in turn causes the influx of karmas (*asrava*) which further strengthens the bondage and so on. This is *sansara*, the mundane existence in the cycle of rebirths, and the soul caught in this process experiences the physical and mental suffering on account of birth, disease, old age, and death. The bondage too, i.e., lack of unfettered freedom, is the cause of suffering. The sum total of the fundamental elements in the universe is forever constant; not a single particle can ever be increased or decreased.

Knowledge (or sentience) is the essence of *jiva*, but this is restricted on account of the limitations of the internal organ and the body. Once the mortal sheath of the body and the internal organ have been cast away for good, the soul is free, and in this state it is omniscient and has full and comprehensive knowledge of all things through direct intuition; at this stage the knowledge could come only through intuition as all the physical instruments as are attached to a body and through which the soul experiences the mundane worldly activities, have perished with the body. This is the state of *kevalaya*, and the knowledge acquired is *kevala-gayan*. The main point is that in this state the spirit is omniscient.

The soul follows the process of transmigration, and this happens because of the karmas, or the good and the bad deeds. Karmas are non-souls, (*ajivas*), which get inside ·the soul and çontaminate it, and this contamination is the cause of the spirit going astray, resulting in the cycle of rebirths. *Jivas* are of higher or lower order depending upon the sense organs they possess. Grass, the lowest in the order of the things which have life, has only touch as the sense organ, while a human being has all the five senses and the internal organ.

The soul is not perceptible to the senses; it is not possible to establish its existence on the basis of logical reasoning as logic is limited to only those items as can be perceived by the senses; only intuitive knowledge establishes the existence of the soul. The soul attracts the subtle atoms of karmas, (and thus gets contaminated) by the exertion of its own inherent force. The atoms are of the karmas, performed by the soul during previous births but they exclude karmas which may not have been relevant to the process of rebirth, like routines performed in the honest and simple process of living. Depending upon the types of atoms sticking to the soul, it takes the form, in the next birth, of a human being, or an animal, or an item of vegetation. The process of bondage between karmas and the soul is considered to be beginningless, in that during no time in the past was the soul not liable to be bound by the karmas. But it is not as if the soul is perpetually bound by the karmas and there is no release; in fact, the aim of the religion is to secure the release. The righteous and sinful deeds are not mere social occurrences; they are not governed by systems created by man. They are the products of man's natural instincts, born with him on account of the karmas. The state of liberation, (nirvana), is not the end of the existence of the soul. It is only a change in its state; having been freed from the karma-atoms, now it does not transmigrate, and stays changeless.

Ajivas are devoid of consciousness, and there are five kinds of them, being matter, time, space, the medium of motion and the medium of rest. Matter is of many types, and it is made up of atoms; when the atoms combine, in different proportions, we have things that give the common experience. It has qualities of colour, taste, touch and smell. Sound also is an attribute of matter but only in its composite and not in its atomic form. Atoms are identical but they produce a variety of objects on account of various combinations. These combinations form earth, water, air and fire. All atoms, or aggregates of them, have souls; the whole universe, thus, is infested with life.

Time and space pervade everywhere. All things are in time and all changes take place in it. The universe is considered to be finite from the point of view of substance and space, i.e., both things have a beginning as well as an end. But it is infinite as far as the time and the modification of substance are concerned, i.e., it is forever changing, and its time dimension is infinite.

As stated above, soul attracts matter, and this results in the influx of karma, and bondage is caused. This bondage is the cause of attachment or aversion, and this further strengthens bondage, giving momentum to the cycle of suffering. This process is forever repetitive and bondage is strengthened from stage to stage. This is *sansara*, living mundane life through non-stop birth-cycles. Dharma is what strikes at the root of the cycle of suffering. The first step is to study and practice dharma. Once the right knowledge has been gained, the person develops complete detachment — he is freed from attachment or aversion. Two things happen when complete detachment has been developed: firstly, the person is no longer generating the *bandha* (shackles) of fresh karma, and, secondly, he is shedding off the past karmas. This is the road to liberation, *moksha*. Complete liquidation of *bandha* leads to complete freedom. Forces like time, individual disposition, universal laws, in addition to karma, also influence the capacity of a person to act, but karma is the most powerful of these. Karmas, however, are born from the doings of the person himself, and he has to bear the consequences. He can get rid of the effects of karmas only when they have been separated from the soul after development of complete detachment.

Mahavira, however, did not accept karma as the supreme power, for that would have meant recognizing karma as God, the Creator or the Controller; it would have meant substituting karma for God; he had denied God. He accepted the power of karma in a limited sense only, for, as he taught, karma could be liquidated by spiritual exertion. He accepted the fact that karma influenced man, but emphasized that spiritual exertion, which is in the power of man, has power over karma. There is, thus, a tussle going on all the time, between the past karmas , i.e., fate or destiny, and the power of man in the form of physical, mental and spiritual exertion. Sometimes it is karma and some times it is the personal exertion of man, physical, mental and spiritual, which has the upper hand. The point to remember is that karma is the instrumental cause of man's condition, his pains and pleasures, and not the efficient cause. It is possible to fight effectively against an instrumental cause by adopting suitable counter measures. Pain and pleasure are felt within the person, in his psych, and it is in there that changes have to be made. Thus a person's inside has to be strong, spiritually, to withstand the onslaught of karma, and negate its effects. That is where asceticism comes in; it may even take the form of self-mortification. Mere softening of the external conditions in the form of good deeds or pursuing noble activities, will, no doubt help, to a great extent actually, but this cannot entirely free the person of the effects of karma. For that counter karmic activity is necessary. Mahavira, thus, has not put forth a pessimistic doctrine, as is sometimes believed. He has, in fact, given a clarion call to humanity to not to lose heart, as man has it within himself to surmount any opposition, from fate or whatever else, with his innate capability for spiritual exertion, *purushartha*, which includes mental and physical exertion, including hard ascetic discipline and self-mortification.

Before complete detachment is achieved, a person has to undergo certain disciplines, like getting to know and experience reality, developing faith in truth, inculcating spiritual uprightness and washing off of the accumulated karmas through right austerities. Amongst the important rules of discipline are (i) equality for all living beings, including human beings (egalitarianism), animals and plant life, (ii) non-killing of any living being or causing pain, or enslaving; and (iii) not imposing oneself on any one. The religion emphasizes complete non-violence, mental and physical, and enjoins its adherents to be fearless, free of hatred and flattery, and not be bothered by failure or success, and such like things. Truth is supreme and is the essence of the universe. Do not be angry or covetous or be a thief. Control all desires and keep the needs to the minimum, and be celebate and do not be attached to sound, beauty, fragrance, taste, and touch, and observe the discipline of walking, speaking, collecting food and eating it and keep clean, pollution free environment. All these, along with tough austerities, were the kind of instructions which were designed to be followed by monks and nuns. The religion accepts the equality of men and women and gives them equal status. They are to renounce their household life and accept the discipline of the ascetic. For the householder the regimen is comparatively lighter. Truth and non-violence are prescribed for him. He is not to steal or be incontinent or covetous, and should practice looking inwards into his self, and try and renounce what is not essential for his living, and lead a simple life, freed of all ostentations, and practise detachment and be freed of superstitions and not harbour any fear of any kind, and such like things. All this is Dharma, designed to rid the soul of the karmas of the past as well as prevent generation of new karmas, and thus bring liberation and *kaivalya*, i.e. make the spirit omniscient and restored to its pristine radiance and purity. But to attain this one has to renounce the world and be a monk and an ascetic; it cannot be achieved from the level of the householder.

As will follow from what has been stated in the preceding paras, the religious order lays stress on non-violence and equality, not making any distinction between caste, creed or sex, emphasizing that unless people learn to coexist, violence would continue, and this would bring pain and misery to humanity. It also discourages dogmatism or fundamentalism in any shape, and emphasizes that there are usually many angles to an idea or a viewpoint, and that the requirement is to try and understand these. This could possibly lead to a synthesis, and also a better understanding of the other's viewpoint, and make the process of coexistence easier. This is the doctrine of *Anekantavada* (synthesis), i.e., there is more than one justification for a certain action, activity, situation, proposition, and that it is possible to understand different viewpoints, and avoid being dogmatic or fundamentalistic. Such an approach would lead to synthesis of the different viewpoints and remove uncalled for tensions between individuals and different elements of the society.

Vardhman Mahavir laid great stress on the need to look inwards, for, he said, he who did not, would not realize the self. Such a person's knowledge was acquired either through verbal testimony or through the medium of sense-organs and the mind. To practice religion, a knowledge of the self was important, for otherwise the person would not secure freedom from attachment, aversion and delusion, and, therefore, would not achieve emancipation, or reach the stage of *moksha* or *nirvana*; the very first step for *nirvana* was self knowledge. Mahavira said, 'See the truth. Do not depend only on what I say, but develop your own spiritual vision.' He was against being dogmatic. He wanted a person to follow the conclusions of his own judgement and experience, and be convinced that whatever he had undertaken was, in fact, the right course for him.

Buddhism

Sixth century BC was a period of intense religious and intellectual activity in Asia. This is the time of Confucius and perhaps, Lao-tzu in China, Zoroaster in Iran, the greatest of the Hebrew prophets, Deutero-Isaiah in the Middle East, and Pythagoras in Greece. This was also the period of Greek's Golden Age when Greek thinkers were looking for a single principle to explain the material world. In India it was the time of Buddha and Vardhmana Mahavira. In fact, with the silent revolt that the philosophy of the Upanishadas was spearheading against the ritualism of the Brahmanical religion, many new teachers had emerged in the Gangetic basin, Buddha and Mahavira being just two amongst them, and not the most popular ones either. Gautama, also called Siddhartha by the devout, is the author of the doctrine of Buddhism. He belonged to a Sakya tribe (for that reason he is also called Sakya Muni), who spoke Aryan language and claimed to be Aryans, though they had no Brahmans or *varanas*, i.e., class distinctions on the basis of colour of skin. They lived at and around Kapilavastu, an area around 150 km north-east of the city of Varanasi and around 50 km south of the Himalayas, and were agriculturists whose livelihood depended mainly on rice and cattle. They were under the Kosala empire. Persenajit was the emperor during the earlier days of Buddha; emperor alone had the power of life and death. The chief of the tribe was probably elected by rotation. Gautama's father, Shuddhodana, who, apparently, was the chief, had two wives, both sisters, daughters of a neighbouring Koli chief (Kolis had the kol tree as their totem; they claimed Buddha's ashes). But both the ladies were childless, till in her 45th year, Maya, the elder lady, gave birth to Gautama, in a *sala* grove, after a bath in the adjoining sacred tank (*pushkara*, the artificial lotus pond); *sala* tree was considered sacred to mother goddess *Lumbini* and was the totem tree of the Sakyas. But she, Gautama's mother, died seven days later. The goddess is still worshipped as Rumminidevi at the same spot though Buddha is forgotten. There are a number of views on Buddha's date of birth but the commonly accepted date is 563 BC. He lived for about 80 years and died in 483 BC.

Young Gautama was trained as a Kshatriya prince in the handling of weapons and state craft. He was married at the age of 16, to a Sakyan princess, Yashodhara, and , in course of time, got one son, Rahula. Early in life he was reflecting on the human vanity, and the sorrows of disease, old age and death. At the age of 29 he left his home, wife and child, in search of an answer to the riddle of life, and, along with five others, spent six years seeking guidance from scholars and teachers of eminence, but without receiving satisfaction. Ultimately he decided to do his own reflection, favouring a middle course. At this stage his five companions left him, but he found them again, at Sarnath, near Varanasi, after enlightenment, and they accepted his philosophy and were his first disciples. After a lot of study, reflection, meditation, and penance, he had received the knowledge of the ultimate truth, the enlightenment, while seated under the Bo-tree (peepal), on the bank of river Neranjara, near Gaya in Bihar; the place probably had been a humble cult spot. During his later years a young disciple, Ananda, who was also his cousin, looked after him, and after he was gone, Ananda repeated from memory many of the discourses of Buddha. Buddha preached mostly in central Uttar Pradesh and portions of Bihar and Nepal, and converted Yakshas, a powerful non-Aryan tribe, and befriended Bimbisar, the Maghadan king, and a host of other noted people of his time. Brahmins were his leading disciples. The Sangha, the Buddhist order, owes its growth, early philosophy and organization to them. During the final days of his life a blacksmith, Chunda, served a special dish of mushrooms to him and that brought a relapse of an earlier attack of dysentry which led to the master's final illness. The end came while he was resting between two Sala trees at a grove at Kushinagara, a place in the city-state of the Mallas, on way to Rajgir from Savatthi. His birth, enlightenment and *parinirvana* (the end), came on the same day.

Buddhism had a wide acceptance and steadily spread to all the four corners of Asia. In south-east Asia, China, Japan, Korea, Mongolia, Manchuria, it is the prevalent faith of the majority of the people to this day. Its spread to south and west Asia was almost immediate. The writings ascribed to an ascetic Mediterranean community, first found in 1747, the Dead Sea scrolls (dated 250 BC to about 70 AD) containing Hebrew and Aramaic scriptural texts and liturgical system of public worship, appear to be of Buddhist origin.

The practice of living in a monastry located atop a cemetry is very Buddhist; the teacher of righteousness, as mentioned in the scrolls, is the precise title of the Buddha. There is a prevalent belief in the east that, in effect, Christianity took off from Buddhism and some of Christ's miracles, such as walking on water, were, much earlier, ascribed to the Buddha. The legend of Barlaam and Josaphat is, in effect, a direct adaptation of Buddha's life story. In fact, in the story of Christ's life not much detail is available about him from the time he was twelve to the time he was thirty. One view is that he spent whole or part of this period in the Buddhist monastery of Himis, located on river Indus, some 25 odd kilometres north-west of Leh, in Ladakh, India. It is claimed that documents in Buddhist and Pali languages, which at one time were in the possession of this monastery, told of the days that Jesus spent here, and where he was not only a welcome student but also a teacher. His Sermon on the Mount contains a strong Buddhist flavour. In fact, belief with certain scholars is that the 'promised land' of Moses was not Palestine but Kashmir, that out of the 12 tribes that set out from Egypt under Moses, one, in fact, did make it to the promised land; Semitic Kashmiris are believed to be the descendents of this tribe. The remaining 11 tribes were in fact lost in the desert, and had perforce to settle in the Palestinian waste land; no one could call a desert a promised land! According to this view, supported by extensive quotes and references, Jesus did not die on the cross, that after his wounds had been treated he was well again, but since he was a man hunted by the Jews, he had to flee, along with his mother, to any hospitable land prepared to afford him shelter. He found none in the Middle East, and had to ultimately emigrate to Kashmir where he felt he would be well received. It was, it is stated, a long and arduous journey, performed during nights or in disguise, and on the way Mary, the mother, died and was buried at a place called *Mai Mari ka Asthan* (the resting place of Mother Mary), in the town of Murree (the town is named after her), some 50 km north-east of Islamabad in Pakistan. Jesus, the account narrates, lived for many years, greatly respected by the people with whom he lived, and was buried at Rauza Bal, in Khaniyar locality of Srinagar in Kashmir. The tomb standing there is stated to be of prophet Yuz Asaf, but, according to the account, that was the name Jesus had taken to conceal his identity during the flight and his stay in the valley.

Anyway, the point being made is that Buddhism had an extensive spread in Asia, including West Asia, and that there is a lot of commonality in the Christian and Buddhist teachings, which suggests that the former respected Buddhism and extensively borrowed from it. As stated above, this was a period when a number of thinkers and philosophers were looking into the meaning and purpose of existence. Already the Hindu orthodox doctrines had come into being. Jainism had laid a lot of emphasis on severe penance, essentially for those who had adopted the course of renunciation and asceticism. There was stress on abstinence, control of breath and the body posture. This possibly led to the development of Yoga doctrine. Charvaka followers felt there was nothing like soul or the impact of the deeds after death. Makkhali Goshala was teaching that, notwithstanding the karma, a soul went through innumerable cycles of pre-ordained rebirths, and his conclusion was that the right course was to make the best while one lived. Buddhism struck, so to say, the middle course.

The doctrine took a leap forward when, around 210 years after the *parinirvana*, the Buddha's passing away, Asoka (ruled between 274-232 BC), the great Magadhan king, lent his support to it; he sent emissaries to different countries with Buddha's message; he sent his own son, Mahindra, and daughter Sanghamitra, to Lanka, modern SriLanka, with a sapling from the Bodhi tree at Gaya (the tree under which the Buddha had achieved his enlightenment), and they, with their zeal and enthusiasm, converted the whole of the island to the Buddhist faith. The religion reached China by the first century AD, Korea in the fourth and Japan in the sixth century AD.

The doctrine denies self or a continuous subject of thought, or soul or *atma*. It denies God working in the manifold phenomenon of the universe. It denies any real matter. But it believes in gods. The doctrine believes that the entire cosmos is filled with infinite trains of consciousness, but these are not souls, having their own identity or existence. Each train is, in fact, a succession of moments of consciousness, each moment a direct resultant of the preceding moments. At a point of time a train gets infected by karma, and no sooner that happens, ego is born, and that brings in ignorance and consequent engulfment by *maya*. At this stage conformations come into being, i.e., potentialities of love and hate and such like weaknesses of the spirit which are the resultants of acts committed in past lives and which shape and direct the acts to be committed in the future (*sanskaras*). The stage is now set for the birth of the sentient being. The first to appear is the consciousness, and this is followed by name and form, or the development of a finite world of particulars. Then the sense organs develop, and these provide the capability of contact with the apparent world, bringing in — the experience of sensations; the growth of desires; and attraction and attachment to individual life and finite existence, all in that order. The existence finally passes through birth, disease, sorrow and death, at the last stage the karmas leave the material body to ride another train of consciousness.

The Buddhists say that there is no existence as such of a sentient being. What we see is only an outward appearance, a phenomenal personality, and this comes into being through the combination of name and form (*nama, roopa*). In 'name' they include all the four subjective phenomenon of thought, viz., (a) feelings; (b) conformations (*sanskaras*) which, in fact, are potentialities of love and hate and similar emotions born out of the deeds of the past lives and which bear a strong influence upon the deeds of the future; (c) general notions like the concept of a definite world of particulars, and (d) definite consciousness. These constitute four *skandhas*, aggregations, (*khandhas* in Pali). The fifth *khandha* is 'form', born out of the four elements of the physical nature i.e., earth, water, fire and air. The force that binds the five *khandhas* into an individual or personality, is karma. Karma here include mental, physical or oral deeds, though involuntary or inadvertent acts are not karma. But the karma is not imposed by some mysterious power. A person has the freedom to act in spite of the influence of the karmas of his past lives, and, thus, has the potential to achieve naishkarmya , freedom from karma, which leads to Arhat-ship and thence to nirvana. To achieve this final state there is need to practise spiritual discipline, and do contemplation, and cultivate the four noble virtues which give a foretaste of this state, the virtues being — universal love, compassion, sympathetic joy, and equanimity. At death all the five khandhas perish. Only karmas remain, which get onto another train of consciousness and assemble another set of *khandhas*, and a new life comes into being. Karmas, in effect, is the link that preserves the identity of a being through all the countless changes that it undergoes during its journey through *sansara*, the chain of re-births. It is the karmas that determine the type of being to be born. This is the doctrine of *pratitya-samutpada*, the doctrine developed to explain how individual existence and consciousness evolve in the cosmic process. What has been given here is but one of its interpretations; there are others, equally plausible, by other authorities.

The goal for the monastic order is *nirvana* while that for the lay devotee, or the householder, it is rebirth in a higher heaven. To achieve the goal it is necessary to comprehend the four noble truths, and follow the noble eight-fold path of the fourth noble truth. The four noble truths are:

First, Life is evil (leading to persistent suffering).

Secondly, Ignorance is the source of evil (suffering). Ignorance (*avidya*) is about the true nature of a being, that it is phenomenal, in a state of flux, constituted by the force of the karmas by uniting five *khandhas*, which perish at the time of death. The karmas, however, survive and they force another set of *khandhas* to start another life; only in nirvana the process ceases.

Thirdly, Evil (suffering) can be overcome. After the coming into being of name and form, as stated above, there is evolution of sense organs which establish contact with the apparent world and there are feelings and sensations, leading to desires, to attraction for and attachment to individual life. This is the finite existence, which goes through disease, sorrow, death and thence to rebirth; rebirth is also caused by the unfulfilled cravings, so that these may be satisfied during the next life or the lives following. But the main reason for the rebirth is karma.

Fourthly, Evil (suffering) is overcome by following the noble eightfold path. The path defined is considered to be the middle path between the two extremes of self mortification , as recommended by Jainism and some other schools following similar philosophy, and self indulgence as advocated by the followers of the Yogchara school and its variants. The steps to be followed have been logically thought out and the seeker progresses from stage to stage without encountering undue contradictions and repetitions. The steps are :

(i) The right view. Cleanse your mind of all superstitions, animism, primitive rites, and consider animal sacrifice to be a sin. Regard all human beings as equal, and give up your faith in a prime creator of the universe, and depend upon your own powers of reasoning. The Buddha disapproved violence in any form, including sacrifices in which animals were killed, or wars where people killed each other. He placed forbearance above the bravery of the man who killed defending a cause, a principal, or a law, howsoever sacred. He wanted every man, including the common folk, to be virtuous and wise. He preached the dharma for the welfare and happiness of every man. He was not advocating a system of prayers, or rites, or rules. He was showing a way of life which emphasised on the purity of thinking, speaking and acting. He asserted that every man was his own saviour and that no outside power could help or hinder in his journey through life on earth, or in the process of seeking the ultimate deliverance from the cycle of re-births.

(ii) Right mental resolve. Having cultivated the right view, this would be the next step.

(iii) Right speech; this follows once the mind is set on the right lines.

(iv) Right action, after having trained in 3 above.

(v) Right livelihood, on the basis of right action.

(vi) Right effort, basically for own mental and moral elevation.

(vii) Right mindfulness, in the form of attention to the activities and weaknesses of own body and mind.

(viii) Right concentration, by fixing the mind on a single object; without this no progress is possible in any field.

In substance all this means is avoidance of all sins, and acquisition of all merit, and steadfastly maintaining an absolute purification of the mind. This is the essence of the middle path.

It appears Buddha was indifferent to the philosophy concerning the deepest mysteries of life; he did not encourage his followers to unnecessarily waste time pondering over such issues as they were irrelevant to the goal, which was attainment of Nirvana. For lay followers it was rebirth in a higher heaven. The Buddha is believed to have said that nirvana could be achieved by love and faith as well, and also that all questions could not be solved by reasoning alone. Critical approach, no doubt, was important, but it had its limitations, and beyond that it was only the teacher who could show the way. In this world, he is believed to have said, there were so many things which were not accessible to ordinary intelligence, but their existence could not be denied for that reason. He was silent on the origin of karma, and the condition or the state in nirvana, and when pressed for an exposition, he is believed to have said that it was not possible to know anything about nirvana. It is a state, he said, where there is neither element of extension, cohesion, heat or motion (the four elements of nature), nor sphere of infinity of space, nor sphere of infinity of consciousness, nor sphere of nothingness, nor of neither perception nor non-perception, neither this world nor the world beyond, nor sun nor moon. There is neither coming nor going, neither staying nor passing away or moving, or arising. This indeed is the end of suffering.

Is nirvana eternal existence or eternal annihilation? One view is that it is not the annihilation of the self but only of the self-hood. But Buddhists recognize no self as such, as in the Hindu doctrines. For them it is just a train of consciousness in flux, getting caught by karma which forces the five *khandhas* around it and generate life, a being. Nothing finite exists in itself; every living thing is a collection of *khandhas*, temporarily united; or, we can say, everything is phenomenal. All data of finite experience is subjective phenomenon corresponding to no objective reality. The truth is that nirvana is both eternal existence and eternal annihilation. In this state the train of consciousness has finally been delivered of the karma and has been freed and it joins the overall content of consciousness, like space contained in a vessel becomes one with the infinite space after the vessel is broken. In this state it is eternal existence. But it is eternal annihilation as well because the space in the vessel has forever lost its existence. The Buddha called the abode of nirvana as void, *shunya*. It is that which is selfless and can be realized only by those who have ended craving utterly, and have entered solitude based on the sphere of neither perception nor non-perception, and have then moved to the state of concentration of mind wherein awareness and feelings cease. This is the condition when the seeker is completely free and enters the utterly purified and incomparably high void. Otherwise there are voids at every stage, like solitude of the forest means a void of human beings, only solitude of the forest remaining, and void of the forest means only earth remaining, and that of the earth means only infinite space remaining, and so on, till the highest void has been attained. In real terms, however, it is difficult to distinguish between void and Brahma, for the distinguishing characteristic of each is the absence of any characteristic at all; each is other than Being, and other than non-Being. In each case *neti, neti* (not this, not this), formula has been used in the description attempt.

In fact, it cannot be said with certainty that everything attributed to the Buddha did, in fact, emanate from him, or had his approval. With time Buddhism broke off into branches and there was a lot of inter-mixture of ideas, and backward and forward movement of views, and, in the process, some stuff which, in fact, had not originated from him, got the treatment as if it had. Otherwise the Buddha's attitude was clearly that of a positivist and an agnostic. His main aim was to remedy the world's sorrow and teach his followers to escape from their karma and thereby, *sansara* (wanderings of the spirit through the cycle of rebirths). He has emphasized that man himself, being the master of his will, is the master of his karmas, that he alone has the capability to achieve the state of nirvana for himself. The main cause of the major split, however, was the rather cut and dried formula that the religion presented to its followers for securing release. The formula tended more for intellectualism than devotion or emotional gratification. During that period Vaishnav *bhakti* philosophy was prevalent all around and in its midst Buddhism was experiencing difficulty in satisfying the needs of the common followers. The common man needed a deity who could serve as a father figure, an all powerful, omnipotent, omniscient god whom he could visualize in an image familiar to him, i.e., human image, and worship with love and devotion to satisfy a powerful emotional urge, and to whom he could turn in the hour of distress for relief and succour, and who would generally be helpful in his pursuit of the final goal. Besides, the entire religious and moral activity of the individual was conducted for securing the personal release from the cycle of rebirths, and this was considered to be a selfish pursuit. Once a person had acquired that degree of excellence at the moral and religious level, he ought to be working not only for his own emancipation but also that of his fellow beings. In addition, the common man wanted to believe in some kind of antiquity of his faith, something that would give him the belief that what he followed, originated from a mysterious, divine source and not from the thoughts of a mere human being who was not only like them but was in their midst only the other day. There was need for mythology. All these factors, and the positivistic course upon which Buddha had already set his followers, lead to the birth of Mahayana Buddhism.

It would be interesting to have a look at a Buddhist account of the creation; this is one account, and there could be others in the books of different Buddhist schools. According to this account any view regarding the soul (train of consciousness) or the universe being eternal is wrong. It states that after a lapse of many ages (*yugas*) the system of the universe comes to an end and the spirits live in the zone of radiance and rapture. Then the universe begins to develop again. Of the various planes that there are, there is one of God, but it is empty in the beginning, till some being, because his life in the zone of radiance has come to an end, or his merit is exhausted, falls from that zone and is reborn in the God-plane, and there he lives, made of mind and feeding on rapture. Many ages pass and this being feels lonesome and desires company, and in course of time other beings also drop upon this plane, having finished their lives or exhausted their merit and are reborn, made of mind and feeding on rapture. The first being who has the longest life and is endowed with maximum power and beauty, now thinks that he was the creator of the beings who came later because he wished their coming there, and believes he is God. Other beings too recognize him as God Almighty. Then a being drops from the God-plane and is born as man, and when he becomes a recluse or is otherwise disheartened or needs to imagine of an all potent father figure, he can think only upto the God-plane. That is how soul and the universe are partly eternal and partly not eternal.

In order to formalize the teachings of the Buddha into a religion and maintain their originality and authenticity, the first council of the leading monks was held at Rajagriha (modern Rajgir) immediately after his *parinirvana* (the Final Release). In this Ananda, who had attained to *Arhatship* on the eve of this council, played a significant role.

The second council was held at Vaisali after a century of the *parinirvana*, essentially to look into the legitimacy of some of the practices followed by some sections of the monks, particularly those of the Vijji country, like accepting gold or silver as alms, drinking buttermilk after meals, or taking intoxicants, and such like matters.

The third council was held at Pataliputra (modern Patna) under the aegis of the great Magadhan emperor Ashoka, around 236 years after the *parinirvana*. It was summoned by a learned monk Tissa Moggaliputta, again to rid the brotherhood of heresy; it was under the influence of this monk that the emperor had accepted Buddhism. It possibly was not a general council but a meeting of a particular school of the Order.

The fourth council was held under Kanishka, around 100 AD; numismatic evidence suggests that the king converted to Buddhism from some Iranian religion. The council was summoned under the king's instructions in order to remove anomalies and contradictions in the Buddhist scriptures, and was held either at Jalandhar or Kashmir. The king ruled a vast country extending north-westwards from western Uttar Pradesh to Afghanistan, including Punjab, Sindh and Kashmir. Southern Buddhists do not recognize this council and there is no mention of it in the Sinhalese chronicles. Also there is no evidence that Mahayana Buddhism was represented; this branch came into prominence only after Nagarjuna, and that happened much after the time of this council. But it is clear that by this time Buddhist schism was complete. One notable feature of the council was the adoption of Sanskrit as the language for the Buddhist literature. Councils were also held, from time to time, in different countries to which Buddhism spread, essentially to ensure that the Buddha's teachings did not get coloured or corrupted by the local cults or lores.

The two main branches into which Buddhism split, are the Mahayana, the Great Vehicle, and the Hinayana, the Little Vehicle

— Teravada to the people who follow this branch, for they do not like it classified as the 'Little Vehicle', a name given, rather pompously and presumptuously by the followers of the Mahayana church. Teravada is the popular religion of the people of Sri Lanka, Burma and Thailand. Further south-east, along the coast and in the north, it is the Mahayana. Buddhism spread along the coast of south-east Asia, and the silk route through Central Asia. In China it nestled with the ethical system of Kung-futzu or Confucius (551-479 BC) and Lao-tzu's mystical religion of the Tao. Tao means 'the way', the way of the universe; the requirement is to be in harmony with the Tao by practising quietude. While the latter two were religions followed essentially by the richer and the well-to-do people, the former was the religion of the common folk.

In the older doctrine Buddha, though risen above the status of gods on account of his enlightenment, was like any other man who had passed away from the world forever and could no longer wield any influence upon it. His recorded teachings could, at best, serve only as a guide. His nirvana was no different from that of any other person who might achieve it, and he could exercise no power to bring about the nirvana of any of his followers; a monk had to have the will to achieve it, and he had to be in the monastic order for this purpose. In other words, in the older order Buddha was essentially a Guru who had shown the way; but he had, in the process, created many more Gurus who were there to show the way to the followers. The school follows the old view that everything exists as a series of continuous changes, over a length of time, till, at the end of the length of time it is no longer there. When an idea constituting a particular self disappears with that self, it leaves behind its mark and thus the self of the next moment is informed of the past happenings, and a kind of a continuity is maintained. This is how the moral responsibility for an act is considered to be of the individual who performs the act.

Mahayana took off from the thought that Buddha had set into motion a train of gurus who continuously helped the members of the brotherhood to improve their lives and, as a final step, attain nirvana. The concept of *Bodhi-Sattava*, a being endowed — with wisdom, now got formulated: he is that who has gone past the stage of Arhat-ship and is ready to enter the realm of nirvana, but has held back his entry for the good of others, to help them and to get them to achieve the ultimate goal of nirvana. Buddha now became god of the first order and was multiplied to infinity. Below him there were countless Buddhas, having domains being run by *Bodhi-Sattavas*. With time, Buddha receded into the background and Buddha Amitabha, 'He of the infinite light' took over, and all Buddhas became active dispensers of grace. The heaven of Amitabha is *Sukhavati* (place of well-being), the happy place, fairyland tenanted by divine population in perfect bliss. Amitabha's chief administrator is Avalokiteshvara — a *Bodhi-Sattava* who has taken a vow not to enter nirvana till he has rescued the whole world. The ideal in Mahayana system is to strive for the nirvana of the fellow creatures. Their Buddhas are associated with Taras — saviour ladies, and sexual opposites — typifying their consorts' energy of grace.

According to Mahayana Buddhists the train of consciousness, or self, is but a stream of ideas. Being and thought are, thus, one. Everything that is conceived or can be conceived by the mind is only subjective imagination existing by virtue of karma. There is no permanent reality except the void; this is a reality too vast, a truth before which thought is stilled. It is not possible to define it except as *neti, neti* (not this, not this). Otherwise everything is in emptiness, and is of it, with no beginning and no end. The five *khandhas* are empty. Form is empty and emptiness form. Perception, name, conception, knowledge are all empty. The doctrine, thus, recognizes two spheres of reality, viz., the absolute reality, which is the void, corresponding to Hindu Brahma, and relative truth, which is everything that is perceived by the senses and is in the sphere of which doctrines and myths are worked out. This latter is the truth in a mutual relationship of things, as it obtains at the mundane level. Being and thought, as stated above, are one, according to this school of Buddhism: "In the objects of thought there dwells no reality except the thought that conceives them. The highest Being is the 'Void' and the understanding of this is the 'highest truth', the 'enlightenment' (*bodhi*) or 'perfect wisdom' (*prajnaparamita*), which is the peculiar possession of a Buddha. This knowledge is actually realized by a Buddha in the ecstasy of his nirvana, where he dwells forever in the utter stillness of infinite thought. This enlightenment in nirvana, actual or potential (potential in the case of *Bodhi-Sattavas* who have held back their entries to nirvana for the general weal of the fellow beings), together with the 'void' which is its object and, therefore, is identical with it, is the Dharma-kaya, the 'Body of the Law'."

The need for history and myth are satisfied by the Mahayana school by introducing two more concepts, viz., *Sambhogakaya* or 'Body of Enjoyment' and *Nirmana-kaya* or the 'Body of Magical Form.' Every Buddha has a domain of his own, *Buddhakshetra*, a universe under the rule of the Law preached by him, the magnificence of which is determined by the nobility of the deeds performed by the ruling Buddha when he was a *Bodhi-Sattava*. He is revealed to the attendant *Bodhi-Sattavas* in absolute spiritual radiance; the latter also appear in similarly transfigured bodies. This beatific form is *Sambhog-kaya*. This is the reward for the virtue and suffering that the Buddhas and the *Bodhi-Sattavas* undertake while performing deeds for the well-being of the earthly creatures. Finally, the Buddha enters the final nirvana, and the stupa or the monument sanctuary, appears in recognition of this; the Buddha now rests in perfect stillness. However, this transfiguration is essentially illusory, for once the Buddhas have passed into nirvana, the void, they are identified with the 'Body of Law' wherein there is no finitude. But the merit of their good deeds lives on in the finite world and that works for the well-being and happiness of other creatures, in the process creating in the minds of holy *Bodhi-Sattavas* the conception of *Sambhog-kaya*, i.e., their Buddha revealing itself for their joy and instruction in beatific form.

The 'Body of Magical Form' (*Nirmana-kaya*) explains the appearance of Buddhas and *Bodhi-Sattavas* in the world of mortals. In fact, as the concept goes, they never really appear, they are mere illusions which they, in their 'Body of Enjoyment', create in their compassion in order to help and instruct the beings of the world. Just as *Bodhi-Sattavas* get visions of their transfigured forms in heaven, so also the people of the earth get the visions of Buddhas and *Bodhi-Sattavas* teaching the law. To the Buddhists the object and subject of thought are really one, so that *Dharma-kaya* represents both the infinite, and the understanding of the infinite. Likewise *Nirmana-kaya* is also the universal intellect, and when under the influence of *sanskaras* or 'conformations' resulting from former births, it conceives its object as universe of finite forms. Thus universal intellect gets the individual minds to believe that they dwell in finite worlds under the dispensations of the Buddhas. This seeming individuality and finitude is the illusion of the lower orders of the creatures from which Law of the Buddhas alone can uplift them to union with the Absolute. It will have been seen that in Mahayana also nirvana is achieved only when envelopment of consciousness caused by karma has been eliminated. The soul of man, the train of consciousness, reflects faintly the divine glory. In the stillness of transcendental unity of joy, love and peace, all spirits are one.

According to Yogchara school, there is only self, conceived as a stream of ideas. Reality is reduced to thought. There is inseparable connection between knowledge and object. Object is a form of knowledge and is distinguished from other objects by the mind on the basis of former impressions collected by it during previous experiences. The diversity apparent in different objects is also caused by the nature of the impressions from previous experiences. The main problem with this kind of doctrine is that it abolishes distinction between truth and illusion and considers all experience as if it were a dream. In real life dreams become false when compared with the waking experience. But if the waking experience itself is false, then how is falsity established; by comparing with what? Again, by rejecting all external objects, even people get rejected, and the inevitable conclusion would be that there is only one reality, the self, and that rest is all a figment of the mind.

Madhyamika school, a forerunner of the Mahayana, denies any reality, of the external objects as well as of the self, the argument being that both physical and the mental phenomena have so many complications and contradictions that they cannot be accepted as real. While general Buddhist view is that everything has a cause of origination, Madhyamikas do not accept this and call the notion of causation as a delusion; conclusion is that the universe itself is illusionary. Nagarjuna, the greatest exponent of this school, says: "there is neither being nor cessation of it, there is neither bondage nor escape from it." This is the doctrine of 'void' (*Shunya-vada*). But the doctrine accepts that delusion is only from the ultimate point of view. In the day to day activity there is reality between the subject and the object. But, although we know, feel and act in the course of our daily activity, the ultimate significance of this amounts to nothing. The ultimate reality of the Madhyamikas is *shunya*, which amounts to being nothing because it is incomprehensible. It is defined as neither 'is' nor 'is not', nor both 'is' and 'is not'. In other words, it is beyond conception; very much like the Hindu or the Jain view. Thus, they accept an absolute consciousness, though undefineable, in addition to the particular egoes.

Both Hinayana and Mahayana accept the doctrine of momentariness, i.e., nothing lasts longer than a mere instant: there is a constant and continuous change to which everything is subjected. All things are, therefore, impermanent; reality is a flow; it is not static. However, as opposed to Hinayana, where the goal is freedom of the train of consciousness from the hold of the karmas and then merging with the infinite consciousness, and thus be freed from the cycle of *sansara*, in Mahayana it is to merge with the absolute which is the 'void'.

Zen Buddhism asks the followers to look into the mind to find Buddhahood, and emphasizes meditation for attaining spiritual enlightenment. According to them intuition rather than reasoning, is what is important for the achievement of the goal, which is salvation and which is possible only through self-enlightenment. They say that all human beings have already been enlightened, implying that every spirit has the potential for self-enlightenment; everyone is born a Buddha; he has to strive to uncover this reality.

Blacksmith Chunda's mushroom preparation brought the final illness of Buddha, but he told Ananda to tell Chunda he had done him as great a favour as had been done by the lady Sujata before he had reached the supreme wisdom, for Chunda's cooking would be the cause of his attaining nirvana, like Sujata's offering had preceded his attaining the enlightenment. But he had given strict instructions for the burial of Chunda's dish after he had consumed a part of it. To his monks he said: "I have nothing more to tell you except that all that is composed is liable to decay! Strive after salvation energetically!"

He said: "Nirvana is a territory in which there is no earth, no water, no light, no air, no sky, no directions, no time, no

Seven

The Religion

Hinduism is the oldest religion of the world. It is essentially a growth, and not a construction, in that it is not based on the sayings or teachings of any single person, a messiah or a prophet. It is an accumulation of religious thoughts over the ages, like 'the frail bark of each passing epoch, put together by the hand of the past, desiring to make over its treasures for the use of the future. This is a religion which, over the ages, provided such emotional and religious satisfaction to its followers, that they have steadfastly respected its injunctions in preference to the alternatives that other religions or creeds offered. It is possible, for instance, to reconstruct the contribution of the people of the Nile to the world as we know it, but those people irretrievably relaxed their hold upon their past and broke the continuity and brought to a halt a process which should have made a significant contribution to the development of civilization and learning. The qualities of stubbornness, the dogged loyalty, the conservatism, are the criteria of a strong national genius, and in India these have been steadily maintained since the beginning of history.

Hinduism is an immense synthesis, deriving its constituents from a hundred different directions. It has within its ambit diverse practices like earth worship, sun worship, nature worship, sky worship, honour paid to heroes and ancestors, mother worship, father worship, prayers for the dead, mystic association of certain plants, trees and animals : all these and more are synthesized in the broad structure of Hinduism. The ideas have originated from the people who arrived in this subcontinent since time immemorial, and from time to time religious leaders have emerged who have tried to synthesize these thoughts, or parts thereof, into a rational whole, accommodating different practices in recognition of the fact that these thoughts and practices possessed a capability to provide emotional and psychic satisfaction to their adherents. The religion is, thus, a conglomerate of such ideas and practices, some of which even conflict with one another. For example, the idea of ancestor worship goes directly against the concept of transmigration of soul based on deeds performed over a number of previous lives, which means that during the migratory process the soul has no identifiable existence as such. Its form and identity changes from birth to birth and the ancestor just does not exist in the form which he possessed when he was the ancestor. Ancestor worship, on the other hand, visualizes ancestors enjoying alongside the gods, in the *pitri loka* (the region of the ancestors), all the boons and comforts as are available to the latter, implying that after death the soul just uplifts and gets into the joyous and peaceful environs of the *pitri loka* and stays there, almost eternally, till it is its turn to once again make another visit to the earth — but that happens after a very long interval. Another example could be the myth behind the purificatory baths at certain places, during certain auspicious times to secure a place in heaven (*svarga loka*); this also goes against the grain of the karma philosophy. The mythological legend, a basic one in the Vaishnav aspect of the religion is that, under the instructions of the Creator, Vishnu, the gods (also referred to as *suras*) and the *asuras*, the malevolent beings, engaged, with a view to extracting ambrosia, in churning the ocean of milk (*amrita manthana*) using the mountain Mandara, for the churning rod and the king of serpents, Vasuki, as the rope with which to do the churning. After a long toil when ambrosia surfaced, Dhanwantari, a god, fearing that *asuras* might forcibly take possession of the beverage of immortality, picked up the vessel in which it was contained, and bolted. He was chased by the *asuras* and the situation was saved in favour of the gods by Lord Vishnu himself, by assuming the form of a pretty damsel and, thus, distracting the pursuers, thereby gaining enough time for Dhanwantari for delivery of the item to the gods and its subsequent consumption by them. But during the chase some ambrosia got spilt at some spots on the earth, and the belief is that if a bath is taken at an appropriately auspicious time in the water-tanks where the spillage took place (Ujjain in Central India is one such place), the soul of the bather straight ascends to heaven after death. The karma theory, on the other hand, visualizes nothing of the sort, the basic concept being that as you sow, so shall you reap, and the process of rebirth shall continue unabated, without any reprieve, no matter how many times one bathed and where.

But, in spite of the contradictions, believers are free to follow the concepts that provide them solace and contribute to their spiritual well-being. Every activity or thought that follows dharma is supported, including that which contributes to the well-being of the community, nation, country. There are differences in different thoughts and practises but, there are no serious disputes. The concept of the supreme God itself varies in different situations. He is beyond any human description or understanding in the ultimate analysis, but at the mundane level he is worshipped almost in human form, as Rama or Krishna, or Vishnu, or Shiva or in the form of mother goddess, Durga. Then, there are gods and goddesses, a pantheon, in whom people have faith and to whom they take their mental and psychic woes and from whom they draw solace and comfort which makes the process of living bearable and easier for them. It would be a mistake to compare the different methods of worship, for worship is a very personalized, individual affair; when practised at the level of the community it tends to become more of a political and social activity. All this, however, is not to suggest that the freedom to an individual is unbridled, dharma defines the limits either way.

As has been stated in chapter 2, the Negritos and the Proto Australoids believed in animism and the power of the spirits, and worshipped, in addition to the spirits, certain trees and plants (tribal totems), stones and rocks which they believed were endowed with special powers, sun, and moon and so on. They also had zoomorphic deities (also tribal totems), including the serpent deities. In the Vaishnav religion's legend of creation, Vishnu, the creator of the universe, reclines in eternal bliss on the coiled body of the Shesha, the king of serpents, with latters thousand headed hood forming a canopy over former's head. In the philosophy of the religion, however, Shesha is the eternal matter contained within Vishnu before the start of the process of creation. Then there is the *makara*, the crocodile, and the tortoise, also given as the incarnations of Vishnu, for He, after assuming its form, went under the ocean of milk to support upon His back the Mandara mountain when the ocean was being churned with it for ambrosia. Monkey god Hanuman is given out as the son of the Aryan god of wind, while the elephant-headed Ganesha is the son of another partly Aryan god Shiva. All this, whole or in parts, has been synthesized under systemization impulses that took hold of the heterogeneous society from time to time, with a view to bringing unity and harmony amongst the people and to veer them on to a broader thought process, the kernel of which contained the essential elements of the religion and philosophy, and served as its foundation. The essential elements of this basic belief are :

(a) There is a power that creates, then ascends to its zenith and finally collapses unto itself, all this based on dharma, the law. After an interval which is as long as the time during which the creation lasts, this power once again stirs into action and the process of creation begins anew. And so it goes on eternally.

(b) The essence of the soul is freedom and bliss, but it gets trapped by the matter because of a certain inherent attraction between spirit and matter. Once there, ego develops and that brings in all the ingredients of ignorance, which causes the performance of deeds and the cycle of rebirth and, consequently, suffering. To get out of this cycle and get back the original freedom and bliss, it is necessary to cast off ignorance and understand the reality and perform good and expiating deeds including those that promote dharma.

(c) Everything in the universe, spirit or matter, is in a state of flux, changing continuously and eternally; peace, rest, bliss is the prerogative only of the free and blissful souls.

(d) All organic matter has life, or capability to generate or sustain life. From simple grass to the complex human being, life is endowed with varying sense organs, minimal in the lower forms—like grass has only touch—and, increasing gradually, to maximum in human beings. What form of life a spirit will adopt depends upon the deeds, Karmas, performed by the combine of the spirit and matter during the previous human existences; Karma is what causes *sansara*, the unending wanderings of the spirit.

(e) Even though the force or the energy that creates is beyond definition and human understanding, *nirguna* Brahma (Brahma without attributes) as it is called, there is no objection to worshipping this power in a form that is comprehensible to the individual intelligence and understanding, *saguna* Brahma (Brahma with attributes), so long as this does not violate the tenets of *dharma* and the adoption satisfies the religious and emotional needs of the person; this need appears to be inbuilt in the human psych.

Subsequently, Dravidian speaking people, which include the near black Palaeo-Mediterraneans, the darkish Mediterraneans and the light complexioned orientals brought in the worship of Rudra, later Shiva, and the mother Goddess who under the synthesis process becomes the consort of Shiva. Originally the two deities were entirely independent of each other, worshipped by people who had little commonality in their cultures or religion, although some authorities have placed the origin of both the deities in the times of the Proto-Australoids. Linga worship almost certainly dates to the period of the Australoids. The idea possibly took off from the practice of tilling the fields with a wooden pole. It does appear plausible that the basic Hindu religion is the religion of the Proto-Australoids and that this has been appropriately modified by the clans, races and people who wandered in later, each one making contributions to provide a more universal appeal to the original concepts.

Witness, for example, the Vaishnav branch of Hinduism. Four out of the ten incarnations of Vishnu are zoomorphic, bearing the stamp of Australoid culture, though this could also have been a way to put across the idea that the evolution first started with marine life. The literature where the mythological legends of different shades and hues, originating amongst different peoples and cultures that flourished on the Indian sub-continent from time to time during the ancient period, have been integrated, comprises the Puranas, the *Ramayana* and the *Mahabharata*. The legends contained in them bear evidence of decisive Australoid influence, for the fact is that the people who came subsequently, including Dravidians of all types, and the Aryans, and any one else, were all in distinct minority when compared to the Australoid group. The latter were well entrenched in their way of life and no outside culture or religion could outright overwhelm them. Even to this day by far, the largest number of people inhabiting South Asia as well as South East Asia, are of Australoid extraction.

However, the first recorded religion is that of the Aryans, and their first work of surpassing interest is the Rig Veda, a work of such lofty dimension as has not been produced anywhere during such an early stage in the development of civilization. The gods of their pantheon are all *devas*, emanating light, splendrous beings associated with the most glorious natural phenomena: the all encompassing Sky, the Sun in its utter brilliance, the omnipotent Thunder cloud, the divinely beautiful Dawn, the roaring Storm. For this pantheon no temple is visualized, though the gods have been so personalized that they receive sacrifice and listen to prayers and hymns, and dwell in a region of unapproachable light, beyond the sun and the stars, living in immortal joy.

Indra is the most powerful and, the greatest of all the gods, who nourishes and sustains his devotees by bringing rain to the parched land so that the crops might grow. He is armed with thunderbolts and flanked by maruts, the wild winds, and with his weapons he smites *ahi*, the malevolent god whose effort it is to keep the rivers and lakes dry and keep the land thirsting for water so that there might be misery and the human race and the beautiful creation might perish. In later times, Indra came to be associated with omnipotence, and became the great war god of the conquering Aryans. From this stage the concept of an almighty Creator who in His benevolence supports the creation, was just a step ahead.

Next in importance is god Agni, Fire, the high priest of gods and men, who accepts the offerings made to the gods and takes them heavenwards, who purifies the hearts of men, purifies their dwellings, and the air they breath, to bestow upon them the gift of health and prosperity. Alongside him is Soma, originally intoxicating juice of a plant, regarded essential for oblations, but later deified to a god who was sought after for wish fulfilment. He is considered to be effective and potent, and many hymns have been written in his praise, particularly in the Sam Veda. Then we have Surya, the Sun, and Savitar, Pushan, Vishnu, are just different forms of this god. Ushas is the Dawn, fair and blushing maidens, and Ashvins, sons of the Mare, are the light bearers of the morning sky. Rudra, the Roarer, is the god associated with storms, while Vayu is Wind. The ancient divinities which fell into the background are Dyaus (Zeus) and Prithvi, Heaven and Earth respectively. Yama, the first mortal to discover the path followed by the righteous after their death, to join their ancestors and gods, is honoured as a god. In course of time he came to be regarded as the arbiter of the deeds of the people, the one who decided whether a spirit had to go to hell or heaven. He is also believed to despatch his underlings to snuff out the life after he/it has lived its duration, and accompany the spirit to his regions where both hell and heaven are located. In this concept heaven has all beauty, joy and plenty, and is the reward for valour in battle, for generous gifts to priest class and for austerity and deeds amassing merit, besides, of course, for deeds upholding dharma, while hell has scorching heat, misery and suffering.

Another group of gods are the *Adityas*, the seven sons of Aditi, Eternity. We do not know the names of all of them, except for Varuna, Mitra, Aryaman, Bhaga. Nor are we aware of the source of their origination. They are the highest of the divinities, particularly Varuna and Mitra, and are conceived as the power behind other gods, rulers who have set the path for others to follow. In the Rig Veda, Varuna is the noblest of all the gods. He was the centre of the theistic movement of the Indo-Iranian age, and represents the loftiest thoughts connected with the divinity of that time. Originally conceived as the 'all embracing heavens', he soon acquired the status of the creator and sustainer of the universe, and that is how he has been praised in the hymns contained in a section of the Rig Veda. He is Omniscient, the protector, the compassionate helper, the Holy One from whom *Rta*, the cosmic order, emanates, and who rewards the righteous and sternly punishes those who violate dharma. There are hymns which seek his pardon, and release from punishment for violating his laws: 'whether we have sinned consciously or otherwise', or for 'whichever of thy laws, known or unknown, we have broken'. At one stage he is pretty close to the concept of God as visualized in Christianity or Islam, and many a scholar has felt distressed at the fading away of this divinity to the status of the mere god of waters, a second rate Neptune, overtaken, first, by Indra, the great war god, and later by the impersonal Brahma (the One beyond good and evil, immanent in all beings and all things of the universe,who, in fact, is the universe itself), and still later by Vishnu and Shiva. As for the idea of rebirth, only in the tenth book of the Rig Veda, are there two passages which vaguely suggest the idea. Apparently, this was not the belief of the Aryans, and developed only in India towards the end of the Rig Vedic period, possibly after the intermixing of their ideas with the religious and philosophical concepts of other racial groups.

The Rig Vedic Aryans were polytheistic, but each of their gods enjoyed a status comparable to that of the supreme god. With time, all the attributes of the gods of the pantheon got transferred to one deity and there was monotheism, till, finally, non-dualism, or even monoism, was also accepted. But that was many centuries later, during the Upanishadic age. Otherwise, the original religion was based on sacrifice and chanting of the Vedic hymns. The family gathered in the open, along with the priest, around the altar comprising shallow trenches cut according to rules and filled with sacrificial grass. Close by burnt the three sacrificial fires where the priests chanted the incantations and made offerings of butter, milk and grain. The animals were sacrificed at the shallow trench, again to the chanting of hymns, and the prayers were made to the gods beseeching them to accept the sacrifice and grant the wishes of the householder.

The religion of sacrifice reached it peak during the period of the *Brahmanas*, and that attracted the adverse attention of quite a few thinkers and scholars, the majority of them from the Kashatriya class. Along side this the thoughts and ideas of the earlier people also exerted their influence. As a result the religion of the Aryans modified itself in regard to animal sacrifice, and the old faiths based on Mother Goddess worship and the worship of Shiva, became substantially prominent. Upanishadic religion of the Aryans, mostly work of forest dwellers who had come in extensive contact with the proponents of ancient religions, and who recorded their views and findings in Aranayakas, the forest texts. Instructions to be imparted in the seclusion of the forest had almost completely broken off from the religion of animal sacrifice. The Upanishads, in most cases, are either contained within the specific Aranayakas, or they form their supplements; some of them are independent works also. Aranayakas are appended to *Brahmanas*, and have the same style of language and content, except that they have put across the idea that the sacrifice as detailed in the Vedic texts has only allegorical meaning, and is not meant to be physically executed; they have expressed extensively on the mystical meanings of the *Sanhita* text. There are a number of ideas that emanate from Upanishads, since each one of them, based on the *Aranayaka* or otherwise, had a different author or commentator. In fact, these documents are like theses. They are research works on the ontological and the eschatological aspects of the creation of the universe. Some of them have pretty poor religious or philosophical merit. But some have put forth perceptions which have had impact on the philosophical thinking not only in India but even elsewhere. The one concept which runs through all of them is that of one atman (God). Chandogyo Upanishad states: "Verily this whole world is Brahma. Tranquil let him worship it as that from which he came forth, as that into which he will be dissolved, as that in which he breathes." Aitareya Upanishad talks of One atman who is everything, i.e., Brahma, Indra, all the gods, the five elements, things born out of an egg or a womb, all organic life, static or moving, and so on. This is complete non-duality, *advaita*, as we have seen in the preceding Chapter on Systems of Philosophy, and to acquire complete understanding of this one has to practice austerity, self-control, including negation of all passions, and even then it may not be forthcoming, unless the Great Self chooses to reveal it'. The result is a complete union with the Creator:

As the flowing rivers in the ocean

Disappear, quitting name and form,
So the knower, being liberated from name and form,
Goes unto the Heavenly Person, higher than the high.

> And then: He, verily, who knows that supreme Brahma, becomes very Brahma. He crosses over sorrow and sin. Liberated from the knots of the heart he becomes immortal.

When Sakalya the disciple asked Yajnavalkaya, the great Upanishadic master and teacher, as to the number of gods there were in the pantheon, the latter gave the conventional number of 33 major gods and 3306 *devas*, or lesser deities. But when pressed, he reduced the number successively to six, three and so on till he finally gave the figure as one, and he called this as the parana, or the life force, or the breath of life.

The Upanishads' time was the age of intellectual and spiritual fervour, and it is certain that the entire literature of this time has not found its way to posterity. *Kena Upanishad*, one of the shorter works, expounds the doctrine of prevenience of Brahma, who, though inscrutable, precedes and conditions all that there is:

> The power behind every activity of nature, and of man, is Brahma, and after this truth has been realised, man becomes immortal.

The *Katha Upanishad*, one of the highly popular works, describes the divine reality as invisible, all pervading but hidden deep inside, and only intense spiritual effort, and not any kind of reasoning, including philosophical, can bring about the mystical experience which gives an idea — only an idea — of this Great Reality. The secret of immortality, it says, lies in the purification of the heart, in meditation, in realization of the identity of the self within, and Brahma without. For immortality is union with God. The Prasna Upanishad is concerned, essentially, with the psychological aspects of the human personality, dividing it into 16 parts. It also has the hymn in praise of the life force. Man is composed of such elements as vital breath, deeds, thought and senses, all of them deriving their being from the self. They have come out of the self, and in the self they ultimately disappear, like the waters of a river disappearing in the sea. Mundaka Upanishad condemns the practice of animal sacrifice, and castigates it as a profession of fools. It emphasizes that the knowledge of the Divine Reality can be had only through proper instruction and self-discipline. Action alone is not enough as all actions of men are only phases of the universal process of creation. The seeker has to distinguish between knowledge and wisdom. Former is of things, acts and relations, but latter is of Brahma alone. Beyond all things, acts and relations, He abides for ever. The wisdom lies in becoming one with Him. The *Mandukya*, a small Upanishad, is revolutionary in more ways than one. The life of man, it says, is divided among waking, dreaming, and dreamless sleep. But transcending these states is the fourth one of the super conscious vision. The philosophy has been explained in terms of Ishwara, which is God with attributes, i.e., God as visualized by a person. Dreamless sleep, according to it, is ignorance, and within this exist the states of waking, dreaming, and dreamlessness. Ishwara, in effect, is Brahma associated with *Maya*, (the latter is universal ignorance), while man is associated with individual ignorance, the difference between the two being that while Ishwara controls ignorance, man is controlled by it. It also states that the Divine Reality itself is unperceived, and unrelated to experience, unknowable, unthinkable, unnameable, indefinable, the one in which everything else has ceased. These thoughts have made a major contribution to the later nihilistic doctrines of monastic Buddhism.

The *Taittirya Upanishad* says Brahma realization leads to pure bliss, the quality of which is unthinkable by the mind and unutterable in speech. Man, it says, in his ignorance, identifies himself with the material sheaths that are wrapped around his true self. Transcending these, he becomes one with Brahma, who is pure bliss. Another Upanishad, *Chandogya*, a rather long work, lays emphasis on the entire universe being just the highest self, even though broken into numerous entities endowed with name and form. Brahma is all, it says. From Brahma come appearances, sensations, desires, deeds, etc. But all these are merely name and form. To know Brahma one has to experience the identity between Him and the self or the Brahma dwelling within the lotus of the heart. Only by so doing can there be escape from sorrow and death, and only thus can one merge with the subtle essence beyond all knowledge.

Brihadaranyaka Upanishad, essentially an *Aranayaka*, and a rather longish treatise, is notable for its stress on the devotion to the Essential Self, but explains that duality is an illusion, that devotion to the Self is not an 'I-Thou relationship' but an identification which is the quality of pure bliss. It also stresses the need to love all beings of the world, and says that all beings experience this bliss, solely because the great self is the final cause of all of them. Almost all the *Bhakti* movements in this country have their foundation in this literature. Even Buddha's essential teachings have emanated from this Upanishad.

These works are essentially research papers wherein seers and masters have noted down their mystic experiences, and their considered findings as to the nature of the ultimate reality. There are differences, no doubt, in views and perceptions. Some of the works talk of Brahma as the lord of the universe, its master, and operator of the systems that run it, while some others postulate Brahma also as the inner essence of man. What has, however, not been elaborated upon sufficiently is as to how the multifaceted universe has emerged out of the single great self, or how its reality can be considered to be spiritual or based in the consciousness attribute of Brahma. This, one surmises, is where intuition comes in, or is realized by mystical experience. *Isha Upanishad*, a work of extreme brevity, most profound but very difficult to understand, is categorical about the need to surrender everything to the Great Self, whom it calls Isha. Life in the world and life in the spirit, it says, are not incompatible. Work or action is not in the way of acquiring knowledge about God, Isha, in fact, when performed without attachment to reward, is a means to it. Again, renunciation implies renunciation of ego, selfishness, and not of the activity of life. The aim of all work, as also of renunciation, is to know the self within, and Brahma without, and to realize that the two are the same. The self is Brahma, and Brahma is all.

Filled with Brahma are the things we see,
Filled with Brahma are the things we see not,
From out of Brahma floweth all that is:
From Brahma all; yet he is the same.

What the Upanishads have put forth — and it is a discovery of the Upanishadic seers — is that there is no difference between the identity of the highest reality and that of the innermost self of man, that the entire universe is Brahma, including everything around us, that our thoughts, our being, our experience, all originate in Him, and in spite of the apparent diversity, there is only One Ultimate Reality and both the microcosm and the macrocosm unite in that Reality.

As stated earlier, the religion of the Indo-Aryans was the religion of sacrifice. By the time of the Sama and the Yajur Vedas, and the Brahmanas, the sacrifice had so dominated that even the gods had receded to a position of secondary importance. The incantations contained in these books were considered to be potent enough to bend the gods and compel them to grant the wishes. Some minor deities of the Rig Veda had either vanished out of sight or been diminished in status. Prajapati (Lord of the created beings) has been visualized in the Brahmanas as the creator and preserver of the universe, there are numerous invocations addressed to Him. He is believed to have brought about the creation by practising severe austerities and indulging in self torture and mortification. But there are other creation legends as well. In some Prajapati himself is a created being and the creation is given out as having been caused by primeval waters, or Brahma, or the force or energy which has been called as the non-existent. Desire is the germ of existence, the motive power of all creation.

The Shaivas

Prajapati is not the god of the people, Rudra is, as can be deduced from the incantations addressed to him in the Yajur Veda Sanhita and important Brahmanas of the time, like the *Aitareya, Kaushitaki* and the *Satapatha*. This Rudra, though a god mentioned in the Rig Veda, is, in fact, a deity of much older times. He is a god of the non-Aryans, who outnumbered the Aryans, he is a deity of the masses. We have seen that Indus Valley seals have a horned ascetic, with erected member, seated in meditation, covered with bangles and surrounded by wild animals, *Pashupati* (Lord, protector of the cattle). The erected member is typical of another very old form of this god, Lakulisha. Horns were a symbol of divinity in Egypt and the ancient Near East, while in India they have been used as emblem, in the early Pallava sculpture, for the figures

The Hindu Trinity, Brahma (the Creator), Vishnu (the Preserver), and Shiva (the Destroyer). Elephanta, Mumbai, 6th century A.D.

Shiva, the ultimate abodė of all Creation, the Sea of Tranquility. Elephanta, around 6th century A.D.

shown as attendants on Shiva. On another seal the same god — or so it appears — is again shown horned. His matted hair falling on his back, and he is revealing himself between the branches of a tree, and a priest, accompanied by a bull with a human face, is kneeling before him, and in the foreground seven votaries with conical head-dresses seem to be executing a ritual dance. Rudra as Bhutapati (lord of malevolent, evil spirits) is a dreaded god. He appears at the sacrifice in black dress and claims the sacrifice victim. The Dravidians, it seems, refined the concept connected with this god of Proto-Australoid origination, and gave him the epithet of 'Shiva' (the Auspicious One), or Mahadeva (the great god). The details of the philosophy of Shaivism as given in the *Shvetashvatara Upanishad* reflects the transition of the concept from the time of the *Atharva Veda*. *Shiva Purana*, in its sixty-ninth chapter gives more than a thousand names to this god, each meant to define an attribute of his. He is the lord of the universe, the creator, the destroyer who assimilates the entire creation unto himself when it is time for this stage to occur. In fact, he himself is the very time who, from the moment of creation, while sustaining it on time basis, is causing its motion towards its final annihilation.

The phallic symbol of Shiva, the Linga, also appears to be of Proto-Australoid origin. We know they had upright conical stones as objects of veneration. The idea appears to be a take-off from the digging stick used by them as a plough. The digging implement then becomes the symbol of fertility, the male element, and what it has dug into is regarded as the female element of the activity of reproduction. By the time the Dravidians had finished with the idea, — and it had been further examined and refined in later times by the Aryans attempting to synthesise the viewpoints (of earlier people) which had rich content of high philosophical value, — the Linga was representing the consciousness component of the power that creates, the Supreme Self, while what it is dug into is the material aspect of the creation, *Prakriti*, that which is active, and is the major player in the creation process, but which, in effect, draws its action potential only from the Supreme Self, the ocean of consciousness. By itself it is inert, it has the potential but that is activated only in the presence of the Supreme Self. Together the two represent God: the consciousness element, the Linga and the material element, the *yoni*. The story is told of a wonderous pillar, a fiery column without beginning or end, source or summit. The gods puzzled over its mystery for a long time, but they were unable to resolve it. They prayed to the Supreme God to grant them wisdom to understand the meaning of the effulgent shaft, and in answer to their prayer a radiant Shiva, *Lingodbhava* (in the shape of Linga), emerged out of it, and the gods were filled with awe and veneration at what they saw, and bowed, and acknowledged that Shiva indeed was the infinite, the greatest of all. The great column, in fact, was the centre of the Universe, as also the Creator of the universe, the *Nirguna* Brahma. The shape of Linga, it may be noted, together with the lower portion into which it is embedded, *yoni*, is like the silhouette of a person in deep meditation, the torso representing the linga portion while the lower cross-legged seated portion, the *yoni*. It represents the Creator in profound contemplation, in the process of creating, sustaining, and folding up the universe.

The universe, the Shaivas believe, is born of *maya* (illusion) and is to be the scene of countless rebirths, and of actions both good and evil. An earthen pot has clay for the material cause, the potter's wheel for the instrumental cause and the potter himself for the first or the efficient cause. Likewise, for the universe the material cause is *maya*, the instrumental cause, the energy or the potency of Shiva (Shakti) — mythologically Shakti is the consort of a deity, and Shiva's Shakti is Parvati, and the efficient cause is Shiva Himself.

Linga Purana explains the objects of life, viz., *dharma*, *artha*, *kaama* and *moksha*, that is, be noble and good to fellow beings; generate wealth through trade, commerce and industry; enjoy pleasures of life but within the ambit of dharma; and, finally, work for the liberation from the cycle of rebirth. The treatise contends that its author is none other than the Great Shiva Himself. At no stage in this Purana has Linga been connected with sex, and nor has this happened in any other book, including the Puranas, of the Shaivas. Some western scholars and Christian missionaries, Abbe Dubois amongst them, have likened the symbol to the Priapus of the Romans and the phallus of the Egyptians. That is not correct. In the remotest past, some eight to ten thousand, or more, years ago when the traces of the idea appeared for the first time, the symbol might have represented the human generative organs, likening the process of creation to the way the manifest creation multiplies itself. But with time the concept has modified into depicting the creator as a force, power, of two essential attributes: the one constituting matter and the other consciousness. Linga is consciousness, while the source of creation, the *yoni*, which could be represented as the female generative organ, is matter, its power activating only at the command of consciousness. They function together, in harmony. The symbol as a whole is the creator, the creating power with its attributes, in absolute ecstasy while in the creation process.

Another representation of the Great God in the process of creation is Shiva in the dancing mode. Here, he is the creation itself, the universe, emerging out of the ring of fire, the expression intensely solemn, enacting the *tandava*, the dance of creation and destruction. He has four arms, and under his right foot Muyulaga Kali, the demon of ignorance, disorder and chaos, lies in subjugation, and his left hand carries the flame, the torch of knowledge which alone provides the means of liberation from the birth-death cycle. The left foot, raised in the dance posture, signifies the orderliness of the creation process, while the beating hand-drum in one of his right hands is time. His other right hand is raised in the gesture of blessing, exhorting his believers to be fearless and be above all false knowledge, including superstition, and be part of the orderly creation process. One of his left hands pointing to the rhythmic left foot, tells the followers that the creation is governed by Dharma, the law. It tells them that life is not a simple game, but a delicate act where each movement has to be carefully balanced so that it is not out of consonance with Dharma. Shiva is the soul of all, and his dance is the creation, preservation and the annihilation process. The dance is ceaseless and eternal. The dance has been variously interpreted by different authorities. It represents Shiva as the source of all movement within the universe, the ceaseless movement causing the five acts of creation, preservation, destruction, embodiment and release. The place of dance, Tillai or Chidambram, is in fact the human

Shiva Natraj

heart, and the release is secured once the knowledge of the reality has been gained. Sometimes, it is given out that the dance is enacted in a burning ground, that He is 'the terrible' and 'the destroyer'. This is surely a carry over of the idea from the days of the Proto-Australoids or even earlier. But later Shaivites have modified this concept to say that the meaning of the burning-ground is the heart of the devotee, waste and desolate, where the self and its deeds are burnt away, including all else except the dancer himself.

In the iconography of the Shaivas he is also shown as the *Ardhanarishvara,* right half male and the left one female, both together forming one whole, signifying that he is both the male as well as the female polarity, all in one, like in a seed, and that the manifest universe emerges out of this seed, it signifies that the two polarities are not different entities but are the attributes of one God. The icon is also believed to signify desire, the simultaneous experience of longing and union, with left female side merging softly and unobtrusively with the right side representing male. Desire, along with fervour, is the germ that initiates the activity of creation.

The great Shiva is the reality, *sat* (being), hidden behind the folds of appearance cast by that attribute of His which creates the phenomenal universe. He is visualized in deep meditation, sustaining, among others, the dance of the phenomenal creation.

The concept of Shiva, then, starts off as *Lakulisa* of the Proto Australoids, and it has stayed thus for a few thousand years. He is the god of fertility, the great impregnator, the creator, the sustainer, emanating total harmony, ever in acute ecstasy and deep meditation, having grown braided hair in the process, and wearing a hide, generally benevolent but could be even terrible when he has to be propitiated, for otherwise in that state he brings down all the suffering. The Dravidians of the Indus Valley somewhat sublimated the concept, and, may be, placed more emphasis on his positive virtues, on his being Shiva, the auspicious one, the supporter of good, the destroyer of evil, the great redeemer who takes care of his followers, gives them abundant crops and protects their cattle, the Pashupati, whose ride is a bull and weapon a trident.

Then in the Rig Veda we find a few early hymns devoted to god Rudra, literally 'the howler'. He controls the destructive features of nature, like floods, storms, lightning. His abode is in the mountains, and he is rough and terrifying, and has to be worshipped in order to stay protected against his malevolence. Not before long, however, this god merges with Shiva who is supporting a cult of his own wherein he is more the 'auspicious one' rather than the malevolent, terrifying one. This is the time when the second layer of the Hindu religion is finding its place. In the later portions of the Veda and in the *Svetasvatara Upanishad* he is the lord of the universe, the simple god whose one concern is the well-being of his creation. Then the mythologies of the different sects of Hinduism start getting intermixed. Like Vaishnavites who give the highest place to Vishnu in the pantheon of gods, followers of Shiva, and the Shaivas, who regard him as the highest of the high. He is time, justice, fire, water, the sun, the destroyer, the creator. He is riding a white bull as god of justice, signifying the purity of justice. When the gods and the non-gods together churned the mighty ocean of milk for the nectar of immortality, the first thing to surface was the deadly poison, and it was Shiva who swallowed this poison to render the nectar pure. In the process his throat turned blue. He is, therefore, also called *Neelkantha*, the one with the blue throat. This is the third stage in Hinduism when the mythology, thought and the philosophy of the different sects start getting synthesized, to eventually develop homogeneity. Though the Shaivas and the Vaishnavas continue to air the greatness of their respective deities, there is little difference between the two in so far as the basic concepts and philosophy are concerned.

Shiva's hair has a light reddish tinge (like the hair of the Proto-Australoids) and these are thickly matted and gathered above the head in a bun, like the hair of an ascetic. He is mostly shown with four arms, looking after the four directions in which the universe is spread, and seated in the meditation posture. He has three eyes, the third one in the centre of the forehead, all three together taking care of the three divisions of time: the past, present and the future. He holds a trident in one of his hands and this, according to some, shows him as the master of all waters. Some believe that the trident signifies his being the creator and the sustainer of the universe and also the one who eventually folds it up. The hand-drum in the other hand shows him as the creator and the annihilator of time, as also its astronomical regulator. He carries a crescent on the bun of hair on his head to denote the measurement of time by the phases of the moon; the serpent around his neck shows the measurement of time by years. Sometimes he is shown carrying a necklace of human skulls, this denotes the lapse and re-emergence of ages, and the extinction and succession of generations of mankind. Sometimes he is shown totally covered with serpents to denote immortality. His followers call him the lord of the universe, the creator, sustainer and destroyer. He is the time, the conqueror of life and death, the cause of life and being, the dispenser of tears of mortals. He is the Great God Mahadeva; the creator Sadasiva; Lord of the universe Jagesvara, and eternally in meditation Yogesvara; supporter of the moon Somnatha; Chandrashekhara; and of the milkyway, the universe Gangadhara; the divine dancer Nataraja; the victor over evil tripurantaka; and over death Mrityunjaya; the gracious Siva; the terrible Bhairava; the Destroyer Mahakala; the lord of the demons Bhutanatha. In the final version, however, 'Shiva is all, and all is Shiva'. All that is seen, heard or perceived is but a manifestation of the great God, he is in everything and everything is in him.

The *Shiva Upa-Purana,* essentially a Shaiva manual and not a Purana in the real sense, written in the form of a discourse to ascetics and Rishis, covers the rules for the Linga worship, and the prayers to be addressed to Shiva, including the times of the day, month, year, and the places and things sanctified by Him, i.e., when, where, or with what things such prayers could be made for maximum effect. It narrates about the birth of Vishnu and Brahma, the creation and the division of the universe, and about the creation of all things from the Linga. It has the details about the flower offerings to the Linga, the method of practising Yoga and the rules for the various observances in honour of Shiva. It glorifies Varanasi and some other places where the god can be worshipped with effect. The second part of this manual is almost wholly devoted to Shiva stories.

With the devotional mode of worship gaining popularity

during the few centuries prior to Christ, Shiva is God with attributes and is worshipped in the male human form. The matter is the inseparable part of Shiva and becomes the source of all energy when activated by the latter. This is termed as the Shakti, Shiva's Power, and gets personified as his spouse, the Great Goddess Mahadevi, Maheshvari, the glorious Gauri, emitting fire from her mouth, *Jawalamukhi*, having eyes full of love, Kamakshi, Minakshi, the great beauty Mahalakshmi, the daughter of the mountains, Parvati, devoted wife Sati, virgin (kumari) Durga, mother Uma, Umbika, the great force Mahashakti, of creation Maya, and also the terrible Bhairavi, the destroyer Kali, Chamunda, goddess of epidemics Sitala and so on. He is adored as a loving husband Kalyansundra, of her spouse. While the Immanence of Shiva is eternal, unperishable, each of His shaktis becomes manifest only during a period of creation and merges with Him at the final dissolution. There are quite a few of them, signifying each period of creation. They also denote the different attributes of the great energy that creates.

But the rivalry between the Vaishnava (also called the Bhagvatas) and the Shaiva sects remains unabated, each incorporating the good points of the philosophy and the teachings of the other, till in their essence the two are hardly distinguishable. After the synthesis process, although the sects maintained their distinctions in smaller matters of detail, at the broader, higher levels of philosophy and religion they came to be regarded as the emanations of the supreme divinity of the Hindus and together with Brahma formed the triad wherein Brahma, Vishnu, and Shiva came to signify the attributes of creation, sustenance and the final annihilation respectively, of the Creator.

Religion evolved essentially at the psychical level. As Joseph Campbell says in his book *Myths to Live By*, mythologies and their deities are productions and projections of the psyche, like the kind of stuff the dreams are made up of, and because all human beings have evolved from a common background, the stuff they dream of or put in their mythologies, is strikingly similar throughout the world. The essentials of most religious thoughts and philosophies are based on these mythologies. The Linga of the Proto-Australoids, the Skambha, the great fiery pillar without the beginning or the end, of the Shaivas, the minarets around a mosque, the dome of the Christian church, are all embellishments of the basic original thought, viz., the male symbol of fertility. The concepts of 'father, son and the holy spirit' and 'shiva, Ganesha and the Cosmic Energy', are strikingly similar. In the beginning, man felt that it were the elements, the floods, quakes, droughts, and similar natural phenomena, which were his worst enemies, and he also noted that most of the time the hardship that he had to bear had little to do with his personal performance or conduct. So he imagined these forces to be the all powerful deities and in order to escape their malevolence he did whatever his understanding or psyche told him. There is, thus, a certain commonness in the behaviour pattern of the followers of all primitive religions. Worship of the motherhood of God came the first and continues, in all religions, in one form or another, to this day. Next came the worship of fertility, and the man turned his attention to the malevolence that stalked him at every step, and he worshipped it so that it might not harm him. That was when he worshipped the gods who, he felt, commanded the forces that could annihilate him. His psyche and his observations told him that in reality nothing ever perished for good. There was only a change of form. The trees shed their leaves which partially turn into dust and partly the food for other vegetation. The elements grind the mighty hills but succeed only in converting them into soil. His conclusion was that the sum total of the material content in the world was for ever constant and from this it was not difficult to deduce that the sum total of the material content in the whole universe was constant; it was eternal, though it constantly changed form. It was febrile, in unbroken agitation, dynamic, and in that context, for ever alive. For this reason earth is referred to as mother — alive, vibrant, sustaining its children, its beings, by appropriate, seemingly conscious adjustments.

If the material content did not ever alter, so did not the spiritual content, the content of consciousness. Such was the logical reasoning and psychical perception of man. He found that although his personal effort had a lot to do with his success or failure in life, it did not account for everything that the result of his effort brought. In fact, that is where the idea of religion was born, idea that there were powers superior to him, in heavens or other worlds, which controlled his destiny. Sometimes he felt his specific behaviour patterns, like the kind of genuflexions he performed, or the way he raised his hands in prayer, or skywards, or the kind of things he did, like telling lies and so on, had a direct impact upon the kind of fate he met with. Not really succeeding to unravel the mystery of life, he resorted to magic and similar activity to secure his safety and the safety of his progeny. He found life to be a harsh, losing struggle. He prayed to whatever god or spirit he thought influenced his well-being; recited words, incantations, prayers, which he thought would be of help; sacrificed, killed, indulged in sexual rituals; in short, he did everything that he thought would place the course of destiny in his favour. While the ignorant and the mentally weak continued with the prescribed practices, the intelligent observers felt that nothing really worked, and came to the conclusion that, like in the visible world where each action precipitates certain results, in the hereafter too this must hold good. Thus was born the theory of Karma. It presumes that nothing ever perishes, matter as well as spirit. At the time of death, the material element in the body goes back to the materials of the earth, while the spiritual element is destined to eventually merge with the overall consciousness. But the deeds of a being, which also do not perish, influence the spirit and force it to pick up the matter again and, thus, push it into yet another birth. What kind of a species that soul manages to raise, depends upon the quality of the deeds. All species other than the human beings, have little volitional capability and the soul goes through this stage of the journey, if it has to perform this journey and not be born directly in human form, mechanically. It is only after it has assumed the human form that it acquires the capacity to fight the deeds and be freed of their hold and attain liberation and join the vast sea of consciousness which is the home of unbounded bliss.Thus, it is the law, the Dharma, which precipitates the effect depending upon the effect-generating activity. Any activity against the grain of Dharma is bound to invite trouble. Man's intuition, perhaps, was mainly responsible for guiding him to these conclusions.

Dharma regulates the universe, but who regulates Dharma? The conclusion is that Dharma, in fact, is an attribute of the Creator, and that, in effect, the entire creation is nothing other than a manifestation of His, for He is consciousness, and matter, and time, and dharma, and anything else that the mind can think of, and all else which is beyond the comprehension of the frail and limited human mind.

Generally the philosophy of the different systems of the Hindu thought have done away with God. The entire universe and its functioning is a system, a system that functions under prescribed laws at the physical, spiritual and intellectual and any number of other levels. To secure peace, health and happiness, it is necessary to understand the system and then flow with it, in harmony, keeping with its rhythm. In a way it is a harsh, unforgiving system, for it does not accommodate weakness. The meek might inherit the kingdom of God, but the weak shall never. With the coming in of the cult of devotional worship, however, the God was allocated attributes which were primarily beneficial to the weak, to their cries of distress, to their pain and misery. But the main philosophical thought, not only of this religion but also of those which branched off from it, like Buddhism or Jainism, supported the 'system' viewpoint. At the other end of the spectrum, are the atheists, not in small numbers, who believe the universe is only a physical system, brought into being by the interplay of material forces of different hues. However, philosophy notwithstanding, most people are theistic, and believe in *Saguna Brahma,* God with attributes, a personal God who is the creator and the ruler of the universe. Alongside, there is a pantheon of smaller deities too, like Hanumant 'in the northern parts of India and Ganesha in the central and southern parts. The general approach is that of the four activities prescribed for an individual, viz., dharma, artha, kaama and *moksha,* (righteousness, generation of wealth, enjoying the legitimate pleasures of life and seeking freedom from the birth-death cycle) the blessings of the lesser deities are beneficial enough for success in the case of the first three activities. For activities of even smaller dimensions, like success in the day-to-day work, blessings of gods of even smaller stature are good enough. But *moksha,* the final liberation from the cycle of births, can be achieved only with the grace of God, which can be secured only by complete and wholehearted devotion to Him. With better knowledge and awareness, though, the pantheon vanishes out of sight and all that remains is the personal God, the ruler of the universe. In the final stages, however, it is only the Nirguna Brahma! the One without attributes, That which is all that there is in creation, which is the creation itself, the one who cannot be divided; everything in the creation is but a manifestation of His.

Thus, Shiva iconography has a glorious aspect and also a frightening one. The latter, born directly out of the religion of the Proto-Australoids, shows him with his *shakti*, Parvati, both black and naked, in ascetic guise, smeared with funeral ashes, their soiled, matted hair wound in buns over the heads, the snakes and human heads serving as their body ornaments, drinking blood from bowls made out of skulls, munching flesh, dancing on corpses to the sound of drums, in drunken ecstasy, in the company of demons, witches and skeletons, around a fire in a lonely cremation ground. This iconography has mystic overtones. The former concept, of his being the glorious God, however, presents him as the Lord of the universe, in His abode on Mount Kailasha, in the company of adoring gods, deities and saints, with his spouse, Parvati, seated next to him, while in the depth of the mountain the demon king Ravana is held in captivity (depicted possibly to emphasize the inferiority of the demoniacal Proto-Australoid deities). In this mode he is showering blessings upon his faithfuls, granting them boons and showing them the way to eternal liberation. There is the story when the god of love, Kaama, tries to arouse desire in Him while He had been in deep meditation for a long time, so that He might respond to the painful longings of His spouse. This so angers Him that He opens his third eye and burns Kaama down to ashes, to the lamentations of latter's spouse, Rati, the goddess of lust. On her pleadings Shiva promises that Kaama shall be born each year for the duration of the spring when the whole world shall turn beautiful and full of desire, in fulfilment of Kaama's role as the god of love.

The devotees, however, worship Shiva's fear infusing mode with equal ardour, for they regard this aspect as inseparable from the other one which is pleasant and acceptable, for they regard the two as different attributes of one transcendental Godhead, like light and darkness, life and death. For Shiva and Bhairava or

Bhutanatha, Gauri and Kali, are the same. Even the Great Goddess is no more than an aspect of the Great God, who is male and female *Ardhanarishvara*, and who ultimately is neither one nor the other; He is Nirguna Brahma, the One Who is beyond comprehension, and beyond definition.

The Mother Goddess

The religion of the Mother Goddess is as old and as widespread as the human race. The first observation of man was about his birth from the womb of a woman, his mother. He imagined the creator to be a woman. The mother not only brought him into the world but sustained him too during the critical young years. It would be wrong to presume that the source of the belief in the motherhood of God is peculiar to any one country or any particular area. This came to man as naturally during the primitive times as his ability to hunt for food. Right from Anatolia in the west, all the way to India, including its southern and eastern areas, there is enough evidence of the prevalence of this practice from the very ancient times. Indus people had terracotta or faience figurines of standing, semi-nude female forms, wearing a girdle or a band around the loins, and an elaborate head-dress and jewellery. Such figurines have been found in many countries in Western Asia. In India they have been used as village or family goddesses. Such deities during the primitive times, and in some primitive areas even in the modern times, were not backed by any kind of philosophy, nor was it that any particular deity had any particular following. They were just mother goddesses, without any specific identity as such, representing the motherhood of God. For this reason, since they were personal deities or, at the most, family or clan deities, no temples were raised for them, not of significant dimensions, anyway. Nor were they spouses of any male god.

A Harappa seal shows a nude, female figure, turned upside down, with legs spread outwards, and a plant coming out of the womb. The reverse side of this seal shows a man in the posture of beheading a woman with a sickle; this appears to be a depiction of a sacrifice to the mother goddess, the goddess of fertility. The concept of the fatherhood of God came in when man settled down on land, in villages, and cultivated, and owned property, and ceased to be a mere nomad. At this stage the physical strength and the capacity to be free to fight, and not be encumbered with either pregnancies or the burden of raising children, became significantly important. The property owner, the warrior male, took charge of the family, clan, race, territory. He was the powerful one, and was looked up at and sung about. The great creator had to be the like of him. But man never really forgot the mother. She was vital to his being brought into this world, and to his sustenance during vulnerable years of his childhood. The thought has travelled down the generations, and man still worships the mother, although in a somewhat refined form. Hindus have her as Durga, Lakshmi or Saraswati, and so on, while to the Christians she is Mary, and to the Buddhists, Tara. Prophet Mohammad's main revolt was against the religion of the Mother Goddess, against the idols of this deity that people worshipped in the privacy of their homes.

Worshippers of the Mother Goddess have their own pantheon of female deities. These have already been mentioned earlier. These deities, in fact, represented different aspects of the Great Mother. She created, and sustained the universe, although the concept was not similar to that about Shiva or Vishnu as creators. She was the destroyer too and is represented as Kali or Chamunda, or as Shitla, the lady of the epidemics, and so on. There are different attributes of the Goddess that take care of the entire human activity.

During the Indus Valley culture the predominant deity appears to have been the Mother Goddess, although the male factor in the creation process appears to have been recognized and given importance. But he was only the silent fructifying agent, all else was accomplished by the Great Mother. With time the male aspect came to be recognized as immanence, the female as the transient creation, male the spiritual factor, the female as the material one, male as the consciousness, and the female as matter, as everything other than consciousness. Together the two came to be regarded as the power that causes creation, the two were regarded as the twin aspects of this power. Thus, came into being the symbol of the Linga and the Yoni.

There is no evidence of the linga-yoni worship during the Indus culture. They seem to have confined themselves to the worship of God in the form of Mother, or Lakulisa, possibly worshipped by the primitive people who constituted the work-force primitive people. It is likely that the idea of the latter deity was conceived and developed by some kind of a sect, like the Siddhas, who have placed great emphasis on celibacy. The institution of the Siddhas was, most probably, anterior, in time, to the onset of the Indus culture, and could have been the contribution of the Proto-Australoids; in eastern India, amongst the people bearing the characteristics of the Proto-Australoids, Siddha tradition is in practice even to this day. Siddha, the perfect ones, renounce the world, practise celibacy and meditative mode of worship, live away from human habitations and absolutely forbid themselves any covetousness, concupiscence, love and hatred, or participation in any worldly activity. They observe austerities in their worship, even to the extent of self-mortification. A branch of Indian medicine system owes its origination to the Siddhas; the system is particularly popular in the south. In north India the followers of this system are called sadhus, although the term now applies to any hermit. Amongst many others, their one belief is that the human mind and the body have latent energy which, when harnessed, can endow a person with extraordinary powers over himself and others. They say that with proper control of breath and concentration in the meditative posture, the individual can attain the capability to survive without food, or withstand climatic fluctuations without clothing or proper shelter, attain mental bliss, and freedom from sensual desires as also from the pain of hurt, infirmity or grief, attain true knowledge about his being and the universe, acquire the capability to walk on the air or be anywhere without physically travelling, take to repose at any time and at any place.

The sect believes that each human being carries within himself a psychic force, *kundalini*, (the nearest equivalent modern expression would be 'libido') which, in the normal course, lies dormant, coiled like a serpent, at the bottom of the spinal column, and that, if activated, or awakened, this force can achieve all that has been mentioned in the preceding para, and more. The awakening is achieved by practising kundalini Yoga under the guidance of a Guru. This Yoga is a combination of ordinary yoga practices, breath control exercises and meditation. During the awakening course the seat of the energy rises gradually from the bottom of the spine to the level of the lower abdomen, then abdomen proper, heart, throat and finally to the cerebral level. The common explanation is that an ordinary person is a being essentially of the senses, engrossed entirely in the process of eating, secreting and procreation, like any other species, thus is he born, and performing the same functions he passes out of this world. With the *kundalini* awakening he becomes aware of the pattern and purpose of creation, the aspect of the universal nature of consciousness, and as he rises higher, above the abdominal stage, he enters the level of intellect and finally that of wisdom, which is the same as Brahma realization. At this stage he is ready for final liberation. *En route*, he collects *Siddhis*, the capabilities as enumerated above, but he is advised not to get distracted by the power of the rising *kundalini*, and continue on course till the end of the journey, at which stage all his organs and the faculties integrate into one complete whole, resulting in spiritual joy, *ananda*.

It is, however, not to be believed that the entire doctrine, (and these people have put forth mutually supporting ideas in the fields of religion, medicine, astrology, astronomy), is of pre-Indus time. Indeed the ideas kept flowing into it (the adherents being totally freed from all worldly problems and given entirely to thinking out the phenomena of creation, sustenance, death and so on) for a long time, till almost the end of the Vedic era.But it can be said that the *siddhas* made a significant, contribution to the basic Hindu thought and philosophy. Most religious ideas originating in this country bear the influence of the *siddha* teachings, be it Buddhism, Jainism or Sikhism. Indeed, even the original religion of the Aryans was almost completely wiped out by them. The adherents, the *sadhus*, are not confined only to the south, they are fairly evenly sprinkled throughout the length and breadth of the country. A vast majority of them wear simple saffron clothes and were a highly respected clan in the past, but in recent times so many of them have been caught committing fraudulent acts, and exploiting the gullible, or following ideas laced with a lot of magic or which are follow up of illogical tribal traditions of a hoary past, that those of them seen in the midst of people are viewed with suspicion, as a rule they are expected to live in seclusion.

As stated above, their contribution to the central Hindu thought has been significant. They have lived as celibates, away from the people, without elaborate shelters or clothing, and have thought and debated and, now and then, have communicated those thoughts to the less gifted people with a view to telling them about the meaning of life and how happiness and contentment can be brought into it. Because of the flow of ideas from these people, the Indian religious thought has emphasized the aspect of pain and suffering in the human life, that the cause of it is essentially the desire to possess, that to be delivered of it there has to be renunciation, of everything, including love, hate, attachment, anger, covetousness, sex, and that there has to be emphasis upon activities promoting the welfare of the community. The requirement is to perform to the best of the ability, but in an impersonal manner, without undue involvement, and to learn the truth about the Creator and Dharma, and worship the former with a devoted heart. Some amongst them attained great fame and were exalted to the position of *rishis* or *sages*. They contributed to the Vedic literature too and enjoyed a kind of status which put them above the level of the common folk. It was, for example, quite in order for the wife of a sterile male to approach a member of this class for the purpose of begetting a child, a function later usurped by the priestly Brahmin class. As for their literature, a lot of it appears to be meaningless gibberish, replete with formulas about sorcery and magic, and description of powers attained through austerities, meditation and yoga, but they have put forth some sterling ideas too. A known votary of this genere was Gorakhnath (early second millennium AD) whose sect practised magic and yoga and who enjoyed great following amongst the people of Proto-Australoid background.

Generally, however, the Sadhus have maintained their distance from the common folk and have practised their austerities with fanatical zeal, often indulging in self mortification whenever they felt they were straying off course. They have emphasized the importance of purificatory baths during certain specified times, particularly at certain spots, tanks or confluences of rivers, for attainment of heaven. Their belief in the Karma philosophy is not entirely defined. It is, however, a fact that, when compared to the

Shiva as Ardhnarishwara, embodying both the male and the female principles. Bhubaneswar, 10th-11th century A.D.

Durga as Mahishasuramardini, slaying the evil of lust and power. Bhubaneswar, 10th-11th century A.D.

requirements of a common human being, they survive in climatically hostile environments with much less protection in the form of food, clothing and shelter.

However, Siddhas, or some such people, appear to have developed the concept of the Linga-Yoni symbol. This is a stage, where no supremacy has been assigned to one or the other aspect of the total Creative Power. Male and the female are just two poles, equal in importance, in power, and capability, two harmonized parts of one complete whole, at the ultimate stage they are but one.

But, in the mundane world, away from the world of the hermits, the story was a little different. Here God was a male, ruler of the world, the Great King, for He was viewed in the image of the patriarch, the females of the palace were his subordinates. The Great Shiva, representing immanence, the male aspect of the fertilization process, came to be regarded as all powerful, the cosmic soul, the sea of Consciousness, and Durga, or Parvati, or many other aspects of the Great Mother, for all of which different names had been assigned, came to be considered as playing the second fiddle, getting activated to participate in the creation process only at the bidding of her Lord and Master. The modification made the doctrine almost congruent with the doctrine of theism, except that it retained the concept that at the ultimate level the Creator and the visible creation are, in fact, one and the same thing.

Durga, the Great Mother, must have evolved from the concept of the motherhood of God, as represented by the numerous figurines of the female deity found from the Harappan sites. Initially the goddess was, perhaps, a family or, at the most, a village or a clan deity, not much associated with any complex philosophy. She was just the benefactress who took care of the interests of the devotees, like a mother did in respect of her children. But as the boundaries of human imagination expanded, it became clear that the creating or the guiding, or the annihilating force was the same for the entire universe. The horizons assigned to the deity expended, gradually embracing the whole world and, finally, the universe. Possibly for a long time Durga, or a supreme female deity going by any other name, remained the unfettered ruler of the universe in the minds of the people imbued with religion, till the male God overtook her and reduced her to a secondary position, or even totally eliminated her, as in Islam.

In the mythology spun around her, she is the Great Mother who, in fact, came to be called Durga after she had slain a mighty demon who went by that name.That was where she, the embodiment of good, annihilated the evil for the beneficence of her devotees. She have a tough and a sanguine fight to another demon, Mahisasura, who had been bewitched by her beauty and wanted to rape her, and ultimately destroyed him after she had retreated to the famous cave of Vaishno Devi in the state of Jammu and Kashmir. In eastern India she is the Great Goddess who visits the earth for ten days, before the onset of winter, to bless her devotees and shower beneficence upon them. The occasion is celebrated as *Durga Puja*, worship of Durga, when the devotees pay obeisance to her and sing her praises and pray. In the present day context, however, Durga is the consort of Shiva and at the end of her visit to the earth she goes back to him. The noteworthy feature, however, is that the worship is directed towards the Great Mother, as the Mother and not as the spouse of the male God Shiva; it has nothing whatsoever to do with Shiva.

An important legend in this lore, as contained in the *Vayu Purana*, is that of Daksha, a celebrated *Prajapati* born from the thumb of Brahma. *Prajapati* is the Lord of the creatures, the primordial God, father of gods and all beings. He is the one to whom all sacrifices are made and all prayers addressed in the Brahmanas. One of his daughters, Sati, an incarnation of Parvati, was married, to Shiva. Both Shiva and Sati were not invited by Daksha to a great sacrifice that he conducted, for he considered Shiva an uncouth mendicant not fit for the kind of function he had organized. Daughter Sati was distressed and, against the advice of Shiva, decided to attend the function even when she had not been invited. During the course of the function Daksha and his sons ridiculed Shiva as a beggarly person, keeping the company of demons and snakes and other despicable beings, and this so incensed Sati that she flung herself into the sacrificial fire and burnt herself to death. Shiva was displeased with Daksha for this, and he sent Vir Bhadra of one thousand hands, created out of a lock of his hair, to destroy the sacrifice. This the latter did, but the perishing of Sati had so saddened Shiva that he held her dead-body close to himself and endlessly flew about the heavens to get over the grief. With time the limbs of the Goddess dropped off bit by bit, and wherever they fell those places have become sacred to the worshippers of the Mother Goddess. Pilgrims visit the places to seek her blessings. Here too the Great Mother has been separated from the Great God and is required to be worshipped as such and not as the spouse of Shiva. In some other accounts Daksha also gets killed by Vir Bhadra and only after entreaties of Brahma and Vishnu is he revived by Shiva, but with the head of a ram, for his own head could not be found at the site of the sacrifice. The incident illustrates a kind of a stage where the followers of Shiva, people of the Dravidian group of races, have secured supremacy over those of Brahma or Vishnu, i.e., people following the Aryan religion, for apart from the vanquishing of Daksha, a number of other Vedic gods get mauled or hurt in this episode. The definition of 'sati' is derived from this episode and implies a widow's consent to be bound with the corpse of her husband, once that has been done she has perished as his wife. She does not have to be actually burnt with the corpse.

Alongside the concept of the motherhood of God, animism, i.e., belief that natural phenomena and things, animate or inanimate, possess individual innate souls, also flourished, and that made gods out of phenomena like winds, fire, stones, trees, animals and so on, and brought in zoomorphic deities like Hanumant or Ganesha of the elephant head, or Nagas or Yakshas. With the fatherhood of God, these deities were mostly visualized as males. As property oriented, patriarchal societies developed, and the fatherhood of God became the accepted norm, the motherhood concept got relegated to a secondary position. In India this branch of religion has extensive following in the eastern, north-eastern and the western and the north-western parts of the country, while Shiva is widely worshipped in the Himalayan foothills and in south India, although he has a following, which may not be very extensive in some places, almost throughout the length and the breadth of the country. In fact, most Hindu temples of today are dedicated to all the different important branches of

Hindu religion, and provide facilities for the worship of all the major deities.

The Shaktas

This branch of Hinduism professes faith in Shakti, the force that creates the universe at the behest of Shiva. Shiva and Shakti are the two aspects of the Creator that combine to set the creation process in motion. While Shiva represents immanence, wisdom or consciousness, the dormant but the all-pervading principle, the Shakti is the active principle, representing the power of creation, and the belief of the Shaktas, the followers of Shakti, is that when prayers to the Great Goddess are addressed with a certain methodology, the path for the realization of the ultimate goal, which is to secure liberation from the cycle of births, *sansara*, becomes shorter and the chances of achievement become more certain. The original idea, perhaps, is of pre Indus Valley times, and may have been the contribution of the *Siddhas*, but in its modified form it is not older than 800 to 1000 years. In this style of worship the emphasis is on recitation of specified incantations and worship of the goddess with grain, flowers, grass, etc., placed at different spots on the sanctified alter, on geometrically drawn triangles and circles, which are made with flour or powdered colour, mostly red or saffron. This worship is called *puja*, and is distinct from the worship with fire and sacrifice which was the practice followed by the Aryans.

During the later stages of the Vedic religion, the Tantric method of worship had not only been accepted, but even given a higher place by some authorities. The system is, however, not to be confused with the practice of devotional worship of Mother Goddess. In fact, it is not the kind of worship in the normal sense. It is an interplay of magic formulas alongside certain prescribed activity, under the watchful eye of a preceptor, all calculated to speed up the process of union with Shiva, for Shiva is the seat of bliss and peace, for He is that level where nothing can be added, and wherefrom nothing can be deducted; this level has the aspect of externality, constance, a no-agitation situation. It, thus, is an ocean of unbounded peace, a being in total bliss, the ultimate goal in the process of liberation.

This worship is a complicated, time consuming process, it is not something that one might take on alongside other mundane occupations, or during the time that one might have after attending to the normal daily chores. The *Siddhas* possibly could do it, for they had all the time to themselves, at least the senior ones in a group or a monastery. The details of the practice are contained in books called the *Tantras*. The system is built on the belief that Shiva and Shakti are in fact one whole, that in the creation process the active aspect is Shakti, and that the path to union with Shiva, or Brahma, the Immanence, where the store-house of bliss is, is through Shakti, this active principle.

The core literature sometimes is contained in esoteric writings, *Sandhabhasha*, often including erotic expressions. Broadly the approach is not fundamentalistic; the individual has been allowed to select a course which he considers to be the most suitable to his background and temperament. Before, however, the person gets down to the higher stages of the worship, he is required to acquire a masterly grip over the important religious literature, which include the epics, the *Ramayana* and the *Mahabharata*, the Vedas and the important Upanishads, and so on. Ritual has a very high place in the Tantric mode of worship, so much so that even activities like pilgrimage or circumambulations are considered as important as meditation and Yoga. The system of worship requires the concerned person to pray to his favourite goddess with full devotion and love, under the guidance of his preceptor, all the time toning up his system with the help of Yoga. This gives lasting purity to his body and mind, and all base and unclean thoughts get banished.The next stage is meditation, during the course of which he awakens the *kundalini* energy and finally, through the medium of a lot of rituals, prayer, recitation of incantations, some or all of which might have been taught by the preceptor, and Yoga and meditation, he reaches the goal. The *kundalini* energy that rises from the base of the spine is visualized as female, while the brain centre where to it rises is identified with Shiva, the Absolute Wisdom. This union of the female and the male principles is often described in esoteric and erotic language.

Apart from the emphasis on following the details of rituals, Tantras stress the need for spiritual discipline, sadhna, the need to follow the course leading to enlightenment in accordance with the laid down rules. Its aim is to eliminate the distinction between the phenomenal and the absolute world in the mind of the disciple; this is achieved through constant contemplation till he sees the whole as one reality. This kind of thought is basic to the monoistic doctrine of Hinduism as well. The difference is that the tantric, the person practising tantras, experiences the oneness of the two modes, that, at least, is the claim. He experiences the fact of his own being, including his mind and intellect, to be non-substantial, and that leads to the realization that it is, in fact, all Brahma, 'I am Brahma', *Ahm Brahm Asmi*, for his own non-substantiality in effect resides within the substantiality of the ultimate Creator. There is hardly any difference in the tantric and non-tantric philosophy except that the tantrics are talking of the actual experience. Theirs is a psycho-experimental interpretation of the non-tantric view of the phenomenal and the absolute worlds. To know the truth the tantric experiments and while doing so he is not rigidly following the conventional moral or social norms. They claim that the course they follow is dangerous and radical, but that, along it lies the short-cut to liberation. 'I', the ego-stuff, is the product of the mind, the thought process, *manas*, when it is experiencing the materialized world. But when this *manas* turns its attention away from the world perceived through senses and ponders over the primordial cause of its own being, and that of the universal source of all consciousness, it becomes aware of its own transient status, and realizes that beyond the transience lies the wholly substantive Brahma. This revelation is not secured through analytical thought or logical reasoning. It is achieved by bringing the mind, *Manas*, to complete rest and relinquishing all thought-activities. The process takes the person through a series of rising dimensions of spiritual awareness which, though it cannot be described, is experienced with the hitherto undeveloped organs of intuitive consciousness, into which manas is transformed after it has turned away from the activities of the outer senses and broken off from the discriminatory activity of the intellect. At the final level it is the experience of infinity and the merging of the phenomenal and the absolute worlds. It is the experience of the union of the two poles and of the oneness of Brahma/Shiva and His creation.

This is achieved through meditation, by closing the mind to the thoughts provoked by the senses, as also the analytical activity of the intellect and, as Lama Anagrika Govinda says, "by reversing the direction of the inner vision from the manifold to the unified, the limited to the unlimited, intellectual to the intuitive, till all else is banished and it is only infinity." Success in the meditative process is achieved with *mantra*, incantation, mystical utterance. A *mantra* is not a hymn or a psalm. It has been variously defined by different authorities, but in essence it is a composition of certain letters, purposefully arranged to produce a sequence of sounds, designed to confer upon the reciter magical or spiritual powers. To have the desired effect it must be intoned in the prescribed manner. It does not necessarily have words which might have meaning in the ordinary sense; to a lay observer some of the words are totally meaningless. But to an adept or the aspirant, it is a pronouncement containing an experience content which operates in the realm of the gods and of mystical powers. This *mantra* is imparted by a guru to a disciple, in secrecy, during the course of a specified ritual. Otherwise, mere recitation of a collection of words, which may normally be labelled as a *mantra*, mean nothing. In the non-tantric religion, however, the *mantra* by itself has the necessary potency as long as it is recited along with the prescribed ritual.

The essential purpose of the *mantra* is to seek the support of good and harmful gods for a fruitful, happy life for own self and the family or the clan, or to secure things in life which are not easily available otherwise, or are not available at all, or (as in the Tantra system) to identify oneself with the object of prayer, e.g., *aham Brahm amsi,* (I am Brahma). The *mantra* normally has a portion where the words have meaning, and together these words make pithy statements designed to impress upon the reciter the purpose for which it is there. But it also has within it syllables which make no sense; these latter are called the bijas, e.g., word 'Om', which forms part of most *mantras*, has no meaning as such, (word *Bija* means seed). The origin of these *Bijas*, it is broadly agreed, has been through some super sensory perception during a successful meditation, it is revealed in a flash, never in part but always as a complete unit, and, this is considered to be the most powerful portion of the *mantra*. Not everyone, however, agrees about the potency of the *bijas*. Materialists of the Charvaka School term them as meaningless gibberish. Most traditionalists do not accept the claims about their efficacy. The *tantrics*, on the other hand, say that *bijas* produce vibrations within the psyche which lift the *manaś* to the level of intuitive consciousness. This is claimed to be particularly true of the *mantras* which are used for meditation, the ones which are imparted by a guru, and also of those which are used in a ritual, like purifying a place of all evil influences before the commencement of anything auspicious, like, for example, meditation. There are a whole lot of *mantras*, claimed to have been revealed by none other than the Great Shiva Himself to suit all purposes, compiled in a book called the *Mantra Shastra*. These *mantras* fall in two broad categories, viz., *Hadi* and *Kadi mantras*. The former are used where the principal aim is liberation i.e., union with the all pervading Immanence, while the latter are used for mundane purposes.

Mantra then is the means of getting the mind detached from the senses or the wandering of the intellect. It is through yoga that mind acquires the discipline and capability to concentrate only on *Mantra* and banish all other thoughts or feelings, and eventually reach the state of deep meditation. There are four types of Yoga, namely :

(a) *Mantra* Yoga, aimed at securing the concentration of thought by repeating mentally the *mantra* and fixing the thought upon it, holding it there and not letting it go astray,

(b) *Hatha* Yoga, comprising a number of physical exercises which condition the body, and make it healthy and fit so that the mind within can concentrate and not be bothered by physical frailties, the exercises comprise body postures in different positions: lying, sitting, kneeling, standing and so on, and breathing exercises which, it is claimed, awaken the dormant *kundalini*, and further the deep meditation process,

(c) *Laya* Yoga, the third stage, when the mind is fully and deeply absorbed in meditation on the deity, when the seeker's *prana*, the vital breath, the breath of life or the life force holding the body together, merges with the cosmic consciousness, and he acquires the power of directing this life force to any part of the body — which in fact is a miniature universe. This is the stage when he has attained the full knowledge of the total creation, and developed the power to have his desires fulfilled if so required; this is the essence of *shakti sadhna,* when the life force is fully controlled, the individual is now a *shakti sadhak,* one who has attained Shakti, power, in the form of *siddhis*.

(d) The final stage of Yoga is termed as the Raj Yoga, the ultimate stage wherein the seeker or the *Sadhaka* concentrates the mind through the control of the vital breath and goes in a state of trance, *samadhi,* and loses his own identity in the Cosmic Consciousness, in the process experiencing indescribable peace and the limits of ultimate bliss. He is now free from the cycle of rebirth. He has merged with the Great Shiva. The ecstasy of this state can be assessed from the story of Shiva who, when disturbed in this state by the arrow of *Kaama,* the god of love, beauty and pleasure, was so incensed that He opened His third eye and in utter rage and reduced the poor god to cinders. This is the stage beyond which there is nothing to seek.

Initiation, *diksha,* of an adept is done by a guru with the imparting of a *mantra*; this, of course, is done in secrecy. A guru is one who should have been initiated in his time and should have gone through the *sadhna,* the spiritual discipline, and should have secured results. He has to be a learned man of some repute, and should possess spiritual maturity, and have the experience and maturity to guide his disciple. Before a person receives *diksha,* he must have the urge for the 'spiritual experience'. This would make him visit renowned teachers and eventually select for himself the one from whom he would accept the initiation. He then visits this person, listens to his discourses, gets known to him, and then states his purpose, and if the guru feels that the disciple would measure up to his expectations, he would agree. There are any number of accounts of gurus who were followed by seekers for long periods, and who were even rough with them, and who agreed only after they had been satisfied, after prolonged observations, that the seeker was genuine. The guru would normally compare his own horoscope with that of the seeker to decide whether the intended relationship between the two was likely to bear fruit. He then makes an assessment of the spiritual qualification of the person and decides upon the *mantra* to be imparted, and then, on the basis of astrological calculations, decides upon the time, place and the manner of conducting the initiation, the place for this purpose is generally the guru's residence, but it could also be a cowpen, mango tree, temple, garden, river-bank, foot of a mountain, or the bank of the Ganges. Such places greatly enhance the chance of success. After the ceremony the disciple departs after he has made the offering of guru's fee, *dakshina*, and lain at his feet in humility and respect, and has circumambulated him three times, and accepted the *prasad* (a small quantity of eatables from a plate that has been touched by the guru). He then gets down to meditate upon the *mantra*. It is the belief of the *tantrics* that without initiation no amount of worship has any merit.

Meditation on the *mantra* brings results because, firstly, by resting the mind upon it all thoughts are progressively banished. The mind then is like a clean slate which would have the capability to sense or experience the divinity. Then, the words of the *mantra* have certain sound-vibrations which are in harmony with those of the deity being sought for, and attract him. For this reason the words of the *mantra* have to depend upon the deity and the purpose for seeking him. The *mantra* also establishes a direct link between the guru and the disciple and secures the support of the former in attaining the goal. Through its medium the guru inspires him, keeps his spiritual urge alive, and does not let him lose faith in his capability, or in the efficacy of the *mantra*, it also inspires confidence in the power and beneficence of the guru. *Mantra* is the vehicle that takes the adept to his goal.

The Vedanta system postulates that the ultimate reality is indivisible, non-dual. But in essence it concedes the existence of two aspects within this non-duality, viz., the spiritual aspect comprising wisdom, experience of the supreme reality and the joy and bliss flowing therefrom, and the non-spiritual aspect comprising compassion, method (adopted to reach spiritual enlightenment), energy and the like; the former may be termed as the static aspect and the latter the dynamic. In the scheme of things the static aspect has been given the male principle while the dynamic the female principle. How exactly this allocation has been arrived at, it is not possible to say with any degree of certainty, it could be purely intuitive. But it is also an established fact that in the creation of life the more important, crucial role is played by the female, though without the male life cannot evolve. In fact the oldest system of Indian philosophy, the Sankhya, as outlined by Kapila (circa 8th century BC), postulates that the universe consists of two principles, viz., inert nature, *prakriti*, (the later day female principle), and pure consciousness, *purusha*. The universe evolves through *prakriti*; consciousness has no role in this, it is only a spectator. But *prakriti* is inoperative in the absence of *purusha*. In other words *purusha* energises the dynamic principle and after having done so lets the latter perform unhindered. Consciousness is the master but is only the indulgent onlooker of the performance of the dynamic principle. Although Sankhya system visualizes two distinct principles in the creation process, the later day Vedic religion combines the two into one non-dual aspect, describing the two as two poles of the same whole.

The Shakta religion is about this dual aspect of the source of creation. It recognizes that the approach to the final experience is through the dynamic aspect and advises the seeker to latch on to it, as it were, till it transports him to the regions of the psyche, beyond the level of senses and the intellect, and he experiences the merging of the two aspects into one whole, and enjoys bliss and beatitude, and secures liberation from the cycle of births. In their iconography they have the male principle, Shiva, being trampled upon by the female principle, Kali. The idea is to emphasize the predominance of the female principle in the creation process. 'Shiva without Shakti is a corpse...' goes the belief of the Shaktas. The male principle, though all pervading, lies dormant, wrapped up in layers of *prakriti*. There are others who claim it by symbolizing Shiva's method of restraining Shakti from adopting an excessively dialectical, materialistic, and punishing approach towards the total creation, particularly the beings blessed with intelligence. She is in great rage, out to demolish any and everything that has violated Dharma. The only way to make her think and relent in her blinding ferrocity, was for the Great Shiva to lie at her feet and thus stop the dance of destruction, even though the destruction was being effected in respect of that element of creation which was in discord, out of harmony, with Dharma. Suddenly she is upon His prostrate body, and suddenly the movement of her feet ceases, and she becomes aware of the wish of the Lord lying at her feet, and breaks into a kind smile and her upper right hand rises in assurance of protection to all creatures against any danger or fear while the lower right hand rises in a gesture of blessing. Earlier she was destructive and that is shown by the raised sword in the upper left hand and the severed head of a demon in the lower left hand. But Shiva's entreaties for mercy, even for the sinful, are conceded provided, of course, the sinners mend their ways during the hereafter. There are yet others who suggest that Shiva, *Mahakaal*, rolling under Her feet suggests the annihilation of time and space, (*Mahakaal* is time and space), which ultimately get assimilated into Her, before she gets assimilated into the infinite sea of consciousness.

Of the Hindu religious literature *Tantras* are the most liberal and cosmopolitan in their teachings. They have laid down the broad course which might be followed by the seeker, but they do not bind him down to any fundamentalistic observances or rituals. They have given full liberty to the person to do his own study and strike his own course. In fact the belief is that no two persons while moving towards the final goal can delineate identical treads. These will vary, howsoever insignificantly, depending upon the physical constitution and mental and psychical make-up of the individuals concerned. Therefore, once the initiation has been done, it is for the individual to decide how best he would cope with the problems on the course he decides to follow. The system accepts that religious urge is a common emotion of all mankind and is not peculiar to any one class or group of people. It, therefore, lays down that no one, not even the so called Shudras, or women, may be denied the privilege of receiving the *Mantra*, or seeking the benediction of Shiva, or following a course that may open to his/her view the nature of the ultimate reality. In short, there has to be no distinction between a person and a person for any reason whatsoever. This, naturally, led to the different authorities interpreting the *tantric* injunctions in their own way, practising, experimenting with methods which ranged between the completely orthodox, laying stress on complete celibacy and a strict regimen for food and other habits, and almost totally unorthodox, which disregarded the accepted religious norms, and advocated seeking union with the infinite even through sensual practices.

A lot of *Tantric* instruction is in esoteric, erotic language, commonly termed as *Sandha Bhasha*. Of this Eliade, as quoted by Agehananda Bharati, says "...the Tantric texts are frequently couched in intentional language — a secret, obscure language with double meaning, wherein a particular state of consciousness is expressed in erotic terminology." The purpose, the author feels, is to camouflage the doctrine against the non-initiates, and to project the *yogi* into the situation which is indispensable for his spiritual training. Another view is that as a devotee progresses towards his goal of experiencing the divinity of Shiva, a stage is reached when his mind and senses are totally purified and his prayer becomes contemplation and the mind is illumined, and he soars beyond the time and space limits, at the intuitive level. He is part of the Great Shiva, a witness to all, having an experience that he would never be able to describe in the language in normal use. That is when he borrows the language of carnal love. Yet another view is that this is a way of representing the experiences of meditation in the form of easily comprehensible outer events. There is, therefore, no question of attaching any sexuality to the yoga practices of the *Tantras*. The underlying object of the instructions or the details of experience, is to guide the seeker to a stage where he comprehends *shakti*, intuitively, and experiences it, and moves even higher in spiritual realization, till he experiences the merging of *shakti* in Shiva.

Primarily, however, this *Sandha Bhasha* could be a code language designed to repel a casual seeker, create, may be, in his mind a sense of abhorrence, and dissuade him from taking on the course when his inner self is not thirsting for it. For example, term *Bodhi Chitta* in normal writing would mean *Bodhi* mind, or illumined mind, but in the intentional language, *Sandha Bhasha*, its meaning is believed to be semen virile. Lama Anagarika Govinda quotes a passage from one of the treatises: "...all women should be enjoyed by the *sadhaka* in order to experience the *Mahamudra*. Quite clearly this passage cannot be taken literally, it obviously is referring to that higher form of love which is not restricted to a single object. Another passage in the same genre translates: "*Sadhaka* who has sexual intercourse with his mother, his sister, his daughter, and his sister's daughter, will easily succeed in his effort to secure the ultimate goal." Here too literal meaning is not intended to be followed, the instruction is conveying in esoteric language something remarkably relevant to the *sadhana*.

But there is another angle to this mode of worship. After the adept has gone through the preliminary stages of the discipline and acquired the basic capability to concentrate his mind on aspects beyond the realm of the senses and intellect, he has, preferably, to proceed further by having a female alongside him during the worship ritual. He is then equipped to unite with Shiva, immanence, the eternal wisdom, the sea of consciousness, through the medium of female polarity, the *shakti*. For, to secure complete experience he has to have his *shakti*, like Shiva has His. During the ritual, if the female sits on his left side, the ritual is called left-handed and when she is on his right side it is right handed. The principle difference in the two types of *sadhanas* is that in the former case the objects as prescribed for the ritual are to be actually used, while in the latter case these are either substitutes or the ritual proceeds with meditating upon them.

Not all, but some followers and adepts of the left handed *Tantric* mode of worship emphasize that sexual contact is an essential ingredient for obtaining the complete experience. The other prescribed objects for this practice, in addition to *Maithuna*, (the sexual contact), are: *madya* (wine), *matsya* (fish), *mansa* (meat or flesh), and *mudra* (ordinarily gesture but also kidney beans or parched grain). All these put together are called the *panch makaars* the five Ms or the five essentials. Barren women and impotent men are forbidden from participating in such rituals. At the face of it, the idea appears to be to consume high protein items and build assured sexual potency before going in for the sexual contact. No doubt elaborate ritual accompanies the consumption of the ingredients, and, as the *tantrics* say in defence of their practice, if the idea was just to have sex there are many such simpler ways of doing so. After taking the first four essentials, with due elaborate rituals, the adept is ready to go in for the fifth, which is *maithuna*, the sexual contact. His *shakti* is invited at this stage and the adept bathes her and dresses her up in red garments and there is a lot of ritual, and reading and reciting of the *mantras* and describing this or that *mandala*, but in essence the entire process goes through a brief courtship, and then foreplay and, finally, the fornication, at the culmination of which the yogi releases his semen virile into his *sakti* as an act of sacrifice and, thus, experiences the merging of the dynamic, phenomenal aspect with the eternal wisdom. The ritual is gone through in the presence of the guru and, where applicable, his wife, if they are available; they do not have to be witnesses to the final act. In guru's absence the function is presided over by the senior *sadhaka* of the group.

The ritual is gone through in single pairs or in *chakras*, circles, in which case a number of pairs participate simultaneously, each male of the pair being the equivalent of Shiva and his female partner Shakti. In the right handed practices the five Ms are not actually used. Either substitutes are taken, like milk for *madya*, wine, or the ingredients are just in the mind while going through the ritual of reciting the designated *mantras* and performing the meditation. The left handed practice is, thus, described as dangerous and only the most accomplished are advised to take it on. The basic yardstick to decide whether the adept is reasonably mature and versed in the *mantra*, yoga and meditation, and has the capability to focus the mind upon the object of worship, and has succeeded in unfolding the *kundalini* and developed the capability of merging with cosmic wisdom when appropriate means become available, is done by assessing his *Bhavatraya*, disposition. There are three classifications of the dispositions: *Pushu Bhava* (animal disposition), *Vir Bhava* (heroic disposition), and *Divya Bhava* (divine disposition). This last one is the highest in the order, but the animal disposition is not to be considered as something of negative value. The very fact that the *sadhaka* has qualified to be considered in this light, shows that he is on the road to progress, though he may yet have some way to go, and might not yet be suited to participate in the *panch makaar sadhna*, or spiritual disciplines. Generally, green disciples or Brahmins were put in this category, Brahmins because they were thoroughly opposed to the left handed practices, also referred to as *Vamchara*, and called them diabolical and unethical, practised and taught by people of lose morals. In the normal parlance term *Vamchara* is used for unrestricted fornication.

The disciple's progress from the lower to the higher disposition depends upon his ability and the intensity of his desire to seek the knowledge. The general indicators in this process are— hatred, fear, backbiting, doubt, shame, or feeling of family or racial superiority, or a lack of capability to break from the established tradition. Bound by these characteristics the person is still striving on the road to progress, but freed he ranks with the very *Sadashiva*, the highest phenomenal aspect of God Shiva.

Once the person has reached the *Vir Bhava* stage, he has acquired the capability to control his senses and has been freed from the chaotic wanderings of his intellect, and has stepped into the region of intuitive. At this stage he has uncoiled the *kundalini* and can direct it for union with the eternal wisdom. He is now fit for the *Panch Makaar Sadhna*, and after a series of successful spiritual rituals he attains the *Divya Bhava*, the divine disposition. According to *Bamakeshwar Tantra*, propensity for *Pashu Bhava* dominates a person till he attains the age of sixteen, and thereafter till the age of fifty it is *Vir Bhava*, and after that it is *Divya Bhava*. At the ultimate level the three *Bhavas* unify to precipitate a state of the mind called *kulachara*. At this level man becomes godlike, and is liberated, he is *jeevan mukta*.

The essential doctrine and the practical teachings of the Buddhist and left handed Hindu tantras are quite similar; in both cases sexual contact is central to the *sadhna*. However, while the Buddhist allocate the male principle to the active aspect, i.e., energy, compassion, method *upaya*, and the female principle to the static aspect, i.e., wisdom, realization, beatitude, the Hindu *tantras* have done just the reverse. But in spite of the subtle differences in the concepts of the male and the female principles, the practices followed in either case do not vary much. While some authorities like Lama Anagarika Govinda have suggested that sexuality as such plays no part in the Tibetan mode of the *sadhna*, others like Agehananda Bharati say that tantric practices, particularly of the Vajrayana School, show but few differences from the left handed Hindu Tantric system.

It is fairly certain that both the religious practices have had some common source. There have been suggestions that Tibetan brand of Buddhism could have had its source in Taoism of southern China, or in the pre-Buddhist Bon religion of Tibet which had its source in Mongolia. But on scrutiny these hypotheses do not hold, and it seems that the source was in India itself. On the basis of the evidence of the Harappan seals we know that, apart from the Mother worship, the Indus Valley people were well acquainted with the ideas of *Pashupati*, yoga, and asceticism. During the flowering stage of their culture, which, possibly, happened much before the flowering of the Indus Valley civilization, the Proto-Australoids had already organized themselves in village communities and their priests, who probably were the *Siddhas*, possibly performed the same kind of functions as the shamans. There possibly were no temples as such, but these shamans, or the *siddhas*, with time, seem to have developed a cult that gave a lot of importance to the male semen, and the female's capability to bear a child. Related, possibly with the male semen were the yogic exercises which, they believed, helped the body system to stay healthy and retain the capability for fertilization. Both, i.e., the child bearing capability, and the male semen, were considered by them to be divine, important aspects of the Great Power that precipitated the Creation.

It is possible that over a few thousand years the concept got modified so that by the time of the Indus Valley civilization, the worship, possibly, had taken a more sophisticated form. In the earlier version the Mother was goddess Kali, a pitch black female demon who needed the basic substances of the created world in order to be propitiated, and this included blood in the form of animal and human sacrifice, and, of course, a host of other items as are found grown in nature, like water, grains, flowers, fruit, etc. With time *bijas* also appeared, the portion of the *mantras* that makes no sense. These possibly did come to the shamans psychically and they did use them in genuine faith in their efficacy.

With the arrival of the later strains of the Dravidians, things started looking up for religion. The idea of human or animal sacrifice was condemned by these people, who achieved a high degree of cultural sophistication as evidenced by the Harappan finds. The religion of Shiva evolved with them, and with time the merging of the Shiva and the Mother Goddess concepts took place, and, may be, later the linga-yoni symbol got finalised.

But the original religion of the Australoids stayed, for these people constituted the majority. The sophistication in the Dravidian religion appears to have been restricted essentially to the urban centres. Rural centres, where the impact of education was minimal, continued to be under the spell of the shamans. This state of affairs lasted, to a large or small extent, till the early years of the 20th century. Even today the land is not entirely free from old influences. Surprisingly, even some educated people believe in the old practices. The gods of the Australoids were visualized as some kind of despotic criminals who could be won over to commit any kind of crime, with appropriate offerings. Practices of *thuggee*, loot, arson, plunder were legitimized, and before the start of any of these criminal activities the Kali, her blood thirsty tongue ever hanging out, was propitiated with sacrifice, even human sacrifice if the task was onerous, and sex rituals. The shamans claimed they could precipitate success in any sphere with their *bijas* and correct gestures and sex rites. On the other hand, the *Siddhas* who had generally retired to the seclusion of the forests, pondered over the issues and, as claimed, went through experiments to seek the knowledge of the ultimate reality. But before that they had to know what the systems of philosophy were. The conclusion in some cases was that the *Panch Makaar Sadhna* did cut down the time required to reach the final goal. This was not religion in the strictest sense, it was more like enunciating methods to achieve a certain predetermined goal, the methods, no doubt, had been evolved on the basis of experiments, or so it was believed. The idea of a modern type of religion where each detail has been set forth for the followers, possibly just did not exist then. After having set the *sadhaka* on the broad course, he was left to himself. It was emphasized that the narrow track to the final destination had to be discovered by the person himself, that no two persons could traverse a common track to reach the same goal. When the *Sadhna*, they claimed, was progressing along the right course, the experience of going along it was indeeded exhilirating.

Shakta concept accepts the Sankhya view that *prakriti* or *shakti* is the cause of the creation and allots it the dynamic principle, but then adds that ultimately it dissolves into Shiva. *Purusha*, Brahma, whose constituent part it is, and re-emerges at the time of the next cycle of creation. Yoga of *Patanjli*, which is considered as almost a part of the Sankhya system, talks of the rising power of *Hatha* Yoga, from the physical level to the higher intellectual and spiritual levels, or higher levels of awareness and consciousness, which make a person realize the reality of the *purusha* and *prakriti*, and he experiences the ultimate bliss and peace. But no polarity, male or female, has been allocated to either of them. *Prakriti* is not female, nor is the *purusha* male. They are the agencies of creation, *Prakriti* creates, and it does so in the presence of *Purusha*, put together they are just two attributes of energy. But Shaktas, while broadly accepting this, have visualised *prakriti* as the dynamic principle and the female aspect, and *purusha*, the quiescent principle and the male aspect. This division has, apparently, been done on the basis of some kind of intuitive wisdom; *tantric* literature does not give any reason. Having allocated the polarity, Shaktas say that awakening of the *kundalini* puts the female energy at higher levels of consciousness, and makes it climb to the still higher ones of wisdom, till it, the physical energy, *shakti*, completely loses itself and merges with this, wisdom, as would happen at the time of the dissolution. That is the state of liberation, absolute bliss. The short cut to this state, according to them, is achieved through the practice of the *Panch Makaar Sadhna*.

Sometime around the beginning of the Christian era when reading and writing had become more extensive, these ideas were reduced to writing. Such writings and ideas had extensive circulation by the early centuries of the current millennium; the assimilation was a slow but a sure process. The ideas were particularly popular amongst the people of Australoid extraction.

It is difficult to say whether the persons who followed these ideas did eventually realize the *Para Shiva*, the Creator, under the monolistic philosophy, but it can be said as a fact that drugs like cannabis, marijuana, or hashish, produce euphoria quite similar to that as is claimed to be experienced during the awakening of the *kundalini*; a lot of *Sadhakas* take just that and believe they are on the progress course. From about the twelfth or the thirteenth centuries the Shakta ideas started asserting and openly ridiculed the Vedic rituals, strongly denouncing the caste system that the latter supported, and its injunctions forbidding the lower classes and the women from reading or practising the Vedic teachings. This revolt, no doubt, was in keeping with their teachings, but their concepts had too many generalities which gave too much freedom to an individual and contained loopholes which led to outright exploitation. The followers never had it so good:— to secure liberation from the birth process, and forever live in the regions of peace and ecstasy, by committing unrestricted fornication. The religion told them they would possess the *sukhas* (comforts), of both the worlds. People came by the droves, and all varieties of gurus and godmen sprang up. They too never had it so good, for they enjoyed a position and status that in earlier years had not even been dreamt of by people in similar vocations. Men, ranging from water-bearers, road-sweepers and the like, to officials and dignitaries, and even the kings and maharajas, were amongst the seekers. Fornication became the rage of the time. A rot set in. The vitality of the Hindu nation got sacrificed in the form of the *Panch Makaar Sadhna* at the altar of the Great Goddess. The Muslim invaders had no problem in subjugating the areas of the land where such form of worship was common, and in later years the British conquerors took the whole of the country with just a handful of their own soldiers. Indeed, they encouraged this form of religion, and wrote great treatises extolling its virtues. The idea was to perpetuate their rule over a population divested of its spunk and self respect by inducing them to keep following this religion of dissolution.

Today, extensive Vedic and modern Western education has struck at the root of this religion of carnality, which is what it has sunk into in spite of the prolific arguments to the contrary by its proponents, and their strong protestations. But that is only a part of the Shakta religion. Its other part of the right handed rites, with its practices of Yoga and meditation, is perfectly in line with the mainstream Hindu thought.

Vishnu on Shesha, around 600 A.D.

Sarasvati — 1000 A.D.

The Vaishnavas

The branches of Hinduism which have so far been covered had their base or foundation in the faiths which were prevalent amongst the people who inhabited this land before the arrival of the Aryans. The Vaishnava branch developed during the Vedic period, although it has borrowed ideas from the earlier cultures. It is the most popular and the most practised branch of Hinduism. The concept of Vishnu worship of the Vaishnavas is perhaps a carry-over from the idea of sun worship, for in the Vedic hymns he is the lord of light and life. The question that the sun worshippers had to naturally consider, once the religious thought had achieved a degree of sophistication, was: sun took care of life and light on this planet, but who took care of the sun? And so the question progressed till it finally rested at the level of Vishnu. He was the Creator and beyond Him there was nothing. He was the supreme God. It was this kind of thinking that eventually erased, almost completely, the Aryan pantheon of gods, including Mitra, Varuna, Indra, Agni, Vayu, and so on, and greatly contributed to the theistic dualism of the Vaishnavas as preached by Ramanuja and Madhava. Monotheism has come into being on the basis of the divine authority of the Vedas. Brahma who in the earlier Vedic literature signified the supreme God, by the time of the Brahmanas was being referred to as *prajapati*, the lord of the creatures, and generally signified prayer verses and formulas in the Veda which gave power to a person to get the gods to fulfil the desires and wishes. Later, however, it came to mean *Trayi vidya*, i.e., knowledge of the verses and formulas contained in the three Vedas. The Atharva Veda was excluded, for the learned Brahmans did not accept it as of divine origin, it is essentially a collection of the magic formulas and rites of the Proto-Australoids. *Trayi*, it was believed, was the first created, for it was the word of God, *shabda*, breathed by the self-existent to the inspired seers, who in turn, transmitted it for the good of the mankind, by word of mouth, from teacher to pupil, in unbroken sequence, over untold generations. Thus, word was the first, in importance comparable with God Himself, for it was His breath and it communicated what the creation was all about. The thought, therefore, contemplated that which was the cause of the *Trayi*, and then of all creation, i.e., Vishnu. This is the time of the *Brahamanas* and *Aranyakas*.

Vishnu by this time was the all important deity to whom all important sacrifices were addressed. Another parallel concept is that of Narayana, which means 'that, whose dwelling is far in the deep' or that 'where every thing eventually rests.' Like Vishnu, the origin of Narayana can also be traced to the Rig Veda. The relationship between Vishnu and Narayana concepts was established in the *Taittiriya Aranyaka*, in course of time, however, both concepts almost coincided: Narayana is in everything, and everything is in Narayana. There is little change in other gods of the pantheon. *Shesh Naga*, the lord of the serpent deities of the Proto-Australoids, is elevated to a position around Vishnu Himself. In the creation legend Vishnu, as absolute consciousness, rests in eternal peace, tranquility, bliss, upon the coiled body of *Shesh Naga* floating upon the sea of cosmic waters.

Another important strand of the Vaishnava faith is the teachings of Shri Krishna, who, it appears, was a great reformer and philosopher, operating in the area of the Jamuna basin of north-west India, sometime before the advent of Buddhism and Jainism. He called the Supreme God, *Bhagvata*, i.e., the adorable, glorious, and venerable Lord. The term can also be used for holy persons. His followers were called the Bhagavatas. The Bhagavata literature is contained in a book called the *Bhagavatam*, while the essence of the teachings are contained in the *Bhagavad Gita*, the song of the Supreme God. In later years Shri Krishna was deified as an *Avatara*, incarnation of Vishnu; his teachings as contained in the *Bhagvad Gita* form a very important part of the Vaishnava faith.

The essential details of the Vaishnava faith are contained in the *Vishnu Purana*. The total work is divided into six books. The first of these is essentially ontological, covering details of primary and secondary creation, *Sarga* and *Pratisarga*. It generally follows the Sankhya system of philosophy and explains how during the *Sarga* stage the universe proceeds from *prakriti*, the eternal crude matter, a kind of chaos, and then how during the *Pratisarga* stage the form of things are developed from the elementary substances previously evolved, or how they reappear after their temporary destruction at the end of a *kalpa*. The crude eternal substance is hewn into shape and form by the forces of *Rta* and Dharma, giving rise to phenomenal universe which lasts for one *kalpa* which is one day of Brahma, equal to 4.32 billion years. Likewise one night of Brahma, when He rests, is also equal to the same number of years. Life of Brahma is 100 years, each of 360 days and 360 nights. After 100 years another Brahma takes over. The process of creation and annihilation is, thus, interminable. Both types of creations are periodical. The termination of the *Sarga* takes place at the end of the life of Brahma, when everything gets annihilated, including the gods, and the elements merge into the primary matter, *prakriti*, besides which only the spiritual being, Vishnu, exists. The termination of *Pratisarga*, however, takes place at the end of every *kalpa*, and affects only the forms of lower creatures and lower worlds, leaving intact the substance of the universe and the sages and gods. A detailed description of time over which these events take place is included in this first book. A lot of the detail originally contained in this book has been lost, but its cosmogony is known to be 'of high antiquity'. While essentially based on the Sankhya system of philosophy, the Purana nevertheless postulates that it is *maya*, the power that creates illusion, that *prakriti*, the energy that manipulates matter, as thoroughly independent except that it precipitates creation in the presence of *purusha*, in the absence of which it is totally inert. Simply put, the Puranic postulate suggests that the material creation, even when it takes place in the presence of *purusha*, is non-eternal, constantly changing so that all its forms are like passing shadows. Actually, in essence the Vaishnava concept makes a departure here from the Sankhya system and accepts the Vedanta system of non-dualism. *Advaita*, for it is repeatedly stated in the Purana that Vishnu is all embracing, that he is the *purusha*, the spirit or consciousness, and *pradhana*, the crude matter, *vyakta*, the visible form, and *kaala*, time. While Vishnu *Purusha* is eternal and without attributes and is central to the creation process, the other three elements together constitute His *Maya*, the non-entity, which is what causes the creation. At the time of dissolution *maya* along with its constituents merges with Vishnu. He is both male and female, like in the concept of the *Ardhanarishvara* Shiva which emphasizes the transcendental nature of God, and shows that in Him he has the characteristics of all the pairs of opposites. He is in everything that is created through His

Maya, and everything thus created has its source in Him. In the creation legend Vishnu, the ocean of consciousness, is reclined in eternal peace on the coiled body of *Shesha Naga*, and out of His navel is born Brahma, destined to be the creator of the universe. Vishnu, the Eternal Being, thus, is the material and the efficient cause of the total creation, but he does not perform the deed as such, for that is agitation, a continuous process of changing form, a continuous state of non-eternality. The job is performed by Brahma, born out of Him, for a tenure of 100 cosmic years, after which time another Brahma takes over while the previous one goes back into the store house of consciousness, merging once again with His Creator. For Vishnu is beyond *Prakriti, Maya*, and He is beyond Brahma, *Purusha*. He is far away, in the deep, the final resting place, the abode of eternal peace and bliss.

Three functions have been ascribed to the Supreme God, namely creation, preservation of what has been created, and then the final annihilation. On the basis of Rig Vedic hymns a view has been taken that these functions are performed respectively by Brahma, Vishnu and Shiva. At the face of it, it appears to be an attempt to elevate the three deities to the same level of importance, possibly to cut out bickerings between their followers. But both the Shaivas as well as the Vaishnavas have rejected the concept. For them the God they venerate the most is the Supreme Lord; He is the Creator, Preserver and the Destroyer, all rolled into one. Vaishnavism believes in non-dualism at the *nirguna* (without attributes) level, but at the *saguna* level it becomes theistic, as will be seen from the expositions of Madhva. At this level, where God has attributes, He becomes a personal God, the ruler of the universe, and intense love for and devotion to Him are advocated if deliverance from the birth cycle and permanent merging with the eternal consciousness is being sought for.

It can be said that barring the mythologies connected with Shiva and Vishnu, the differences in the teachings and philosophy of the Shaivas and the Vaishnavas are not significant.

According to the first book of Vishnu Purana the human race originated from the 'will-engendered' sons of Brahma. For this purpose Brahma has two facets, namely male and female. Daughters are also begotten who are married to the *Prajapatis*, and then there are the seven sages in the line, and they have wives, and the human race originates. The first pair are the Manu Swayambhuva, the son of the self born or the uncreated, and his wife Satarupa. However, the entire mythology connected with the origin of the human race is allegorical, woven around the point that it all started from a single pair, that the *rishis* and other learned men were historical personages who authored 'the Hindu system of social, moral and religious obligations' and studied the heavens and 'developed the science of astronomy'. The first book also has stories, like that of Prahlada or Dhruva, which seem to have been borrowed from other sources, like the pre-Aryan folk lore. It also describes the earth as having been under the rule of kings, and people who introduced agriculture and civilization.

The second book continues with the prominent personages, and kings of the first Manwantara, one of the best known amongst whom being Bharata of the Bharata clan, after whom India has been named as Bharatavarsha, the land of the Bharatas. Manvantra is a period during which one Manu presides over the affairs of the world. The book also gives the geographical description of the subcontinent, particularly its northern part, and also planetary details, and details concerning astronomy. It contains a lot of mythology. The third book deals with Vedas and other sacred literature, and also sages like Vyasa, and the duties of the castes, and obligations during different stages of life, the laws of Manu, and so on. The book is a work of a period earlier than most of the other Puranas and, for this reason, contains no sectarian prejudices.

The fourth book is about the ancient history, and has a comprehensive list of dynasties and persons and events. From a historical point of view it is an important work. It may not be possible from the details given, to work out exactly when an incident took place or an important personage appeared in that distant past, but it is possible to have a good idea of their antiquity. The likely date, for example, for the Mahabharata war, from the Puranic detail, would work out to around 15000 BC, and for the establishment of the first regal dynasty in northern India to around 2700 BC. This would put the age of stable monarchies, following one another in continuous successions, very comparable with monarchies anywhere in the world.

The fifth book is exclusively devoted to the life of Krishna, from his birth to the time he destroys the demon king, Kansa. Krishna has been mentioned in the Vedas only once, and in the *Mahabharata* where he plays a prominent role, his divinity has only been alluded to. In none of the works he has been described as God incarnate, playing the kind of naughty pranks as have been given in this Purana. There is, thus, a suggestion that, possibly, this part is of a later date, and about a person different from Krishna of *Mahabharata* or Dwarka. Similar stories about Krishna appearing in Brahma and Bhagavata Puranas and Hari Vansha are definitely of a comparatively later origin.

The sixth book is about dissolution, in the minor and major cataclysmic aspects. End of all things by fire and water, *Pralaya*, and then the aspect of its rebirth. It also covers the aspect of metaphysical annihilation of the universe by the withdrawal of the spiritual component from the physical existence.

Bhagavad Gita

This is an important work of the Vaishnava faith. The book gives the gist of the doctrine and the practices followed by the Bhagvatas, a sect of the Vaishnava religion. It is in the shape of answers given by Krishna, revealed as the supreme God, to Arjuna, the valiant Pandu prince of the *Mahabharata*, one of the five sons of Pandu. The battle lines are drawn at Kurukshetra between the sons of Pandu (collectively called the Pandus) and their cousins, the Kurus, sons of Dhritarashtra, Pandu's half brother. Arjuna requests his charioteer, who is none other than Krishna himself, to station him between the two armies so that he might see the people arrayed against each other, and the soldiers and commanders he would be fighting against. Once there, he realized what a difficult operation it was going to be, for there was hardly any one in the hostilely poised armies whom he wished dead or bodily harmed. In fact, there were any number of them in the opposite ranks and files whom he knew to be his friends and well wishers, who had played a role in his upbringing, who had trained him to be the great soldier that he was. Even those he did not know, had done him no harm. They were innocent human beings, standing there facing his army because it was their duty to do so.

He decided, a fight would be a grievous wrong, and he communicated this view to Shri Krishna, his charioteer. Krishna, however, does not agree and tells him that it was his duty to fight in defence of righteousness, no matter who got killed or harmed in the process. There follows a discourse of 700 verses in which Shri Krishna explains to doubting Arjuna the meaning of life and death, the creation and annihilation, the role of Dharma and the need to uphold and defend it, the need to be above petty attachments while performing ones role appropriate to one's station in life — all this against the backdrop of the Sankhya and other systems of philosophy. Finally Arjuna's mind is clear, his doubts are gone and he is ready to give his best.

At the ontological as well as the eschatological levels the Vaishnavas generally accept the Sankhya system except that they believe that the universe is brought into being by the force of *maya* which is about the same as *prakriti* except that it has as its constituents, *pradana*, the crude matter, *vyakta*, the visible form, and *kaala*, time, all the three together creating a kind of an illusion of creation, in that they generate ever changing, non-eternal forms, in a continuous, unbroken process till it is time for dissolution, when every thing merges with the cosmic consciousness. At the level of the *purushas, Geeta* accepts that there are numerous souls interacting with *prakriti* in the creation process, but places a Supreme God beyond the levels of *prakriti* and *purushas,* into which every thing merges when the universe ultimately folds up. This supreme God, if that is the name one would give to this force, is *nirguna,* without attributes, incomprehensible. But at the mundane level He is *saguna* with attributes, so that the believers might visualize Him mentally, more so while engaged in loving devotion towards Him. At this level He is the personal God, the Lord of the universe. The *Geeta* thus synthesizes the essential thoughts of *Advaita, Vashishta Advaita, Dvaita* and *Sankhya*. The last named becomes only one part of the total philosophy as put forward by *Geeta,* but each of the other three is accepted in full. The suggestion is that there is no contradiction in the three systems, only the levels of comprehension are different. At the initial level only dualism as preached by Madhva will work, but with higher levels of perception in the course of contemplation of the ultimate reality, the adept will pass over to the level of qualified non-dualism of Ramanuja, and finally to that of actual non-dualism of Vedanta, as taught by Shankra.

There are three ways to achieve the ultimate reality, namely, *karma yoga*, the path of action; *gyan yoga* the path of knowledge; and *bhakti yoga*, the path of devotional worship. The view on the *gyan yoga* is about the same as was later expounded by Shankra in *Advaita*, i.e., non-dualism, that there has to be the realization that every constituent of the universe is a part of the Ultimate Reality, that He is in every thing and that every thing is just a part of His. Once this realization has been attained, and experienced, the liberation from the birth cycle and union with God is secured. The main point is that non-duality has to be experienced, mere theoretical knowledge is not good enough. For this, start has to be made with the recommended Vedic way of worship, gradually moving on to yoga, renunciation and meditation.

In the *bhakti yoga* there has to be the experience of love for God. There are five varieties of love in varying intensities: first, the love of the servant for his master, humility and the desire to serve selflessly and with ardence are the prominent aspects in this type of love; secondly, the love of a friend for a friend, the chief characteristics here are sincerity and faith; thirdly, the love a parent feels for the child; what stands out here is the desire only to give and take nothing, and indulge in the pranks and foibles of the child; fourthly, the love as develops between spouses; when love is true they are one in body and mind: and, finally, the illicit love; this, for obvious reasons, is the most intense. Devotional love for God has to progress gradually till it reaches the intensity as is experienced in illicit relationship.That is where emancipation lies. For *bhakti*, God is *saguna*, with attributes, for it is not possible to feel love for something which cannot be reasonably imagined, not in the initial stages, anyway. This process requires the aid of the idols as well the idol makes it easier to visualize the deity.

To obtain final liberation and union with God it is necessary that only God, Lord Krishna, is worshipped, for those who worship lesser gods manage to reach only the lesser levels, and after exhausting the merit accumulated during their sojourn on earth, get reborn, they do not reach the final destination. So intense have to be the feelings during the worship process that the devotee gets to believe that the idol he is worshipping is indeed the deity, and he expresses his feelings before it as if he were doing so before the deity itself.This intensity is not easily acquired, it is experienced when God is benevolent, it is His grace, His *prasada*. Metaphorically speaking, the devotee in this situation is like a baby monkey, it clings to the mother and is saved; no doubt the process of successful clinging is achieved through the little fellow's own effort. This is Bhakti. The other angle to the devotional worship is passive, called *prapatti*.Here the person completely surrenders to God in a humble attitude of trust. This is likened to the little kitten who completely abandons itself to the care of its mother, the latter moves around carrying it in her mouth; the kitten is making no contribution to its own survival process. In this situation the emphasis is on genuine piety in the completeness of surrender rather than on the intensity of Bhakti discipline.In the latter case the grace of God is earned so to speak, while in the former it is a complete bestowal.

Karma Yoga, the path of action, of the performance of deeds, is central to the philosophy of *Geeta*. The point emphasized is that it is action which caused the total creation, and this creation is a manifestation of a force no element of which is ever static. No existence, no life, is possible without activity. The fact that action or activity cannot be avoided, is thus settled. The only question is about the type of action which would be conducive to the cessation on the reincarnation process. *Geeta* suggests that the deed has to be performed without the desire for reward, for if thus done it will not accumulate merit or demerit for propelling the cycle of life and death. It is not that rebirth is a retributive process. In fact, like many other laws in the system of creation, this also is believed to be one. Nothing perishes in this universe; there is only the change of form. Solids, liquids, gases, change form when subjected to external influences. Likewise, thoughts do not perish either; they only precipitate a change of form under certain specialized conditions in keeping with the particularized laws of creation. No one, it seems, has succeeded in ascertaining the dimension of these laws or of the details as to how thoughts or karmas influence the change of form of an organic being, but one thing is reasonably clear: it is not an inexorable process. Prayer has its effect; prayer, after all, is a thought too.

There are corrective mechanisms in the total creation process. Prayers, good behaviour, truthfulness, generosity and the like are the ones at the micro level. Incarnations, *avatars*, perform this function at the macro level in so far as the living world is concerned. *Yada-yada hi dharamasya*, (whenever there is decline of good, and unrighteousness tends to prevail, I arrive in this world to restore the supremacy of righteousness). This happens as part of the corrective process. Deeds which precipitate noble results, which are the cause of happiness and contentment all around, or in the performance of which the person does not hanker after rewards, or which uphold dharma and righteousness, or which are performed while discharging one's duty as required due to the station of life in the community or society, do not contribute to the cumulative effect of the force that propels rebirth, though when such actions pander to the ego or desire for results, these would make the contribution. These are *sattava* qualities, that is qualities that support righteousness. *Rajas* qualities, of mundane worldly activity, that is, those like sexual lust, anger, greed, attachment, pride, definitely cause rebirth, while *Tamas* qualities which generate stupor, indolence, ignorance, tightly bind the soul and fling it into the worst forms in the hereafter. Only that person who has rid himself of the three *gunas*, or the set of qualities, can get past the incarnation cycle, for all these sets of qualities are of *prakriti*. Once across, the soul merges with the infinite consciousness.

Geeta does not say that in order to be good one has to be a non-violent being, as preached by the Buddha or Mahavir Jain. *Geeta* is neither for war nor against it. To uphold dharma and righteousness if there has to be a fight, then that must be taken on, and the negative forces must be destroyed, even if the process might cost ones own life. On the other hand, fighting or violence that causes the spread of injustice, or misery to innocent human beings, would be a criminal act, and all supporters of Dharma must do their very best to defeat such evil or nefarious activity. Having thus spoken to Arjuna (as contained in the *Geeta*), Sri Krishna advises him not to accept whatever has been told to him just because it has been so told by Sri Krishna Himself. He has to ponder over what has been said and accept only that of which he gets convinced. (verse 63 Chapter 18)

Mahabharata

Geeta has been set against the backdrop of the Mahabharata war, which is placed between 1200 and 1500 BC by different authorities. Epic Mahabharata in its present shape has over 100,000 verses. According to experts this huge and great work originally had only 8800 verses and was called 'Jaya Sanhita', song of victory. Gradually there were additions and at one stage it had 24,000 verses when it was called 'Bharata'. Later, however, further additions were appended and it became *Mahabharata*. The central story in the finished work is about the fued between the princes of the Lunar race of the clan of the powerful king Bharata who ruled from Hastinapur on the bank of the river Ganges, a place not far from the present Delhi. Twenty-third in the line of descent was Shantanu, who had married twice, once to Ganga, a lady from a royal house, and then to Satyavati, a fisherman's daughter who had been living, without marriage, with a Brahmin, Prashara by name, from whom she had a son, Krishna Dwaipayana, who grew up to be a great scholar, and sage and came to be known as Vyasa, and was the compiler of the *Mahabharata*, the epic and, possibly, *Geeta*; the word *Vyasa* is derived from a Sanskrit verb which means "to fit together" or "arrange".

Satyavati, it seems, was a lady of great charm and beauty, for after her husband Shantnu's death some well-known rulers, warriors and scholars of that time sought her hand in wedlock. But their designs were thwarted by Bhishma, Shantnu's eldest son from Ganga. Bhishma had taken a vow never to marry so that there might be no heir to the throne from his side, for Satyavati had put this precondition for her marriage to the aged Shantnu: that only a son born to her would inherit the throne. Two sons were born to her. Chitrangada, the elder one, ascended the throne first, but, apparently, died unmarried. Vichitravirya, the second son, was married to two daughters, Ambika and Ambalika, of the king of Kashi, modern Varanasi. Bhishma had abducted these girls for his half brother, from the midst of a gathering of princes who had arrived from different states to compete for the hands of the fair maidens. In age, Bhishma was way ahead of his half brother and enjoyed the status of the patriarch. He had abducted a third daughter, Amba, as well, but she insisted that she would marry none other than Bhishma himself, and when the latter refused as he was bound by the vow of celibacy, she immolated herself in protest against Bhishma's outrage in preventing her from selecting a spouse of her choice from the gathering of the eligible princes. The accounts say she was reborn as Sikhandi, a eunuch, who caused Bhishma's defeat and death at the Mahabharata battle. But Vichitravirya died too before any child was born to any of his two wives. He was barely 23 then, and possibly died of tuberculosis. The only surviving male who could claim the throne at this stage was Bhishma, son of Ganga, but he would not, being bound by his vow. The custom of *Niyoga* under which a woman who had not conceived from her husband for any reason, could seek pregnancy from another man, normally of her choice, but usually one from the clan of the husband, was then prevalent amongst the Bharata clan, and under the circumstances Bhishma or some other prince of the clan would have been the right choice. But Bhishma was bound by the vow, and Satyavati did not approve of another person. She, instead, asked her son from Prashara, Krishna-Dwaipayana Vyasa, to perform *Niyoga* with both the widows. As a result, to Ambika was born Dhritarashtra, but blind, and Ambalika got Pandu, but with some kind of a terminal disability which in his youth turned him sterile and put him in poor health. He spent his last days, even though young, as a forest dweller in the company of his two wives. The throne of Hastinapur had come to Pandu as his elder brother, Dhritarashtra, was blind. In the early years of his rule Pandu embarked upon an ambitious plan of conquest and was eminently successful, but not long thereafter the disease, which might have been contagious, like leprosy, forced him to relinquish the crown to his blind brother. Vyasa had performed *Niyoga* with a maid of the house too, who held a wifely status, and out of her was born another son, Vidura, who played an important role as the peace maker between the sons of Pandu and Dhritarashtra. To Pandu's first wife, Pritha or Kunti, were born three sons, who were from three gods, Dharma (Yama), Vayu (Wind) and Indra, who were respectively named as Yudhishtira (firm in battle), Bhima (terrible) and Arjuna (upright), and to the second wife, Madri, were born Nakula (mongoose) and Sahadeva (a twining plant); the last two were from Ashvini-Kumaras or the twin sons of sun. The suggestion is that all these conceptions were immaculate, untouched by any sexual contact. In actual fact these children would have been begotten by the two queens through *Niyoga* with men of their choice, and since the conceptions had Pandu's sanction, they were treated as his own sons, that was the prevalent law of the time. Kunti had another son, Karan, born to her before her marriage with Pandu. She had conceived him from sun god, but to hide her shame, had floated him in a cradle down the Ganges, when a person of inferior station had found him and later brought him up as his own son. This lad grew up to be very brave and highly skilled in the martial arts, but the circumstances so developed that he was alienated towards the Pandavas, and Duryodhana of the Kurus was too happy to take him in his camp, where he remained, with all his loyalty, till the very end when, during the Mahabharata battle, where he scourged the Pandavas, he was killed by Arjuna, at a time when a chance occurrence had deprived him of his weapons, and in accordance with the code of fighting, he was entitled to re-arm himself. But Arjuna, on the advice of Krishna, took no chances; little did he know that he was slaying his own half brother. Karan is a significant player in the Kuru-Pandava feud.

To Dhritarashtra were born 102 sons, the eldest being Duryodhana, from Gandhari, a princes from Gandhara, present day Afghanistan. Besides, Dhritarashtra also had a Vaisya maid-in-waiting and other wives and concubines to have fathered so many sons, collectively they were known as the Kurus. Ever since the time Pandu repaired to the forest to nurse his illness, and Dhritarashtra ascended the throne, Duryodhana, his eldest son, had decided that being the eldest son of the ruler of the time he was the legitimate heir to the throne. This view, however, was not shared by his father who felt that he (father) was only a substitute ruler, that the throne, in fact, had been given to him by Pandu because the latter had to retire to the forest to secure treatment. Therefore, when after Pandu's death Kunti and the five sons of

Pandu, collectively called the Pandus, returned to Hastinapur, Dhritarashtra not only received them well but also arranged for their education and training alongside his own sons. Madri, Pandu's younger wife, had immolated herself on the pyre of her deceased husband and had become a sati. But the rift between the Kurus and the Pandus grew with time and ultimately there was the battle at Kurukshetra, in the modern State of Haryana, which was joined by all the major northern kingdoms of the time. The battle lasted for eighteen days and resulted in the complete rout of the Kurus, though Pandus too suffered heavy casualties. The latter were sad at the outcome and after ruling for some years, left the state to the charge of the only survivor, Parikshit, Arjuna's grandson, and along with their common spouse, Draupadi, left on an arduous pilgrimage into the Himalayas where one by one they all perished; only Yudhishtira survived to the end because he had never committed a major sin, and ascended directly to heaven.

Only one-fifth of the 100,000 verses that the present *Mahabharata* has, are devoted to the Kuru-Pandu feud. The rest are digressions covering unconnected episodes, legendary history, philosophy and mythology. The burden of most of the remaining work is the need to uphold Dharma even if that involved going through tough trials and tribulations; in the end Dharma triumphed over the agencies that caused suffering and sorrow. It has eighteen voluminous books; the original work is attributed to Vyasa. *Geeta* is a small part of this large work comprising just 700 verses arranged in eighteen chapters (note that Mahabharata lasted eighteen days), but it is undoubtedly the most read portion, it has been translated into almost all the languages of the world. As stated earlier, along with Vishnu Purana, it is the most important work of the Vaishnava faith.

Unlike Brahmanism, the Vaishnavas made no distinction on the basis of class or sex. Krishna in *Geeta* says that no matter what the class of a person is, whether he is born out of the womb of a sinful woman, or belongs to the traders' community or the servants' class, or be the person a woman: all these will attain me and secure liberation if they worship with loving devotion and take shelter in my grace. (*Geeta* 9/32). For this reason Brahmans have not accorded the status of *shruti*, revealed literature, to *Geeta* and have called it

Lingaraja Temple, Bhubaneswar. 1114-15 A.D.

Sun-god, Konark, around 1300 A.D.

a *smriti*, traditional literature. Vaishnava temples are open to any and every one, without any distinction. The concept of *avatara* incarnation, is peculiar to this religion; Shaivas do not accept this. Again, unlike Vedanta, where the experience of the knowledge of the self and the Absolute Self is enough to secure freedom from the bondage of rebirth, here this is achieved by devotional worship and right actions dedicated to God and performed without the desire for reward. Geeta is set against the backdrop of a war, and it lays stress on the fight to the finish in support of the cause of Dharma. Such deeds, karmas, not only do not add to those which cause rebirth, but, in effect, absolve the individual from previous misdemeanours. Geeta is the beacon of hope for those who are not born as Brahmins and are not well versed in the Veda, or those who were born as women, or those who were born as Dvijas, twice born, i.e., those who did not belong to Brahmin, Kshatriya or the Vaisya classes; at the time of the first birth all beings are equal, but at the time of the wearing of the triple cord the menfolk of the three upper classes become twice born and become entitled to read and listen to the Vedas and the connected literature. Women are debarred from wearing the cord. The triple cord is made of three strings of thread put together in the shape of a loop, and worn over the right shoulder and under the left armpit. Vedanta advocates renunciation of the world in the final stages, to experience Brahma: *aham Brahm amsi* or I am Brahma! *Geeta*, though not denouncing the idea, says that this is but one of the ways to secure *mukti*, liberation. *Geeta* accepts that it is not possible for a householder to renounce the world, and says it is not necessary so long as the karma marg, the philosophy related to the concept of human activity, is understood and followed sincerely.

Vedanta postulates that there has to be a keen desire in an individual to seek liberation, that is the first step. It begins with the person being convinced of the verity of the scriptures. He then has to develop stable character with the help of common sense, practical logic and by performing religious ceremonies and works, and perform his duty as laid down in the *Shastras*. All this is what Shankra terms as the lower knowledge, and once this stage has been covered, the devotee is ready to move into the field of higher knowledge where he attains the capability to receive the direct intuition of *Sat-Chit-Ananda*, i.e., Reality-Consciousness-Bliss. A number of steps, or practices have been prescribed for this, the salient ones being :

(a) restraint of inner and outer senses, and fixing the mind on the 'Self', with complete faith in the Guru, and comprehending the meaning of *Tat-tvam-asi* or that thou art;

(b) Yoga practice, and renunciation, and experiment on the basis of the knowledge that involuntarily springs up in the mind, then experience that which is eternal, in which all limitations vanish. The soul gets liberated or achieves *mukti* during the process of this experience itself; it does not have to wait till the perishing of the body.

> That which is real in the absolute terms, immutable, eternal, all pervading, exempt from all change, all-satisfying, undivided, whose nature is to be its own light, in which neither good nor evil, nor past, nor present nor future, has any place: this incorporeal is called liberation.

> Geeta's view is that meaningful action takes precedence over inaction, including inaction suggested by *sanyása*, or renunciation, as postulated in Vedanta. Whatever action your duty calls for, perform it, for it is better to act than not. No physical life would sustain if there were no action. (8/3)

> He, who is the Creator and pervades the universe, is worshipped through the performance of one's duty; indeed this way does one achieve perfection in one's profession. (46/18)

> You are a being of action, but to the rewards of those actions you have no right. Therefore, act in keeping with the duties that have come your way, and are enjoined upon you by dharma, and do not ever harbour any attachment to inaction. (47/2)

On the karma kand, i.e., worship in accordance with the Veda, or worship of sacrifice, the Geeta view is that it has merit but the final destination is not achieved through this. Shri Krishna says:

> Those who are proficient in the knowledge of the three Vedas, and desire to secure heaven by worshipping me with sacrifices

> and oblations of the soma juice, indeed attain heaven and enjoy the pleasures of the gods. But once their merit is exhausted, they are back; the Vedic mode of worship keeps them in a to and fro movement between the heaven and the earth. (20/9 and 21/9)

Is a being then stuck hopelessly in the grip of the past karmas? Not at all, says *Geeta*. Where a person has the necessary will and the determination, there is nothing that can stop him from achieving whatever he wants, including liberation. It is like swimming across a stream. The current, the eddies, the whorls and so on, that the swimmer comes across during the process are due to the past karmas, but the skills, the strength, the stamina, the determination and such like factors constitute his own effort which, if pressed resolutely, would get him across. In a game of cards, the cards that are dealt are karmas, but the proficiency of the person in the game, constitutes his personal effort. Like in the case of the swimmer, both factors together precipitate the outcome. Should a person have, however, landed up in a real bad patch, there is always the next birth available to try again. The point to remember is that it is only in the human form that the volitional capability is available. Once this form has been lost then the next time can only be when this form has again been secured after due expiation. According to Vaishnava belief there are 8,400,000 different sets of species into which life might move after the human form has been lost, and the soul may have to move right from the bottom, steadily to the top, or it may bypass some of the stages, depending upon the performance during the human existences. It, however, cannot be said that all life outside the human form is miserable. It definitely is not. Nor is all life in non-human form an existence of joy or pleasure. But all life does not necessarily attain human form; a lot of it stays non-human, possibly till the very end of creation. That is where human form assumes importance, for once this has been secured, the opportunity to gain release from the reincarnation cycle opens up, and once that release has been achieved, it is all peace and bliss, for ever, in the abode of Vishnu.

On devotional worship or *bhakti*, Shri Krishna says in *Geeta*:

> Fix your mind on me, and worship me with devotion; if you so discipline yourself, then you will attain me.

There is no set methodology for devotional worship. It is an affair of the heart and it has to be sincerely and forcefully felt there.

> Devotees can come to me following any course, and practising any mode of worship. I accept them, so long as they have the desire to come to me and possess the necessary intensity of devotion. (11/4)

Thus *Geeta* is totally open on the mode of worship. If the desire is sincere, it does not really matter what method of worship is adopted. The Hindu belief, therefore, is that no one must ever pile insult or humiliation upon another for his method of worship, nor preach hatred for this reason. This could be the greatest disservice to the glory of God, for it is His creation, and He takes care of it regardless of the views on the manner in which His grace is sought for. Diversity, in fact, is the essence of creation.

While *Geeta* accepts the path of knowledge as one of the ways to achieve liberation, it also accepts that it has limitations: a whole life time is required to assimilate the knowledge, follow the disciplines and then experience immortality. It postulates that the pathways of selfless action where the person is not hankering after rewards, and sincere devotion, are equally efficacious. These can be followed by any one who has the inner urge, and the person does not have to renounce one's family and the community and become a non-entity for them.

Krishna was the author of *Geeta*. One opinion is that he was a religious reformer, and was defied by his followers after his death. The other view is that he, in fact, was a mythological personality and that the author, or compiler of the work was Vyasa, that it is a work which falls in the category of Upanishads, albeit one for the common folk, for its concern is for the house-holder and his family, for the lower castes and women, who have been denied access to the Vedic literature and mode of worship. It categorically states that before God all creatures are equal, that the only cause for visible distinction between man and man is the karmas, and emphasizes that arduous study of the Vedic literature, though desirable, can be dispensed with for seeking union with God; devotional worship as also performing deeds without hankering for the rewards, are equally effective. The stress is upon the need to secure perfection in all performance.

The Krishna legend, it would appear, has been put together by combining three different legends, the first amongst them being that of boy Krishna growing up in the midst of cowherds in Vrindavan-Gokul, on the bank of Yamuna, around eighty miles south-east of Delhi. The highlights of this legend are :

(a) Destruction of malevolent forces that made abortive attempts upon his life when he was still a baby.

(b) Overpowering serpent-king Kaliya. Serpent worship was a common practice amongst the pre-Aryan people. Vaishnavas, who had no hesitation about admitting these people to their fold, by this mythological story have established the supremacy of Vishnu over non-Aryan gods, including their king of serpents. They, thus, emphasized that Vishnu and only Vishnu needed to be the object of worship.

(c) Lifting of mountain Govardhana so as to provide shelter to the people of Vajra (Gokul-Vrindavan) from the fury of storm and rain unleashed by Indra when people, on Krishna's advice, stopped offering sacrifices to him and, instead, changed to the sacrifice-free worship of Vishnu. The point being emphasised is that the Vedic form of worship has limited merit, and that complete and permanent liberation cannot be secured without Vishnu's selfless worship.

(d) Killing of Kansa and his followers to give hope to the righteous, and affirm that whenever evil gets the better of the good then to guard the righteous and destroy the evil doers and to re-establish the law or dharma, I take birth, age after age.

Another highlight of this legend is Krishna's fluting and dancing with the *gopis* or milkmaids, and the bond of love between Radha and Krishna, Radha is a married woman. This dance is allegorical where, for the Vaishnavas, Vrindavan, where *Krishna Leela* or Krishna's play, takes place, is the human heart, and the sound of the melodious flute is the rise in the human heart of an intense love for the divine Creator, while Radha is the human soul, longing for union with Krishna. It appears that *Krishna Leela* lore originally was of some scythian tribes who had settled in

Gujarat and present Rajasthan. Boy-Krishna represents the local god of these people. Names Gopala (herdsman) and Govinda indicate his origin as a god of flocks and herds. With time the concept possibly got expanded and was used by the Vaishnava saints to emphasize the idea of loving devotion to the one and only God in the form of Krishna.

Then we have Krishna of the second legend, the one who revealed the *Geeta*. The *Geeta* philosophy takes both the *Sankhya* (enumeration) as well as the *Vedanta* systems in its ambit. Like *Vedanta,* it postulates God, the ultimate reality, to be the material as well as the efficient cause of the universe, but, unlike it, it believes in the Karmas to be the cause of rebirth; in *Vedanta,* the realization that the person is the part of the ultimate reality, and then experiencing that reality, is the essential requisite for liberation, and not good karmas. Thus, according to *Geeta,* both *purusha* and *prakriti* are components of God. In the *Sankhya* system the creation manifests when *prakriti* becomes active, although it can create only in the presence of *purushas*. In *Geeta, prakriti,* also called the *yog maya* or just *maya,* illusion, is manipulated by God to effect creation. In other words this is His agency He uses to fashion creation. But *maya* is not to be understood as some kind of a mirage where all that manifests is just an illusion or a dream. All it implies, as has been explained earlier also, is that the visible universe is non eternal, and is in constant flux. Whatever appears as real and genuine today vanishes out of sight in no time so that, as one ponders over what has gone past, the feeling is that that was only an illusion. This *maya* has three *gunas* or modes, being *Sattava, rajas* and *tamas*, or lightness, movement, and heaviness when viewed at the material level, and goodness, passion and dullness, when related to the psychical phenomena. During *pralaya* the modes are in perfect equilibrium and there is no creation, but during the *kalpa* stage these modes start interacting and there is loss of equipoise. This is the cause of creation. By implication, when interaction between the modes is at a low key, it is comparative peace, but as this pace of agitation goes up, so do the problems of sustenance and survival (witness the march of time from *Sat Yuga* of peace and happiness to *Kali Yuga* of relentless conflict).

> Three *gunas* or modes appear from *maya* or *prakriti*, being *sattva* or goodness, *rajas* or passion and *tamas* or dullness, and these bind down the imperishable spirit residing in the body. (Geeta 5/14)
>
> O Arjuna, God is omnipresent, and abides in everything, and is the cause of all action, and He effects this through His *maya*. (Geeta 61/18)

Finally there is Krishna, the ruler of Dwaraka, the seaport on the west coast, on the Arabian sea. The legends connected with this king bear little connection with the doings of the child Krishna, and whatever connection that has been detailed in the accounts in Puranas with the expounder of *Geeta*, or even the personage who acts as Arjuna's charioteer in the Mahabharata war, is at best tenuous. The account crediting the king of Dwaraka, belonging to the Yadu clan of the lunar race, with sixty thousand wives and eighteen thousand sons who ultimately perish fighting one another, makes perplexing reading, unless it is allegorical and meant to convey something subtle. The king himself gets killed while reclined under a tree, his one leg resting upon the other bent at the knee, by the arrow of a hunter who mistook the illumined spot in the sole of his foot, for the eye of a deer. There is an element of historicity attached to this personage: he possibly defeated hordes of invading Scythians or some other tribesmen and threw them out of the country, and it is likely that exaggerated accounts of his prowess and bravery were composed and sung by bards and minstrels. This king might well have participated in the Mahabharata war.

Krishna of the *Geeta* also has a historical perspective. He has been mentioned in the *Chhandogya Upanishad* as Krishna Devakiputra. He is also known to have been a disciple of Ghora Angiras, and a major proponent of the Vasudeva or Bhagavata religion. The system of the Bhagavatas, i.e., the worshippers of Bhagavan, the supreme Lord, is called *pancharatra* and *Satvata*, and is believed to have been composed by the famous seven *rishis* or sages. It doctrine of creation, *Vyuha* or expansion, visualizes the supreme reality as Vasudeva who in his fourth form creates the indestructible Sesha, called Sankarshana, the primeval matter or *prakriti*. Out of this is born *Pradyumna*, the cosmic mind or *manas*.

Cosmic self-consciousness, *ahankara*, as part of the supreme reality, then takes birth as Aniruddha, and out of His naval springs forth Brahma (seated on the lotus), from whom come all creatures, mobile and immobile. Thus does the creation come into being repeatedly at the beginning of every kalpa. Creation and annihilation succeed each other like sunrise and sunset of this world. This simplification of the Sankhya philosophy was, apparently, done for the benefit of the common man, for the Vaishnavas often refer to Krishna as Vasudeva, and Balarama, his brother, as Sankarshana, drawn out, for he was drawn out of the womb of his mother and placed in the womb of Rohini, his father's second wife. Krishna's son in the Vaishnava accounts is Pradyumna and Aniruddha is his grandson. There is evidence to suggest that, like the worship of Mother Goddess, who represents *prakriti*, in the Sakta religion, Sankarshana was worshipped in the era before Christ.

In the Vaishnava faith, Krishna is worshipped not as the king of Dwaraka, but as the child God incarnate; as the friend of the cowherds of Gokul and Vrindavan; as the conqueror of the serpent king Kalia; as the protector of his people from the torrential storms unleashed by Indra, which he did by uplifting the Govardhana mountain to afford them shelter; as the slayer of the tyrant Kansa even though the latter was his own maternal uncle. He is also worshipped along with Radha, the milkmaid whose loving devotion had made her a part of him, made her a kind of his *shakti*. As stated earlier, symbolically Radha represents the human soul totally absorbed in the contemplation of its Creator, totally assimilated unto him. In the *Geeta*, Arjuna is the human soul in a state of bewilderment, seeking guidance from the supreme self, abandoning the chariot of his body to his Lord. This imagery too is revered, like the imagery of the boy Krishna, but worship is offered only to the latter, Krishna of Gokul and Vrindavan. It is at His lotus feet that the devotee seeks whatever he seeks.

Krishna as briefly mentioned in the *Chhandogya Upanishad* (C 600-500 BC), is certainly of the pre-Buddhist times, for there is no mention of Buddhism in *Geeta* or any of the literature connected with it. In verse 20 of Chapter 9, the mention is only of three Vedas, and it is possible that at the time of its first writing, the fourth Veda, the Atharva, just did not exist, though it is also possible that its omission may be on account of the non-recognition of its magic formulas by the intelligentsia of the time. Thus Circa 600-500 BC can be reasonably accepted to be the time of the first writing of the *Bhagavad Geeta*, though subsequent modifications of the original text cannot be ruled out.

Balakrishna, or boy Krishna, was born to Devaki, daughter of a king of a pre-Aryan race, and Vasudeva, a noble man of an Aryan clan called the Yadus. She was his second wife, the first one being Rohini, Devaki's cousin Kansa ruled Mathura on the bank of the Yamuna river, while the Aryans controlled the land to the south, across the river. Kansa was a despotic, cruel man who had acquired the throne of Mathura after deposing and imprisoning his own father. He had been told by a sage that a son born to Devaki would be the cause of his overthrow and death. He, therefore, captured Vasudeva and Devaki and kept them in prison where he killed all the sons born to the couple. The seventh son, Balarama, also an incarnate divinity, got transferred, through divine intervention, from Devaki to the womb of Rohini, and survived. Kansa had not imprisoned Rohini. Krishna was born as the eighth child, during a pitch black, thundery night (Krishna means black) when the guards had mysteriously been overtaken by deep slumber and the prison locks and gates had fallen open. Vasudeva took the child and crossed over to the Aryan territory after negotiating a swollen Yamuna, and went to the house of an influential person by the name of Nanda, and exchanged the male baby with the baby girl just born to Nanda's wife Yashoda. He then was back in the prison before daybreak, and when the guards awoke they found everything in order. Kansa nevertheless decided to execute the girl child, but as he did so a heavenly voice told him that the being who would be the cause of his destruction was already born. Thereupon Kansa decided to execute all the male children born to people around that time, including the children born in the Aryan territory across the river; for this he had to depend on deceipt and subterfuge. But the baby, and later the boy Krishna defeated all the moves aimed at his life, and finally, as an adolescent, he killed Kansa.

Krishna is God incarnate for he destroyed the evil which was

Kansa and his henchmen and restored order or dharma. He is also God incarnate for being the author of Geeta, a remarkable synthesis of the religious philosophy of different schools, and the way of life they supported. His teachings, which were easily assimilated by the common folk, brought about a revolution in the Hindu thought, and crossing the barriers of cast and ethnicity, produced a unity of religion, culture and way of life. He is also God incarnate for being the just and kind and a very brave and victorious ruler of Dwaraka; the city went under the sea after He was gone from this world.

However, not all that has been written or said about him has been maturely understood. The *raas leela*, his fabled dance in the company of the *gopis* or the milkmaids, has been interpreted by some European writers who have gone about studying mythology as if they were handling history, as his sexual escapades and have questioned the morality of it. They have possibly not understood that a lot of stuff in this genre is essentially allegorical or mythological, put across either to drive home a point, or, sometimes, just to give vent to whatever was contained, as a result of intense devotional love, in the deep recesses of the psyche of the writer, singer, devotee or the theologian. It is not history. Some have expressed the view that accounts of Krishna's dissolute frolicks with the *gopis* provided religious sanction to some kind of Hindu immorality. The view is rash. Hindu ethos all along has been very orthodox in matters of sexuality, an attitude which has primarily contributed to according a lower status to the woman. Considered as a possible source of promiscuity, she was denied the freedom that, it was believed, could cause sexual misdeeds in the society. The Puranic account of Shri Krishna having sixty thousand wives or eighteen thousand sons is also an allegory, and not history. The point never to be missed is that He is God incarnate, and He takes human form to re-establish Dharma. The allegorical accounts are only establishing his Godhood, and are there essentially for the benefit of the laity, the common folks whose capability to grasp complex religious philosophy is limited.

In the Hindu religious thought, the ultimate reality, the incomprehensible entity, is untrammelled by anything conceivable, is in absolute freedom, the ocean of consciousness, reposed in absolute peace and bliss. He is *Nirguna* or without attributes. In effect there is no 'He' as such. It is a reservoir of boundless energy which in essence is consciousness and has matter as its inseparable component. It is not a kind of a person or a grandsire or a benevolent monarch or a father, who is constantly monitoring the doings of the human beings, or issuing punishments and rewards, or coming to their succour when they have been wronged. It is just that sea of energy and it operates on the basis of *Rta* and Dharma and puts forth its corrective mechanisms automatically when the situations so warrant, and thus keeps the system of the universe going from the moment of its creation till it is finally dissolved. Of course, *Rta* and Dharma are in operation during the *pralaya* as well, i.e., the period between the dissolution and the re-kindling of the creation process. The concept of the father-like figure of God is also there, but then He, the *Saguna* Brahma, is a figment of imagination, only a stage from which the *Nirguna* aspect is realized and experienced. But the efficacy of communion with the *Saguna* Brahma is not denied.

Then what end does the ultimate reality seek to achieve by going through periodic creations and extinctions? Why does the creation come into being in the first place, if it has to be effaced eventually? As has been stated already, the ultimate reality is totally incomprehensible. Shankra called the cycles of creations and extinctions as the sport of God, His *leela* boy Krishna's symbolic play with the *gopis*, or his frolicksome activities in the company of boy cowherds, are also designed to emphasize the same point. This kind of depiction possibly was to invoke a feeling of love in the hearts of the devotees for God in the form of an innocent, naughty child, while also stressing the aspect of sport being the likely purpose of creation. Otherwise the incomprehensibility factor remains. The question just cannot be answered.

Ramayana, or the adventures of Rama, is the other important epic of the Vaishnavas. It is the story of Rama on the line of Manu Vaivasvata (c. 3100 BC), whose son Ikshvaku of Solar dynasty was the first king of Ayodhya, and according to the Puranas this line came all the way down to king Sagara and then to Bhagiratha, Raghu and Dasharatha and, finally to Rama around c. 1950 BC. Historicity of Rama is well founded on the basis of the accounts of the Puranas. He was a great king who was just and very concerned with the well-being of his subjects. He vanquished the pre-Aryan and aboriginal tribes and brought security to his subjects, with the consequent flourishing of trade and commerce and spread of general prosperity and happiness. Even today the term 'Rama Rajya' or Rama's Rule, is synonymous with the rule that provides justice, contentment and happiness to the citizens.

In the *Ramayana* story, Dasharatha, the noble and brave king of Ayodhya, a descendant of the illustrious king Raghu (originally from Ikshvaku's line, but now the line was called *Raghuvansh*, or Raghu's dynasty) had four sons from his three queens. The eldest was Rama born to Kaushalya, while Sumitra the second wife had Lakshmana and Shatrughana, and Kaikeyi, the youngest and the favourite wife, had Bharata. Although all the four brothers were attached to each other, Rama and Lakshmana were particularly so, so that whatever task was assigned to Rama, Lakshmana always joined in. The first achievement of the two brothers was the vanquishing, at the behest of sage Vishwamitra, of the aggressive pre-Aryan tribes, who were opposed to the Aryan system of worship. This, one might say, set in motion the process of Aryanization of the subcontinent. Rama then won Sita as his wife in a show of strength where he broke (by some legends he just strung it) the bow of Shiva, held in the charge of Janaka, king of Mithila and Sita's father. The legend has it that Sita was in fact daughter of Mother Earth and was found by Janaka in a furrow ('Sita' means furrow). At the time of the contest Rama and his brothers were in late adolescence. During the wedding of Rama and Sita, other leading princesses of the royal house of Mithila were given away to the other three brothers, and a huge marriage procession eventually arrived in Ayodhya to the delight alike of the royal house and the public; Dasharatha and his sons were held in high esteem by the subjects.

Once Kaikeyi, who was the most charming of the three queens and favourite of the king, had accompanied her husband to a battle, and at a critical time had rendered to him service of such signal importance as had turned the very fate of the battle in his favour. The king was happy and told his wife to ask for any favour. The queen, however, said that whatever she had done was only out of her duty and love for him, and told him to think nothing of it. But the king insisted and the matter was set at rest only after the queen had promised to ask for the favour at some time in the future. After the return of the princes from Mithila, Dasharatha decided to appoint Rama as the crown prince. This was where the trouble first started. Kaikeyi felt that she, being closest to the king and his favourite wife, ought to have secured the throne for her son, Bharata. She remembered the promise the king had given her and demanded that instead of Rama, her son Bharata be made the crown prince, and that Rama be banished from the state for a period of fourteen years. Bharata and Shatrughana were then out of Ayodhya and were not aware of the goings-on, and Rama, in spite of the protestations of Dasharatha, decided to leave, to redeem latter's pledge. Dasharatha died heart broken at the turn of events. Bharata and Shatrughana were summoned post haste to take over the affairs of the state, and when the former learnt what his mother had done he was filled with sorrow and shame, and went after his brother and caught up with him in course of time and requested him to return and be the king of the country. But the latter refused, for their father's pledge had to be redeemed; Rama's wife Sita and brother Lakshmana had also joined him in the banishment.

Rama spent the first thirteen years of the exile in the Vindhyas and central India. Many other people of Aryan extraction, including colonisers, traders, workmen and Brahmans, had preceded him; renowned sage Agastya had been touring the Vindhyas and other areas of central India way before Rama set out of Ayodhya. These secular and religious people had established working relationship with the inhabitants of the areas: there were trade and commerce activities, and inter racial marriages, and the Brahmans were putting across the essentials of the Aryan religion, culture and beliefs. A lot of positive interaction was in evidence between the pre-Aryan people and the Aryans. Rama consolidated the gains of these colonizers and missionaries.

During the fourteenth year Rama, his brother Lakshmana and wife Sita moved to the area of Panchvati in the central Deccan plateau. This area and the southern peninsula were under the influence of Ravana, the powerful king of Lanka (present Sri Lanka). Aryans referred to him and his race as *rakshasas* or malevolent and cruel people. Aryans planted such epithets upon any race, clan or class who were opposed to them or their ideas, e.g., *asuras, daityas, danavas* and the like. Not before long Rama, as the symbol of Aryan expansionism, came in conflict with Ravana. *Rakshasas*, as the Aryans liked to call them, were unhappy about the Aryan presence, for the Aryans were not only winning over the tribes of whatever areas they went to, through their way of thinking, they were also instigating them to resist the expansion of Ravana's influence. Ravana was disturbed and he dispatched two of his brothers to establish outposts to check the infiltration into the territory which, for all practical purposes, was under his suzerainty. According to the story, along with the brothers also came their sister. Rakshasas now increased their inimical activity against the Aryan religious men and women and the Aryan-friendly local populations. The oppressed people approached Rama for help and in the ensuing conflict a number of *rakshasas* got killed. At this stage Ravana's sister appeared on the scene and attempted to seduce Lakshmana, who, offended at the affront, cut off her nose (it, we are told, was mended by plastic surgery by Susruta, the renowned surgeon of that time). That angered her brothers, the commanders of the force, and in the fight that followed, they met their end. When the news of the disaster reached Ravana, he was besides himself with rage, and himself arrived at the site to take stock of the situation, and, through subterfuge, abducted Sita, Rama's wife, and took her all the way to Lanka, and imprisoned her there. Rama had no alternative but to march on Lanka with whatever support he could command locally. Enroute he secured the alliance of tribes, who were mostly known by the names of their totems, like Vanars (literally monkeys) whose important war leader Hanumant (literally monkey god) has been given out, in the mythology, as son of *Vayu*, the Aryan god of air. These people had been won over by the Brahmin missionaries who had not only educated them about the Aryan way of life, but had also introduced them to organized agriculture and other rural trades. Aryan pattern of life was not imposed upon these people, only their willing cooperation was sought for and secured, till they had come to believe they were part of the Aryan milieu. It does not have to be stressed that Brahmins and traders could operate only under the protective umbrella of the Kshatriya leaders, soldiers and princes, and Rama was one such personage.

With this army of allies, Rama arrived at a place later named as Rameshwaram, on the gulf of Mannar, and there the allied army constructed a bridge and crossed over to Lanka. This was a rich kingdom, known as the Lanka of gold, for Ravana was a wise ruler and had worked assiduously to enrich the state and his subjects. There was bitter fighting between the two armies and there were ups and downs for both of them, but eventually Ravana and his army were routed. Sita was liberated and after enthroning Bhabikshana, Ravana's estranged younger brother who had been won over to the Aryan religion and way of life and had joined Rama in this conflict, Ram left Lanka for Ayodhya where his brother Bharat handed over the throne to him. This is where the main story of Ramayana ends.

There is a later addition, *Uttara Khanda,* which is about the banishment of Sita. Rama banished her because he learnt that his subjects were not happy to accept her as their queen, for they felt that she was open to defilement by the Lankan king or any of his henchmen, during her stay in former's custody for a period of almost one year. Sita was pregnant when this happened, and a pair of twins, both sons, were born to her when she was in exile in the hermitage of a non-Aryan sage, Valmiki, the acknowledged author of the original *Ramayana*. These sons, under the tutorship of Valmiki, grew up to be highly accomplished and brave youths, and while still in adolescence, they roundly thrashed some of Rama's generals when the latter were guarding the horse which Rama had set at large for the horse sacrifice (*Ashvamedha Yagna*); anyone who dared to challenge Rama's imperial overlordship had to capture the horse and, thus, risk a conflict. Rama himself arrived at the scene of conflict to persuade the youngmen to release the animal, for he felt they were too young to face him. But they, not knowing he was their father, defied him, and in the contest that followed, even defeated him. At this stage Rama learnt the truth from sage Valmiki and was very happy, and brought the youngmen over to Ayodhya. The court requested Rama to terminate Sita's exile, and she too was invited. The whole of Rama's court and the prominent citizens had assembled to receive her, and there she came, the resplendent goddess, and stood in their midst, her mind filled with the agony of having once been banished by her own people, and, her supplicant arms raised, in a voice loaded with anguish, she prayed to Mother Earth, whose daughter she was, to take her back into her fold, for she could no longer endure the torment she was experiencing. The earth then parted and out of it emerged a beautiful throne, and seated upon it was Mother Earth, her arms extended towards Sita who just went into them, and then, within everyone's view, including the all-powerful Rama, the throne descended and the earth closed over it. This was the moment of sadness and retribution for everyone for having laid a foul blame on a woman who was as chaste and pure as the Mother Goddess herself.

Story of Rama was apparently a popular folklore even before Valmiki compiled his version of it in verse form. In some versions of the folk lore Rama is reluctant to accept his wife after she had been in Ravana's custody for a period of almost one year, and this in spite of her admonitions and protestations. This caused Sita's banishment. In some versions Rama instructs Lakshmana, his younger brother, to take Sita to some remote forest and put her to death, the problem had arisen since his subjects were not prepared to accept her as their queen. Lakshmana, however, out of pity and respect for the unfortunate queen, does not carry out the order, but to convince his brother, shows him a sword smeared with the blood of some animal. To some believers of the time this was a rather harsh ending to an otherwise great and heroic sage. Valmiki got over the banishment problem by bringing in the fire ordeal when, to prove her fidelity and purity, Sita enters a burning fire and comes out unscathed. But, apparently, so strong were the feelings related to the fidelity and purity of the women, that in spite of the fire ordeal brought in by Valmiki, the banishment chapter stayed, it was not compiled by Valmiki. Feelings have been strong in either camp. The feminists all through the ages have been unhappy with the banishment chapter, *Uttarakhand*. Additionally, there have been disagreements with some alleged rulings given by Rama during his reign, on the status of and the treatment to be meted out to the *Shudras* and the untouchables, although these appear to be later interpolations. Some scholars of religion have, for these reasons, expressed the view that Rama was God incarnate only upto the time when he vanquished Ravana, the king of Lanka. Thereafter he was just the king, ruling his country in accordance with the rules and customs of the time, though he is supposed to have done that so well and justly that it is to this day considered to be the ideal rule, for it brought all the happiness and prosperity to the citizens.

Rama never married again, and ruled for many years, and after he felt he had accomplished whatever he had come for, he left this world. As stated above, historicity of Rama is pretty well established. He was deified for his being a just king, who lived essentially for the well-being of his subjects. Rule of Rama, the *Ram Rajya*, is rule of justice, truth, nobility, contentment, and plenty, in terms of fulfilment of needs, desires and aspirations of the subjects, from where all criminal activities have been eliminated, and where all people have others good at their hearts, and so on. This was Rama's example for posterity. He caused the spread of the Aryan religion and culture throughout the subcontinent, and that was possible only because he was a brave king and he valiently supported all progressive moves, moves which not only brought modernity into the lives of the people, but also laid the foundations of a uniform culture for the subcontinent, and brought homogeneity and a uniformity in the way of life and religion. He was the epitome of nobility, generosity and bravery. He was a great king, and a kind and a just man. And for all this he was deified.

All this was achieved around 1950 years before Christ. But once deified he ceases to be the Rama of history, and is way above the range of human weaknesses and foibles. He is God incarnate, with attributes of God. The devotee is not worshipping the Rama of history. He is, instead, worshipping God whom he calls Rama in stead of God. Therefore, any comment on the basis of some historical detail, corroborated or otherwise, about the life of Rama, would be totally out of place. It shows a sheer lack understanding of the concept behind the idea of *avatara*. The basic point is that the divine spark present in this human being, Rama, assumed the brightness of the ultimate reality itself and activated forces of good which eventually annihilated evil and restored Dharma. It is this divine spark which is worshipped and not the human being possessing it.

The idea of incarnation of God or Avatara, in the human form, to put mankind on the Dharma course and eliminate that which threatens the growth of the human society, is one of the basic beliefs of the Vaishnava faith. Although both Rama and Krishna are considered to be incarnations, the two strains of religion which so accept them, viz., the Vaishnavas and the Bhagavatas, are much older than this idea. It is completely absent from the old Upanishads, though it is present in popular religion from about the second century BC. In the Vedic literature too there is no mention of Rama or Krishna as divine beings. In fact, Rama is never mentioned at all, and Krishna is mentioned but once and that too as Krishna Devakiputra, a mere man, a Vedic student. In Bouquet's view the *Avatara* concept found its way into India from Iran. The Buddhists too, he suggests, borrowed some important concepts from there. *Bodhisattava* Amitabha apparently resembles significantly a divinity of the Zoroastrian religion.

Ramayana is a work of about 24,000 verses arranged in 500 cantos. The original work is by sage Valmiki and corresponds with Books II-VI of the present *Ramayana*. There is no reference to Buddhism in this work and there is hardly any mention in it of the philosophy of the Upanishads. That gives the latest date of its writing or being composed, around 600 BC. The earliest could be much earlier. In Valmiki's epic, Rama is a brave, noble prince and not God incarnate. There is no suggestion that people so considered him, or that he knew he was such a divinity. On the other hand Krishna knew all along he was the *avatara* and acted accordingly. This difference has to be kept in mind when going through the two epics. The despair and grief that Rama went through when confronted with difficult situations, did not have to be experienced by Krishna; the latter just straightened out the problems with a view to establishing the supremacy of Dharma. *Ramayana* is not history or biography as C. Rajagopalachari says. Essentially it is part of Hindu mythology. To understand Hindu Dharma one has not only to study the *Ramayana*, but also understand the different characters who form part of it. Mythology is an essential strand of a religion, like philosophy or ritual, and to get a proper grasp of it, a sound understanding of all the three is essential.

A brief *Ramayana* is also contained in the Buddhist *Jatakas* or the birth stories. But the rendering which has the greatest distinction and religious significance is the work of Tulsi Das, the sixteenth century poet. It is the image of Rama contained in this work which is recognized as the incarnation of Vishnu, and not the image as depicted in the *Jatakas*, or any other accounts. *Valmiki's Ramayana* has enough mythology to place Rama in the category of *Avatara*, *Tulsi Das's Ramayana* is based on this. As stated above, once Rama has crossed into the *avtara* region, any comment on him on the basis of some detail which might be containted in the Buddhist *Jatakas* or any other writing and given the status of a historical truth (most *Jataka* stories are just stories with little historical relevance), makes little sense. He is God incarnate with attributes as detailed by poet Tulsidas. Any detail about him as a being of history, which may or may not be based on facts, is not relevant.

The *Ramayana* has been translated into all the major Indian languages, and is read by the devout not merely as a work of fine literature, but as a sacred text which would bestow upon them religious merit and uplift them mentally as well as spiritually. Shankra, the *Advaita* exponent has said that to secure freedom from the stranglehold of karmas one should have Rama in ones heart and meditate upon Him. The date of Rama as c. 1950 BC is based on traditional accounts contained in the Puranas and not on genuine historical facts which, here and there, do not quite back the traditional accounts. Although Rama is not mentioned in the Vedas, some earlier or later kings have been, and it is with reference to them that the Rama period has been worked out. One important mark in traditional history is the Dasharajana or the battle of the ten kings, which ultimately brought victory to Sudasa, a king of the Panchalas or five tribes, in a pitched battle on the bank of river Ravi (Parushni) against a confederacy of ten kings, who ruled areas between the present day Punjab, and Afghanistan in the north-west. The ten kings had got together to check Sudasa's territorial ambitions. This battle was fought not much after the Rama period, and around 400 years later was fought the Mahabharata war. Thus, if Dasharajana was 1800 BC, then Mahabharata would be 1400 BC. But by some other accounts the Mahabharata could be as late as 1000 BC, and if that be so then the genuine period of different events and persons would change accordingly. Dasharajana has been mentioned in the Rig Veda too, but we know that by the time of this Veda the Aryans had not gone much beyond the line of the Saryu (Ayodhya) in the east and the Vindhyas in the south. But by the Ramchandra period the Aryans seem to have traversed virtually the whole of the peninsula. Now, if the Dasharajana was soon after the Ramchandra period, and if that was the time of the Rig Veda, and if Rama preceded Mahabharata, as he did, then there is error in assuming c. 1950 BC as the period of Rama. The confusion is caused by assumption that the territory under the Aryan control during the Rama period is in excess of that during the Mahabharata period. Panini (c. sixth century BC), the great Sanskrit grammarian, mentions Deccan in his book *Ashtadhyayi*, but not the south. But Katyayana (c. fourth century BC) in his commentary on Panini, has covered most of south India. Conclusion could be that Aryans came in contact with the people of the south some time between the sixth and the fourth centuries BC.

On the other hand, it is not necessary that people to people contact has to find place in an academic work like the grammar of Panini. Aryans may have been there in the south during the Rama period, right from c. 1950 BC or even earlier, but after the Rama-Ravana war their presence was merely marginal, and they made no contribution of historical significance in the region during that period or the period following, as might merit mention in the annals of history, or inclusion in the oral Puranic lore or epochs. It is well-known that in the south the Aryans met a civilization which was already well developed and pretty insular to their culture and the religion of sacrifice. That the south resolutely maintained its identity in culture, religious thought and languages is clearly seen today in the spread of the Aryan and the Dravidian ways of life in the present day north and south India.

India is a land of many people, races, clans, groups, communities. They arrived, primarily from the west, over a long period, and brought with them many religious ideas, and social customs and practices. Due to leaders and reformers who appeared on the Indian scene from time to time, over the millennia, there has been a lot of synthesis of the ways of life of the different groups so that today it is fairly possible to define an Indian archetype. Nevertheless, the diversity is evident. After every couple of hundred kilometres, there is a perceptible change in the cultural pattern, and religious concepts, the social behaviour and values, language and dialect, customs, dress, even the physiognomy of the people. Despite the togetherness of the millennia and a certain uniformity in certain aspects of the day to day life, under the surface, differences persist; each group in its own way struggles to maintain its so called identity. During the second millennium AD, an age marked for decline in the Hindu religious, cultural or social values, a lot of literature edited or authored by second rate, sometimes even bigoted, thinkers, got churned out, and many negative social and religious practices, new or based on some past custom or tradition, received the approval of communities, which not only took pride in following them but considered them vital for their identity. A section of the Kshatriyas, for example, particularly of the landlord or the ruler classes, followed the custom of sati whereunder a widow immolated herself upon the pyre of her deceased husband. The custom at one time was prevalent amongst the warrior classes of Hun or Scythian extraction, like the Rajputs of Rajasthan. Generally these people fought their battles to the finish and if faced with defeat they preferred to die fighting rather than bear the ignominy of being taken as slaves by their enemy, and their women immolated themselves and became satis rather than be distributed as war prizes amongst the enemy soldiers. Here and there an odd widow immolated herself even when it was not war, but, by and large, there was no pressure on her for this. But with time the practice of the woman immolating herself became a custom amongst these tribes even when the man died normally and not in battle. At the other end of the scale was the custom of *nyoga* (levirate), followed by some communities in northern India. Under this a widow had the option to pick on a man, generally from the brothers of the deceased husband or his other close relations, for begetting a child, particularly a male. Such like practices, including child marriages, killing of the girl child, temple prostitutes, assigning a lower status to the woman, were in vogue amongst different groups of people. Some are still there, to a lesser or greater degree, though a number of them have fallen by the wayside and are no longer relevant in the modern context.

Apart from the four main branches of the religion as described above, viz., the Shaivas, Shaktas, the worshippers of the Mother Goddess, and the Vaishnavas, there are innumerable who have their own gods or deities, or who worship trees, or stones, or just some specified spots on the ground, or their gurus (like the followers of Guru Gorakh Nath), or some deceased head of their clan, or graves of some sufi saints or religious men, or just a grave of any one, and so on. But such people are in a minority, and with each passing day their number is dwindling. Then, of course, there are those who feel compelled to preach the oneness of all religions, the inherent goodness of all religious thought, the need for every man to be good towards people of other faiths, and to forever be good in own personal thoughts and deeds. They preach that every one should follow every religion, and develop respect and regard for everyone's deity. The number of these people is indeed insignificant, but some out of them have made a name, like Ramakrishna Paramahansa.

Eight

The Caste System

The most complex phenomenon of Hinduism is its caste system. Generally, caste comprises an endogamous group of people, speaking a common language and having common social customs and religious beliefs or practices, this last aspect only at the micro level, such as having own priests to conduct ceremonies like marriages. Where the caste group is a large one it has a number of smaller groups which are the sub-castes. In such a situation, endogamy is the norm only within the sub-caste. Even mutual social intercourse and common or community feeding or drinking, or smoking, here is permitted within the members of the sub-caste only. This sub-caste has an identity of its own, and has a graded position within the caste structure, which structure, has a graded position within the overall Hindu hierarchy. The sub-caste is an important constituent of the Hindu society and generally has its own system of management of its internal affairs; some, particularly the lower castes, have *panchayats*, a body of generally five elected representatives whom all controversial matters are referred to for resolution. In his book, *Caste and Class in India*, G. S. Ghurye has observed that to get a sociologically correct idea of the caste system, it is the sub-caste which needs to be recognized as the basic or the fundamental unit upon which the system rests.

Caste or sub-caste is not a racial group and exclusivity between castes and sub-castes is not necessarily on account of racial loyalties or prejudices. It is true that racial factor made significant contributions but there are other factors too, some easily identifiable, others obscure and perplexing. The population diversity has made its own contribution to the evolution of the caste system. But why and how this diversity has divided the population into rigidly compartmentalized sections is still not clear. Why, for example, there is such a lot of stress on endogamy. Even in the same racial group people of different castes, when staying in close proximity, should be emotionally, culturally, and economically, closer to each other, as compared to those of their caste staying in different far away areas. Yet, when it comes to marriage, it is the caste and not the race that will decide the issue.

In caste system there are at least two hundred groups which can be and are called castes, with distinct caste names. The number of sub-castes, which are endogamous, is around two thousand. The birth of an individual in any of these not only decides how and where he or she would marry but also the profession that would be followed and the social status within the society. One feature of the caste was a common priesthood. The castes sometimes lie scattered over a number of villages performing the functions of their station, like village cobbler, the blacksmith, the carpenter, but sometimes they are in communities, like weavers. A number of factors combine to decide the caste of a person, and perhaps the most important is his profession. A Brahmin's job is to perform the religious functions of the community sincerely and efficiently. He has also a role in promotion of education. A *vani*, the *baniya*, is a trader. He supplies the consumer items to the people of the village, and also takes care of the sale and purchase of the surplus agriculture produce. Kshatriyas, who have any number of castes and sub-castes within their *Varnu*, are the people who form the military; the kings gave them large tracts of land where they could train and maintain contingents for war. In the order of the castes the Brahmin had the top position since he was the guru, the preceptor, the teacher and the religious guide who taught religion and helped the people of the community to establish communion with God. The Kshatriyas came next in the order, for they were the rulers and safeguarded the integrity of the state. Vaisyas, the Vanis, came next, while the last place went to the Sudras who were the workforce, the labour, the artisans, the people who served the other three *varnas*. A large number of castes in their case went by the name of the professions they followed, like *lohars* iron smith, *tarkhan* carpenter and the like.

The other factor that contributed to the caste formation is the tribal or ethnic identity, like, for example, Mahars, Santhals, Bhils, etc. Then, some religious movements have also given their names to their followers and these have, with time, consolidated into castes, e.g., Bishnois or Aryas. Some castes are known by the name of the localities the caste groups originated from, but these are generally sub-castes from well-defined castes and the rule of endogamy does not strictly apply here. There are cases where the progeny of spouses coming from different castes started yet another caste. But there is a provision where, if the male belonged to a higher caste, the descendants could get back into the caste of the male after a gap of a few generations. Geographical isolation of groups in this large country because of poor, undeveloped communications, also contributed to the caste factor. Some tribes performed tasks which were regarded as contemptible, like scavenging by the *choorha* community, or disposal of carcasses of animals after skinning, by the *chamars*. Such tribes were regarded as untouchables even though the *chamars* formed the backbone of the leather industry.

The system, however, was not so rigid in the earlier stages, and even today the local traditions vary substantially. The system definitely existed during the days of the Indus Valley Civilization, but could be older. There is evidence of the existence of organized labour, as also of the guilds of artisans, and that the working classes were segregated from those with better vocations. The untouchables, possibly, lived outside the city limits. Recent excavations have suggested that the Indus culture was pretty widespread in northern India and was not restricted to the Indus basin. Caste distinctions, thus, existed well before the arrival of the Rig Vedic Aryans.

The *Varna* system of the Aryans was for securing apartheid and is not to be confused with the system of the castes and sub-castes. But dilutions had crept into this system as well. For example, it will not be wrong to assume that some of the great *rishis*, the seers, of the early Vedic days were not the fair skinned Aryans. Krishna-Dvaipayana Vyasa, almost the greatest of them all, was born to Satyavati, the daughter of a non-Aryan fisherman, from Prashra, a Brahmin, with whom she was living till she caught the eye of the local king, Shantanu, and got married to him. In the caste hierarchy, a fisherman, and that too a non-Aryan, was a Sudra, and yet Shantanu, the Aryan king, had no qualms about marrying her, even when he knew she had borne a son to the man to whom she was not even married. Nor did the people he ruled raise any objection to this wedlock. Likewise, Sumitra, one of the three queens of king Dasharatha, father of Rama, is stated to be a Sudra. Yet Dasharatha married her, and this fact inflicted no social disability upon her sons Lakshmana and Shatrughana when they were married to the princesses from the royal house of Mithila. But the people of Ayodhya were not that unconcerned when it came to accepting Sita as their queen after her return from Ravana's captivity. They were more particular about the chastity and character of their women rather than their *Varnas* or castes.

In the earlier Rig Vedic hymns there is no mention of the four *Varnas*; only three, namely *Brahma*, *Kshatra* and *Vaisha*, are mentioned, the first two being the poet, priest and the warrior respectively, while the third had the rest of the population in its ambit. Only in the Purushasukta, a later hymn about the creation emanating from the sacrifice of Prajapati, the Primeval Being, is it stated that Brahmins came from his mouth, the Kshatriyas from the arms, the Vaisyas from the thighs and the Sudras from his feet. This has been often quoted in the later Brahmanas to support the order of precedence between the four *Varnas*, thus giving the precedence a divine justification.

No sin could be greater than that of killing a Brahmin. The books of religion laid down that no taxes should be imposed on this community, that gifts should be freely given to them on all occasions, from birth to the death, (the more liberal the gift the greater the merit), that they should not be tried for criminal offences, and if anyone had to be, then the punishment must be light. Kings and conquerors generously distributed the war booty to the Brahmins as a reward for their prayers for victory, and this included whatever land and women were captured. The Brahmana literature emphatically laid down that no sacrifice had any merit unless it had been presided over by properly qualified Brahmin priests.

Otherwise, Veda does not impose any restrictions on priesthood. Communities could have their own priests, which was the practice followed during the early Vedic period, e.g., Vishvamitra, a Kshatriya of eminence, was Sudas's official priest.

But it is not as if the Brahmins were absolved of accountability. A very strict code of conduct had been prescribed for them. They had to be well versed in the Vedas, the Adi-Vedas, Vedangas, Dharmasutras, Smritis, and all the other connected literature. Not all priests, however, managed to achieve this. The minimum they had to know was the Mantras affecting their immediate vocations, e.g., the *purohita* who presided over events like births, marriages, and so on, had to know the appropriate Mantras and the connected literature, or the *acharya* who took care of the rituals for the dead, had to be versed with the correct rites and procedures affecting his task. Though the Brahmana literature forbade death sentence to a Brahmin, other literature relating to law and justice placed him on equal footing with the commoner. He was required to be pure of thought and deed, and do all the right things and not be part of activity which may even remotely be sinful, dress simply but properly, and so on. Since his activity often was non-remunerative, his survival very much depended on whatever gifts or charity he received from the clients he served, which was not always much. As the population of the Brahmins increased, the situation became even more difficult. Thus, barring a minority of them who enjoyed the patronage of kings and courtiers, and rich merchants or landed gentry, the community was generally poor. Their poverty is underscored by the *Mahabharata* story of Sudama, Krishna's Brahmin friend of boyhood days, who, in spite of his high qualification in the Veda, had fallen on such bad times that he had to seek Krishna's help so that his starving family might get a respite. Yet it is to the credit of this community that in spite of the hardships they stuck to their profession, and not only led religion, its culture, philosophy and civilization, to a high mark of distinction, but also played a stellar role in synthesizing different religious, philosophical, and cultural thoughts that disparate groups of people brought with them into this country. Later, when the very foundations of Hindu faith were threatened by Islam and Christianity, they were the frontrunners in staking their everything to hold it together, convincing even the most neglected Sudras that what they possessed in terms of religion and culture was the best. When Buddhism and Jainism posed a serious threat, essentially by decrying the cult of sacrifice as enjoined in the Brahmanas, they were quick in their appraisal and promptly shifted emphasis to devotional worship, *Bhakti*, no longer stressing sacrifice, and accommodating the low caste Sudras by emphasizing that knowledge of Vedas was not necessary to attain the highest merit and freedom from the cycle of rebirth. This could equally effectively be achieved through intense love for the deity, the *Saguna Brahma*. There was no religious activity which could be regarded higher than the activity of pure *Bhakti* and no scriptures or elaborate knowledge of religious literature was required for this. All that was required was a surge of desire.

Caste played an important role in resisting proselytization by Christians and Muslims, for no individual could act against the wishes of the fellow members of the caste group. In agrarian environments it just was not possible to survive outside the fold of the community. If boycotted, the person had no chance to find work, or the wherewithal to secure the means for the survival of his family. If there had to be conversion to some other religion it had to be by the whole community. Even a part of the community seeking conversion would be up against problems; even a whole community up against an opposition of other communities would not have it easy. The castes and sub-castes were too proud of the legacy of their forefathers to even think that what their elders had handed down to them, in terms of religion and culture, was in any way inferior to whatever was being preached by the aliens, or that there was anything wrong with their traditions or with whatever they had learnt. Only the dispossessed, people of indigent means, kind of vagrants who belonged to no community that could censure them for this or that reason, whose boycott by any institution for any reason really made no material difference to them, and who stood to gain by changing their religion and aligning themselves with the power of the time, converted. There have been cases, though, where parts of certain communities, like weavers and fishermen, converted *enblock*, essentially to secure financial advantage from the ruler of the day. Otherwise the castes and the sub-castes stayed pretty insular to outside influences and tenaciously held on to their age old traditions and culture and religion.

As stated above, in the early stages the Aryan society was divided into only three *Varnas*, viz., Brahmins, Kshatriyas, and the Vaisyas. The idea of the Sudra, the fourth class of people who basically served the other three classes, apparently came up later and included every one who served, like the farm-hands, the artisans, labour, the menials, and all such like people who served and whom no one served. Originally, term 'Arya' was used for a person of Nordic origin, a fair skinned person, a person of the race that originally emigrated to north-west India from Iran. But with time a number of pre-Aryans, particularly in the professions of traders or soldiers or government officials, got assimilated in the Aryans society and the meaning of the term changed to imply a 'noble man'. But with the accommodation of Sudras in the Aryan fold, the meaning of the term further changed, it was used to indicate a person who followed the Brahmanic religion and, possibly, used Sanskrit language. The four *Varnas* now included people of parallel professions of the pre-Aryan people, irrespective of the colour of their skin. Additionally, there emerged classes of people who were placed even below the Sudras, like the Chandalas, and the untouchables. While the former were the classes comprising people whose parents had married outside the caste, violating the caste law, essentially when one of the parents was born from the union of a high caste woman with a man of low caste, the latter were those who performed the lowly jobs of scavenging or handling dead human or animal bodies. Such castes were definitely outside the Aryan fold.

During the early stages, it seems, the system was not that rigid, and some mobility from a lower to a higher caste was possible. But with the hardening of the religion of the Brahmanas, greater emphasis came to be laid upon the fundamental aspects and that brought in the insistence upon the purity of everything that was offered in sacrifice, or to *agni* (Fire). If there was infringement of the basic rules, insisted the Brahman, then not only was the merit of the sacrifice lost but there could in fact be a reverse effect. Thus, whatever was impure was forbidden, as also the activities of impure beings, in places or rituals which had sacred status. House was a sacred place, so also the human body, and the things one fed on, and the clothes one put on, and any number of other items of daily use or chores. All this tended to place greater emphasis on keeping a distance from the low castes and untouchables.

While the Aryans devised the broad division of the society into four *varnas*, the *jati*, the caste or the sub-caste had a somewhat different connotation. Apart from the limitations imposed by the *varna* classification, there were restrictions which came about because of the caste, like taboos and commensality. Each of the *varnas* is a kind of an umbrella under which numerous *jatis* or castes/sub-castes performing jobs appropriate to the *varna*, are clubbed. In northern India, for example, both the Jats and the Rajputs are in the Kshatriya *Varna*, but the Rajputs consider the Jats to be lower in the caste ranking and do not marry in their community, they do not even drink water from their wells. Jats are essentially tillers and their rightful place according to *varna* definition should be with the Vaisyas. But they claim to have been warriors since the days of the Mahabharata, and say that they took to different vocations like agriculture, or trade, or some kind of work as artisans, only to survive during the non-war period. The artisans have been classified as Sudras. Even the Rajputs followed a similar vocational pattern for their survival. Even within the Brahmins there are sub-castes, like people who perform only the rites at the time of the death, or those whose job it is only to memorize certain portions of the Veda, or those who accept only alms in the names of gods, and so on. All these form sub castes.

The older a tribe, the more particular it is about endogamy and commensality and maintaining its ethnic identity. In this it influenced by concepts regarding fertility, human sacrifice in one form or another, and infanticide. It is not possible to exactly define the caste or sub-caste. They have originated from various factors, not all of which are relevant to the forming of any one caste. According to Hutton, the description of caste, which could be called as quite comprehensive, is the one given by Senart, a noted French anthropologist; he said:

We must conceive of a group, united, closed, and at least in theory hereditary, provided with a measure of organization which is traditional and independent, with a headman and with a council, a group that meets when need be, more or less in full assembly, often at the time of certain festivals, and is bound together by a common occupation, and share common customs in regard particularly to marriage, the consumption of food and drink, and to various cases of pollution (brought about by eating the wrong type of food or with wrong type of people or doing anything proscribed by the community's customs and tradition). Finally, it is a group which has the power to maintain its authority by means of a jurisdiction which, though not overbearing, is capable of making the power of the community effectively felt by the imposition of various penalties, the most important being permanent or temporary banishment from the group.

One factor that contributed to the stability of the system, was the intercaste gradations. It has been said that Brahmins were at the top of the ladder, and so on. But the sub-castes within the castes also carried a degree of ranking. There were various factors that decided this, one amongst which, and an important one, being the type of work that the sub-caste carried out, e.g., a family chaplain, the *purohita*, ranked higher than the Brahmin whose hereditary function it was to perform the last rites for a deceased being. Another important factor was the status of the parental marriage. Offsprings of marriages which had the sanction of the prescribed law ranked higher than the offsprings of mixed marriages, i.e., intercaste marriages. The latter gave rise to new castes or sub-castes. Broadly these new castes are put under the category of *Anuloma* and the *Pratiloma*, the former being those who beget sons on women of their own mixed caste or the caste of their mothers, while the latter (mixed castes) beget sons on women of castes different from that of their fathers or mothers. *Manu-Smriti* lays down that children born to parents of the same caste have the same status as that of their fathers, but those born from women of higher castes and men of lower castes are not considered to be of the Aryan society; Sudra's son from a Brahmin wife is a Chandala, the lowest in the caste hierarchy. By the time of this Smriti, however, the Aryans had ceased to be a community, there had been intermixing between the Aryans, the Dravidians and the pre-Dravidian people and the Aryans as such were more like a socio-religious group based on Sanskrit language.

Another factor that needs to be considered in the context of the caste system is whether a society is patrilineal or matrilineal. Like the worship of the Mother Goddess, the matrilineal system had a widespread practise amongst the pre-Aryan societies. Where a tribe has originated from a mother, the system of the caste and its taboos is strong for various psychological, psychic, sociological, shamanistic and other reasons. The woman impinges her personality upon her children more strongly than does a father. Most matrilineal tribes moved over to the south under the pressure of aggressive incursions from the north-west of this country. For this reason south today has more such tribes than the north, and the caste system is stronger there. In the north, however, the arrival of the patrilineal tribes provided the opportunity for the intermixing of the two systems. In a matrilineal house the woman enjoys the same freedom as the man under the patrilineal system. But the code of Manu (of the patrilineal system) forbids to the woman the status of man. Thus, when a man from patrilineal background marries a woman from the matrilineal set up, he feels the need to restrict her freedom and, thus, preserve her virtue and fidelity, because these characteristics are his property. He achieves this by putting her in the veil, behind the *purdah*. It is for the same reason that the girl is married off, in some communities, when she is a mere child, sometimes even when she is a mere infant. In this process the father is handing over his charge, in so far as her virginity, purity, character, are concerned, to another patriarch, the boy's father who, once the body has grown up sufficiently, gives her over to him, all with properly designed ceremonies. But in the overall context she remains the charge of the tribe, community and, finally, the family; the husband is only one segment in this process. The laws of Manu lay down that a girl, or a woman must not do anything independently, even in her own house, that in her childhood she has to be in the charge of her father, in youth of her husband, and when her lord is dead, of her sons; a woman must never be independent. These were the laws in a totally patrilineal society. However, in the south where there is a strong admixture of matrilineal ideas even amongst people following patrilineal systems, neither a woman is forced to be in *purdah*, nor has she to be given away in marriage when she is a mere child. Only the tribal customs regarding taboos and commensality are more rigid. The tribal laws in any system are complex and stringent and a love marriage is virtually out; it has to be in accordance with the tribal traditions.

However, in another view the child marriage is attributable to the belief that any father who failed to marry her off would assuredly land in hell, for a woman was created to bear children, and any one who denied her that function was a sinner. The father had to ensure that a good, healthy husband was found for her in conformity with the tribal laws, and the husband had to ensure that she bore children. She grew up believing that there was nothing more unfortunate for a woman than being barren. Women unsuccessful with their husbands even sought *Niyoga*, or even illicit relationship. A male progeny was the most essential requirement, for, according to the belief his participation in the family rituals is essential for the well-being of the family in this world and the hereafter, as also for the well-being of the community. By the time of the later Vedic age the belief was that a woman was like a field whose function was merely to nurture the seed dropped into her by the man. For that reason too her status was lower, although there also was the appreciation that seed without the soil was useless. However, because of the onerous responsibility that befell a father to find a suitable husband, he sometimes did away with her right at her birth rather than suffer the ignominy of being unsuccessful and face the prospect of hell. Besides, in some communities the father had to pay heavy dowry to get his daughter wedded, and often he found it difficult to meet the demand. Not infrequently, the daughter was so ill treated by the inlaws that she became an object of tragedy. Sometimes she was turned out, to the utter disgrace of her parental house. Amongst the poorer castes the girl child was unpopular because she was an additional mouth to feed *vis-a-vis* the boy who was a potential bread winner. Her father's house considered her as the trust of her future inlaws for whose benefit, they felt, they brought her up. They had to ensure she stayed a virgin, well trained in handling the household chores and utterly humble and respectful towards the family of her husband, for her vulnerability was so apparent. For this reason she was told that she would enter the house of her husband on a palanquin, but leave it only on a bier, no matter what atrocities were committed upon her there. This was the traditional view irrespective of whether the girl's father was a prince or a pauper. But essentially the compulsions for early marriage or even infanticide were markedly prominent amongst the castes following the patrilineal customs. Amongst the matrilineal castes, infanticide was resorted to by poorer castes, essentially for reasons of poverty. Otherwise the position of women amongst them was much better. The situation has markedly improved in modern times, but the old customs are still there.

It is a custom amongst some tribes to make an offering of the hair to their deity. This practice was brought by tribes from the countries of the Mediterranean rim and southern Europe where they made such offerings to their goddesses in the belief that there was association between the hair of the head, and the fertility of the soil and of the body. The practice is still prevalent, with modifications, amongst a number of castes, although in the south it is more extensive. In the same genre is the case of *devadasis*, (females engaged in the service of the temple god), a custom followed by an odd caste. These women are married to the god but may have children from men. This custom too seems to have arrived in India from the Mediterranean rim, although there the women served the goddess and not god. Though these women are in the service of the god, on specified occasions they are required to cohabit with strangers. Here again the belief is in the connection between the fertility of the soil and coitus between strangers in the presence of the god. It is visualized that the fertility of the soil, and the prosperity of the community serving the god, are related to the body and its mating.

Originally agriculture was the main economic activity, but with the development of trade and industry the requirement for the division of labour became necessary, and the commonality of interest between people of the same profession tended to bind them into a caste. An amplification of this view suggests that as the guilds grew they developed self governance, giving rise to smaller groups which tended to be endogamous and possessed all the trappings of a sub-caste. In support of this view Blunt suggests that a functional caste is made up of sub-castes which are endogamous, whereas non-functional castes are endogamous as a whole and not as sub-castes, infact, quite often endogamy within non-functional sub-castes is positively forbidden, though there are non-functional sub-castes which practise endogamy. A caste whose members follow a common vocation would be a functional caste, e.g., carpenters, blacksmiths and so on, while castes like Rajputs where members are not bound by a common vocation, or the Jats or Ahirs, would be classified as non-functional.

One belief is that the colour of the skin and hereditary function caused the caste system. Senart, however, is of the view that though the colour played an important part, it was not the over-riding factor. He traces the commensality factor to the family meal and worship and comes to the conclusion that it was the tribe and the clan, that formed into a caste or a sub-caste. This does not, however, appear to be the case, for a caste is never based on a common ancestor and, therefore, is not a clan or a tribe. He has said that the Aryans arrival in India ultimately produced two types of mixed races, one laying stress on the purity of descent and the other on the purity of occupation. This led to the formation of new groups and, consequently, castes. The priestly class emphasized the purity of descent for themselves and, thus, exercised moral power over others. Colour certainly does not appear to have been an over-riding factor, for the untouchable *chamars* of north-western India, people who skin the dead animals as they being treating their hides to make leather, have, in many cases, near European complexion. This is also true of a number of other Sudra castes. As stated earlier, race and colour have no doubt made a contribution, but there are other reasons as well.

Hocart interprets caste in purely ritualistic terms. He has said that the ruler, petty or otherwise, and the community needed people for the essential, purificatory rites, like *dhobi*, (washerman), or the *naai* (barber), and as the number of such people grew they got classified into castes. This, however, does not explain the taboo on commensality and endogamy, unless it is taken for granted that a ritual was considered as spoilt if the person performing it was contaminated by association with people who were not entitled to perform it. This brings in taboo, magic and *Mana*, the last mentioned being the personal spiritual power of the being performing the ritual. In Slater's view, caste system existed in India in the pre-Aryan period, from the time when professions became hereditary, and endogamy became necessary in order to preserve the trade secrets. The Aryan arrival strengthened the system and also, may be on the basis of colour, led to some kind of a gradation of social precedence amongst the castes. The priest magician of the pre-Aryan times had delineated the caste structure. Mixed in this, as explained by Ghurye, was the belief of the primitive people in the power of food to 'transmit qualities'. The idea of untouchability arose from the need for ceremonial purity, possibly applied to the aboriginals in the first instance, in connection with sacrificial ritual, and to 'theoretical impurity of certain occupations' later.

Considering taboo, *mana*, commensality, and magic, it would seem that the origin of caste in India is from the time of the first arrival of human beings here. As the vast tract of land of the subcontinent was interspersed by jungles, rivers, deserts and mountains, there was geographical isolation of areas; in the earlier stages the means of communications were virtually non-existent. The smaller groups survived on hunting and food gathering but moved to other areas during famines and floods and other natural calamities. The leaders amongst a group, including their families, formed a different sub-group, and possibly had their own magician-priest. They controlled the means of production and exploited the rest of the group as their labour. Both had, in course of time, developed their own taboos, the sense of commensality, and endogamy; in much of this the isolation caused by the geographical factor must have played a decisive part. Into this the magician-priest who must have guided, if not dictated, the social and political life of the community, must have brought the totems. The groups were thus formed, each believing in its own taboos, and having its own magician-priest, leading to commensality and endogamy. Then came trade and industry and, as in the agrarian economy, groups got formed here too, of people of same trades, basically to protect their financial or survival interests. All these became castes, of people in same or similar trades, of the rulers in trade and industry and agriculture, of the serfs in various grades of employment, of menials and scavengers, all having faith in their magician-priest, and totems, and taboos. Food was what they all essentially worked for, and it was considered sacred and had a special significance in the religious and social structure, in the totemic and primitive belief it was considered to possess the capability to readily convey injurious qualities.

Agriculture brought villages and settled, organized life, and a stability in the social system. But even then the caste system could not have been that rigid and some mobility, upwards or sideways, should have been possible. Education by itself does not appear to have played much of a part in the evolution of the system. Hypregamy, on the basis of colour or profession, must have created new castes. The arrival of the Palaeo-Mediterraneans would have disturbed the existing balance and given rise to further combinations, and the lighter skinned orientals and emigrees from southern Russia would have made the situation even more complex.

However, the rigidity of the system, its endogamy, and the emphasis on commensality, has a lot to do with the primitive belief in totems and consequent taboos, magic, *mana* and what Hutton calls 'the soul stuff' which in effect implies 'the life force', that which is the essence of whatever comprises the creation. The belief was that wherever there was the excess of the life force, there it was abundance of everything that made life happy, and to deny a person success it would help if his or his community's *mana* was diminished: *Mana* is the power residing within each person, including his belongings, and collectively it had, it was believed, a decisive influence upon the fortunes of the tribe. The eclipse of an opposing tribe was sometimes sought to be achieved by performing acts which were tabooed for that tribe, thus decreasing their *mana*, like serving them proscribed foods or foisting upon them forbidden trades, and such like acts. Even the inert tools of the worker were believed to possess *mana*. The artisans worship the tools of their trade, howsoever briefly, every time they take them out for work, and at least once in the year elaborately, on the *Vishwakarma* day, around the time of *Diwali*, the Hindu festival of lights.

The ideas of sacrifice, human, animal or otherwise, and head hunting and cannibalism, are based on this belief. By decapitation, the *mana* of the victim was sought to be secured. Likewise, by eating the flesh of another human being, the people doing so were, in fact, partaking of his *mana*. Additionally, the magician priest had devised other methods also to achieve the same results, like preserving the placentas of the women of the community, or eating the flesh of the dead elders before their burial, or seeking fulfilment of wishes by offering prayers at the graves of dead people who possessed recognizable wish fulfilling qualities when they lived. Though graves of even ordinary people are venerated, for the power of the 'soul-stuff'; the idea is to prevent the loss of *mana* of the community for its own benefit, or for personal benefit, and make use of the power of the 'soul-stuff' for gains and to ward off any evil or hardship. Movement of an individual of a tribe to another one was considered to be a loss of *mana*, a kind of a betrayal, which the tribe resented and resisted. This could also be the argument for endogamy amongst the tribals.

Thus, we see that the foundation of the system lies in the Proto-Australoid, or earlier, belief in *mana*, magic and the soul stuff. This had already brought in endogamy and commensality. With the development of trade and industry guilds of artisans and tradesmen got formed, some of Dravidian extraction, but a large number from the pre-Dravidian people. This gave a new dimension to the caste system, bringing in groups based on professions, which eventually coalesced into castes. Another superimposition came with the advent of the *varnas*. The Brahmanical religion emphasized the purity of the race and the sacrificial ritual, and also the aspects of pollution, i.e., how pollution was caused by the proximity of people who were physically not clean, or did not wear clean clothes, or performed unclean jobs, or, in some cases, did not belong to the *varnas* of the twice born. All this tightened the caste classification. The Karma concept of the later Vedic period also contributed and gave it further rigidity. Although the Vaishnavas, the Buddhists and the Jains, tried to break this rigidity, they failed, for the roots of the system were far too deep and firm.

Food had a decisive influence on the system of taboos. Tools of the artisans perform jobs, or at least are an aid in that direction, and are considered to possess soul stuff or *mana*, for their usefulness, like the usefulness of a house, a boat, a machine, is proof of its soul-power. Likewise food also has soul-power, or *mana*, and it is important that this power is not lost by pollution. When food is served by strangers, or by people with whom eating is tabooed, there shall be loss of power. Besides, foods from sources outside the possessions of a tribe, are considered harmful. Generally, however, accepting food from the twice born castes could be in order, though normally this is not permitted for fear of loss spiritual power, *mana*.

To sum up then, the factors as enumerated below may be considered relevant to the evolution of the caste system:

1. Geographical isolation of the peninsula, and the mutual isolation of its regions on account of difficult and varying terrain. The isolation of the subcontinent prevented extensive interaction with neighbouring countries. The tribes with different cultural backgrounds generally tended to nurse their prejudices and that coupled with difficult terrain and underdeveloped communications, lent to isolation and contributed to the growth of sectarian societies.
2. Development and perpetuation of primitive customs and concepts about totems, *mana*, — soul-stuff, magic and power of food and the working tools and other items of utility including the home and hearth. Even words of the magician-priest were believed to have power, *mana*. His incantations became *mantras* which were believed to have power. Movement out of the tribe was loss from the collective *mana* of the community. In fact, even abandoning the family, or improperly eating outside with people of other families, or disregarding own totem or ancestor worship, was believed to adversely affect the *mana*.
3. With the onset of industry there was evolution of guilds of artisans. Trades and professions became hereditary as the tribes and families tended to become insular on account of their belief in totems, magic, etc., which brought in endogamy and commensality. There was, thus, restricted inter-tribal or inter-family contact and the need was felt, on account the primitive beliefs, by the family to keep the mechanics of its

trade a secret, loss of the trade was like loss of its inner strength. Consequently, opportunity to pick up trades from people outside the tribe was minimal.

4. The ideas of purity, and pollution, and ablutions, in ritual sacrifice.
5. Colour, race, and civilizational antagonism. Incoming people overpowering those already living here, considered themselves superior and made every effort to preserve their own purity of race by strictly keeping away from the local inhabitants, while the local people tightened their insularity to maintain their integrity and identity. Under this head the clash between the patrilineal (like the Aryans) and the matrilineal (a large number of pre-Aryan tribes were matrilineal) societies is also covered.

The Sudras were classified as *sat* and *asat* Sudras, i.e., those of higher denomination in the caste hierarchy, and the rest. They were denied the privileges of the twice born and were not permitted Vedic rites for birth, death, marriage and the like, nor could they use the sacred mixture made from cow's milk, curd, clarified butter and its urine and dung. But the *sat* type could take the help of the Puranas, this was called the *Namas* method. They were enjoined to perform all the daily sacrifices too on the basis of *Namas*, and execute welfare works and be charitable. Those who wanted to gain merit were advised to be virtuous. By the time of the later Vedic period, however, the *sat* Sudras, which category included people like carpenters, masons, goldsmiths, or people who owned substantial land or other property, or followed respectable vocations, or were pre-Aryan people of good means and education though outside the Aryan fold, were treated well and were allowed the services of the Brahmin, though the ceremonies had to be based on the Puranas and not the Veda. In fact, during the post Buddhist period the good Sudras were being equated with the Vaisyas, one amongst the many arguments for this equation being that both the Sudras and the Vaishas originated from the lower part of the body of Prajapati, i.e., thighs and the feet, as opposed to the Brahmins and the Kshatriyas who were born from the higher, superior portion, i.e., mouth and the arms. Besides, both the *varnas*, i.e., the Vaisyas and the Sudras, essentially provided service to the people of the higher *varnas*, and, therefore, there was little justification to place one higher than the other. According to Kautilya, the issue of a Vaisya from a Sudra wife is to be treated as a Sudra; in fact, according to his *Arthashastra*, a work compiled during the post-Buddhist period, the issue of a Brahmin from a Kshatriya wife is also to be considered a Sudra, which is directly against the laws of Manu which allow such an issue to be treated as a Brahmin. However, a Brahmin now could accept food offered to him by a good Sudra, as he could from a Vaisya. The *sat* Sudras could engage in trade, like the Vaisyas, and agriculture.

However, it is not to be visualized that Sudras accepted the rule of Brahmins timidly, or they accepted the authority of the *Smritis* or the *Dharma Shastras*. In fact there always was resistance and in quite a few cases aggressive Sudra tribes managed to claim higher *Varnas*, e.g., the Nandas ruling from Pataliputra were Sudras, while imperial Guptas and Harsha Vardhana were of Vaisya origin. Having risen from the level of robbers and dacoits, many militant Sudra tribes ruled vast territories, and got their leaders proclaimed as kings and their kinsmen and other supporting elements as Kshatriya Rajputs, literally, sons of kings. Any one daring to contest their pretensions, or any Brahmin refusing to issue religious proclamations in their favour, was ruthlessly eliminated.

Vaishnavism is tolerant towards Sudras and advocates non-discrimination and emphasizes the importance of sincerity in seeking the divine reality, and a purity of heart and goodness of deeds, irrespective of caste. They recognize every individual's right to worship and, consequently, his right to enter a temple. Both Jainism and Buddhism do not recognize any caste distinctions.

However, a large number of the original inhabitants continued as "Asat Sudras", generally as scavengers, village menials, or those performing the last rites for the dead people, or handling dead human beings or animals. They continued to serve as the underdogs right up to the modern times. Often they were referred to as the *Ad-Dharmis*, i.e., the followers of the original religion, which implies people who follow Hindu faith but are not part of the Hindu society. This has in some cases led them to adopt other faiths, like Islam or Christianity, but even after conversion the stigma of low birth has generally remained. Quite often humiliating restrictions have been imposed upon them. In the south, where caste system was strong as compared to the north, the low-caste people, particularly the untouchables, were forbidden from wearing ornaments of gold; or their males from wearing their clothes below their knees; or wearing formal clothes like coats, shirts or vests; or using umbrellas against rain or sun, or getting a haircut; or their women from covering the upper portions of their bodies or using flowers for personal decoration. They could use only earthen utensils, and could never ride a horse, for whatever reason. Their children were forbidden from getting education and were required to only tend cattle. The families were required to be at the beck and call of the high-caste people, and were required to work on measly wages, and not own land, nor use music in their marriages and so on. In northern India, however, the restrictions were not so severe, and the people were generally alive to their utility and valued the services they provided, and were not only tolerant towards them but even provided them the essential wherewithalfor survival, like land to build a house or the food grains. Where such largesse was not forthcoming, because the village community could not utilize the services, generally on account of over-population amongst these Sudras, they tended to turn into criminals. In eastern India, particularly in the hill areas of Assam and adjoining states, the majority of the tribes are an admixture of Proto-Australoids and the northern Mongoloid people. They are treated as external castes. But being in majority as compared to the high-caste Hindus, they do not suffer the disadvantages to the same extent as the people of the external castes in the rest of the country.

It is, however, not to be assumed that untouchability is observed only by the caste Hindus towards the exterior castes. Mahars, an exterior caste of Maharashtra, do not like to be identified with Chamars, also an exterior caste whose people are concerned with the disposal of dead animals. Chamars in turn have distanced themselves from the Bhangis, the scavengers, and so on. Taboos and endogamy are strict amongst these classes. Caste Hindus do not permit any of them to enter the temples, or accept food or water which may have been touched by them; even a shadow of these people falling on food or water is enough to pollute the items. Brahmins do not officiate at their marriages or other religious ceremonies, nor are the barbers working for high-caste people allowed to cut their hair. Because they are generally illiterate and do not always have profitable vocations, some amongst them are poor, and have to borrow from the higher castes to survive, or to meet expenses of essential ceremonies. This often ties them down to the moneylender as farm hands or servants, often for their whole life. They constitute the bonded labour.

Since Independence, however, successive governments have taken steps to ameliorate their lot. Untouchability is banned and a large number of government posts are reserved for them, as also vacancies in the educational institutions. Gandhi was a strong champion of their cause, and today, because of the media, they have effectively united and wield reckonable political influence.

The depressed classes (scheduled castes and scheduled tribes) constitute almost 30 per cent of the total Hindu population, and ethnically they are either of pure Proto-Australoid extraction or are mainly a mix of the Proto-Australoids and the Palaeo-Mediterranean Dravidians. Essentially they are pacifists, and dislike violence, and have borne the humiliations and hardships brought upon them by their low social status, timidly. May be for this reason some anthropologists have expressed the view that Proto-Australoids have, possibly, evolved from a subhuman species within south Asia itself. Their pacifism has bred amongst them extreme tolerance and an attitude of giving in to adversity, blaming it upon factors beyond their control, including Karmas, and turning to magic to induce the hostile influences to relent their hold, rather than adopting a discerning attitude to enquire into the cause of the suffering, and devising appropriate resistance and remedies. This has been the cause of almost total absence of the development of science and technology amongst these people. Being at the receiving end most of the time, life to the thoughtful amongst them appeared a painful journey through suffering and sorrow, and the religion they evolved was essentially based on this premise.

The systems of endogamy and commensality that the primitive people evolved, stayed in practice till about the modern times; to a lesser extent, amongst some tribes those are in vogue even today.

In the distant past some tribes had subsisted on food gathering when people around them had become food producers. The gathering groups mostly depended, and consequently, concentrated on the type of food that was available in their areas, which could be fruit, fish, birds, insect and so on, and this became the favoured food. Totem, and its gathering was accompanied with celebrations, and rituals, including sacrifice (even human). With time the clans exchanged food, on a kind of barter basis, and that brought contact and marriages between totem groups, improving diet, and genetics, and developing language, and increased the population of the clans that thus intermixed; others possibly became extinct. With the increased sanctity attached to the totemic symbol, certain taboos relating to it were enforced and that, (or possibly for some other reason as well) forbade sex relation within the totem clan. A tribe had several of such clans and marriage was permitted only within the tribe and not outside it, but it was not permitted within the totemic clan. However, the limited intermixing notwithstanding, the tribes were generally self-sufficient in the prevalent salubrious climate and felt little need for extensive movement or learning, or improving the living conditions by developing scientific temperament. For this reason the culture of these people, including of those who had been relatively more mobile and had learnt the use of metals and evolved viable social systems, remained, to a large extent, obsessed with religion and superstition. Whatever verve and scientific culture got generated, it was due to the incursions by outsiders. Time stood still as far as these Proto-Australoid or the Palaeo-Mediterranean tribes, or the tribes born out of a combination of the two, were concerned. And they forever lived in deprivation.

During the post Buddhist period it was the accedence of Brahmanism, but the hold of the high castes over the low castes was relaxed to some extent, though in the south the relaxation was comparatively limited. But in spite of this, the hold was oppressive enough for any radically progressive initiative that the depressed classes, or their supporters, might have taken. There were various reformers, and some movements, which sprang up from time to time to redress the wrong done to them. The governments, particularly during the post Buddhist period, even after Buddhism had been overwhelmed by Brahmanism and put in effort to improve the lot. During the golden age of Hinduism, during the reign of the Guptas, fourth to sixth centuries AD, a lot of time and resources were devoted to their welfare. Guptas and later Harsha Vardhan, though Vaisyas and followers of Brahmanism, were well disposed towards other religions and castes and sub castes. Here and there governments appeared which were non-Brahmanic in character and under them the lot of the lower classes was even better.

During the early years of the fifteenth century, Brahmanism, as interpreted by Sayana, the top Vedic scholar of the kingdom of Vijayanagar, and his followers, mostly restricted itself to the ritualism of the later Vedic period. This could unduly highlight the caste divide. But the lot of the lower castes was receiving attention of the social reformers and religious leaders. Although access to the Vedic literature was not freely granted to them, their right to worship was acknowledged. Both the Shaiva and the Vaishnava saints were preaching equality of all beings before God. About the beginning of the thirteenth century, in Maharashtra a number of Sudra saints had gained popularity for their preaching the path of *Bhakti* for the depressed classes. Some of them made a great name for themselves with their pure lives and their ability to compose religious poetry. Kabir in Uttar Pradesh was one such saint. Namdeva and Tukaram, both non-Brahmin saints, preached the devotional system of worship from their temple pulpits, to the accompaniment of simple music, whereto they invited people of all castes and creeds. Besides, a large number of non-Brahmin saints arose almost throughout the length and breadth of the country to accommodate the aspirations of the lower castes. One prominent amongst them was Guru Nanak in Punjab, while Kabir in Uttar Pradesh was another one. Brahmin saints prominent for supporting this movement were Eknath, and Gyaneshwar and his sister, all of Maharashtra; the former was so fanatical in his belief in the equality of all before God, that he not only openly dined in Sudra houses but during a function in his house gave a higher priority to the Sudras over the Brahmans when it came to serving the meal at the end of the ceremony. All this went a long way in making the life of the Sudras more comfortable, except of course the untouchables, for whom the respite was only marginal, mainly because their professions were considered to be of mean stature and were looked down upon. There is no doubt that the advent of Islam in India had its own impact, howsoever minor, on the caste system.

Private enterprise got a boost with the rise of the village communities, and the traders guilds secured for themselves reckonable power in the society. But the guilds never were organized to provide all the services the village required. The problem was solved with villages having their own set of artisans, and that made the village communities tight and closed, though viable and self-sufficient. This development hit the guilds adversely; it weakened them and with that came the break of interaction between artisans, and weakening of mutual competition and the innovative and scientific temper. The prosperity achieved could, therefore, focus on nothing other than the religion. The wealth generated had little utility in developing science and technology for more extensive trade and commerce, and got locked in the rich images of gods or the gold and silver that people wore on their persons. There was no incentive for the growth of talent, and with the passage of time even the religious leadership had gone to the ignorant illiterate Brahmins, for there was little else required than religious singing to the accompaniment of simple country musical instruments, and preaching the cult of devotion to the favourite deity. This did not require much education since there was little use for the knowledge of philosophy or the Vedic or other Hindu literature in this kind of worship. Sayana, in the fifteenth century, restricted the total worship process for the high castes to the recitation of the *Mantras* as laid down in the Brahmanas. Some communities even found the Brahmin to be superfluous, for they felt that other men could be equally useful as cult priests. This view was particularly prevalent amongst the lower classes where Brahmins in most cases, were not providing the necessary religious service. All this cut into the sources of income of the Brahmin, and impoverished him. But he retained the job of casting the calender, or forecasting, and such like activities which required minimum literacy.

It may, however, not be assumed that the lower castes did not view disfavourably marrying into higher castes or that there were no restrictions on eating or establishing close social links with them. The ideas on commensality, *Mana*, etc., were strong, and excursions outside the caste were not accepted. In most cases entry of a higher-caste person into the realm of a lower caste was frowned upon with the same vehemence as that of a lower-caste person into the sphere of a higher caste. The caste structure was tight and insular.

Originally all land was village property and the grain produced was distributed on the basis of the requirement of the families. If a person was banished from the clan, he and his family lost the right to the foodgrain that the village land produced. This could indeed be a serious punishment. Later, however, the concept of individual ownership for most of the village land came in, though a substantial portion still stayed under the control of the village, mostly on caste basis. Lands owned by the individuals attracted tax which was collected for the king by a dignitary appointed by him, who kept a part of the revenue as compensation for his services and passed on the rest, mostly in the form of cash or gold or silver. He also served in the king's army and was responsible to provide a specified number of soldiers when required; he raised money for this purpose from his share of the tax collections; he also had the authority to take on local welfare works, like construction of dams to improve the land yield. All this was within the sphere of the activity of the Kshatriyas. The merchants and the manufacturers of the Vaisya *varna* were concentrated mostly in towns and ports, while the artisans of the Sudra *varna* who started of as guilds, suffered the loss of original cohesiveness as they got scattered in different places, in search of work. They could, consequently, operate only from temporary associations, formed for restricted purposes, like for construction of a temple. Merchants' associations, however, regulated competition and received guarantees from the king against interference by feudal lords and minor officials.

Thus, at first it was the caste; it originated from the time of the most primitive people of this subcontinent. Then came the system of the *varnas* which simply superimposed itself upon the existing caste system, but then, under the pressure of the indigenous ideas, started developing almost on the same lines as the caste system. But the castes which evolved from this superimposition were not that fanatical or rigid on the rules of endogamy or commensality.

The position today is that, thanks to the policies of the successive governments, the media attention, and education, the systems of caste and untouchability no longer possess the seriousness of the past, nor the rigidity about commensality and taboos, particularly at the urban centres, though intercaste marriages are still rare. Brahmin community itself has taken to other vocations, some of which earlier fell within the sphere of the Sudras. In the rural areas the trends are similar though the movement is at a slower pace. Because of ease in movement due to rapid progress in transport, there is movement to any centre where money earning capacity develops. Some Sudra artisans are better-off financially compared to the people in higher castes. Their unity has generated a political force that cannot be ignored at any level. Their lot is not much worse than that of the others and daily the situation is turning in their favour. But it will take time before the caste distinctions disappear completely.

Nine

The Historical Perspective

Homosapiens have lived on this subcontinent since the second interglacial period, i.e., for the last 400,000 to 200,000 years. The Ice Age was not as harsh or extensive over the Indian subcontinent as it was in the northern hemisphere, e.g., Europe, in fact the southern and the eastern parts of the country escaped it entirely. Because of the fertility of the soil the growth of vegetation was abundant and there was much larger variety of edible fruits and plants growing naturally when compared to Middle East, Central Asia, or Europe. Thus, people here survived on food gathering even when their western neighbours had turned food producers. Compared to the hunter whose success depends much on the cooperative effort of the community, food gatherers prefer to work individually or in family groups, social intermixing would force him to share his food as well as its source. Again, a hunter moves extensively in search of his prey and has to be alert and ingenious if he has to secure success. There is no such pressure on the food gatherer, though during natural or man made calamities, like, droughts and floods, his situation is pretty hopeless. He has to wander off in search of other sources, but that is not always easy. Besides, the food of the hunter is far more nutritious and, therefore, he is physically tougher.

The period of Stone Age has varied from place to place. This was followed by the age of copper. This metal fairly replaced the stone tools. Copper became the material for tool making because it could be produced from its ore, in kilns no more technical than the pottery kilns, pottery is found along with stone tools in late stone age. Some parts of India, like western Deccan, almost missed the Copper Age, some even the Bronze Age. Progressive stages of development, like moving from early Stone Age to the next one, or moving from there to Copper Age, were essentially brought in by the ingressing tribes.

There is no information as to what happened to the homo-sapien species who lived on this subcontinent during the second interglacial or thereafter. They could have become extinct, or been assimilated by the incoming tribes, like the Proto-Australoids, or the Proto-Australoids may well be the evolved version of these inhabitants. The small statured and almost black Negritos, the first racial group to have been identified on this subcontinent, were possibly here 6000 to 7000 years back. Then appeared the dark Proto-Australoids. Some of their tribes seem to have been fairly well settled in village communities five to six thousand years ago, tending to agriculture, but some amongst them were mere food gatherers. They were followed by the Paleo-Mediterraneans, also a dark skinned people, who mixed extensively with the Proto-Australoids and out came a stock who have generally stayed at the lower rungs of the Indian social structure. They were followed by other groups, the darkish Mediterraneans proper, the light skinned people emigrating from southern Russia, and the Orientals and Armenians and the like, and they caused the flowering of the Indus Valley Civilization, one of the oldest. This culture was pretty widespread in the north-west of India, generally in areas which were served by perennial water sources and were not unnecessarily encumbered by heavy growth of vegetation, for this is the time of the Bronze Age and the man did not possess the means to effectively and speedily clear the forests. This had to await the discovery of iron. The Indus Civilization is known to have been fairly established by around 3500 BC and flourished unhindered for at least one thousand years. Its decline seems to have started by about 2250 BC which coincides with incursions into this country from the north-west, including that of the Aryans. These last named people, though not so numerous as the earlier groups, made a lasting contribution to the culture and civilization of the people of the subcontinent. Broad historical details up to the time of the later Vedic Age of the Aryans have already been covered in the earlier chapters of this book.

The Hindu Factor

By about 600 BC northern India had at least 16 well established big or small states, being Gandhara (Peshawar-Rawalpindi area); Kamboja (south-west Kashmir and parts of Kafiristan); Avanti (eastern Gujarat); Ashmaka (on river Godavari); Shurasena (Mathura); Matsya (Jaipur); Panchala (Bareilly-Farrukhabad); Kuru (Thanesar-Delhi-Meerut); Vatsa (Allahabad); Chedi (area between the Yamuna and the Narmada rivers); Malla (Gorakhpur district); Kosala (central Uttar Pradesh around Lucknow); Kasi (Benares); Magadha (south Bihar); Vriji (north Bihar); and Anga (east Bihar). The states, however, were not entirely friendly towards one another, and smaller states, particularly the republics, felt vulnerable to their bigger and more powerful neighbours. In course of time four out of these emerged as the major powers, being Avanti, Vatsa, Kosala and Magadha. Out of these Magadha held the pre-eminent position.

Magadha as a non-Aryan kingdom of some reckoning, has been mentioned even in the *Mahabharata* epic. This country then also had a strong army, and its ruler, Jarasandh, an ally of the Kurus in the conflict, was a feared and respected potentate. Magadha owed its strength to its fertile and rich soil, and its copper and iron ore mines, like in Singhbhum district. These metals were used not only for the manufacture of agricultural implements but also for the weapons of war. The sand of its river, Sona, which joins the Ganges near Pataliputra, modern Patna, carried gold. Its capital city, Girivraja was enclosed by five hills and with time, came to be protected by a stone wall. During the sixth and the fifth centuries BC it was ruled by Saisunaga kings. Bimbisara, whose father had abdicated in his favour when he was just a lad of fifteen, is about the most remarkable ruler of this line. Immediately upon securing the crown in 545 BC, he got down to expand the kingdom and entered into matrimonial alliances with Kosala and Vaishali and founded the city of Rajagriha, modern Rajgir in the Patna district. He supported and encouraged intellectual activity; both Mahavira and Gautama Buddha preached in his kingdom. His rule brought name and strength to Magadha and was a model of sorts for the kingdoms around, and even for the kingdoms that followed. The line of the Saisunagas went out of history in a couple of centuries.

In his old age Bimbisara got killed by his son Ajatshatru and that provoked the joint hostility of Kosala and Vaishali who had given to him their daughters in marriage. But the new Magadhan king defeated the allies and even captured some of their territory. As part of his defence he fortified the village of Pataligrama; within a couple of generations this fortress grew into the famous city of Pataliputra. He captured Vriji and took Kashi from Kosala; its king Prasanajit, in order to appease him, had to give him his daughter in marriage. Prasanajit was a powerful king. In later years his successor and son is known to have massacred the tribe of the Sakyas. The Magadhan king patronized both Buddhism and Jainism, but in the former case he supported Devadatta, the schismatic cousin of Buddha. Both Buddha and Mahavira died during the early period of his reign. The first Buddhist council was held during his time, essentially to compile the scriptures and codify the discipline norms for the monks so as to censure any laxity in their conduct.

At least four kings of the Saisunaga line were parricides, namely, Udayain, Anirudha, Munda, and Kalashoka. The last named, moved the state capital permanently from Girivraja to Pataliputra, though he was very fond of Vaishali as well, which was almost like his second capital. The second Buddhist council was held there, during the tenth year of his reign, after 100 years of Buddha's nirvana. This too was called basically to tighten the code of discipline and rid the religion of the unnecessary frill it had gathered in the course of the 100 years. Sadly, in the year 376 BC this king got assassinated and the power came to his ten young sons who were all exploited by the powerful officials of the court, at whose behest the princes got down to eliminate each other till by 345 BC, in a matter of 22 years, they were all gone and the throne was captured by Mahapadmapati Nanda, the founder of the Nanda dynasty. This man is said to have been of a low origin, though the Brahmanical *Varna* system was not in vogue amongst the Dravido-Austral people of those times.

Mahapadmapati Nanda turned out to be a man of ruthless ambition, and expanded his empire as far to the west as Punjab and exercized suzerainty over south Orissa and parts of West Bengal. He was succeeded by his eight sons, one after the other, the last of whom, Dhanananda, is known for his riches and a powerful army comprising 200,000 infantry, 20,000 cavalry, 2000 chariots and over 3000 elephants. Some accounts place the strength of the army at a much higher level. All this forced him to impose heavy taxes and that alienated his subjects, and an adventure soldier, Chandragupta Maurya, assisted by a Taxilian Brahmin, Kautilya or Chanakya, took advantage of the prevalent disaffection and overthrew the king and captured the throne of Magadha for himself. Chandragupta, a non-Aryan, adopted the title of Maurya from the caste of his mother who, going by the Brahmin gradation, was of a low origin. By the Buddhist chronicles of Ceylon, Nandas ruled from 345 to 323 BC; of this the major part was taken by the first king. Obviously the palace intrigues, treachery and murders were prevalent and different aspirants ruthlessly eliminated one another in order to capture the throne and the power.

The north-west of the subcontinent at that stage was pretty unsettled. By about the middle of the sixth century BC Iranians had made inroads into the north-west and Cyrus (c 558-530 BC), the founder of the Achaemenian empire, had captured land lying to the west of the Indus river. Darius (522-486 BC), the most notable of this line, expanded his empire up to the present day Rajasthan. This enclave enriched him with enormous annual tribute. However, the Iranian hold did not last for long after Darius, and the area got divided into a number of small free states, of which Pushkalavati (modern Peshawar) and Takshashila (modern Taxila) were important. Both states had flourishing trade and commerce; Takshashila, besides, was known for being an important centre of learning, particularly in the three Vedas and the other connected branches of knowledge. *Mahabharata* is believed to have been first recited in this city.

Alexander of Macedon (Greece) marched into the north-west of the subcontinent in 327-326 BC and eventually returned from the banks of river Beas in the Punjab in 325 BC when his soldiers refused to go any further. During the return journey, all the way to the sea, he had to reduce a number of states. During one of the battles he was badly wounded. On reaching the open sea he divided his force into three columns, despatching one column by sea, and another through Afghanistan, while he himself headed the third, following the difficult route along the Makran coast, eventually making it to Babylon, where he died in 323 BC, the time when Chandragupta Maurya had just about ascended the throne of Magadha.

Brahmins in north-west India were against any incursions into their country by any foreign power. They had played a central role in the eviction of the Achaemenian Iranians and were equally vehemently opposed to Alexander, for which they had to face latter's retribution. Alexander organized the conquered territories into *satrapies* under local or Greek governors, and placed some states under vassal kings. The captured Indian territory was placed under the *satrapy* of Seleucos Nikator who, in 321 BC declared himself independent, and in 306 BC the king. However, the Taxilian Brahmins were not giving in, and one amongst them, Chanakya, a recognized and respected teacher in a Taxilian university, highly disciplined and versed in the state-craft and common law, picked upon Chandragupta to spearhead the movement against the Greeks. At this stage Chandragupta was operating as a leading brigand in the territory around the Vindhyas in central India. He raised an army of mercenaries with the wealth he had collected, and, after Alexander was gone, he recaptured from the Greeks the territory east of the Indus river. Chanakya, possibly, also travelled to Magadha to persuade the Nanda king to join in the battle, but was, it is said, rebuffed. He was incensed and disappointed and, sensing the disaffection of the Magadhans against their king, advised Chandragupta to attack and capture the throne, which the latter did in 323 BC after defeating the powerful Nanda army led by their renowned Commander-in-Chief, Bhadrashala, in a terribly bloody contest. His earlier attempt to capture the Nanda empire with the help of a force raised locally, had failed. Success came only after he had established himself in the north-west and attacked with the army raised there. Chanakya worked assiduously to ensure Chandragupta's victory, using all skills, including bribery, sex, extortion and efficient intelligence: *Daam, kaam, dand, bhed*!

Chandragupta was already in possession of the territory north of the Vindhyas, including southern Rajasthan and the adjoining areas of the present day Gujarat, when he took the throne of Magadha. By about 313 BC he annexed Avanti and Saurashtra, comprising the remaining of Gujarat. In 305 BC he defeated Seleukos Nikator, the Greek king of the *satrapy* of Babylon, and captured the trans-Indus provinces and most of the present day Afghanistan and Baluchistan. Jain records say that he was tilted towards Jainism during his last days, and renounced the throne in favour of his son Bindusara to spend his remaining time as a hermit. This view, however, is not supported by any other sources.

The Indo-Greek contacts helped the growth of trade. Indians exported to Greece and the countries of the Levant, spices, jewels, muslin, turquoise, silk yarn, indigo, in exchange for pearls, copper, dates, gold, and, maybe, slaves from Ethiopia, Arabia and the Mediterranean. Indians also learnt from the Greeks the system of coinage, and they honoured their astronomers. Most visible impact was on the Indian art, particularly in the sphere of sculpture, the notable example of which is works of Gandhara. Alexander had established some Greek settlements in the Punjab, but none of them survived. Those people probably moved over to the adjacent cities and towns and settled down. The Greek officials continued almost undisturbed even during the Mauryan times, although at the eclipse of the Mauryas, the adventurous ones, in concert with their kind from the former Seleucid *satrapies* of Bactria and Parthia, carved out independent kingdoms for themselves.

The first Mauryan emperor developed an effective system of roads to the areas that he annexed, the most important being the *Uttara Path* or the northern highway, also known as the royal highway (the Grand Trunk Road of the modern times), connecting Pataliputra with the north-west of India. According to Greek chronicles, a number of non-Aryan practices were still prevalent in north-western India, while the focus of Aryan culture had moved eastwards. There is also the suggestion that in spite of the powerful Magadhan empire, the system of independent republics was functioning in certain areas. As for the Magadhans of the time, the accounts say that they were of dark colour and preferred white clothes, which comprised a cloth covering the body waist downwards, upto the calves, and another one that covered the upper part of the body, kind of a wrap around it. Rich Indians wore ivory earrings, and elaborately trimmed white leather shoes of thick soles. This made them look taller. They used parasols for protection against sun.

The greatest of the Mauryan kings was Ashoka. He possibly secured the throne after a struggle during which he eliminated his brothers and other claimants. There are varying versions, but it is a fact of history that his anointment as king was delayed by almost four years.

Ashoka, like his forebears, was a great conqueror. After annexing Kalinga, in the twelfth year of his rule, after a pitched, bloody battle, he had under him, except the Tamil country, the whole of the subcontinent, including Afghanistan and Baluchistan in the north-west. He, at this stage, was the greatest monarch the earth had seen till then, and one of the greatest the world has seen even to this day. Whatever was left of the subcontinent, was within his easy grasp, so also the tracts of Central Asia. His empire was a land of settled village agriculture and he had put into operation an elaborate system of administration and tax collection. This system was essentially based on Chanakya's Arthashastra, possibly the world's earliest treatise on statecraft; Chanakya, apparently, was his chief minister during the early years of his reign. But, from this pinnacle of greatness and glory, he suddenly decided to eschew war, and killing of human beings, or destruction of animal life, for he had been highly distressed with his experience of the Kalinga war. Too many people had died then, and too much misery and suffering had been caused. Turning religious he became tolerant towards all religions, although he had the closest association with Buddhism, and impressed upon his subjects the importance of Dharma, not only the Buddhist Dharma, but also Dharma as defined by the Brahmans. He laid stress on the need to be good in speech and thought, clean in body and mind, and to preserve life and not destroy it, whether animal or plant, and live in harmony with nature, in clean environments, and not cheat or tell lies or cause pain and suffering to others through speech or action. He raised a special force whose job it was to teach this to the people at large. In fact, often he took it upon himself to teach

Dharma, the importance of morality and piety. He communicated his message to his subjects through engravings on pillars especially erected for this purpose, and also through engravings on rocks. He organised digging of wells, planting of trees for shade, cultivation of herbs for medicines, erection of hospitals, education of women, and welfare of aborigines and subject races. He encouraged dynamic criticism of the Buddhist religious order so that it could be cleansed of corruption and superstitious accretions. For this purpose the third Buddhist Council was held under his patronage. Of him H.G. Wells has said: "His reign for eight and twenty years was one of the brightest interludes in the troubled history of mankind."

Ashoka was a spiritual giant who turned Buddhism, a local sect in the Gangetic planes, into an Order of a great and renowned world religion. He sent emissaries, which included members from his immediate family, to the nations of South and South-East Asia to spread the message of Buddha; his son Mahinda and daughter Sanghamitta embraced the order and crossed over to Sri Lanka and converted the whole island to the Buddhist faith. For his achievements he had been called Ashoka the Great.

But the experiment of running an empire while following the ideals of Buddha failed, and within a hundred years of his passing away in 232 BC, his great empire had been rendered non-existent. But Buddhism endured for many centuries, alongside Brahmanism, though it eventually lost to the latter and was almost wiped out, but not before it had been firmly entrenched in Sri Lanka and the countries of South-East and East Asia, including Korea, Mongolia, China and Japan, a development for which the great emperor had worked assiduously.

The empire was finally broken by the pressure exerted by the Greeks and the Kushan barbarians from the north-west; a number of their tribes managed to establish kingdoms and dynasties in western and central India. Constant fighting required heavy taxation and that tended to alienate the subjects. By about 187 BC the boundary of the Mauryan kingdom had shrunk almost to the outskirts of Pataliputra. At this stage Pushyamitra Sunga, the Brahman Commander-in-Chief of the last Mauryan king Brihadharatha, beheaded the king in full view of the Army when the latter was carrying out an inspection, and proclaimed himself as the ruler of Magadha; he possibly had the support of the Army and a number of officers of the civil administration and the citizens who were dissatisfied with the heavy taxation, and the string of defeats at the hands of the foreign intruders. The last few kings of the line were followers of the Shaiva faith.

Pushymitra Sunga (c. 187-151 BC) stabilized the north-western border of his empire along the line Jalandhar-Sialkot in the Punjab. The rest of the north-west had been lost to the Greek invaders. He continued to rule from Pataliputra, while his son Agnimitra, stationed at Vidisha, modern Besnagar in eastern Malwa or north-western Madhya Pradesh, looked after the north-west. The latter was soon threatened by the neighbouring kingdom of Vidarbha or Berar. He roundly defeated them, but then came under heavy pressure from the Greeks attacking from the north-west, Kabul, western Punjab and the lower Indus valley had already been lost to the Greeks, and their king Menander had, in addition, taken under his rule the areas of the present day Rajasthan and captured almost the whole of the upper Gangetic plain and was threatening Magadha itself, till Vasumitra, son of Agnimitra, attacked the rear of the Greeks from the Sunga base in Malwa and forced a withdrawal upon them to the line of Jalandhar-Sialkot.

With the rise of the Sungas, the Vedic religion once again bounced back to pre-eminence. But the Sungas could not last beyond 75 BC and even the Kanvas who then took the Magadhan throne, were all but extinct by BC 30, after being wiped out by the Satavahanas. Here and there, however, some pockets of these ruling families sustained for some more time.

Satvahanas ruled Andhra and parts of eastern Deccan till they captured Malwa from the Kanvas. The line was founded by Simuka, and the major expansion of the state was accomplished by Satakarni I after he had negotiated agreements with powerful Maratha chieftains of western Deccan. After Satakarni the empire had set a back on account of Scythian invasions, but the situation was more than restored by Gautamiputra Satakarni after he had driven out the Scythians, the Greeks and Parthians from some of the territories they had annexed. His empire included most of northern Andhra of the present time, eastern Deccan and Malwa. The final spark of the line was Sri Yajna Satakarni who took back whatever territory the Scythians had annexed from his predecessors and brought about an era of great prosperity to his subjects. After this king it is a steady decline for the Satavahanas till by about the middle of the third century AD the line came to its end.

South of the Magadhas there were a number of states, the most notable being Kalinga, which had declared itself independent after Ashoka, and the Cholas, the Pandyas and the Keralas. The most prominent ruler of the Kalingas was Kharavela who established a considerable empire and played some decisive role in the fortunes of the monarchies of south-east India. He was a constant threat to the Sungas of Magadha. However, after him there was a steep decline in the power of the family and not before long the line became extinct. In the south, the Cholas ruled the present Thanjavur-Tiruchirapalli tract, securing remarkable achievements in arts and military conquests during the second century BC; they even conquered Sri Lanka. Pandyas ruled Madurai-Tirunelveli-Thiruvananthapuram and were great promoters of trade and learning; they had embassies in Athens and Rome. Keralas ruled the area along the southern part of the west coast including Malabar, Kochi and Kottayam.

By about the first century AD the Greek rule had been all but eliminated and whatever of them opted to stay back, joined the folds of Buddhism or Vaishnavism. Their ruin had been caused by the Sakas, the Pahlavas or the Parthians and the Kushans or the Yue-chi tribe. Both the Sakas and the Yue-chi were part of the same horde, but on account of conflict of interests, mostly concerning grazing areas, the Sakas were forced out eastwards from the Central Asian plains. They established themselves along the border of Central Afghanistan, *Sakasthana* or the present day Sistan, till, in about the early first century AD, they found the Indian border states sufficiently weak to yield to their pressure. Around the same time the parthians were also exerting pressure on the Indian borders. In course of time the Saka-Pahlavi kings ruled over a vast tract extending from Afghanistan in the north to Malwa and upper Deccan in the south, extending eastwards upto the upper Gangetic plains. It was only after Gautamiputra Satakarni of the Satavahana line had taken them on, that they were held and even made to yield some ground. Rudradaman (130-150 AD), the Pahlava king who ruled from Ujjain, was one of the most powerful of his line, and ruled Sindh and Marwar in the north, going as far as the Konkan in the south. He entered into a matrimonial alliance with the Satavahanas ruling the country to his immediate south, but attacked and defeated them when he was displeased. His successors were not so powerful, and there were family feuds and loss of territory, till a line risen from the sons of the soil, the Guptas (not Mauryas), put an end to their state. However, even before that the Yue-chi nomads had secured the intelligence about the weakened kingdom and had moved closer to the Indian borders, taking Kabul around AD 92. Soon they were on the conquest course, heading towards the Indian interior at a time when branches of this tribe had already hit China.

The great king of the Kushan line was Kanishka. In the Indian history he is a Saka potentate, basically because all the tribes of the Scythian and the Yue-chi line have been grouped under one head. This king ruled for 23 years and laid the foundation of the Saka era of 78 AD. This calendar continued to be followed by his successors for many generations. He ruled from Peshawar (in Pakistan) and his empire extended upto Benares in the east and in the west included most of the present day Afghanistan, and Kashmir. He even threatened the Chinese in eastern Turkestan and secured a limited success. He was a follower of some Iranian faith but later changed over to Buddhism and became its ardent supporter, he constructed magnificent Buddhist monuments throughout the length and breadth of his empire. The fourth Buddhist Council was held during his time at Jalandhar, or, maybe, in Kashmir, in c. 100 AD. Since the followers of the Theravada school did not participate, the Southern Buddhists do not recognise this council. The council adopted the doctrine of the Mahayana (the great vehicle) and recognized it as the main branch of this Faith and accepted a broader view of the Buddha's teachings, permitting local religious lores, ideas and deities into the Buddhist pantheon. This gave mythology to Buddhism. This council also made Sanskrit the vehicle of Buddhist scriptures. Ashvaghosha, the philosopher, poet and dramatist, and the author of *Buddha Charita*, lived during his time and enjoyed his patronage.

Kanishka's successors held on to the boundaries of the kingdom. Huvishka even extended them. Such was the extent of their power that one of the descendants even called himself 'the Kaisar' Caesar, in addition to the other titles he had adopted. By third century, because of the dissentions within the ruling house, there were four different kingdoms formed by the Yue-chi. These were broken by the Nagas, and finally annihilated by the Guptas operating from Ayodhya.

The founder of the Gupta line, Srigupta, was a king of a small state. His son Ghatotkacha ruled Pataliputra and the surrounding areas, but his son, Chandragupta I (AD 320-335), was an ambitious, farsighted, brave and a shrewed person; he founded the Gupta line. He married Princess Kumaradevi of the neighbouring state of the Licchavis. The connection gave him status amongst the rulers of his time. He extended his rule over Magadha and Kosala, and appointed his son Samudragupta as the crown prince, and associated him with the affairs of the state. Risen from the soil, he was averse to the rule of the foreigners and wanted them out, and though he did not live long enough to make a major contribution in this direction, he left behind a tradition and a solid base for his successor to launch from.

Samudragupta (AD 335-380) was the greatest of this line.While an understudy to his father, he had come to the conclusion that lasting peace and prosperity for the Indian people could be possible only under a federation of States under one strong paramount authority. He had observed that small states maintained luxurious courts, well beyond their means, and robbed their citizens through heavy taxation and other repressive measures, and their local chiefs committed predatory crimes against the subjects and not only made their lives miserable but virtually arrested all growth, financial, cultural or educational. Their expensive lifestyle made them easy prey to the monetary inducements offered by the enemies of the state. With such ideas on his mind he set about, to begin with, to cleanse the state while he was still the crown prince. He urbanized the forest tribes around Nepal, Assam and Central India by clearing the land and putting the tribes in permanent settlements. This process had, in fact, been started during the reign of the Mauryas, in accordance with the rules in Chanakya's

Arthashastra, but it was given to Samudragupta to complete it. After getting the throne, and once his own state had been consolidated, he led his armies (330-36 AD) to subjugate the Gangetic plain and Central India. Then he returned to Pataliputra and for eleven years just consolidated his gains, and by 347 AD was ready to take on the powerful south Indian Dravidian states, a task which not many kings, Indian or foreign, had dared to take on.

South India had three noteworthy kingdoms, namely, Pandya, Chola and Kerala (also known as Chera). In addition there were fierce predatory tribes who lived by war and pillage, the most prominent being the Pallavas. They had secured suzerainty over the three Tamil states by c 226 AD. By the time of Samudragupta the Pallavas, with Vishnugopa as their king, were ruling an empire with their capital at Kanchipuram near Chennai, and had available to them, in addition to their own resources, also the resources of the three feudatory states. Samudragupta moving against them, first defeated King Mahendra of south Kosala in the Mahanadi valley, then subjugated the aboriginal tribes further south, in the forests of Orissa. He wanted no problems with his supply line. He then overpowered Kalinga and Vengi between rivers Mahanadi and Krishna, and then attacked and defeated the Pallavas. Vishnugopa was captured, but was released after he had signed the treaty of submission, which was dictated by the emperor personally. Having completed his mission, the emperor returned to Magadha by way of Western Deccan, *enroute* subjugating the states of western Maharashtra and Khandesh, and by the year 350 AD, when he got back to Pataliputra, after covering a distance of over 2000 miles, he was the most powerful king on the subcontinent, ruling over an empire comparable in size to what had been achieved by Ashoka the great. Some historians have likened him to Napoleon, but unlike Napoleon this emperor never lost an engagement.

The king now got down to consolidating his gains. He deposed the incompetent, small rulers of the Gangetic basin. The kings of Nepal and other Himalayan kingdoms were his vassals. To secure his north-western frontiers he entered into a treaty with the Kushan king who still ruled over parts of Afghanistan, including Kabul. Then, in the year 351 AD the emperor moved the seat of his government from Pataliputra to Ayodhya, in north Kosala, or later day Oudh. The decision appears to have been precipitated by the need to be more central in relation to the territory he ruled and also, maybe, because of the connection of Ayodhya with the legendary Rama, a personality central to the Hindu ideology of religion and culture.

India during the days of Ashoka had been mostly Buddhist, while during the Kushan rule it had partly been Buddhist and partly following the religion of the Shaivas. Later Kushan kings were mostly Shaivas. Buddhism was one of the many religious cults flourishing in the Gangetic basin during the sixth century BC, and possibly not the most popular one either for securing a position of pre-eminence. But this was an ideology which was preached by a prince, and in later times it caught the fancy of two of the most powerful emperors of the time, namely, Ashoka and Kanishka. Although Hinduism had been fairly on the upswing since the days of the Sungas, its hour of glory came, after the later Vedic period, only with the rise of the powerful Guptas, many centuries after the reigns of Ashoka and Kanishka. Till then it was in a fierce competition with Buddhism. The Guptas structured it on solid foundations.

Soon after arrival at Ayodhya the emperor performed the horse sacrifice with unprecedented magnificence, and feeding of hundreds of Brahmins, and doling out generous alms to the poor and needy. The following year he concluded a treaty of alliance with Sri Meghavarna, the king of Sri Lanka; the latter sent his envoy to the Imperial court with expensive presents, including exquisite jewels, and in return received permission to build a Sinhalese Buddhist monastery at Bodh Gaya. Ayodhya became an important centre of intellectual activity. The emperor was highly versed in the scriptures, poetry and music, and he had around him the best talent of the country, not the least eminent among whom was the warrior-poet Harisena. The religion and arts flourished under this king.

Both Ashoka and Samudragupta were great conquerors. The former finally chose the path defined by Buddha, and his empire was lost within 50 years of his death. The latter believed in intense military and intellectual activity. He believed that physical and military weakness brought misery and suffering, that intellectual activity propelled religion and sciences. His line flourished for almost two centuries after his death, and made the most signal contribution to the stabilization of Hindu religion and culture. Though the king supported Hinduism, he was equally well versed in Buddhist philosophy, and often presided over friendly religious debates. He greatly respected intellectuals in any field of activity.

He was succeeded by his son Chandragupta II (c 380-413) who in later years assumed the title of Vikramaditya, the sun of power. This king too was a great military leader, a legislator and a patron of arts and literature. His military prowess rests upon the victories he secured against the Saka king based in Ujjain. He founded the *Samvat* era of 58 BC. His reign saw the peak of the Hindu renaissance, a process which introduced many changes and improvements in the religious, artistic and cultural concepts. Kalidasa, the great poet and playwright, flourished during his period. The king had assembled in his court a galaxy of renowned men of art, culture, religion and sciences, and the nine top most amongst them were called 'the nine jewels'. They made formidable contributions in their respective fields. Hindu architecture began to free itself of the Greco-Roman influences and great and beautiful temples, dedicated to Vishnu, came up in most towns. Gupta emperors were devotees of Vishnu, and restricted altar offerings to fruits and flowers and were staunch protectors of animal life as was the practice of the Buddhists. Religion flourished. Even though Guptas followed Brahmanical religion, they patronized other faiths with equal zeal. Hindu religious literature was edited, compiled and rewritten, including a number of Puranas and even Upanishads. The epics got their near present rendering during this period, the systems of Hindu philosophy were formalized, the *Bhagavad Geeta* got its final form, as also the *Vishnu Purana*, the Bhagvata literature, and, may be, even the *Shiv Purana*. The different heterogeneous strings of ideas of Hindu religion were woven into a composite whole. This was a period of effervescence in all branches of knowledge, like sciences such as mathematics, astronomy, astrology, metallurgy and other basic and advanced sciences, industrial technology, military science and connected disciplines, trade, commerce and economics, and art, drama and poetry. Maximum possible attention was paid to education, including Buddhist education. A great Buddhist university housing over 10,000 monks, flourished at Nalanda, near Gaya, financed essentially by royal grants. Around this time China had adopted Mahayana Buddhism and a number of Chinese travellers had become interested in India. Fa-hien, the Chinese traveller who visited during this period, says that, torture as an instrument of coercion, and capital punishment were almost unknown, while those were extensively practised in China.. He speaks of minimum crime, people seldom having to lock their houses, of prosperity, health and education, and flourishing trade and commerce with the neighbouring states as also with countries beyond the Indian shores. The kingdom was involved in extensive trade with Rome, exporting gold, spices, scented resins and woods. Towards the east there was trade with the countries of the Pacific rim, namely, Cambodia, Thailand and Malaysia. The trade led to settlements which, in course of time developed into colonies which significantly influenced the ethos and culture of the region. To strengthen his position the emperor went in for political marriages, like his predecessor. He also gave away his daughter Prabhavati in marriage to Rudrasena II, the Vakataka king of the Deccan, an alliance that helped him in overpowering Rudrasinha, the Saka *satrap*.

The successive Guptas enlarged their empire, defeating their enemies, and defending the state against White Hun (Epthalites) invasions. Under them their soldiers fought with savage ferocity and the Huns who had pulverized the Persian empire in 484, reeled against the Indian counter offensive. Their Chief, Toramana, a Shaiva, was defeated in a fierce battle at Mandasor in Malwa in 528, by Yashodharman, a powerful king of Central India, with the help of his allies. But while the Huns were broken and were absorbed in the Hindu community as Rajputs, the Gupta empire too weakened and by the early years of the sixth century virtually went out of reckoning, but not without having left a lasting imprint upon religion and philosophy, arts and crafts, sciences, literature, and every other field, not only in India but even abroad, particularly the Far East. Each of its emperors was a person of great ability, both in war and peace. Huns wrecked the powerful Sassanians in

THE FIRST EMPIRES

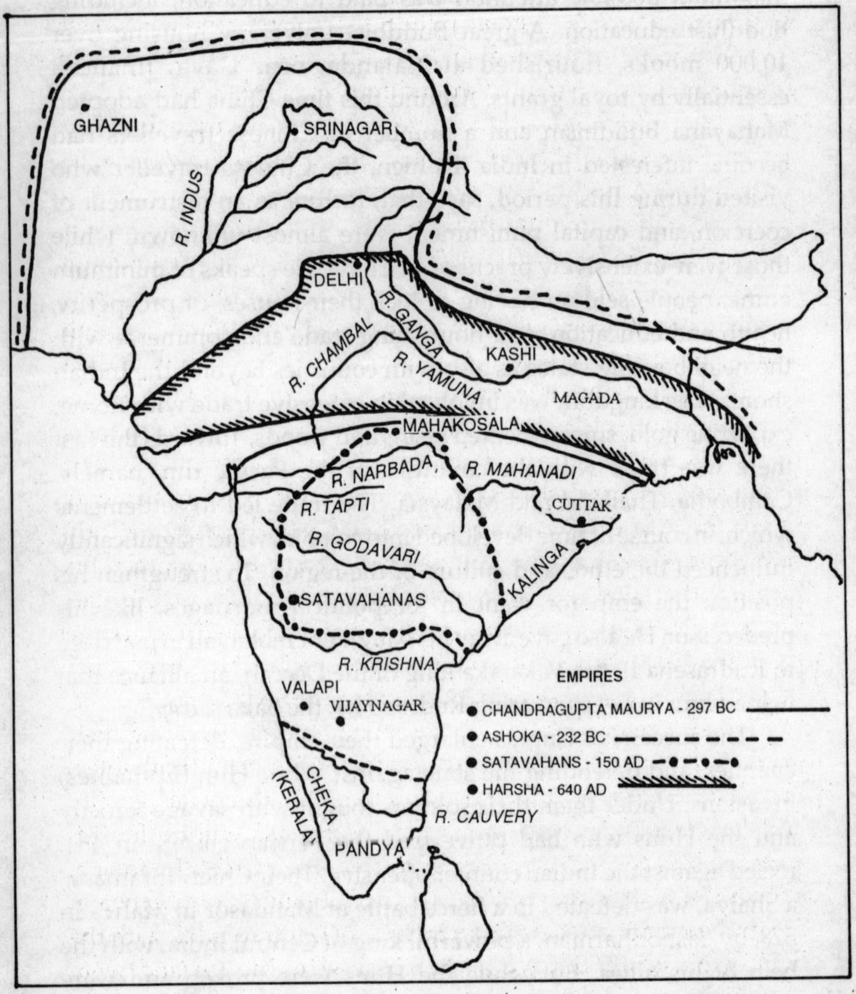

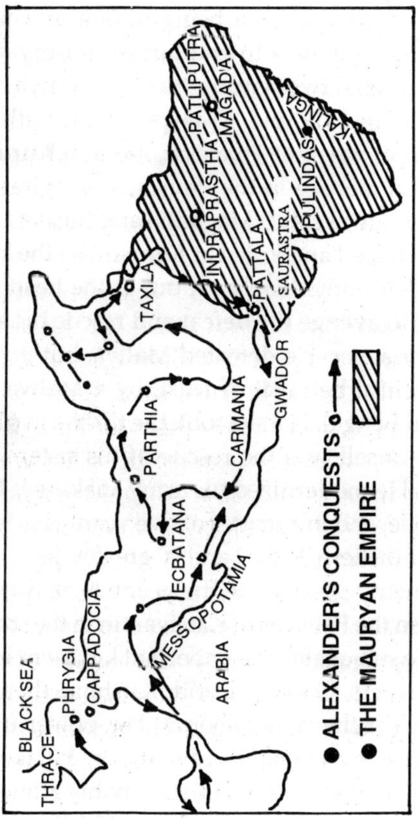
THRACE
BLACK SEA
PHRYGIA
CAPPADOCIA
ARABIA
MESSOPOTAMIA
ECBATANA
PARTHIA
CARMANIA
GWADOR
TAXILA
PATTALA
SAURASTRA
INDRAPRASTHA
PATLIPUTRA
MAGADA
PULINDAS
KALINGA
ALEXANDER'S CONQUESTS
THE MAURYAN EMPIRE

Persia, and quite a few powerful kingdoms in Europe. It is to the credit of the Guptas that they held them and finally broke them, although in the process they got broken themselves. They represent the spirit of India, a determination to stay free of foreign domination. They believed in being strong and just; this, they believed, was the only way to end human misery and suffering.

In the year 604 two young princes, Rajyavardhana and Harshvardhana, ages 19 and 15 respectively, both brothers and from the kingdom based at Thanesar, modern Kurukshetra, were fighting the Hun menace in the Punjab, when Grahavarman, the Maukhari potentate of south Magadha and husband of their sister Rajyasri, got defeated and killed at Kannauj by the king of Malwa. The elder brother immediately set out at the head of an army of 10,000 cavalry, to avenge the defeat and rescue his sister who had been taken a prisoner. He defeated Malwa, but got assassinated, through a deceitful betrayal of trust, by a Malwa ally, Sasanka, ruler of Central Bengal. Harsha took the throne in 612 and the first task he gave himself was the rescue of his sister which he duly accomplished. He modernized his army, making it lighter, swifter and more mobile, and in a matter of five years plus had subjugated the whole of northern India, and a greater part of Bengal and defeated his enemy Sasanka. In the year 620 he was the dominant power, and even the Pallavas of Kanjivaram in the south recognized his strength. He subjugated the important kingdom of Vengi located between the rivers Godavari and Krishna, then attacked the Chalukyas, his southern neighbours. The powerful Chalukyas, a kingdom formed by a Rajput adventurer, Pulakesin Chalukya, and ruled, during the days of Harsha, by his grandson Pulakesin II, a competent monarch who had brought this kingdom to the zenith of its glory, thwarted the attempt. The two armies met on the banks of the river Narmada, and in spite of several determined attempts, the Chalukyas remained intact. Finally, the river line became the boundary between the two states.

Harsha next turned his attention to Valabhi, comprising the whole of the present day Kutch peninsula and most of Gujarat, and by 665 had secured the submission of the ruler, Dhruvabhata, to whom he later offered the hand of his daughter to further strengthen the bond between the two kingdoms. It is possible that he did that as a mark of respect for the house of the Valabhi who claimed direct descent from Rama, the king of ancient Ayodhya.

Harsha ruled from Kannauj which was already a flourishing city on the eastern bank of the Ganges, and had a large number of Hindu temples and Buddhist monasteries. The king, though a follower of Hindu religion, was soft on Buddhism, which tendency got accentuated during the visit of the forty-three years old Chinese traveller Hiuen Tsang, who had come to study Buddhism at the Nalanda University. This did not please the Brahmins who believed Buddhism would weaken the state and be the cause of anarchy, because it supported unlimited tolerance. Besides, they held their own religion in very high esteem. During a joint Hindu-Buddhist festival at Kannauj in 643 AD, organized by the king essentially in honour of the Chinese scholar, where he gave generously to the poor and the needy, and the Brahmins and the Buddhist monks, an attempt was made on his life by a group of Brahmins. The conspirators were eliminated with rare ruthlessness. The Kannauj festival was followed by another one of matching grandeur at Prayaga, the confluence of the Ganges and the Yamuna. Both festivals saw lively interreligion debates but possibly emptied his treasury which could have been resented by his subjects.

Rajyasri, the emperor's widowed sister, who in effect was a joint ruler and exercized great influence over him, was already converted to Mahayana Buddhism. The king followed the creed of Shiva, but under the influence of his sister, and the Chinese traveller Hiuen Tsang, he was very much under the spell of the Buddhists, and this attitude permeated into every limb of the governing machinery. Taking of animal food was forbidden and so was taking of life. But in spite of all this Buddhism was on the decline. For, the ultimate aim of the religion to achieve nirvana was too complex for the common man and difficult to comprehend and did not really enthuse him. An average person desires happiness in this world and in the hereafter. To most of them life was not an epitome of pain after all, filled with grief and sorrow, or devoid of happiness and joy. To them it was a superb gift of God so long as it was not mired in problems. So, they yearned for a deity who could take care of their problems in this world as well as the next one. Otherwise they loved life and enjoyed it, and wanted to continue enjoying it. Hinduism gave them all this: a promise of a happy, healthy life in this world, and a happier one in the hereafter, so long as a few simple rules were taken care of, and Dharma was respected, for Dharma ensured that not only was the individual's personal life fruitful and happy but also that of the whole community he lived and worked with. For the average Hindu, the soul lived with the gods, in the *swarga* or heaven, reposed in ultimate bliss, or it attained *moksha* and got united with the source that creates and which is the fountain without limits, of bliss and joy. In the Buddhist *shunya* it is neither this nor that, neither happiness nor suffering: it is the concept of absolute zero, a vast, unlimited, sea of tranquility. Mahayana Buddhism brought in the concept of gods and compassionate incarnations of Buddha, and developed mythology to attract the common believer, but ultimately it was the nirvana, and for the common man this concept was difficult to comprehend. It required a lot of monastic training and discipline. Besides, the Hindu mythology was related to places he was familiar with, the ideas and incidents he had known from the days almost of his childhood, to kings and commoners who had risen almost from his stock. It was not difficult for him to understand the essence of what was being put across; this mythology was part of his culture; he could relate himself to it. The eighteen rather important Puranas dealt with the stories of the Hindu gods, placing them, in terms of their passions and aspirations, at the level of a common human being, thus creating a mythology which appealed alike to the educated and the uneducated. They were, thus, a part of the Hindu lore and were not comfortable with any other way of life.

Harsha honoured the intellectuals. He himself authored three plays, each of some merit: one about Buddhist religion, and two romantic dramas. Kannauj, his imperial capital, situated on the eastern bank of the Ganges, was strongly defended, and well laid out with gardens, water tanks and canals. People were prosperous, and given to arts and learning. His formidable army was based primarily on horse cavalry and elephants, and he ruled over most of northern India, from the Himalayas in the north to the Narmada basin in the south, including Magadha, Orissa and Bengal. Kings of Kashmir, Sindh and Assam were his vassals. Bana, his Brahman friend and an eminent man of literature at his court, wrote the *Harshacharita* or "The Deeds of Harsha", after the latter's death, in order to immortalize him.

According to Hiuen Tsang, Harsha's army had 60,000 war elephants, 100,000 horse cavalry, and infantry which could be as strong as 20 million. By contrast the Maurya army at its peak did not exceed 9000 fighting elephants, 30,000 horse cavalry and around 600,000 infantry. Yet the Mauryas held a vastly larger empire. Apparently Harsha's army was supplied by his vassals and it was mobilized only during a war, though it is quite possible that Hiuen Tsang's figures are exaggerated and include certain other non-specified elements. The policy of decentralization in every field was successfully adopted by the Imperial Guptas. While the Mauryas believed in a strong central control, Guptas left most state functions to their vassals and feudatories, including supply of soldiers for war, all under their strict control. In return they provided them protection, something like the 'Subsidiary System' which the British followed in India while expanding their empire.

Harsha had no son and the line finished after his death in 646, and the country got divided into numerous small kingdoms. Kashmir, which all along had been governed by one or the other of the major Indian empires, came to its own in the seventh century. In the ninth century Lalitaditya was ruling it. He caused the defeat and downfall of Yashovarman of Kannauj. His rule extended from Afghanistan in the west to Gauda or western Bengal in the east. Famous historian Kalhana served in his court. His great temple at Martand stands to this day though in ruins. The line came to an end around 855.

By 836 Pratiharas were ruling from Kannauj and by the end of the century they controlled most of northern India. Their noble and notable king was Bhoja I. Stories of his concern for his subjects make folk lore even to this day. This king checked the eastward march of Avantivarman, the king of Kashmir of the Utpala line who were the rulers from around 855. The westward expansion of the Utpalas was checked by the Indus kingdoms. In course of time this line was caught in internal strife and the state got divided into a number of fiefs, till in AD 1339 it finally succumbed to the Muslims.

Bhoja's son Mahendrapala expanded the empire, mostly eastwards, for in the south-west he had formidable foes in the Rashtrakutas. Like his father he too was a just king and worked assiduously for the spread of education, and recognized talent. He had the best of the scholars adorning his court. Till about AD 917 Pratiharas were pretty well entrenched in their kingdom, when Indra III, the Rashtrakuta potentate, defeated them and took Kannauj, though help from the Chandella king saved the throne finally. In AD 1018, Kannauj was plundered by Mahmud of Ghazni and the state was severely weakened, and by about the middle of the eleventh century it had gone out of reckoning.

In the south the Vakatakas ruled in upper Deccan, i.e., Berar and the adjoining tracts, or the present day northern Andhra Pradesh. The Pallavas with capital at Kanchipuram near Madras, then ruled over territory comprising present day western Karnataka, southern Andhra and the whole of the Tamil country. Samudragupta had given his daughter Prabhavati in marriage to the Vakataka king Rudrasena II. Vakatakas had matrimonial alliances with several royal houses and that greatly helped to stabilize their rule. They ruled for many generations till they were overtaken by other rising dynasties.

The Pallavas, whose king Vishnugopa was captured and then released by Samudragupta in about the middle of the fourth century, maintained a steady hold over their country till around the later half of the sixth century they had a powerful king, Simhavishnu, who captured the territories of the Cholas and defeated even the king of Sri Lanka. During the reign of his son Mahendravarman I a struggle ensued between the Pallavas and their northern enemies, the Chalukyas, which continued for several generations: Chalukya king Pulakesin II inflicted a crushing defeat upon the Pallavas, which was avenged by Narasimhavarman I of the Pallavas. In the first half of the eighth century the Pallavas were routed by the Chalukyas, and thus weakened they were finally eliminated towards the end of the ninth century, by the Pandyas and the Cholas, their southern neighbours. The Pallavas made a noteworthy contribution to the history of South India. They were the first to build a great empire south of the rivers Penner and Tungabhadra. They supported the worship of Vishnu and Shiva. A number of saints of these sects flourished during their rule. Kanchi, their capital, became a great centre of art and learning. They treated alike the learned men of both the Brahmin and the Buddhist faiths. The cave architecture and sculpture developed during their period, was of high value as also the design and layout of the Hindu temple; all this set in new trends which were extensively followed in later years both in India and the Far East.

Chalukyas were the rulers of Karnataka and had their capital at Vatapi, modern Badami in Bijapur. The line was founded by a Rajput adventurer, Pulakesin I, an energetic and brave king in his own right, who performed the horse sacrifice when he ascended the throne. Their most renowned king was Pulakesin II (AD 609-642) who captured the whole of the territory of northern Maharashtra between the Narmada and the Kaveri, and held his own against Harshavardhana of Kannauj, forcing the latter to accept Narmada as the boundry between the two states. Mahendravarman of Kanchi feared the strength of this king and accepted his domination. Ultimately the Pallava king, Narasimhavarman, the son of Mahendravarman, inflicted upon him a series of crushing defeats leading to the destruction of his capital, Vatapi. His son Vikramaditya I, however, re-established the power of the crown, and three generations later Vikramaditya II did even better when he actually took the Pallava capital. Around 753 AD his son and successor was overthrown by one of his chiefs, Dantidurga, who started the line of the Rashtrakutas. They formed a great empire embracing Karnataka and Maharashtra.

During their hey day the Rashtrakutas were ruling the most of the peninsula, from south Gujarat and Malwa in the north to Tanjore in the south. They had humbled the emperor of Kannauj, though the deltas of the Godavari and the Krishna were not under them. The Arab historians of the time clubbed king Vallabharaja of this line with the emperor of China, the Caliph of Baghdad and the emperor of Constantinople, as the four greatest kings of the world.

The Rashtrakutas were the patrons of arts and learning. The famous Kailasha temple at Ellora was made during their time. In later years their king, Dhruva, subjugated the Pratiharas and the Gauda kings. Under Givinda III, son and successor of Dhruva, they were the most powerful, and extracted tribute from the Pallavas. Under Amoghavarsha (AD 815-877) they were involved in a struggle with the Chalukyas of Vengi. Simultaneously they were engaged in arresting the southward advance of Bhoja I of Kannauj. Three generations later Indra III defeated the Pratihara king, Mahipala, of Kannauj, taking a temporary possession of his capital city. In 973 the dynasty was overthrown by Taila II, a feudatory who claimed descent from the Chalukyas of Vatapi and founded the line of the Chalukyas of Kalyana or Kalyani. The successors of this line got involved with the Cholas of Tanjore, descendants of king Aditya, who had inflicted a crushing defeat upon the Pallava king Aparajita.

The Cholas rose to power under Rajaraja and his son Rajendra Chola. Around this time Bengal was ruled by the Palas who were overthrown by Vijayasena of Karnataka. He formed the new line of the Senas. This line ruled Western Bengal, after defeating the Gauda king of the Pala line. They also ruled north Bihar, Assam and Orissa. Their king Lakshmanasena who took the throne around 1178, conquered as far as modern Varanasi, including parts of Kalinga. He was a patron of learning; Jaideva, the author of *Gita-Govinda*, was of his court. Around this time the Chola armies had visited as far in the north as the Gangetic plain, while their naval power had asserted in the overseas territories including Sri Lanka and other islands. They also overpowered the Kalyani Chalukyas. Around the beginning of the twelfth century the Chola and the Kalyani Chalukya families had united through marriages and the rule of Deccan was shared by families thus united. Vikramaditya VI, son of a Chalukya king from a Chola wife, was a great patron of art and learning and some important works connected with Hindu law were authored during his time. This king also established a new era in place of the Saka era.

After 1190 the Kalyani Chalukya empire split into three kingdoms, namely, the kingdoms of Devagiri, Warangal and the Dorasamudra; the last mentioned was ruled by the Hoysalas. The Cholas also weakened, and its southern part was taken by the Pandyas while Hoysalas and other neighbours pounced upon the rest of the kingdom. Around this time rose the new empire of Eastern Gangas of Kalinga and Orissa.

Yadvas of Devagiri were patrons of learning. They established a college of astronomy to study the works of Bhaskaraacharya, the renowned astronomer. Works of Hemadri, Bopadeva and Gyaneshvara were composed and compiled during their time. During their peak period they were ruling upto as far north as Maharashtra. But they, as also other small kingdoms which flourished in the south after the fall of the Chalukyas and the Cholas, could not hold out against the Muslim invasions of Alauddin Khilji's general Malik Kafur in 1306-1307. By about 1317 Yadava domination of Maharashtra had come to an end, and with that ended the Hindu rule there, which was not restored till the rise of the Marathas in the seventeenth century. Pandyas, after a brief Muslim rule, became a part of the Vijayanagar empire. Orissa formed a strong kingdom and defeated Muslim invasions, till it finally succumbed in 1568.

The time upto the end of the first millennium AD belonged to the Hindus in so far as the Indian subcontinent is concerned. They were about the most accomplished people in the world; China was possibly the only other country where people of matching capability lived. Otherwise civilizations did grow in other places as well but in terms of continuity, uniformity. homogeneity, the depth of its religion and philosophy, this one was unique. They evolved sound and rational philosophical and religious concepts. Shankracharya and Ramanuja expounded the finer points of Vedanta, the former emphasized the unity of the subcontinental culture, i.e., the Hindu culture, by establishing pilgrimage places, which he enjoined every Hindu to visit, at the four corners of the country: Badrinath in the Himalayas in the north, Puri in Orissa in the east, Rameshwaram in the gulf of Mannar in the south and Dwarka on the Arabian sea in the west. A sound system of governance was evolved and the emphasis in religion as well as politics was on simplicity. The subcontinent saw great kings, some of the greatest in the world, like Ashoka, the Guptas, Harsha, Bhoja; they dedicated their lives to the well-being of their subjects.

People generally stuck to the cast they were born in though the cases of switching the caste professions were not uncommon. Position of women in the upper castes was pretty strong though subordinate to that of men. Well to do Rajput classes practised

Sati, though not on a wide scale, while widow remarriage was forbidden. Some castes practised *Niyoga*. Child marriage was not uncommon. Education for women was restricted, but not very much for those of the well to do classes. Importance of education was emphasized right from the village level, though its advantage was derived mainly by the Brahmin community. Most kingdoms had universities for higher education. Present day Bihar had a number of universities (The word Bihar is derived from Vihara, a conglomerate of universities). Nalanda had 10,000 students during its peak time. Patliputra had been a great centre of education. Valabhi in western India, Bahur in the south (devoted essentially to Vedic studies), Devagiri (for astronomy) in the Deccan, were all great institutions of learning. With time the legal system became strict and punitive. The citizens, however, considered justice as their right.

The period also saw the countries of Central Asia being ruled from India. Afghanistan and the area immediately to the west of it was ruled from India right upto the time of attacks of Mahmud of Ghazni. Indian culture, religion and art found extensive acceptance in the countries of South East Asia. Between the second and fifth centuries AD kingdoms of the Malayan peninsula, Cambodia, Annam (present Viet Nam), and the islands of Java, Sumatra, Borneo and Bali were ruled by Shaiva Hindu kings, initially from the Indian subcontinent, and for the best part of a thousand years Hindu culture was dominant in this region. Cambodia and Champa (Annam) were Hindu, with Sanskrit as the court language, and stayed at their peak till long after Hindus had suffered a decline in this country during the later part of the first millennium AD.

Buddhism was readily accepted in the east, but it was also the prominent religion of the countries to the west till it was violently smothered out by Islam (being essentially pacifist it became an easy prey). There is similarity between Brahmanism and Judaism. Buddhism was a revolt against Brahmanism while Christianity against Judaism. Notice the similarity between Buddhism and Christianity in terms of the essential teachings of the two religions, or the resemblance in the architecture of the Christian chapel and the Buddhist Chaitya hall, or the similarity in the way Jesus as also the Buddha, incline their heads in benediction in the ancient theme paintings of the two religions. Buddha wanted to see to it that he was not deified after his death. He said the pleasure originating from colour and form caused desire, which was the cause of attachment and consequent suffering. He emphasized spartan, simplicity and brotherhood of man, in fact a close bond between all life bearing entities. So did Mohammad.

The period also saw growth of trade. Numerous port towns sprang up along the sea routes Arts and sciences developed. Aryabhatta (fifth century AD) worked out that the earth revolved around the sun and also around its own axis, and on this basis the eclipses were forecasted accurately, and Hindu calendar of 12 months and 30 days was worked out. The division of time into smaller units was evolved. Different eras had their own calendars: Vikarmi of 58 BC, Saka of AD 78, Gupta of AD 320, and Harsha of AD 606. In mathematics the Indians had nine digits and the zero, the decimal system, algebra, positive and the negative numbers and the like, and the quadric and intermediate equations. Atom was the basic unit of matter. Metallurgy brought in production of iron and coinage while there were significant developments in surgery, general medicines and the study of the nervous system of the human body.

The Muslim Factor

Towards the turn of the millennium the subcontinent had been divided into numerous small, mutually inimical states, possessing little defence potential, their revenue barely managing to support their flashy, imperious court life. Their defence set-up. whatever of it they possessed, was old and outdated, almost of the Ashokan model. In contrast the Central Asian hordes had well oiled war machines, superior weapons, and high mobility and motivation, and the Hindus were vulnerable to their determined attacks. Besides, the Hindus in general had not appreciated the content, the mode, the likely effects of the differentiations of the Islamic fundamentals. To them it looked like any other religion, where people worshipped God. This latter aspect, in fact, even pleased them. In Kerala they erected a mosque for the worship of their Muslim brethren.

Arabs attacked Sindh ruled by Dahir, (he ruled a small part of the present day Sindh) in 711 AD under their young and energetic leader Mohammad-Bin-Kasim, and secured a signal victory with the help of the disaffected feudatories and office bearers in the court. Their further advance southwards or eastwards, however, was checked by the Chalukyas of Badami and the Gurjaras of Rajputana. The Arabs were generally mild and their rule brought in good trade between Sindh and Arabia. In 714 Kasim got murdered and within 30 years, Sindh had been cleansed of all Arabs, thanks to the stronghold of the Brahmins in the Hindu ethos. Arabs made rapid progress in Iran where the clergy was not well respected.

The first major predatory ingress into India was by Mahmud of Ghazni, and he beat the hell out of the Indian states in the north-western and northern India. He looted the cities, the temples, desecrated the holy shrines, and during each of his seventeen odd destructive visits he carried enormous amount of loot loaded upon caravans of camels. India was a rich country in comparison to the land of the Middle East or Central Asia. In spite of its philandering rulers of the innumerable minuscule states of that time, it had a competent trade machinery, which had been in place from time immemorial, and generated wealth. Mahmud called the country the "Golden Sparrow", and pounced upon it like the proverbial hawk every time he needed money to finance his ventures in Central Asia. In the first attempt in 1001 he was resisted by Jaipala of the Brahmin Shahiya line from Peshawar, but the latter suffered such a humiliating defeat that he immolated himself. It has to be stated to the credit of the kings of this line that they continued to offer ferocious resistance, sometimes rallying the neighbouring rulers so that foreigners might be thrown out of the country, till in 1021-22 Trilochanpala, in spite of leading an army of some allies, suffered a crushing defeat on the banks of Ramganga river and was assassinated, and with the death of his son Bhima in 1026 the line of the brave Shahiyas, whose respective kings had spilt their blood to defend every inch of their territory, came to an end. But their sacrifice had not been in vain, for Mahmud could not establish a firm enough empire along the sub-continent's northern borders, and the country was left fairly alone for the best part of a century and a half.

Next major incursion was by Shehabuddin or Mohammad of Ghauri in 1186. He captured Lahore which had been under Muslim rulers from time to time after the fall of the Shahiyas. Chauhan Rajputs ruling from Delhi were unhappy about this development and a battle was fought between Prithviraj Chauhan, the king of Delhi, and Ghauri, in the year 1186, in which the latter was defeated. But the Rajputs, in stead of chasing the retreating Muslims to complete their rout, let them go. Ghauri came again in 1193 and defeated Prithviraj; the latter died fighting in the battle. Ghauri left behind a governor, Qutbuddin Aibak, a slave of his, who though originally stationed at Ajmer, took Delhi and eventually became its ruler (1206-10). He was succeeded by Illtutmish, Qutbuddin's slave and son-in-law. The line of the slave kings (1206-88) came to an end after Illtutmish's daughter had been dethroned around 1244 and the kingdom was seized by adventurers from the family and outsiders, with a lot of bloodshed. These kings had little authority outside Delhi and could not create a political state. They were no doubt recognized as the dominant power in areas of the present day Agra, Oudh, some parts of Bihar, Sindh, Gwalior, central India and Rajasthan, but the hold was tenuous and restricted only to receipt of taxes whenever conditions were favourable.

The Khiljis ruled for 33 years, from 1288 to 1321. Alauddin (1295-1317) was their strongest Sultan. He was an uneducated tyrant and secured the throne by assassinating the ruling Sultan, his uncle and benefactor, Jalaluddin. He took Gujarat in 1297 and married the beautiful queen, Kamla Devi, of the ruler, Karan Dev; she became his favourite queen. His trusted general, Malik Kafur, a eunuch and a former slave, annexed for him the most of south India, including the east coast and the Tamil land, right up to Cape Comorin, where in 1310 he built a mosque to mark his victories. He took an enormous amount of wealth from this expedition. In 1303 Alauddin had taken Chittor and demanded that their queen be sent to his harem. The Rajputs defied and died fighting; their women, including the coveted queen, burnt themselves to death. By 1312 his health was fading on account of his excesses and the state was virtually being ruled by Kafur, till in 1321 the Tughlaks captured the throne of Delhi.

DELHI SULTANATES

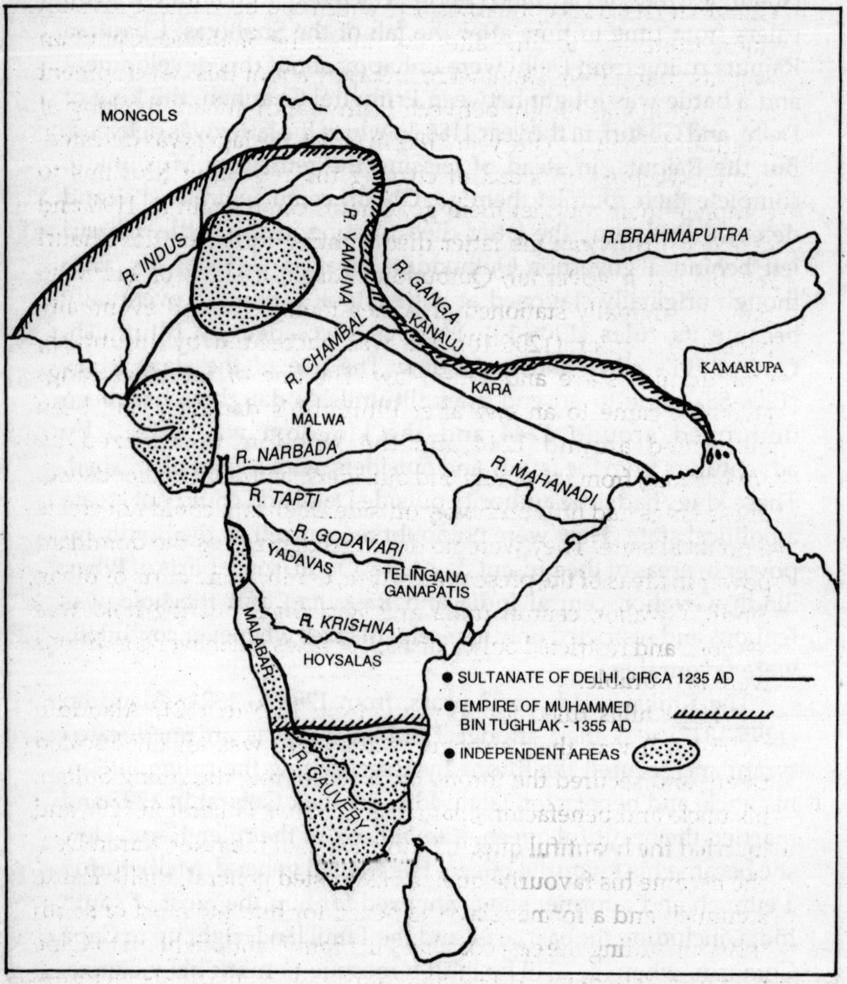

EMPIRE OF MAHMOOD OF GHAZNI

The Tughlaks were on the throne of Delhi from 1321 to 1414. Their noted Sultan was Mohammad-Bin-Tughlak who, like Alauddin, took the throne of Delhi by ingeniously killing his father Ghiyasuddin. He ruled for 26 years, from 1325 to 1351. Being a conceited ruler of a large empire he decided to conquer China. His army perished in the Himalyan foothills itself. He shifted the capital to the southern peninsula in order to be away from the destabilizing menace of the Mongols from the north-west, but nearly lost his kingdom, since this had badly exposed Delhi to the Mongol incursions, and moved back, causing enormous suffering and hardship to his subjects. His reign was marred by famines, sickness, and general maladministration. There were large scale revolts, and running between places to put out these fires he died at Tattah, Sindh, on 20 March 1351. His successor, Ferozeshah (1351-88) though a mild king, was a religious bigot, and in order to please his nobles, persecuted Hindus. Not that the Hindus were spared by the earlier Sultans. Almost all of them had imposed the hated Jizya tax, while Muslim officials plundered the Hindu traders at will, but during the time of this Sultan the persecution attained new levels. This resulted in large-scale dissatisfaction amongst the Hindus, the majority population, and that triggered the downward slide of the rule. Amir Timur (Tamerlane) attacked during the reign of the last Tughlak, Mahmud, in December 1398 and struck such a deadly blow that it caused the demise of this line. After Mahmud the state was taken over by the governor left behind by Timur. Timur was a terrible killer (in Mongolian style he left pyramids of the skulls of people he killed in battle), and a destroyer, and plundered. He took hordes of wealth and numerous artisans to develop Samarkand, his capital city. The rule of the Delhi Sultan had shrunk now to the outskirts of the town. The governors left behind by Timur found it difficult to rule, and fled, leaving the field to the Lodhis (1450-1526). The last of this line was defeated by Babar, attacking from Kabul in 1526, in the first battle of Panipat.

By the time of Babar's invasion, Hindus of India were like a people who might have turned in on themselves. Their caste system had divided the society into irreconcileable units working in mutually compromising directions, with little intergroup interaction, and their fundamentalist traditions had deprived it of

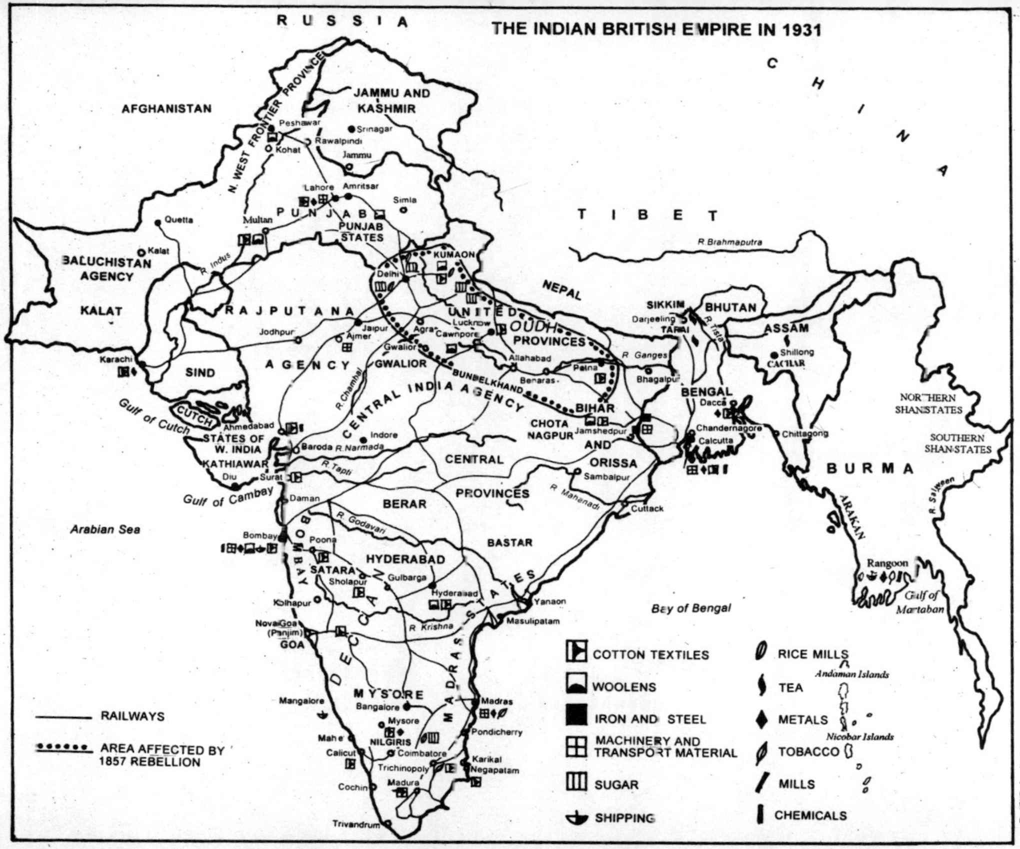
THE INDIAN BRITISH EMPIRE IN 1931
RUSSIA
CHINA
AFGHANISTAN
JAMMU AND KASHMIR
N. WEST FRONTIER PROVINCE
Peshawar
Srinagar
Kohat
Rawalpindi
Jammu
Lahore
Amritsar
Simla
PUNJAB
PUNJAB STATES
Multan
Quetta
Kalat
BALUCHISTAN AGENCY
KALAT
R. Indus
TIBET
R. Brahmaputra
NEPAL
KUMAON
Delhi
RAJPUTANA
UNITED PROVINCES
OUDH
Jodhpur
Jaipur
Ajmer
Agra
Lucknow
Cawnpore
Gwalior
GWALIOR
AGENCY
Karachi
SIND
Allahabad
Benaras
BUNDELKHAND
CENTRAL INDIA AGENCY
R. Chambal
Patna
BIHAR
R. Ganges
Bhagalpur
SIKKIM
Darjeeling
TARAI
BHUTAN
R. Tista
ASSAM
Shillong
CACHAR
BENGAL
Dacca
Chandernagore
Calcutta
Chittagong
NORTHERN SHAN STATES
SOUTHERN SHAN STATES
BURMA
ARAKAN
R. Salween
Rangoon
Gulf of Martaban
CUTCH
Gulf of Cutch
Ahmedabad
STATES OF W. INDIA
KATHIAWAR
Diu
Surat
Gulf of Cambay
Baroda
R. Narmada
Indore
CHOTA NAGPUR
Jamshedpur
AND
ORISSA
CENTRAL
PROVINCES
Sambalpur
R. Mahanadi
Cuttack
R. Tapti
Daman
BERAR
R. Godavari
Arabian Sea
Bombay
Poona
BOMBAY
HYDERABAD
BASTAR
SATARA
Sholapur
Gulbarga
Hyderabad
STATES
Yanaon
Masulipatam
Bay of Bengal
Kolhapur
Nova Goa (Panjim)
GOA
R. Krishna
DECCAN
MADRAS
MYSORE
Mangalore
Bangalore
Mysore
Madras
Mahe
NILGIRIS
Pondicherry
Calicut
Coimbatore
Karikal
Negapatam
Trichinopoly
Cochin
Madura
Trivandrum
RAILWAYS
AREA AFFECTED BY 1857 REBELLION
COTTON TEXTILES
WOOLENS
IRON AND STEEL
MACHINERY AND TRANSPORT MATERIAL
SUGAR
SHIPPING
RICE MILLS
TEA
METALS
TOBACCO
MILLS
CHEMICALS
Andaman Islands
Nicobar Islands

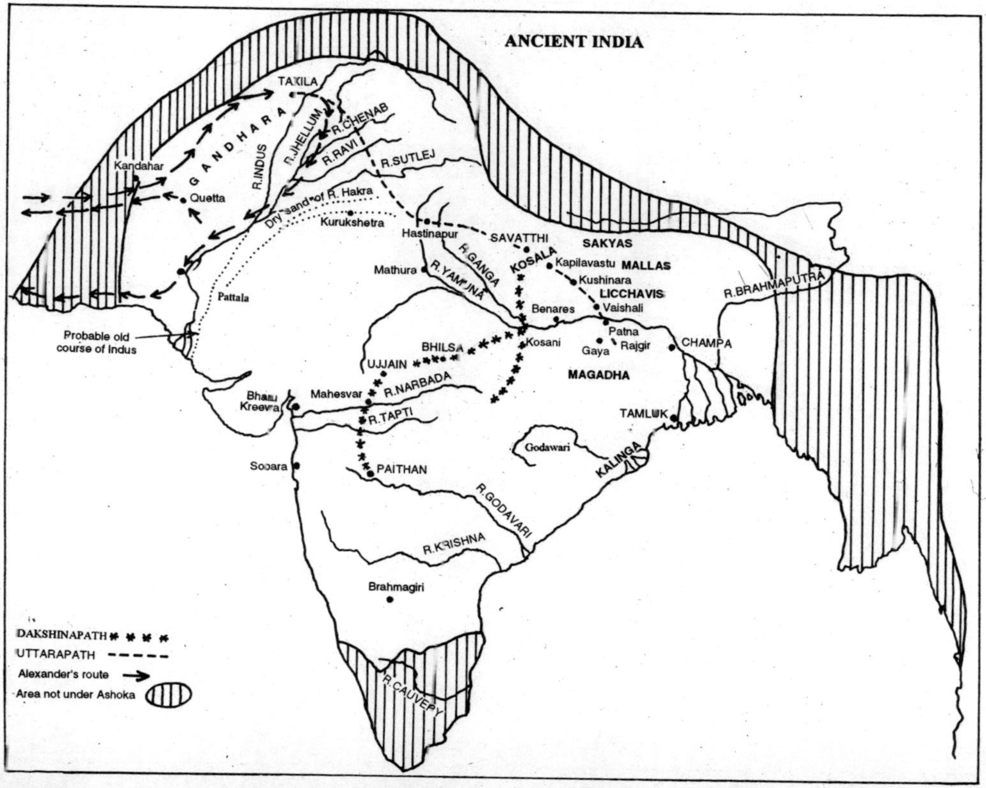
ANCIENT INDIA
TAXILA
GANDHARA
Kandahar
Quetta
R.INDUS
R.JHELLUM
R.CHENAB
R.RAVI
R.SUTLEJ
Dry sand of R. Hakra
Kurukshetra
Hastinapur
SAVATTHI
SAKYAS
KOSALA
Kapilavastu
MALLAS
Kushinara
LICCHAVIS
Vaishali
Mathura
R.YAMUNA
R.GANGA
Benares
Patna
Rajgir
Gaya
Kosani
CHAMPA
MAGADHA
R.BRAHMAPUTRA
Pattala
Probable old course of Indus
BHILSA
UJJAIN
R.NARBADA
Mahesvar
Kreeva
R.TAPTI
TAMLUK
Godawari
KALINGA
PAITHAN
R.GODAVARI
R.KRISHNA
Brahmagiri
R.CAUVERY
DAKSHINAPATH
UTTARAPATH
Alexander's route
Area not under Ashoka

dynamism. It had turned traditionalist and obscurantist and emphasized status quo. It was essentially a pacifist agrarian society, self-contained for its needs at the level of the village, lacking in mobility and dynamism and in the capability to comprehend changes, innovations, inventions or functioning of technical equipment, or to organize complex systems or mechanisms. They meekly took on the humiliations and attrocities piled upon them by their rulers. The society was just not sufficiently united to be able to organize united resistance. This, however, isn't to suggest that they had totally lost the sanguine touch. Far from it, in fact whenever the opportunity afforded they did not hesitate to strike. They had time and again driven the Delhi Sultanates to the gates of Delhi. But the fact that even the Afghanis, who had been ruled from the Indian soil ever since the inception of history, managed to make kingdoms and ride them rough shod, did not show them in good light.

The successive Sultans had parceled out the land into *jagirs* of large holdings and awarded them, including the people living thereon, to their favoured nobles. The latter generally plundered their subjects with impunity. Babar took Punjab in 1524 and was joined by Allauddin Lodi, Ibrahim Lodi's brother. Delhi Sultanate had at this stage extended its hold eastwards, over the Gangetic basin, including a tenuous hold over Bihar, but excluding Bengal which, being the farthest from Delhi, had declared itself independent. Sindh, Gujarat and Malwa were also under the Muslim rule. The Bahmani kingdom in the Deccan had split into five warring sultanates of Ahmadnagar, Bijapur, Bidar, Barar and Golconda. The founders of these states had been mere adventurers.

As for the Hindu states, these included Orissa and Gondwana, the confederacy of the Rajput states of the present day Rajasthan, the powerful state of Vijayanagar south of the Bahmani states, covering the peninsula almost right up to Sri Lanka, Assam, including Kamarupa and Nepal.

Babar defeated Ibrahim Lodi in the first battle of Panipat in 1526 and established the Moghul rule in India. His son almost lost the territory to Shershah Suri. The kingdom was consolidated by Akbar, Babar's grandson who, though went about his conquests ruthlessly, erecting pyramids of human skulls outside the cities he had ravaged and conquered, realized early in his career that to hold his kingdom, the friendship of the Hindu population was necessary. He defeated Hemu, a competent Hindu general of Shah Adil Sur, in the second battle of Panipat in 1556, immediately on taking over the reins of the kingdom. It is significant that at this time, while the Muslims were extensively using gun powder fired weapons against their enemies, the Hindu kingdoms were still organized on ancient models and fighting with outmoded swords and bows and arrows. No wonder they never could withstand the heat of the attacks of the invaders from Central Asia, or even Afghanistan. Akbar's queen, a princess from the Rajput house of Jaipur, gave birth to Jahangir, his successor. Rajputs held positions of pre-eminence in Akbar's court. Akbar's policies were directed at securing the cooperation and the involvement of the Hindus in running the affairs of the state. He introduced a new religious cult which contained good points of all religions, and adopted it; he called it Deen-i-Ilahi. A fundamentalist kind of religion was not important to him. His interest was essentially to hold his kingdom, which he felt he could best do by giving his subjects a competent and just government. He encouraged talent and promoted trade, and organized an efficient revenue system under Todar Mal, the best brain in this field at that time. Like Vikramaditya, he also had nine jewels in his court who worked for the betterment in every field of the government. Though he was almost an illiterate, he supported unrestricted education. His state developed an industrial output which was very comparable to that of Great Britain of that time, and much higher than that of the U.S.A. His Moghul empire was known throughout the civilized world for its prosperity and grandeur. Whatever period the Moghuls lasted for on the throne of Delhi, it was because of the sound foundations that Akbar had laid. He has been called Akbar the Great.

Akbar's policy of cultivating friendly relationship with the people of the majority community, however, got eroded, though gradually, during the reigns of Moghul emperors who followed him. Under the influence of the Mullahs his son, Jahangir (1605-1627), had twice revolted against him, though being the son of a Hindu mother the hold of the Mullahs was not that enduring. But

Jahangir did imprison his son Khusrau for his pro Hindu leanings; the prince died in captivity in 1621. Besides he restored Islam as the religion of the kingdom. By the time of Shah Jahan (1627-1658) the hold of the Mullahs had become stronger, and the Muslims were predominant in all departments of the government, including the army. Mostly only the non-governmental professions were open to the Hindus. Persecution of the Hindus took alarming proportions during the reign of Aurangzeb Alamgir (1658-1707), and this led to large scale revolts and resistance, leading to the folding up of the Moghul empire to the gates of Delhi in a matter of fifty odd years. During the peak period Aurangzeb had the whole of the subcontinent except the Tamil and the Kerala lands in the south. But during the latter part of his rule a number of centres of resistance had arisen, the notable ones being the Marathas in the Deccan, the Rajputs in Rajasthan and the Sikhs in the Punjab. Besides, European trading nations who had been striving to secure the rich resources of India, had also secured a significant presence, and these together with the other rebellious groups caused the downfall of the empire.

The Rise of the Marathas

In 1646 Shivaji started with the capture of the fortress of Torna around Pune, and from then on he was on an expansion mode, and by 1678 when he died he was a ruler of a formidable Maratha state. The same year Raja Jaswant Singh died while guarding the north-western frontiers of the Moghul empire, and Aurangzeb offered to recognize his infant son as the successor only if he converted to Islam. The Rajputs (Rathors) refused and joined the Maratha camp. Sambhaji, Shivaji's son, was a competent successor though somewhat lax in personal discipline. He was caught by the Muslims while he was hunting near Kolhapur and was sent to Aurangzeb who promptly had him beheaded. He was succeeded by Sahu, his infant son, under the regency of Raja Ram, who maintained the pressure on the imperial forces through the guerrilla warfare. Aurangzeb died at Ahmadabad in 1707 at the age of 89. During his last days he was a harried person, running between places to stem the tide of the rebellions against him, with his treasury nearly empty on account of the need for constant fighting.

Often his troops had to be put on frugal rations and spartan discipline to which the Muslim element was not favourably disposed since, being the rulers, they were used to comfortable living. Being suspicious of his sons he never permitted any of them near his bed even when he was dying.

The Peshwa (prime minister) of Raja Sahu did a good job of the governance. But his successors usurped the power of Raja Sahu and put the royal family in Satara, virtually in retirement. By 1733 the Maratha army was controlled by three prominent families, being of Udaji Pawar of the area around Pune, Malhar Holkar of Indore and Ranaji Sindhia of Gwalior. Nadir Shah the Iranian potentate, sacked Delhi in 1739-40, and considerably weakened the Moghul rule. In 1748 Ahmad Khan Abdali or Durrani, an officer of Nadir Shah who had established himself as an independent ruler of Afghanistan after Nadir Shah had been assassinated, attacked the north-western frontier, but was defeated by the Imperial troops. He came again in 1750 and took Punjab. In 1756 Abdali sacked Delhi, he had assumed the title of Ahmad Shah Abdali after the capture of Punjab. The Moghuls could regain their throne at Delhi only with Maratha help. During 1758, Raghoba, the Maratha leader, took Punjab from Abdali. The Marathas now visualized themselves as the rulers of Delhi, notwithstanding the fact that though they were the masters on the subcontinent in the craft of irregular warfare, they had little wherewithal for regular set-piece fighting.

In 1759 the Moghul king Alamgir II got murdered in a palace coup, and in 1760 Sadashiv Bhao, commander of the Peshwa army in the north, took Delhi. This elicited immediate reaction from the Rohillas who wanted Delhi for themselves albeit under Abdali, for they considered Delhi to be a preserve of the Muslims. On 6 January 1761 the two armies faced each other for the third battle of Panipat.

At this battlefield the Marathas suffered the same disadvantages as their adversaries had suffered fighting them in the Deccan peninsula: a long command and supply line controlled the battle; for Marathas the controlling centre was Pune. This led to the development of a poor infrastructure for the battle. The administration had broken down even before the start of the

Bhao's commanders had told him they had long gone past the peak performance capability, that with each day their fighting potential was being adversely affected. Most of all the Marathas were not sufficiently versed in the technique of launching large-scale combined infantry-cavalry attacks duly supported by guns, nor were they good enough in the defence against them.

Marathas fought hard, and almost carried the day when, towards the evening, a fiery attack by 13,000 fresh troops of Abdali turned the battle in his favour; the Marathas had no reserves at this stage. Both sides lost heavily in men and materials, and the Marathas had to withdraw to the line of the Narmada for reorganization. Abdali, weakened and his dream to rule from Delhi shattered, was harried all along the communications line and was forced to withdraw to Afghanistan; in subsequent years he made a few inconsequential forays in the north west and was forgotten. Rohillas ceased to be a force of any reckoning. Marathas failed to establish a Hindu kingdom at Delhi, and Peshwa Balaji Rao died of grief when he learnt of the debacle, and the Marathas split into a confederacy of four power centres, being Gackwad at Gujrat, Bhonsley at Nagpur, Holkar at Indore and Sindhia at Gwalior, all operating under the Peshwa at Pune. In the early nineteenth century they were the major force to challenge the spread of the British, and could have been eminently effective had they been united.

The British Ascendancy

A serious menace was, in the meantime looming over the sub-continent's eastern horizon. In 1757, the British commander, Robert Clive, had defeated Siraj-ud-Daula, the Nawab of Bengal, by bribing his wazir, Mir Jafar, and taken an effective control over Bengal, Orissa and Bihar. This was the time when Portugal, France and the Great Britain were engaged in a struggle to capture the trade and trade routes to the east, and with this end in view had established sea fortresses along the seaways, including the Indian east and west coasts. In 1600 the British East India Company was established and the British had arrived in India with Sir Thomas Roe presenting himself in the court of Jahangir in 1615 as ambassador of King James I. Around 1639, the British had established the Madras outpost on the Bay of Bengal, in 1662 they got the island of Bombay from the Portuguese as dowry to King Charles II and in 1690 they acquired land in Hooghly, Bengal. By the end of the eighteenth century they had defeated the French and the latter had left with only the small enclave of Pondicherry. They had also overpowered the Portuguese and had confined them to their bases of Goa, Daman and Diu. By 1768 the British had taken the Northern Sarkars from the Nizam and in 1775 they seized Benares and Ghazipur from Oudh. Tipu Sultan of Mysore was defeated in 1799, this gave them a continuous block of Indian territory from Malabar to Coromandal. The Moghuls had ceased to be a power of any reckoning after the assassination of their king Alamgir II. Marathas were the only force who could prevent the British from taking the whole of India.

The European mastery of the sea was brought about by their galley type sea ships which originally started with extensive fishing operations, but later got fitted with arms to commit piracy and plunder on sea and land. Being big, these ships carried men and materials to far off lands to engage in warfare. This was how the British came, through the sea routes, and established themselves. The guns on the ships attacked from a direction which had been least prepared for defence. The mastery of the sea routes gave them the unhindered capability to switch forces between the coast-line around Madras, Bombay and Calcutta.

After its capture, Bengal was extensively looted and plundered by the East India Company, and with this loot arriving in Great Britain, started their Industrial Revolution of the seventies of the eighteenth century, bringing to them an era of great properity. To find unhindered sale of their cloth and steel manufactured in the mills at Manchester and Birmingham, the Indian artisan, and the trader was smothered out of existence. This was done ruthlessly; there were instances when Indian craftsmen were even amputated. Bereft of the means of livelihood, people died of hunger and disease by the thousands. They did not possess the means to procure even the bare minimum farm inputs. The crops failed and there were famines, compounding the already tragic situation.

This slide to grinding poverty had its roots in the fundamentalistic policies of the fanatic Muslim king Aurangzeb, and the pathetic passivity shown by the Hindus in taking it lying down. Little wonder that Lord Bentinck (the British Governor-General in India) wrote in his 1834 report (as quoted by Nehru): "The misery hardly finds a parallel in the history of commerce. The bones of the cotton weavers are bleaching the plains of India."

Paul Kennedy in his book *The Rise and Fall of Great Powers* has quoted Ashton's observation made as late as 1947, the year India secured its freedom:

> There are today on the plains of India and China men and women, plague-ridden and hungry, living lives little better, to outward appearance, than those of the cattle that toil with them by day and share their places of sleep by night. Such Asiatic standards and such unmechanised horrors, are the lot of those who increase their number without passing through an industrial revolution.

That is what happened to the Hindus of India, for their passivity, for their failure to keep abreast of the political, economic, military, or scientific, developments in other parts of the world, and to stay vigilant and resist unitedly any external or internal threat. Bengal saw a major famine in 1770, thirteen years after the take over by the Company, and it is believed that a third of the population of this fertile and densely populated region perished. The Indian traders class under the kings and their henchmen had little political force. India, thus had no middle class, the class of thinking elites who were spearheading the industrial revolution in the west. Nevertheless, the Indian trader was, within the limitations of the period he was operating in, a competent performer and had a respectable share in the overall world trade transactions. According to the figures of Paul Kennedy, in 1750 the Indian share of the total world manufacturing output was 24.9 per cent as against 1.9 of the U.K. and 23.6 of the whole of Europe. At the beginning of the Industrial Revolution, India was one of the leaders in trade, commerce and industry, but in a matter of merely 150 years it sank to the abysmal depths of near total deprivation, essentially because its industry never managed to make it to the level of an Industrial Revolution, because the society emphasized only on the state of 'no change' because of lack of modern outlook and education. The surprising part is that the Hindus sought the help of the British military strength from time to time, but never made an effort to develop the know-how for the development of superior weapons of destruction indigenously.

Peshwa Madhava Rao died in 1772, setting off a war for supremacy amongst the Maratha chiefs; the two contenders were Raghoba and Nana Pharnavis. The British stoked the fire of discord amongst the Marathas, and this led to the first Maratha war between them and the Marathas, which brought little gain to either side. There were a few other engagements but they came to nothing. In late 1780 an alliance of the Maratha chiefs and Haider Ali resolved to throw the British out of India, but this also made little headway.

Lord Wellesley took over in 1798 and with that started the era of extensive acquisitions. The declared policy of the Company now was to offer a ruler to become its subsidiary when he felt he was not in a position to hold his own against his real or perceived enemies, internal or external, in exchange for a guarantee of protection of his rule. He was required to maintain a force of specified strength of Indian or British troops under the command of the British officers, and to meet the expenses thereof he had to cede territory, or pay from his revenues.

In 1799 Wellesley swiftly defeated Tipu and then embarked upon the Second Maratha War in 1803-05. The British forces were commanded by General Wellesley, Governor General's younger brother and later Duke of Wellington. Marathas were defeated and had to sue for peace and cede Upper Doab, Rajputana, Broach, Ahmadnagar and south-west Deccan. The subsidiary annexations brought Surat and most of the southern peninsula. In course of time under the subsidiary system British suzerainty was recognized by nearly all the major Indian rulers. In 1803 even the Moghul emperor at Delhi accepted the British protection. This is the stage when the British war machine was at its peak efficiency. The outbreak of war between Britain and France in 1744, had brought the war for the Caribbean trade and the war for Silesia together into a single global conflict that extended from North America to India. The struggle which intermittently lasted till 1815, eventually became a conflict for supremacy between Great Britain and France, and all the kings and rulers in these lands, including Indian, fought as dependent and subsidized allies of these two powers.

Though the British were not the absolute winners they came out better than France in this global conflict.

The British restored Gwalior to Sindhia under a new treaty in 1805 after the departure of Wellesley and that put an end to their conflict. During his term Wellesley introduced some educational innovations, like opening a college at Fort Williams for the training of the new arrivals from England, and to acquaint the prominent Indians with the British culture and civilization. There were some administrative reforms as well, particularly in the legal system.

Wellesley's annexations had created unrest amongst the Indians, and the Company decided it was time for restraint, since its main concern in India was with trade and commerce and not with empire building. The Marathas, however, were not giving in easily. Between 1812-17 they again organized to fight the British, and had mustered the support of the Pathans and freebooters called the Pindaris. Early in 1817 the Governor-General, Warren Hastings, assembled a 1,20,000 strong army, the strongest in those times, and set out to finally finish the Maratha presence. Though the Marathas had the will and determination, and they were incensed at the humiliations suffered by them at their earlier defeats, they were neither sufficiently united, nor working for a common goal, nor did they possess the financial resources or weaponry or the organization, to wage a first grade war. At heart each one of the chiefs was working to enhance his own interests. In fact so poor was the Maratha showing in battle that a contingent of 27,000 men of the Peshwa were defeated at Khirki, near Pune, by a small British garrison of 2,800 men. By the end of the year the Maratha power was finished, and their empire, founded by Shivaji in 1669 had ceased to exist. In the first few days of the year 1800 the Peshwa had been dethroned and the Raja of Satara recognized as the true monarch. He was of Shivaji's line; the power had been usurped by the Peshwas from Shivaji's grandson Raja Sahu in 1708.

The Sikhs also showed their belligerence to the expansion of the British influence towards the Punjab. The first Sikh war was fought during 1845-46 which was lost by the Sikhs and the British troops entered Lahore on February 20, 1846. The second Sikh war was fought during 1848-49. This too was lost by the Sikhs, although

MUGHAL EMPIRE UNDER AKBAR AND IN 1700

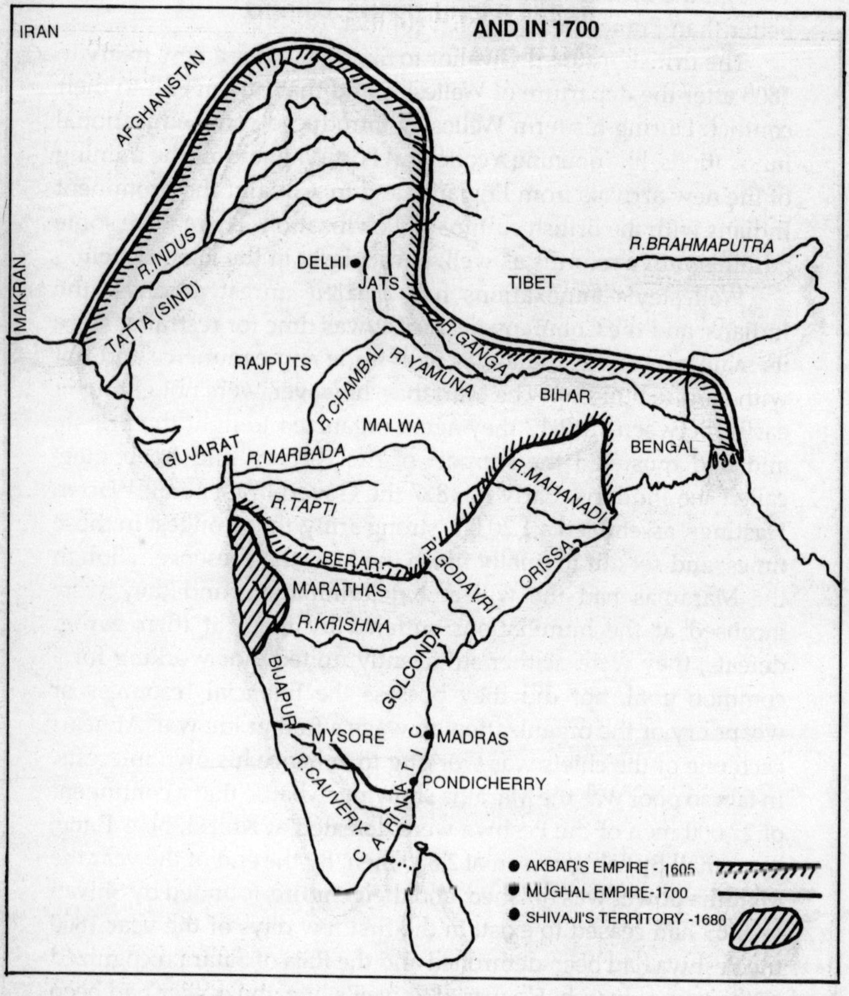

BRITISH CONQUEST BY 1805

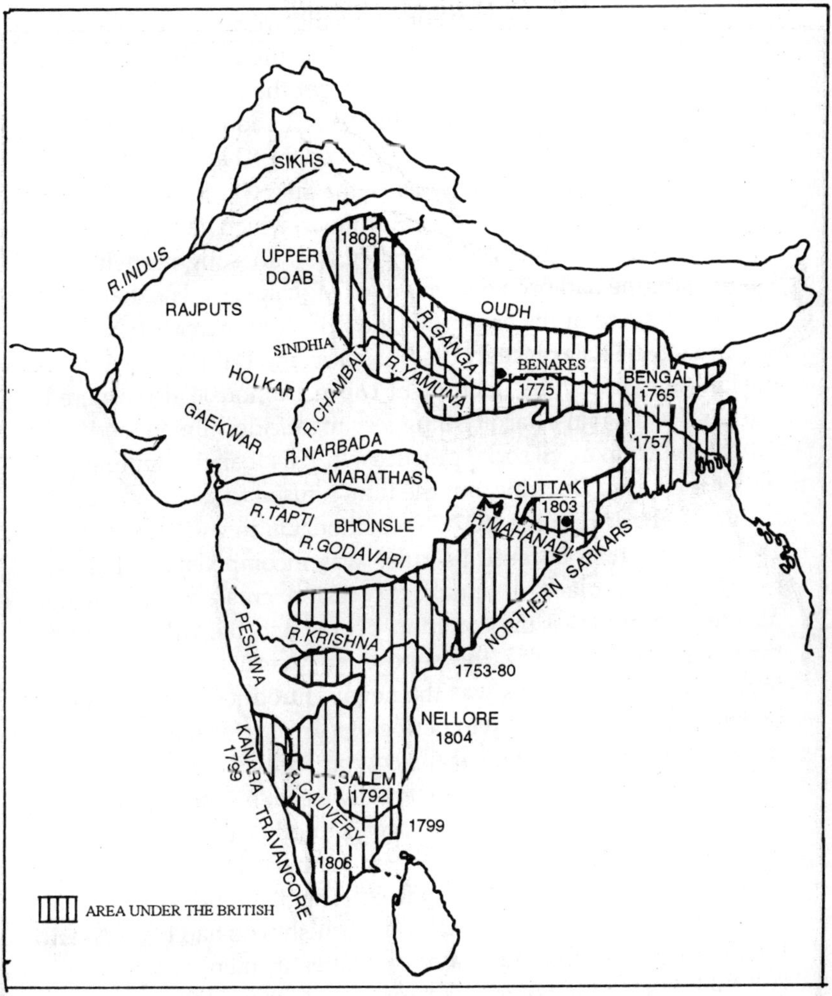

they gave a brave fight at Chillianwala on the bank of river Jhelum. The Sikh weaponry, organization and skills were no match to that of the British. The Sikhs, in fact, were a fractured community with any number of factions, each trying to get the better of the other with the view to capturing the throne of Lahore. On March 12, 1848 Dalhousie annexed Punjab, disbanded the Khalsa army, placed severe restrictions on the activities of the Sikh war lords, and took away the priceless diamond, the Kohinoor, which had been given to Ranjit Singh by Shah Shuja when he had sought shelter at Lahore after he had been driven out of Afghanistan. The diamond now adorns one of the crowns of the British monarch's family.

In 1848 the Raja of Satara died issueless and Dalhousie annexed the kingdom under the Doctrine of Lapse. Dalhousie also ordered a general war against dacoity, thuggee, infanticide, human sacrifice, sati, and such like evil social practices. In 1854 Jhansi was annexed under the Lapse Doctrine, but the Rani refused to relent and gave a tough fight during the 1857-58 rebellion. Oudh was annexed on 13 February 1856 because its ruler was incompetent. All these events taking place in quick succession created large-scale disaffection amongst the common people and the rulers of that time. On 10 May, 1857 the sepoys at Meerut mutinied. The immediate cause for this was the newly introduced ammunition which carried a preservative coating of a greasy substance, which, the rumour had it, contained the cow as well as the pig fat. The talk was that this had been deliberately done to defile the Indian religions. The rebellion rapidly spread to other military centres, including Delhi, Lucknow, Kanpur (under Nana Pharnavis), Allahabad, and the intervening areas. The Sikh and the Gurkha troops generally saved the day for the British who had been taken by surprise and suffered heavy casualties in men, women and children. In Delhi the rebels had appointed the non-effective king Bahadur Shah as their leader, promising him an unfettered rule after the British had been thrown out of the country. The rebels shared a view that only a small force of the British were in control of the whole country, that this was possible only because a large section of the Indian polity was working to protect and project the British interests, that there was general disunity amongst the Indians with different factions vying for personal gains, howsoever petty, and that the British success was due to their policy of 'divide and rule'. By mid June 1858 the rebels had been defeated at all points. The Rani of Jhansi who took a stand to safeguard the interests of her adopted son, and fought the British at Gwalior, died fighting, but not before offering a stubborn resistance and there had been much bloodshed.

On 2 August 1858, by an act of the British Parliament, India ceased to be under the control of the Company and became a territory of the British Crown.

The Indian Independence

The great Indian revolt was quashed, but it brought to the fore the spirit of nationhood, the need to rise above the local, parochial interests and work as one nation. Indian National Congress was formed in 1885 in Bombay, with the blessings of the Government, and though it started as a tame annual gathering of affluent public men, it soon was spearheading a movement to eventually secure full freedom from the British rule. In 1905 it launched an agitation against the partition of Bengal on communal lines. It succeeded, but the British did everything in their bag of tricks to tell the Muslims and the Hindus that they were two irreconcilable groups. Although the Congress party kept emphasizing all along that it was working for the interests of all faiths and classes, in 1947, at the time of Independence, the country was partitioned into two on communal basis.

In retrospect, the Hindu civilization, their religion and culture, is a synthesis of three distinct streams, viz., the Australoid, Dravidian and the Aryan. The interaction between the Australoid and the Dravidian streams in the fourth millennium BC caused the flowering of the Indus culture which embraced the whole of the north-western subcontinent. If it did not travel further south of its southern limit or further east of its eastern limit, this was because it was the age of the bronze and copper tools and implements, and development of farming land and large-scale communications and means of travel was possible only upto a limited extent. It was essentially an agrarian culture, but in its final stages it had turned urban, bringing about an era of extensive trade and commerce and prosperity. The philosophy of the culture was essentially pacifist. It believed in respect for all life and was totally opposed to destruction of any kind. Some of its sections possibly believed that even matter had life, but that it was indestructable. Its atoms in different combinations brought about the manifest world. Both Jain and Buddhist religions were based on the essential thoughts of this culture.

The Sanskrit speaking Aryans arrived towards the end of the third millennium BC. They had a script. The hymns of the Rig Veda were already in composition. They arrived from far off lands, after a wandering of centuries. Their horizons were bigger, and not before long they were talking in terms of the subcontinent being one country under one ruler. Although the Iron Age had not yet set in India, these industrious people cleared the lands in the Gangetic basin and in the country to the south of the Vindhyas, and expanded both eastwards and southwards. This movement had also been effected by the pre-Aryans who had been on the move over a long period, partially in search of fresh areas for food gathering and cultivation, and partially to escape from the insecurity brought about by the ingressing tribes from the north-west. Around the beginning of the second millennium BC Aryans possibly had gone as far south as the Vindhyas and Satpuras. Their king Rama conquered Lanka, the island south of the southern tip of the subcontinent. Even if some details of the Rama story might be mythical, the concept of one whole India had very much been kindled in the Aryan mind. The philosophy of the Aryans was not pacifist, to say the least. They believed in hard conquest; their god Indra wreaked thunderbolts from the heavens against their foes. Theirs was a religion of sacrifice which had taken its final form in the early Vedic period coming up to around 1000 BC. During the later Vedic period (1000-600 BC) the Aryans had started to mellow under the influence of the earlier cultures. With the onset of the Upanishadic period the mellowing process had perhaps been completed. The animal sacrifice was replaced by offerings of grains and flowers.

The pacifist Australo-Dravidian stream, however, had not dried up under the pressures of the Aryan presence. It was only dormant, and surfaced around the seventh century BC, giving rise to Buddhism and Jainism. During the third century BC, Ashoka established a rule which covered the whole of the subcontinent and Afghanistan and some parts of Central Asia. But he wrote off his empire after he had accepted the pacifist doctrines of Buddhism, although it has to be said that running such a vast empire during that period of difficult communications was no easy task either. It is a possibility though that Ashoka supported Buddhism more under the pressure from the majority of his subjects who were from the Australo-Dravidian stock than out of his own preference, for Brahmanism which was well entrenched during his time and was the essential instrument in running the affairs of his state. His empire survived barely 59 odd years after him.

Next the subcontinent, or the most of it, came under one rule was during the fourth and the fifth centuries AD, under the Guptas. Although these rulers were indulgent towards Buddhism (no ruler could afford to be otherwise when a majority of the subjects followed a particular set of ideas), they were adherents of Brahmanism and held their borders firmly, and lasted for over a century and a half. In Brahmanism India is one country, and it is there for the well-being of its people, and that right of the people has to be safeguarded at all costs. The Mauryas were broken by the Kushans and the Scythians invading from the north-west, while the Guptas were engaged in a struggle unto death with the Huns from Central Asia. They destroyed the Huns; it is another story that in the process they got destroyed themselves. Under them the subcontinent saw its best days: peace, prosperity, general well-being, flourishing arts and crafts, and trade and commerce. Possibly the subcontinent never again saw such glorious times.

The ruler of the last of the great Hindu empires was Harsha Vardhana. He was a great king, but he too leaned towards passivity and accepted Buddhism towards the concluding days of his rule. The empire did not last even for a day after his death.

This contest between passivity and aggressive dynamism has been a constant factor on the Hindu historical scene. The majority have reposed faith in truth and non-violence, and have been at the receiving end for most of the time of the Indian history. Arabs took a portion of Sindh in 711 AD, but were thrown out within 30 years of their arrival. But Mahmud of Ghazni, first attacking in 1001, made the first dent in the defence organization of the Hindus.

Muhammad of Ghauri further weakened the borders during his attacks during 1176-93. Had the northern Hindu rulers evolved some system to take on such like raids unitedly, the history of the subcontinent would have been different. After Ghauri the Hindus had virtually lost the control of their north-western borders. The invaders came at will, and the Hindus caved in and cowered before the ruthlessness of their attacks, and displayed little capability to raise the wherewithal to organize an appropriate defence.

During the second millennium Alauddin sent his general Malik Kafur on the conquest of southern India, and for a while ruled the most part of the subcontinent, but it hardly amounted to much, for the expedition was more in the nature of series of raids for plunder than an attempt to found a viable empire. Next came Aurangzeb, but did not quite make it because of the severe opposition of his Hindu subjects; even some of his Muslim feudatories went against him. The British did unite the subcontinent under one rule but they ruined the achievement by dividing it into three countries. Today there are a large number of people who believe in the subcontinent being a single unit, as it was during the Maurya and the Gupta rules.

With the arrival of the Europeans came their more lethal weapons, their superior battle field organizations, and the naval warfare. The Marathas had a formidable presence but little else to take on the new challenges. British presence destabilized the subcontinent, and the constant preoccupation of the Indian rulers to safeguard the boundaries of their states, led to raising larger armies, and emptied the treasuries. The developmental and the welfare works got neglected as also the agriculture and industry, and the country fell into poverty, and to survive the common man opted for crime. Cities and towns languished for want of trade and commerce. In the villages an average person had little else to do than get over occupied with tradition and religion. The outlook became narrower, and since education brought no distinct financial advantage, it got neglected. Customs like sati, infanticide, child marriage, *devadasis*, came into vogue. The society was emasculated. The people who claimed connection to one of the oldest civilizations, whose richness and prosperity had attracted migrants and invaders throughout the course of history, became the poorest in the world; the British, under pressure from their industrial revolution, and the need to finance their wars and industries, sucked away everything that had any value and left this land completely wasted. The intellectual inertia, a lack of scientific temper amongst the Hindus during almost the whole of the second millennium, caused all this.

And then the British masters poured ridicule. This is what Major General Sir George Younghusband had to say:

> It is never wise to stand studied impertinence, or even the semblance of it, from any Oriental. Politeness, and courtesy, by all means, and even camaraderie, as long as these are reciprocated, and all is fair and square, and above board. But the moment there is sign of revolt, mutiny, or treachery, of which the symptoms not unusually are a swollen head, and a tendency to inactivity, it is wise to hit the Oriental straight between the eyes, and to keep on hitting him thus, till he appreciates exactly what he is, and who he is.

Despite all this the Hindus have held on to their religion and culture tenaciously. The conversions into other faiths have been few and those too got effected under extreme pressures of the state. Even today a few cases take place on account of caste differentiations, and possibly this will go on till the imbalance between the different layers of the society are evened out. Hindus did not accept conversions into their faith, but they have changed the stance, and some conversions have been registered. The process can gather speed if the caste and the *Varna* distinctions are done away with.

The Indians have been free for more than fifty years now, and in this time their numbers have simply exploded. Eighty-five per cent of the Indian population is Hindu, eleven Muslim, while the remaining are people from miscellaneous faiths, including Christianity. The Indians today are at the threshold of the Industrial Revolution, 225 years behind Great Britain. It is a peculiarity of the onset of affluence that the populations register a rise, with the fruits of the scientific developments getting available to the common man, when his intellectual faculties have not kept pace with the advancements, and he is still bound by the past customs and beliefs. The situation gets remedied once the level of education improves and he acquires the comprehension to assess his gains and losses and plan his future. Today this factor is responsible for the endemic poverty amongst some sections of the Hindu society.

Hindus have been, and still are, a very tolerant people. Ever since the independence there has been a lot of sabre rattling from the people of neighbouring Muslim countries. The rallying point is their resentment at the loss of Muslim rule in India. They believe Hindus caused it, even though a majority of them are converts from the erstwhile lower classes and were nowhere near the ruling status. Islamic resurgence worldwide, the Pan Islamic movement, also are factors of motivation. But sooner or later the mullah will get exposed and the people will realize the importance of affluent, comfortable life. Today this is available essentially only to the agents of the religion. At that stage trade between the countries of South Asia, and beyond, will be well established. Both India and Pakistan have very old trading classes, dating from the days of the Indus Valley. This class will exert and produce results. With time, religious fanaticism will recede and meaningful trade between India and surrounding countries will be a reality, bringing all round prosperity. Hindus of India are the leaders in ushering the Industrial Revolution in South Asia, and forging trade ties with the nations of the world. Once the population growth is contained the Hindus of all denominations shall be in the zone of prosperity. But there is a lot of hard work to be done to get that stage.

Hindus have a rich culture and civilization, a profound philosophy and religion. It will be good for the subcontinent, and will receive the approbation of the world at large, if they came on their own and took charge of their destiny. They have a major contribution to make in shaping the future of this world.

Bibliography

History and Culture of the Indian People, Edited by R.C. Majumdar and published by Bharatiya Vidya Bhavan, 1951. A compilations of essays by:

Sankalia, H.D. : Prehistoric Age — Paleolithic to Iron.

Pusalkar, A.D. : The Traditional History from the Earliest Times. The Indus Valley Civilisation. The Aryan Settlements in India.

Chatterji, S.K. : Race Movements and Prehistoric Cultures.

Ghosh, B.K. : The Aryan Problem. The Indian and the Iranian Aryans' Relations. The Vedic Literature — The Age of the Rik Sanhita.

Apte, V.M. : The Political and the Legal Institutions of the Aryans. Religion and Philosophy. Social and Economic Conditions.

Ghosh and Apte : Later Sanhitas, Upanishads and Sutras.

John Garret : A Classical Dictionary of India Illustrative of Mythology, Philosophy, Literature, Antiquities, Arts, Manners, Customs of the Hindus, 1871.

Abbe Dubois, J.A. : Hindu Manners, Customs and Ceremonies, 1906.

Alexeev, V.P. : The Origin of the Human Race, Moscow, 1986.

Piggot, Stuart : Prehistoric India, 1950.

Wheeler, Mortimer, R.E. : The Indus Civilisation, 1953.

Kosambi, D.D. : The Culture and Civilisation of Ancient India in Historical Outline.

Ratanagar, Shereen : The Westerly Trade of the Harappan Civilisation.

Singhvi, Nagindas, H. : Ancient Indian History.

Bhasham, A.L. : Studies in Indian History and Culture, 1964.

Chandra, Lokesh : India's Contribution to World Thought and Culture.

Malik, S.C. : Indian Civilisation; the Formative Period, 1968.
Panikkar, K.M. : Geographical Factor in Indian History, 1959.
Suvira Jaiswal : Origin and Development of Vaishnavism, 1981.
Sharma, R.S. : Shudras in Ancient India, 1980.
Dandekar, R.N. : Harappan Bibliography, 1987.
Fair Servis W.A., Jr. : The Roots of Ancient India, 1971.
Goetz, Hermann : India, 5,000 Years of Indian Art, 1964.
Rao, Venugopal, S. : Power and Criminality.
Marx, Karl : Notes on Indian History, 1964. Progress Publishers, Moscow
Bouquet, A.C. : Hinduism, Hutchinson's University Library, World Religions.
Farquhar, J.N. : The Crown of Hinduism, 1913.
Thomas, Wendel : Hinduism Invades America, 1930, New York.
Swami Satya Prakash Saraswati and Satyakam Vidyalankar : Introduction to Rig Veda Sanhita, 1977.
Raimundo Panikar : The Vedic Experience: An Anthology of the Vedas for the Modern man and Contemporary Celebration, 1983, Pondichery, India.
Buhlar, G. : Translation, The Laws of Manu, 1987 Reprint.
Misra, Janardan Doctor, and Misra Jogesh : Veda and Bharat (India).
Tilak, B.G. : Orion, 1893.
Sarkar, S.C. Professor : Some Aspects of the Earliest Social History of India (Pre-Buddhist Age), 1928.
Dange, Sadashiv Ambadas : Sexual Symbolism from Vedic Ritual.
Vivekananda, Swami : Jnana Yoga, 1961 edition.
Swami Nikhilananda : Vivekananda, A Biography, 1953.
Radhakrishnan, S. : The Hindu View of Life, 1927, The Bhagavadgita.
Radhakrishnan and Charles A. Moore : A Source Book in Indian Philosophy.
Anantharaman, N. : Anandalaharistotra of Adi Shankaracharya.
: His Holiness Jagadguru Shri Jayendra Sarasvati Svamigal Shri Shankaracharya of Kanchi Kamakoti Pitha: Our Heritage.
Mahadevan, Dr. T.M.P. : The Naishakarmya-Siddhi of Sureshvaracharya: An Introduction.
Jagadguru Shri Chandrashekharendra Sarasvati : Veda and Dharma.

Jagadguru Shri Jayendra Sarasvati : Brahman and the World.

Essays in Shankara Bharati : The Voice of Shankara.

Anantaanendra Sarasvati Institution : Shankaracharya and Shankarite Institutions.

Sharma, J.M. : Madhva's Teachings in His Own Words, 1961.

Pillay, Dr. V.K. : Quest for Divinity: Based on the Teachings of Bhagvan Shri Sathya Sai Baba.

Gita Press, Gorakhpur : Srimad Bhagvadgita, 1984.

Khwaja, Dil Mohammad : Gita; Lahore, 1945.

Rajagopalachari, C. : Ramayana, 1957.
Mahabharata, 1951.

Vidyarathi, Gurudatta : Commentary on Upanishads.

Dyananda, Saraswati Swami : Introduction to the Commentary on the Vedas; translated from the original Sanskrit by Pandit Ghasi Ram, 1958.

Prakashananda, Saraswati Swami : The Philosophy of Divine Love, 1982, The International Society of Divine Love.

Rajneesh, Shri Bhagwan : Priests and Politics, 1987.
The Rebel.

Hiriyanna, M. : Essentials of Indian Philosophy, 1949.

Prabhupada Swami Bhaktivedanta, A.C. : ḲṚṢNA in two vols, 1970. International Society of Krishna Consciousness.
: Sandesh (The Message).

India Book House Private Limited, Bombay : Dasha Avatars (The Ten Incarnations of Vishnu)

India Book House Education Trust, Bombay : Elephanta

Jagdish Chander, B.K. Raja Yogi : Illustrations on Raja Yoga.

Pabhavananda, Swami and Manchester, Frederick : The Upanishads Breath of the Eternal.

Bibek and Dipavali Debroy : The Rig Veda; Introduction.
The Yajur Veda; Introduction

Govt. of India, Ministry of Information and Broadcasting-The Publications Division : 2500 years of Buddhism, May 1956.
Guru Nanak, 1969.

Sanders, C.W. : The Inner Voice, 1948. The Radhasoami Satsang, Beas, Punjab.

Tulsi, Acharya : Bhagwan Mahavira.

Maurice, David	:	The Lion's Roar; an anthology of the Buddha's teachings selected from the Pali Cannons. Myths of the Hindus and the Buddhists.
Shastri, Doctor Harish-chandra	:	Tantra Darshana; based on a 15th century work.
Anuruddha, R.P.	:	An Introduction into Lamaism, 1959.
Govinda, Anagrika Lama	:	The Foundations of Tibetan Mysticism, 1960.
Bharati, Agehananda	:	The Tantric Tradition, 1965.
Bose, D.N.	:	Tantras: Their Philosophy and Occult Secrets.
Barnett, L.D.	:	Path of Light, A Manual of Mahayana Buddhism, 1909.
Joseph Campbel	:	Myths to Live By, 1972.
Jung, Carl G.	:	Man and His Symbols, 1968.
Alexeev, V.P.	:	The Origin of the Human Race, 1986.
Life-Time International	:	The Epic of Man, 1963.
	:	Early Man, 1970
Bongard-Levin G. and Vigasin A.	:	The Study of Ancient Indian Civilisation in the USSR—The Image of India, 1984.
Powel-Price, J.C.	:	A History of India.
Marx, Karl and Engel, Frederick	:	Selected Works, Vol. I, 1951; Moscow.
Kennedy, Paul	:	The Rise and Fall of the Great Powers: Economic Change and Military Conflict from 1500 to 2000 A.D., 1989.
Lawrence, James	:	The Rise and Fall of the British Empire, 1994.
Sen, Surendra Nath	:	Eighteen Fifty Seven, Publications Division, Ministry of Information and Broadcasting, Government of India, 1957.
Nehru, Jawaharlal	:	Discovery of India, 1945.
Waley, Adolf	:	A Pageant of India
Mohammad Yasin	:	Rauzabal and other Mysteries of Kashmir, 1972.
Majumdar, P.C., Ray-chaudhury, H.C., and Kalikinkar Datta	:	An Advanced History of India, 1978.
Wells, H.G.	:	A Short History of the World, 1946.
Shelat, J.M.	:	Akbar, 1959. Bharatiya Vidya Bhavan.
Hawking, Stephen	:	A Brief History of Time, 1988.
Gleick, James	:	Chaos, 1987
Ghurye, G.S.	:	Caste and Class in India, 1983.
Hutton, J.H.	:	Caste in India: Its nature, functions and origins, 1963. Oxford University Press.

Bhandarkar, D.R., Edited by
Mahatma Gandhi : Backward and Untouchable Classes: Caste System and its Relation to Social and Economic Life.

US News and World Report, 1957 : Untouchables in India.

Caste Discriminations in Indigenous India; Education I:, Radhakrishnan : Nature and Extent of Education in Early Nineteenth Century British India, 1986.

Chakravarty, S.N. : A Guide to the Antiquities of the Historic Period.

Prince of Wales Museum of Western India, Bombay

Archaeological Survey of India : Bhubaneswar, Sixth Edition, 1996.
: Ajanta, Eleventh Edition, 1996
: Konarak

Anand, Mulk Raj and Bharadwaj, R.R. : Ajanta

Tourism Guide : Aurangabad, Daulatabad, Ellora and Ajanta
: Puri
: Konarak
: Khajuraho

Maharashtra Tourism Development Corporation Ltd. : Elephanta
: Ajanta
: Ellora &
: Aurangabad

Essays and Articles of Interest

The Times of India, New Delhi

Dated 19 July 1988, Did Indo-Europeans Originate in Turkey? Review of the Book "Archaeology and Language: The Puzzle of Indo-European Origins; by Colin Renfrew. The archaeological data does not support the view of Indo-European Invasion of South Asia at any time.

Dated 3 October 1989, India's Role in the Study of the Cosmos.

Dated 22 April 1990, Aryans Originated in India.

Dated 27 March 1990, Was Rama's Ayodhya Actually in Afghanistan?

Dated 5 July 1992, Bihar officer deciphers Harappan script; sceptics await more proof.

Dated 31 December 1992, Dead Sea Scrolls out of the Closet.

Dated 1 November 1993, 'Mahabharata' dates to 1350 B.C., Study.

Stanford Observer November 1988 : Sorting Racial Myths from Facts.

Soviet Land : Black Lightning above Mohenjo-daro, Professor M. Dmitriyev

: Research into the History of Indian Philosophy in the USSR, by O. Mezentseva, Researcher.

: Study of Hinduism by Russian Theologians in 18th-19th Centuries, by O. Mezentseva, Research Workers, Institute of Philosophy, USSR Academy of Sciences.

: Meru Mountains: Where are they? By Svetlana Zharnikova, Art Scholar.

India Today, September 15, 1989 : Seismology; Waiting for a breakthrough; How the Indian Subcontinent was formed, by Raj Chengappa.

Span May 1990 Issue : Illuminating the Noble Path; The Buddhist Art of South Asia and Tibet.

: Saying it in Sumerian, by Marion Steinmann - writings on earth tablets.

October 1993 Issue : Once upon the start of Time — The origin of the Universe, by Ann K. Finkbeiner

Readers Digest, June 1991 Issue. The Riddle of Time, by John Boslough.

San Francisco Chronicle; 26 July 1990. Original of Life on Earth and its Evolution. David Periman and Gina Kolata.

The Economist, December 22, 1990 : GAIA (pronounced Jee-e or Gay-a), The veiled goddess; the Greek goddess of earth who bore and married Uranus and became the mother of Titans (primordial gods overthrown by Olympian gods) and Cyclopes (one-eyed giants). The earth is a live system.

Index